P9-CRK-991

LOCKE & KEY

WELCOME TO LOVECRAFT

WRITTEN BY

JOE HILL

ART BY

GABRIEL RODRIGUEZ

Written by: Joe Hill

Art by: Gabriel Rodriguez

Colors by: Jay Fotos

Letters by: Robbie Robbins

Series Edited by: Chris Ryall

Collection Edited by: Justin Eisinger

Collection Designed by: Robbie Robbins

Locke & Key created by Joe Hill and Gabriel Rodriguez

For international rights, contact licensing@idwpublishing.com

ISBN: 978-1-60010-384-1

23 22 21 20   17 18 19 20

Chris Ryall, President & Publisher/CCO • **Cara Morrison**, Chief Financial Officer • **Matthew Ruzicka**, Chief Accounting Officer • **David Hedgecock**, Associate Publisher • **John Barber**, Editor-in-Chief • **Justin Eisinger**, Editorial Director, Graphic Novels and Collections • **Scott Dunbier**, Director, Special Projects • **Jerry Bennington**, VP of New Product Development • **Lorelei Bunjes**, VP of Technology & Information Services • **Jud Meyers**, Sales Director • **Anna Morrow**, Marketing Director • **Tara McCrillis**, Director of Design & Production • **Mike Ford**, Director of Operations • **Rebekah Cahalin**, General Manager

Ted Adams and Robbie Robbins, IDW Founders

Facebook: facebook.com/idwpublishing • Twitter: @idwpublishing • YouTube: youtube.com/idwpublishing
Tumblr: tumblr.idwpublishing.com • Instagram: instagram.com/idwpublishing

www.IDWPUBLISHING.com

  You Tube

LOCKE & KEY, VOLUME 1: WELCOME TO LOVECRAFT. JANUARY 2020. SEVENTEENTH PRINTING. Locke & Key script © 2020 Joe Hill, art © Idea and Design Works, LLC. All Rights Reserved. IDW Publishing, a division of Idea and Design Works, LLC. Editorial offices: 2765 Truxtun Road, San Diego, CA 92106. Any similarities to persons living or dead are purely coincidental. With the exception of artwork used for review purposes, none of the contents of this publication may be reprinted without the permission of Idea and Design Works, LLC. Printed in Canada.
IDW Publishing does not read or accept unsolicited submissions of ideas, stories, or artwork.
Originally published as LOCKE & KEY: WELCOME TO LOVECRAFT Issues #1–6.

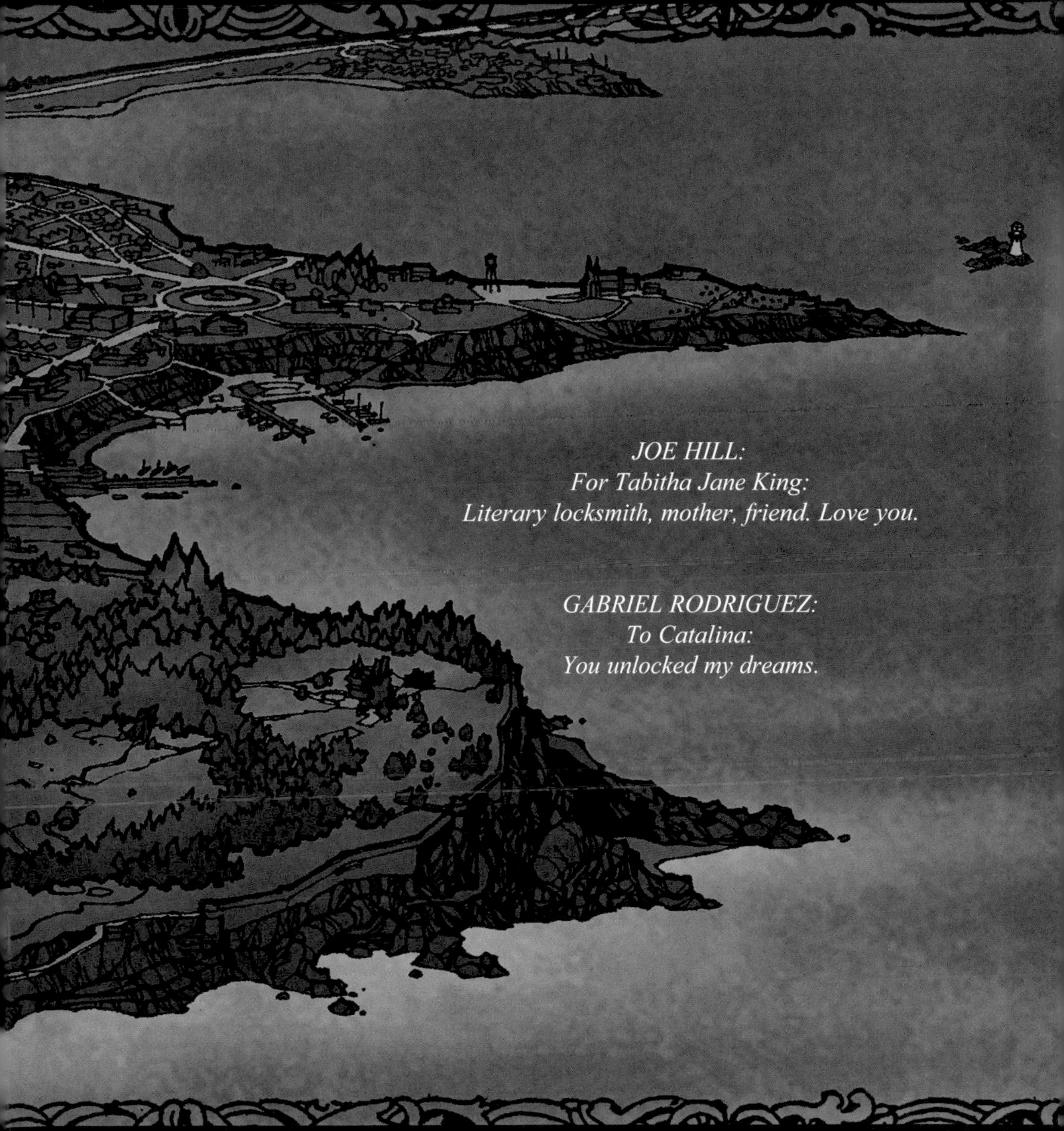

JOE HILL:
For Tabitha Jane King:
Literary locksmith, mother, friend. Love you.

GABRIEL RODRIGUEZ:
To Catalina:
You unlocked my dreams.

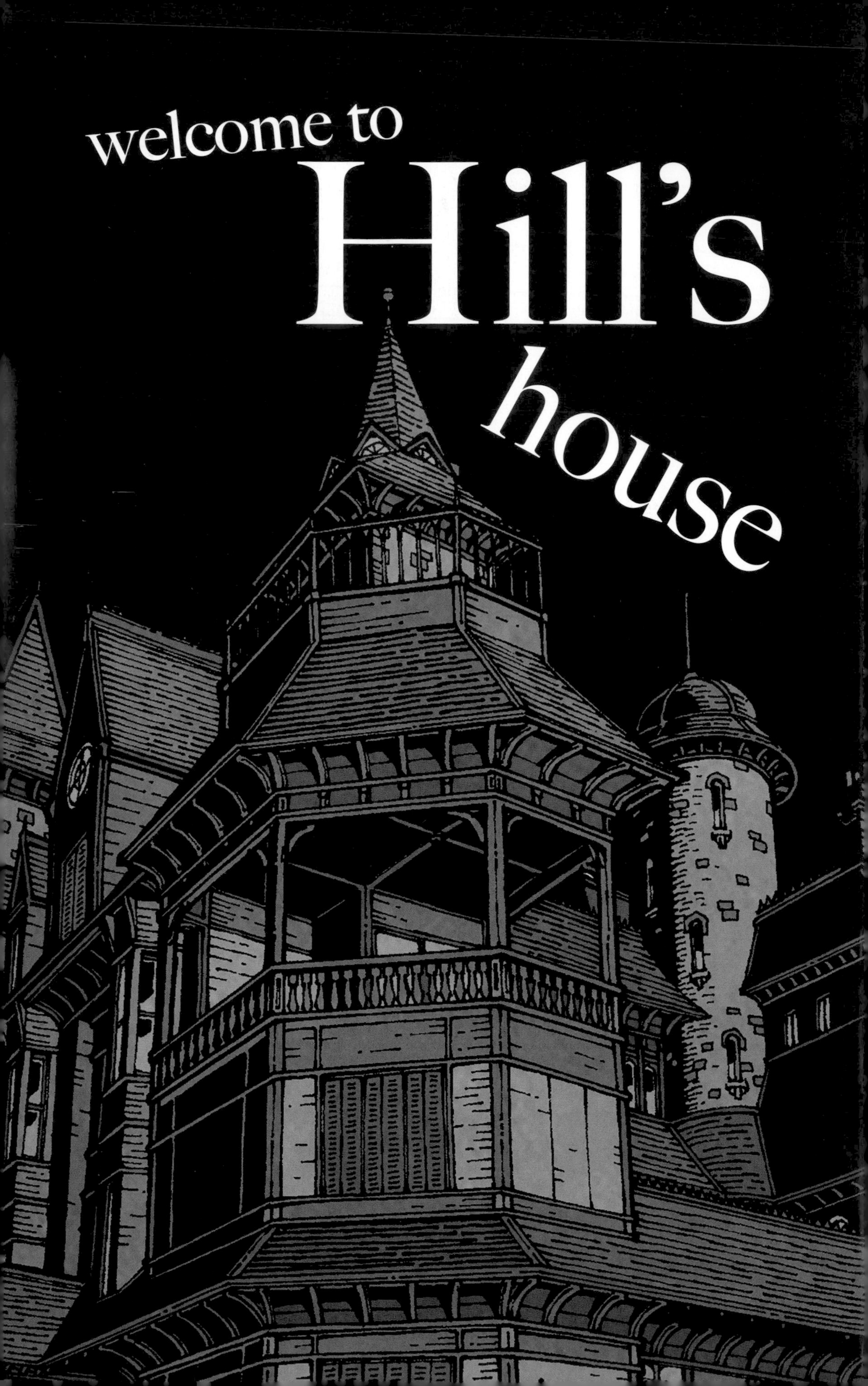
welcome to
Hill's
house

by Robert Crais

I was in London to promote a book called *The Watchman*, slamming between BBC radio interviews and bookstore stock signings when my UK publicist says, "We have another American writer in town. Shall we join up for lunch?"

So the two American writers got together, hunkering down over fish and potatoes in a hip little London restaurant not far from Trafalgar. The other guy was a tall, friendly dude with a thick beard, black duster, and easy smile–Joe Hill.

After swapping a couple of obligatory "touring writer" stories as we got to know each other, we discovered a mutual passion: Baseball. Being from Los Angeles, I bleed Dodger blue. Joe, from New England, is a hardcore member of Red Sox Nation. This was a perfect conversational match because so many ex-Dodgers were then playing for Boston (Julio Lugo and J.D. Drew among them, both of whom would bat over .330 in the upcoming post-season), and ex-BoSox were taking the field in Chavez Ravine (ace starting pitcher Derek Lowe and All-Star infielder Nomar Garciaparra, to name only two). Our British hosts probably glazed over as Joe and I rattled on–not about horror novels and crime fiction, but Derek Lowe's durability, J.D. Drew's commitment to the game, and whether or not the BoSox had the stuff to make it to the 2007 World Series (they did, crushing the Colorado Rockies in four games, much to Joe Hill's no doubt considerable delight).

After lunch, we swapped books as our respective publicists dragged us away for more interviews, and I spent the rest of my tour and the long flight home sucking down *Heart-Shaped Box*. I immediately bought *20th Century Ghosts*, and devoured the short stories. Then Chris Ryall dropped the first three *Locke & Key* scripts on me.

When baseball scouts judge player talent, they consider five tools: Hitting for average, hitting for power, how fast the guy can run, how well he can throw, and how well he can catch. The very best players–think A-Rod or Ken Griffey, Jr.–can do it all: Crack a key single when it counts or slam a home run, steal a base, throw out a runner, or make one of those spectacular hauling-ass-back-to-the-ball-over-the-shoulder catches. Most players in the bigs show two or three tools, but the very best players have all five.

Joe Hill is a five-tool player.

Check it out. A fabulous first novel. The killer short stories, which require a different skill set than writing a novel. And, now, this amazing graphic novel, which is an entirely different form of storytelling than novels or short stories. I'm betting dollars to donuts it won't be long before we see Hill's byline on a major motion picture.

The scripts for the first three issues of *Locke & Key* blew me away. And this was even before Gabriel Rodriguez's stunning art, which has been hauntingly colored by Jay Fotos to achieve exactly the right tone and mood. From Keyhouse's imposing lines to murderer Sam Lesser's listless, watery eyes; in the depiction of Tyler Locke's withdrawal to the pain burned into Kinsey's face, the art and story are perfectly matched to reveal not only the characters, but a steadily mounting tension that will creep you out, surprise you, and is guaranteed to keep you turning the pages.

I read the scripts in a single evening, then pleaded with Ryall for more.

Locke & Key is a graphic novel of the richest kind, presenting a story and characters conceived with all the depth of a full-blown novel, yet perfectly rendered by both writer and artists to take advantage of the graphic medium. Here we have these three lost children–the oldest brother, Tyler, who feels responsible for his father's death; Kinsey, the middle sister, who has already saved her younger brother once, and is now trying to save herself; and six-year-old Bode, who may well be the key, so to speak, to their survival–hauled across the country by their mother after their father is murdered by a homicidal student; these three kids who are at once real because of the secrets they carry, and how the author subtly intertwines their personal stories with the mysteries of Keyhouse and the forces that have drawn them home. (Memo to the Locke family: You want to rebuild your lives, you sure as hell do NOT retreat to a town called Lovecraft.)

Locke & Key works so well, I think, because it resonates with basic fears that all of us share–our loss of innocence; that we might unwittingly hurt someone we love; that revealing ourselves in a moment of weakness might inevitably lead to our undoing. Or worse. This is the stuff of great stories, and when the author tosses in thrills, chills, and the promise of worse things waiting, the reader is in for a helluva ride.

As the Locke family arrives in Lovecraft, Tyler laments that a high school kid can only be one thing–the jock, the slut, the smart kid, or the victim.

If Joe Hill was only one thing, it would be this: An amazing story-teller.

Welcome to Lovecraft.

Welcome to *Locke & Key*.

Welcome to Joe Hill's house.

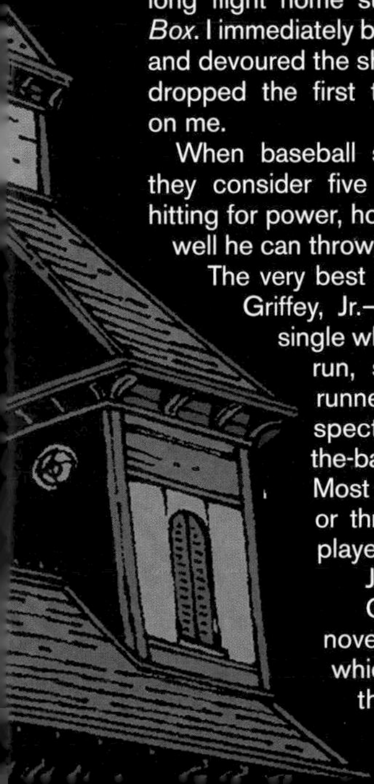

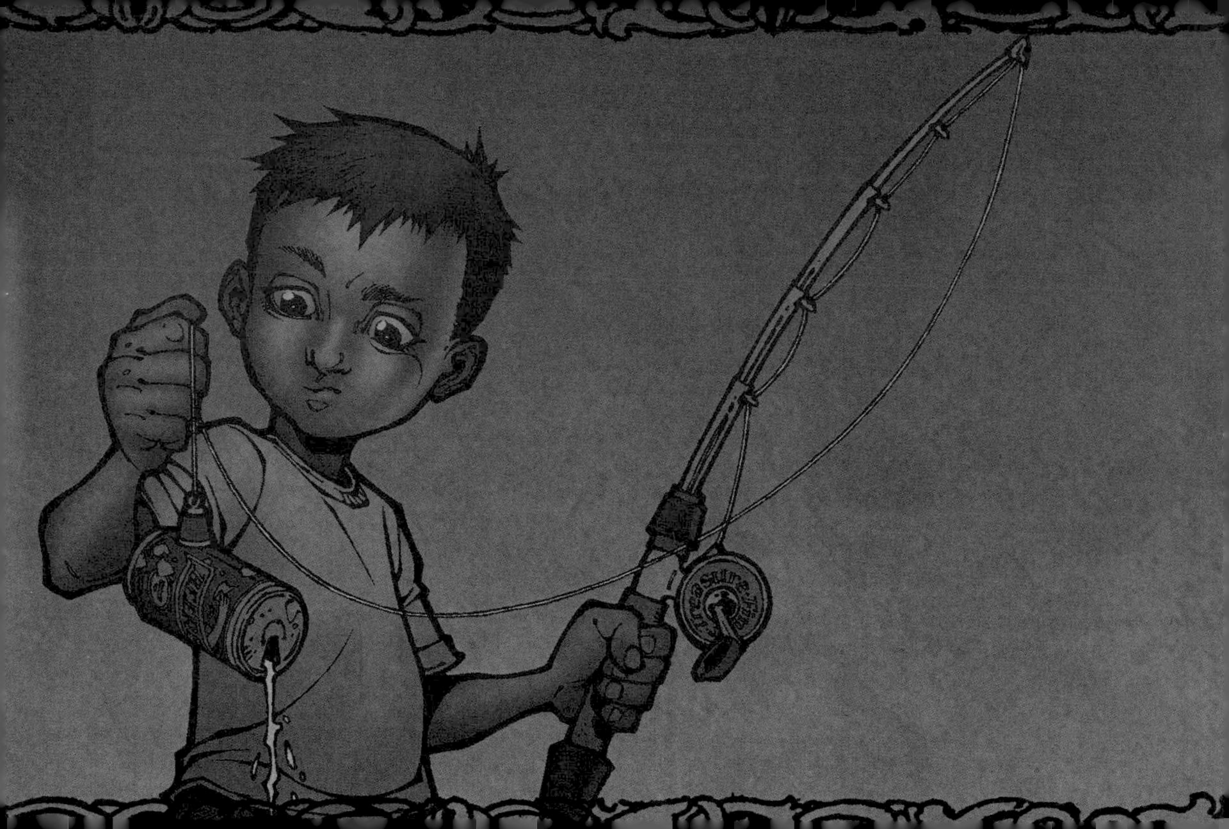

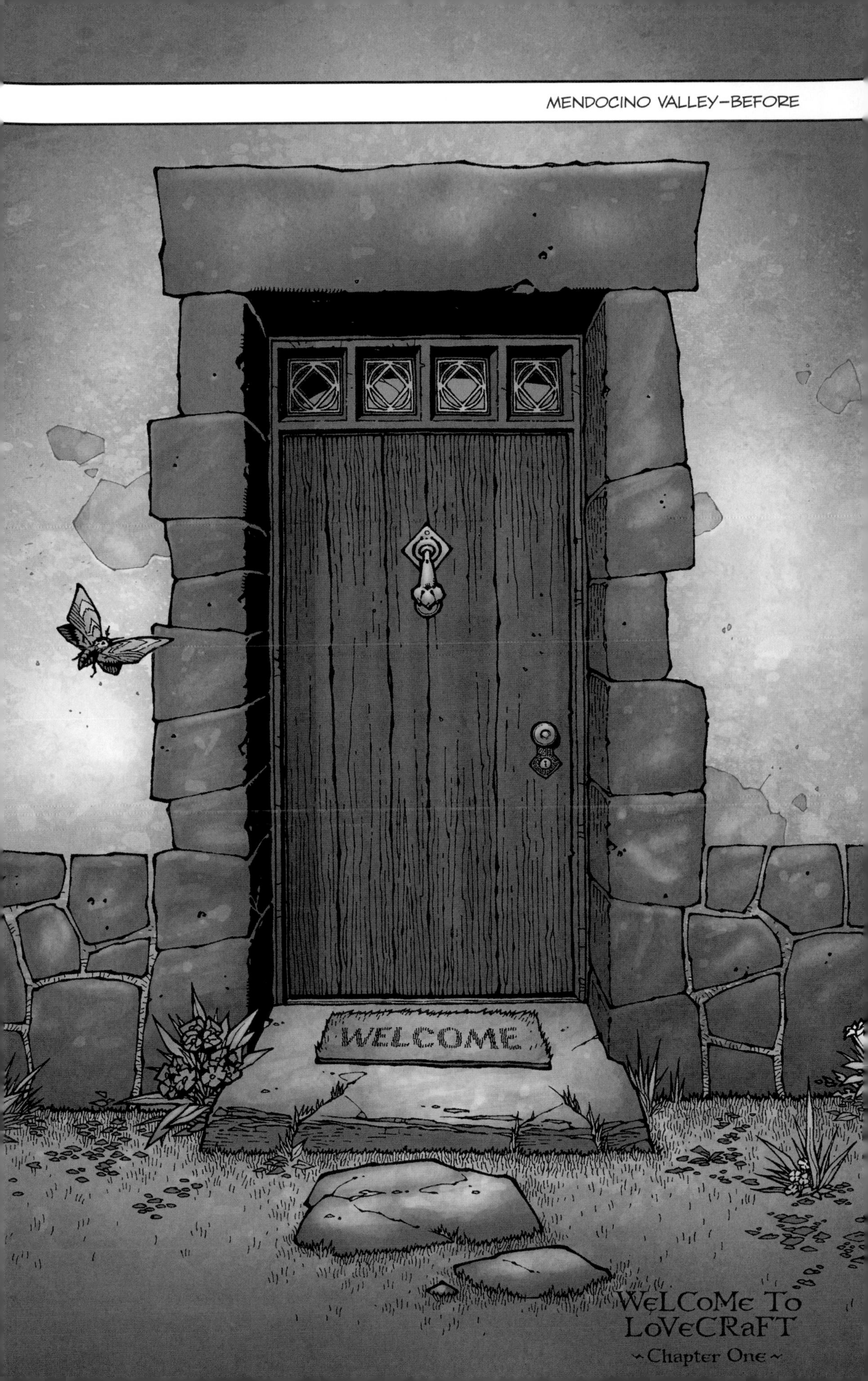
MENDOCINO VALLEY–BEFORE
WELCOME
WELCOME TO LOVECRAFT
~Chapter One~

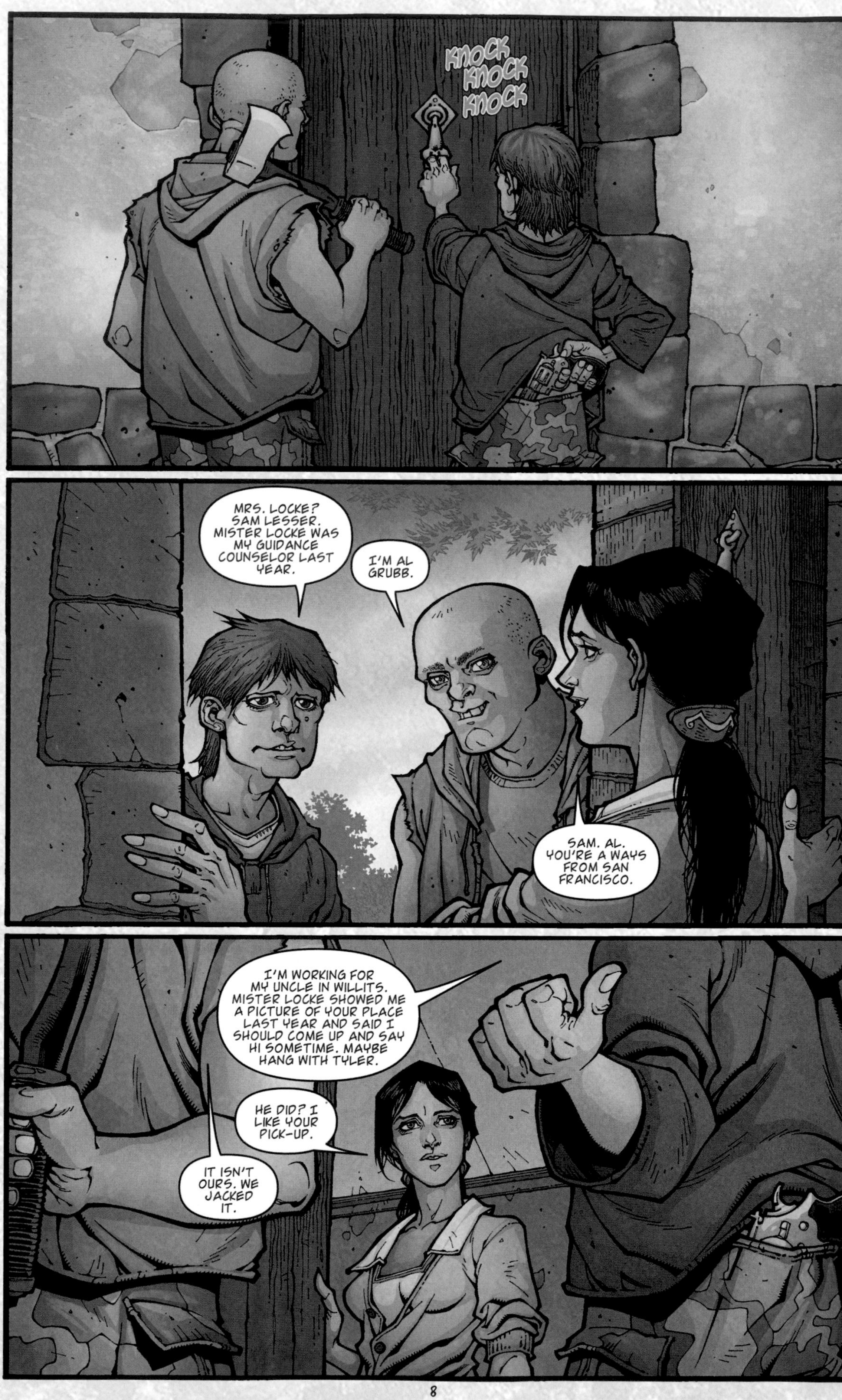
KNOCK KNOCK KNOCK
MRS. LOCKE? SAM LESSER. MISTER LOCKE WAS MY GUIDANCE COUNSELOR LAST YEAR.
I'M AL GRUBB.
SAM. AL. YOU'RE A WAYS FROM SAN FRANCISCO.
I'M WORKING FOR MY UNCLE IN WILLITS. MISTER LOCKE SHOWED ME A PICTURE OF YOUR PLACE LAST YEAR AND SAID I SHOULD COME UP AND SAY HI SOMETIME. MAYBE HANG WITH TYLER.
HE DID? I LIKE YOUR PICK-UP.
IT ISN'T OURS. WE JACKED IT.

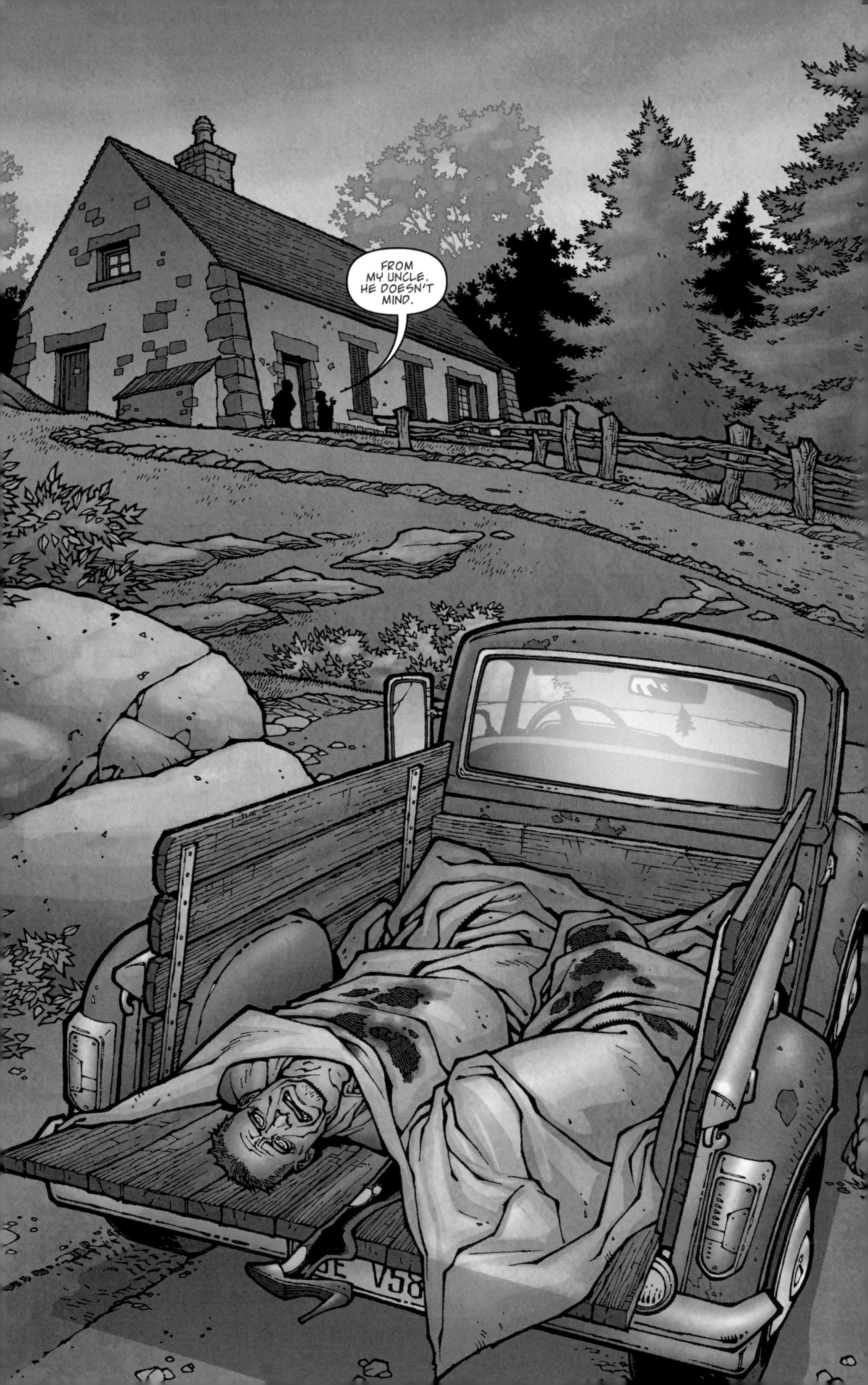
FROM MY UNCLE. HE DOESN'T MIND.

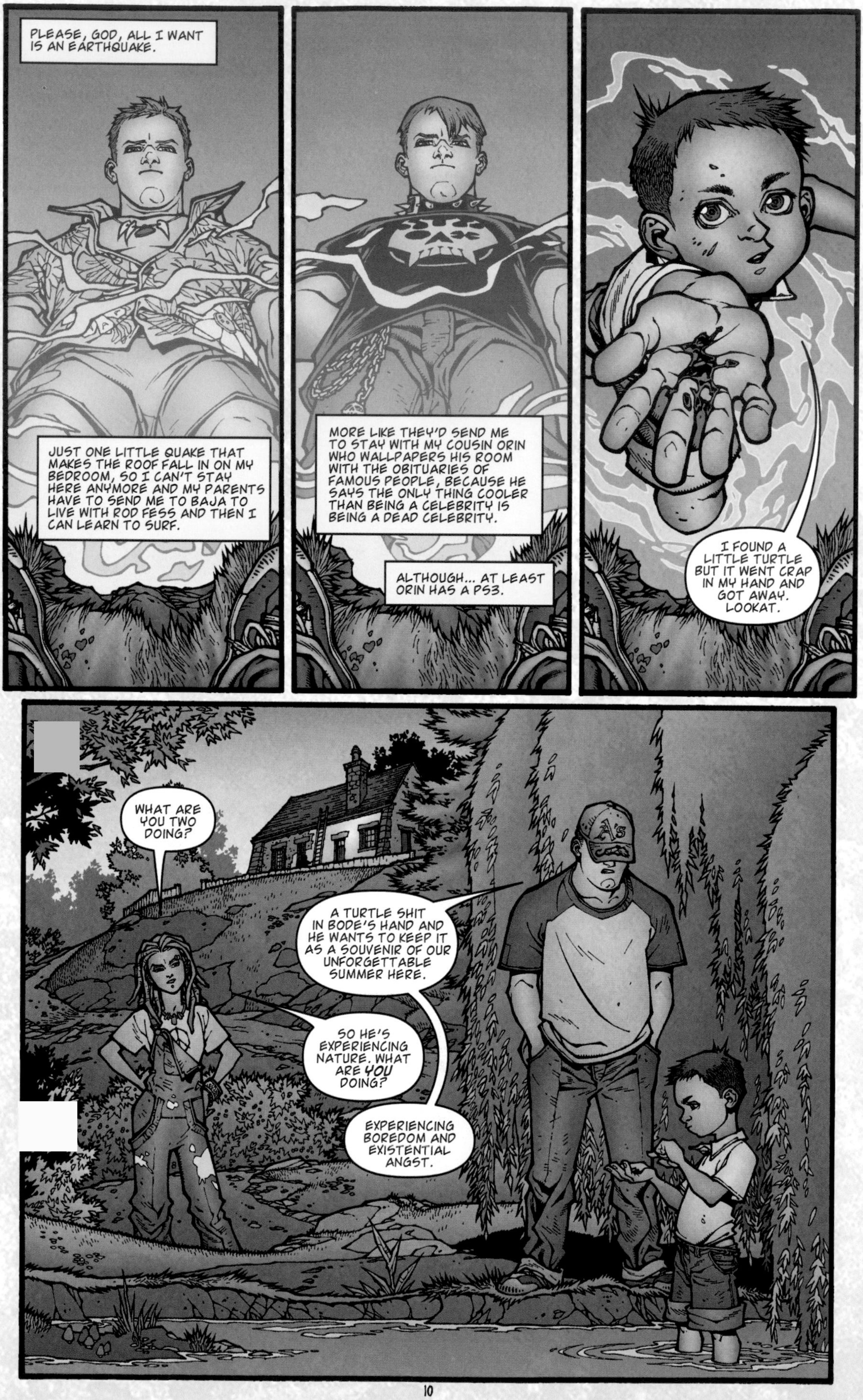
PLEASE, GOD, ALL I WANT IS AN EARTHQUAKE.
JUST ONE LITTLE QUAKE THAT MAKES THE ROOF FALL IN ON MY BEDROOM, SO I CAN'T STAY HERE ANYMORE AND MY PARENTS HAVE TO SEND ME TO BAJA TO LIVE WITH ROD FESS AND THEN I CAN LEARN TO SURF.
MORE LIKE THEY'D SEND ME TO STAY WITH MY COUSIN ORIN WHO WALLPAPERS HIS ROOM WITH THE OBITUARIES OF FAMOUS PEOPLE, BECAUSE HE SAYS THE ONLY THING COOLER THAN BEING A CELEBRITY IS BEING A DEAD CELEBRITY.
ALTHOUGH... AT LEAST ORIN HAS A PS3.
I FOUND A LITTLE TURTLE BUT IT WENT CRAP IN MY HAND AND GOT AWAY. LOOKAT.
WHAT ARE YOU TWO DOING?
A TURTLE SHIT IN BODE'S HAND AND HE WANTS TO KEEP IT AS A SOUVENIR OF OUR UNFORGETTABLE SUMMER HERE.
SO HE'S EXPERIENCING NATURE. WHAT ARE *YOU* DOING?
EXPERIENCING BOREDOM AND EXISTENTIAL ANGST.

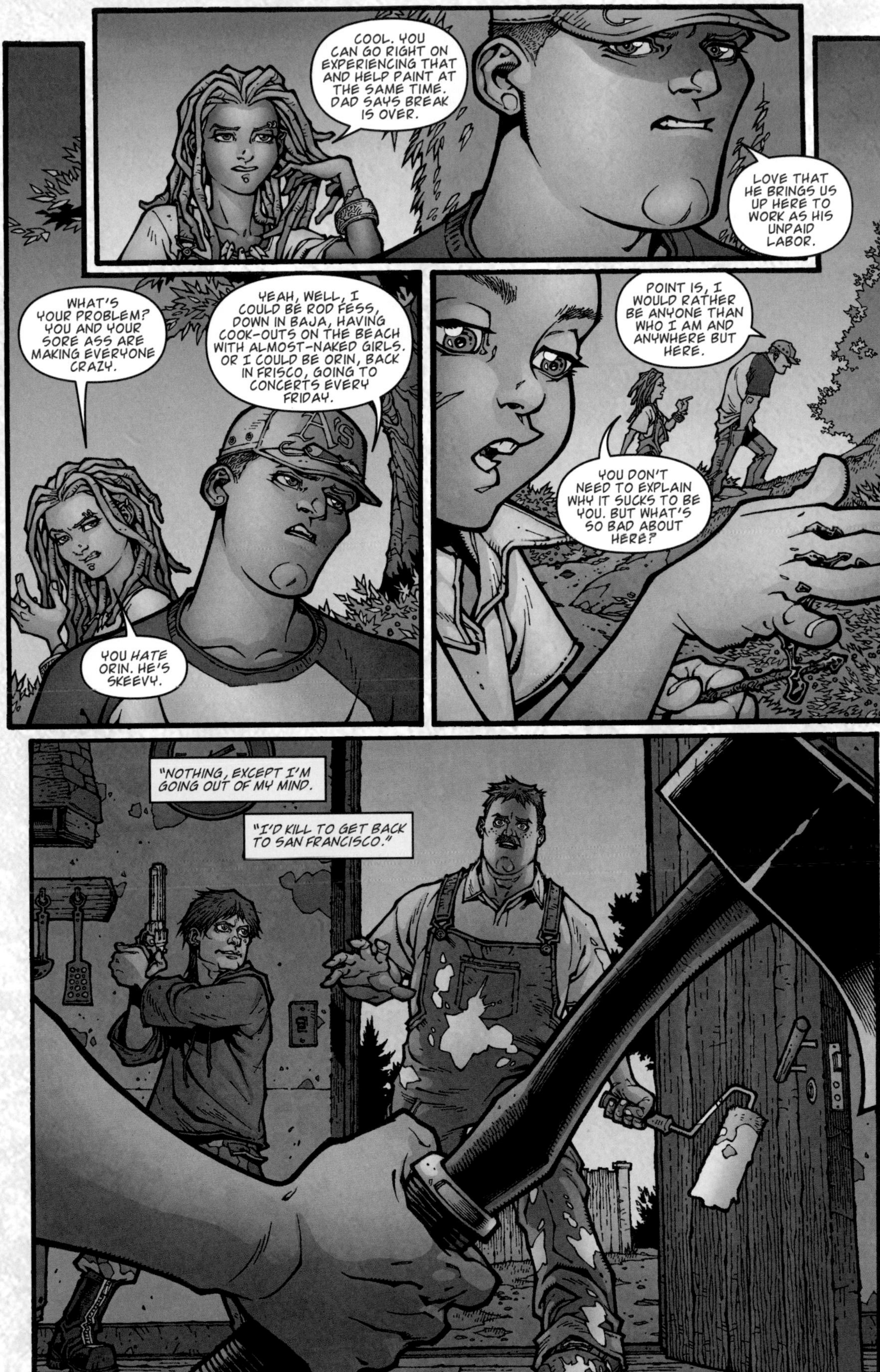
COOL. YOU CAN GO RIGHT ON EXPERIENCING THAT AND HELP PAINT AT THE SAME TIME. DAD SAYS BREAK IS OVER.
LOVE THAT HE BRINGS US UP HERE TO WORK AS HIS UNPAID LABOR.
WHAT'S YOUR PROBLEM? YOU AND YOUR SORE ASS ARE MAKING EVERYONE CRAZY.
YEAH, WELL, I COULD BE ROD FESS, DOWN IN BAJA, HAVING COOK-OUTS ON THE BEACH WITH ALMOST-NAKED GIRLS. OR I COULD BE ORIN, BACK IN FRISCO, GOING TO CONCERTS EVERY FRIDAY.
YOU HATE ORIN. HE'S SKEEVY.
POINT IS, I WOULD RATHER BE ANYONE THAN WHO I AM AND ANYWHERE BUT HERE.
YOU DON'T NEED TO EXPLAIN WHY IT SUCKS TO BE YOU. BUT WHAT'S SO BAD ABOUT HERE?
"NOTHING, EXCEPT I'M GOING OUT OF MY MIND.
"I'D KILL TO GET BACK TO SAN FRANCISCO."

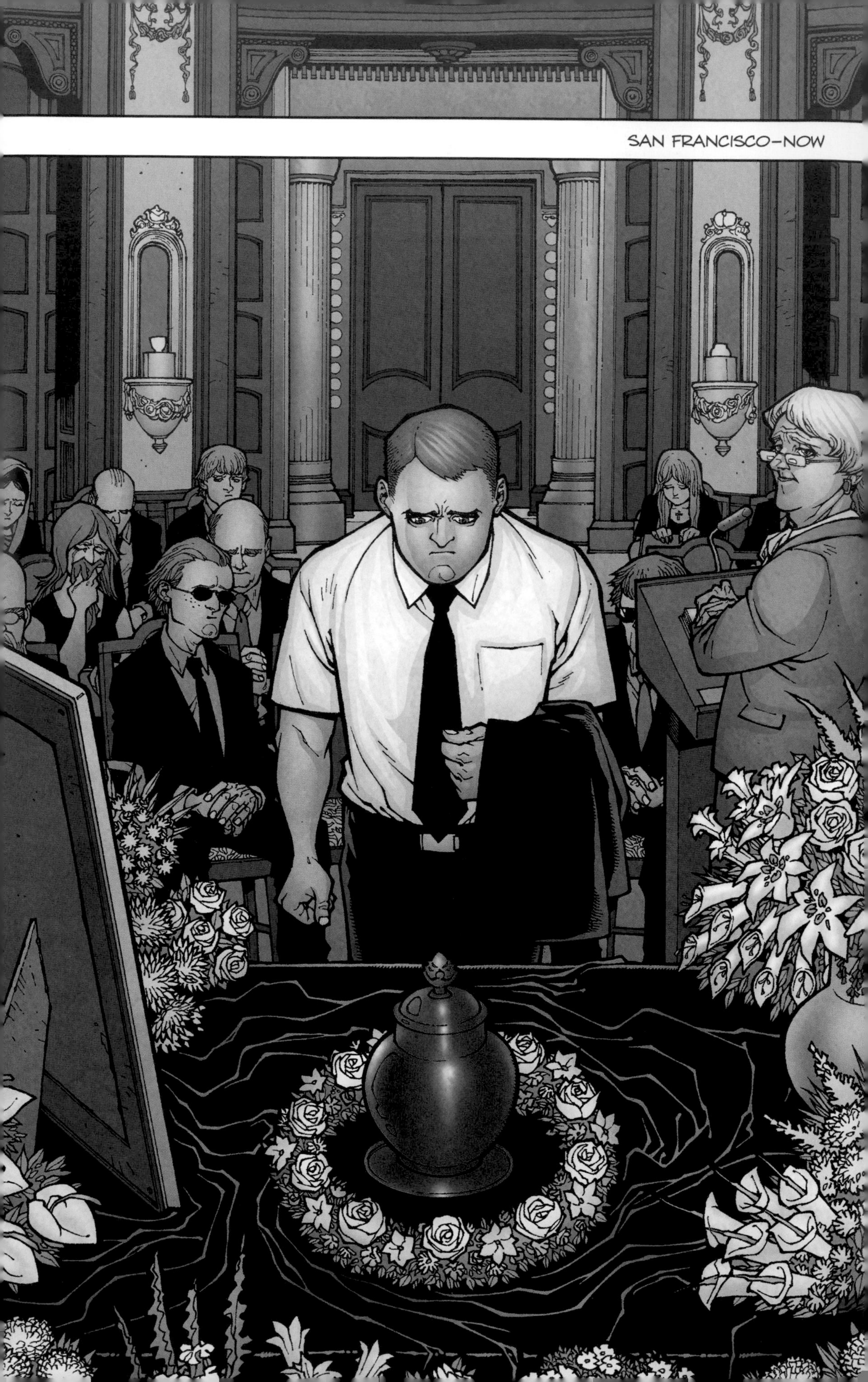
SAN FRANCISCO–NOW

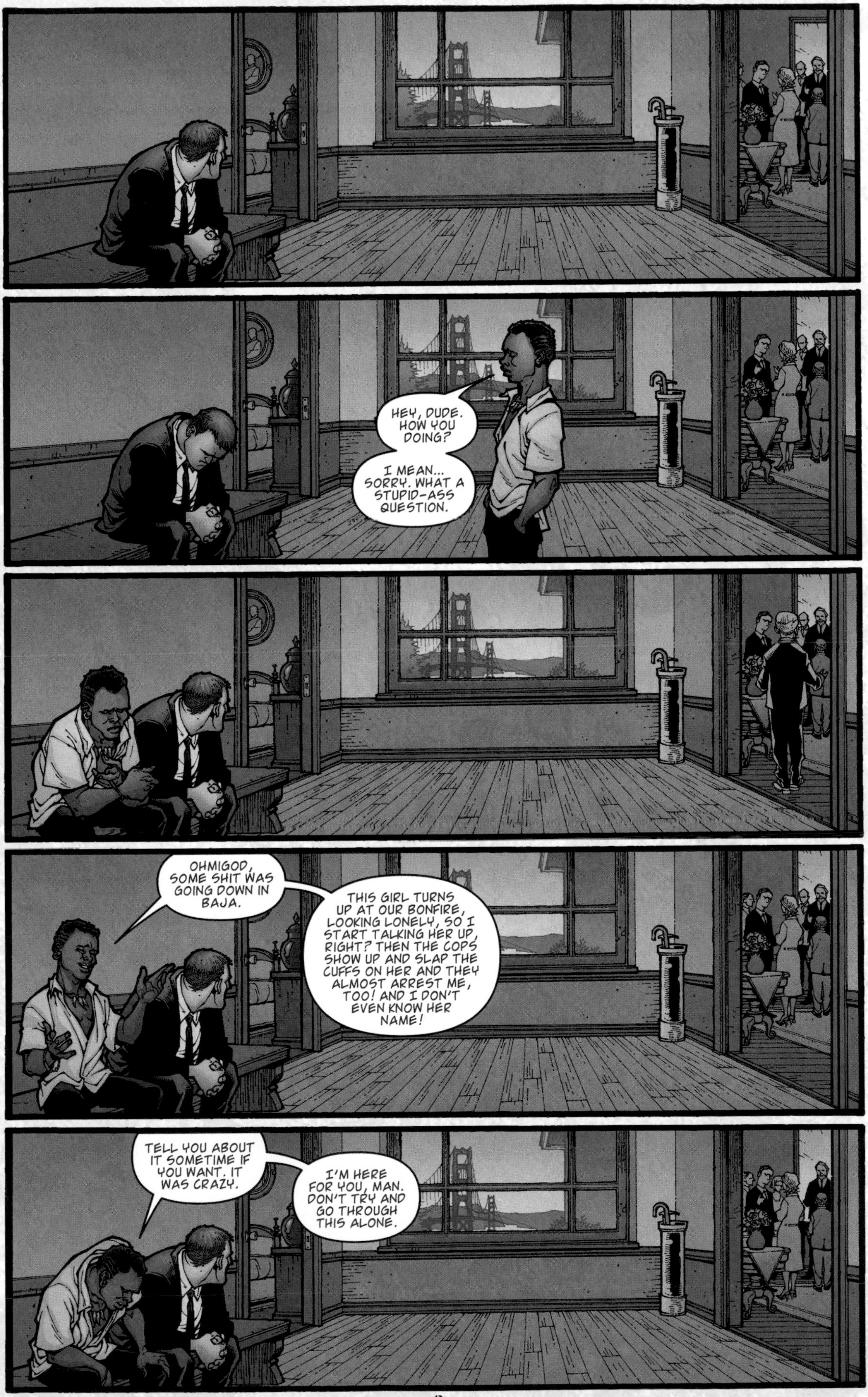
HEY, DUDE. HOW YOU DOING?
I MEAN... SORRY. WHAT A STUPID-ASS QUESTION.
OHMIGOD, SOME SHIT WAS GOING DOWN IN BAJA.
THIS GIRL TURNS UP AT OUR BONFIRE, LOOKING LONELY, SO I START TALKING HER UP, RIGHT? THEN THE COPS SHOW UP AND SLAP THE CUFFS ON HER AND THEY ALMOST ARREST ME, TOO! AND I DON'T EVEN KNOW HER NAME!
TELL YOU ABOUT IT SOMETIME IF YOU WANT. IT WAS CRAZY.
I'M HERE FOR YOU, MAN. DON'T TRY AND GO THROUGH THIS ALONE.

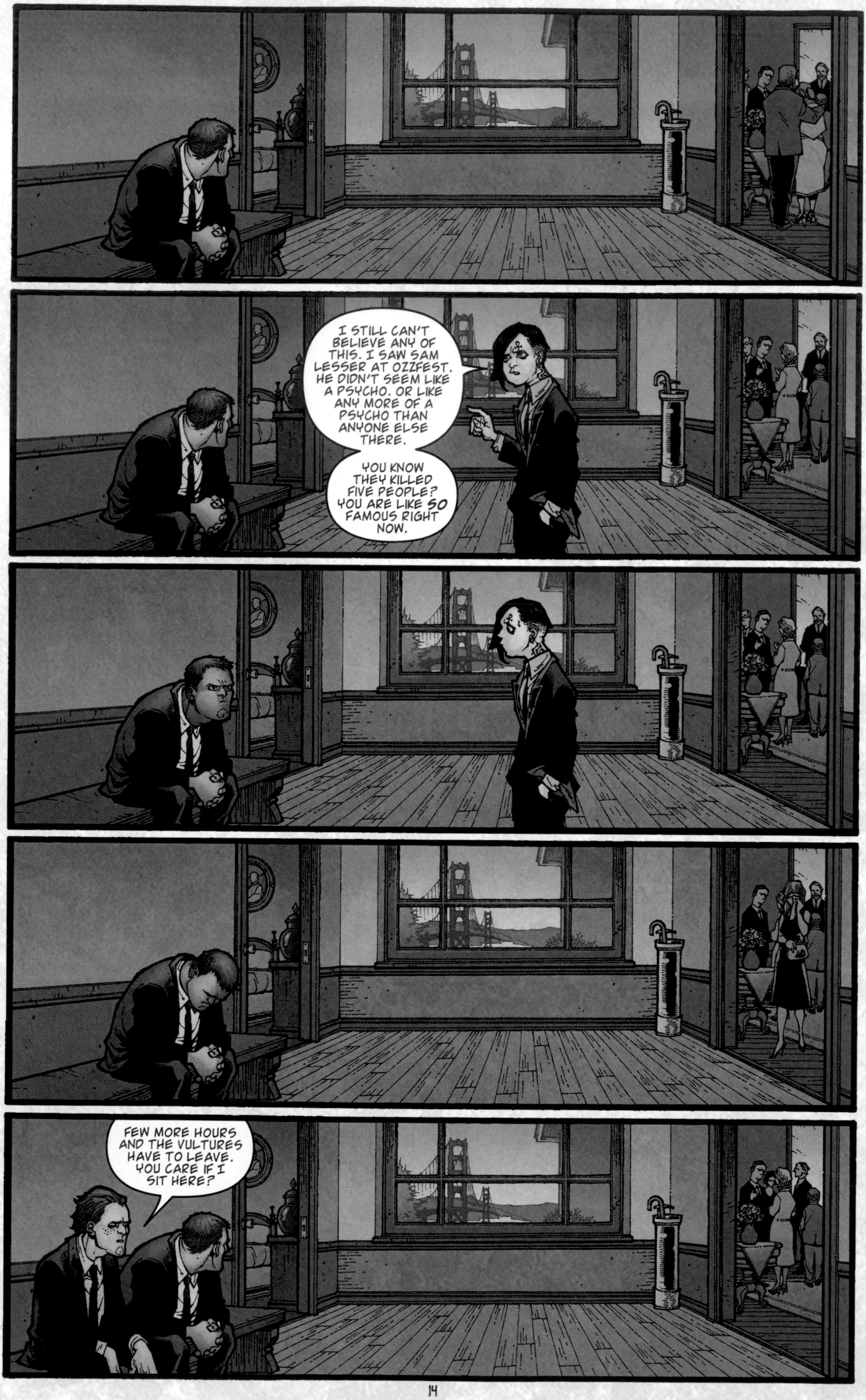
I STILL CAN'T BELIEVE ANY OF THIS. I SAW SAM LESSER AT OZZFEST. HE DIDN'T SEEM LIKE A PSYCHO. OR LIKE ANY MORE OF A PSYCHO THAN ANYONE ELSE THERE.
YOU KNOW THEY KILLED FIVE PEOPLE? YOU ARE LIKE SO FAMOUS RIGHT NOW.
FEW MORE HOURS AND THE VULTURES HAVE TO LEAVE. YOU CARE IF I SIT HERE?

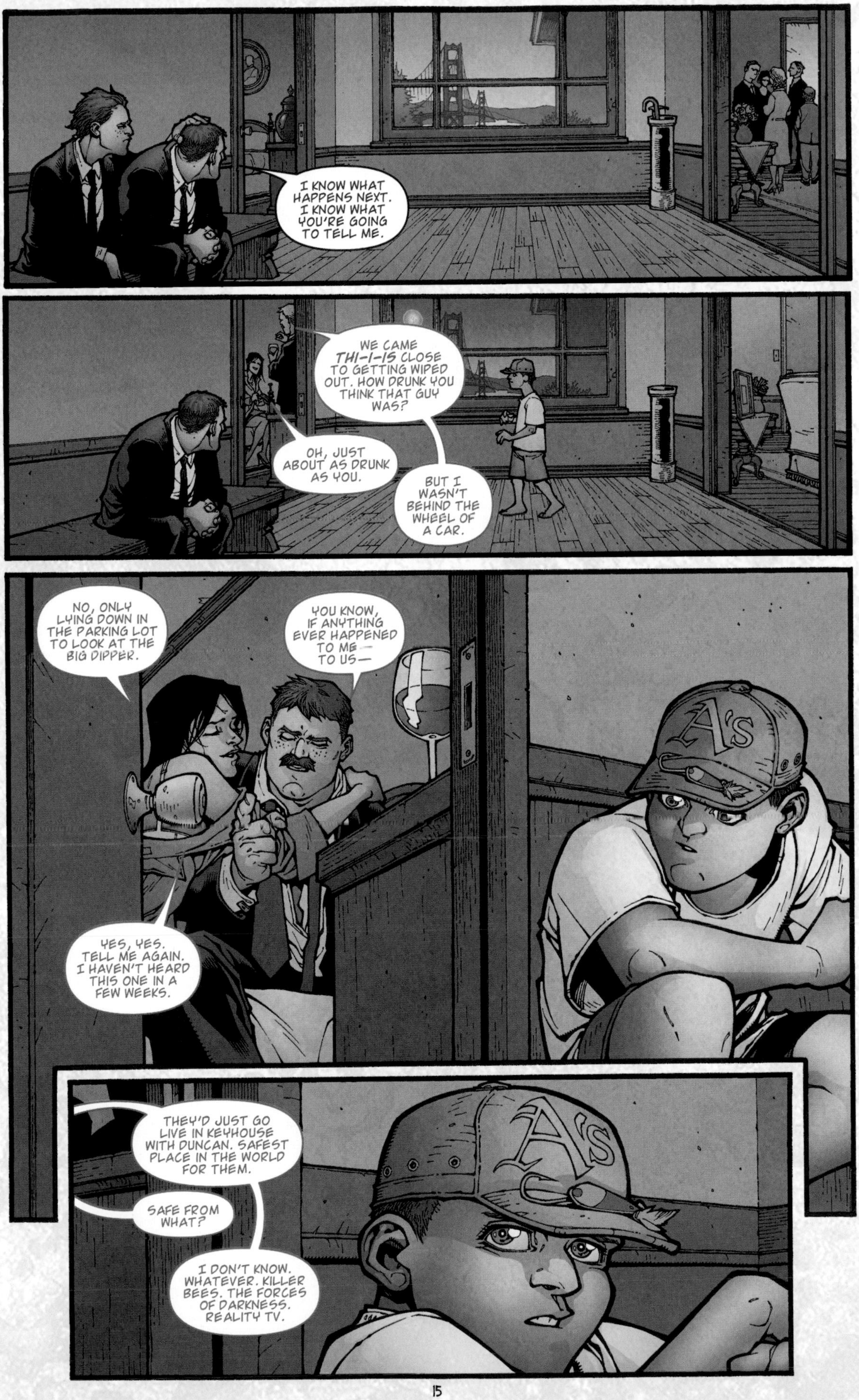
I KNOW WHAT HAPPENS NEXT. I KNOW WHAT YOU'RE GOING TO TELL ME.
WE CAME THI-I-IS CLOSE TO GETTING WIPED OUT. HOW DRUNK YOU THINK THAT GUY WAS?
OH, JUST ABOUT AS DRUNK AS YOU.
BUT I WASN'T BEHIND THE WHEEL OF A CAR.
NO, ONLY LYING DOWN IN THE PARKING LOT TO LOOK AT THE BIG DIPPER.
YOU KNOW, IF ANYTHING EVER HAPPENED TO ME— TO US—
YES, YES. TELL ME AGAIN. I HAVEN'T HEARD THIS ONE IN A FEW WEEKS.
THEY'D JUST GO LIVE IN KEYHOUSE WITH DUNCAN. SAFEST PLACE IN THE WORLD FOR THEM.
SAFE FROM WHAT?
I DON'T KNOW. WHATEVER. KILLER BEES. THE FORCES OF DARKNESS. REALITY TV.

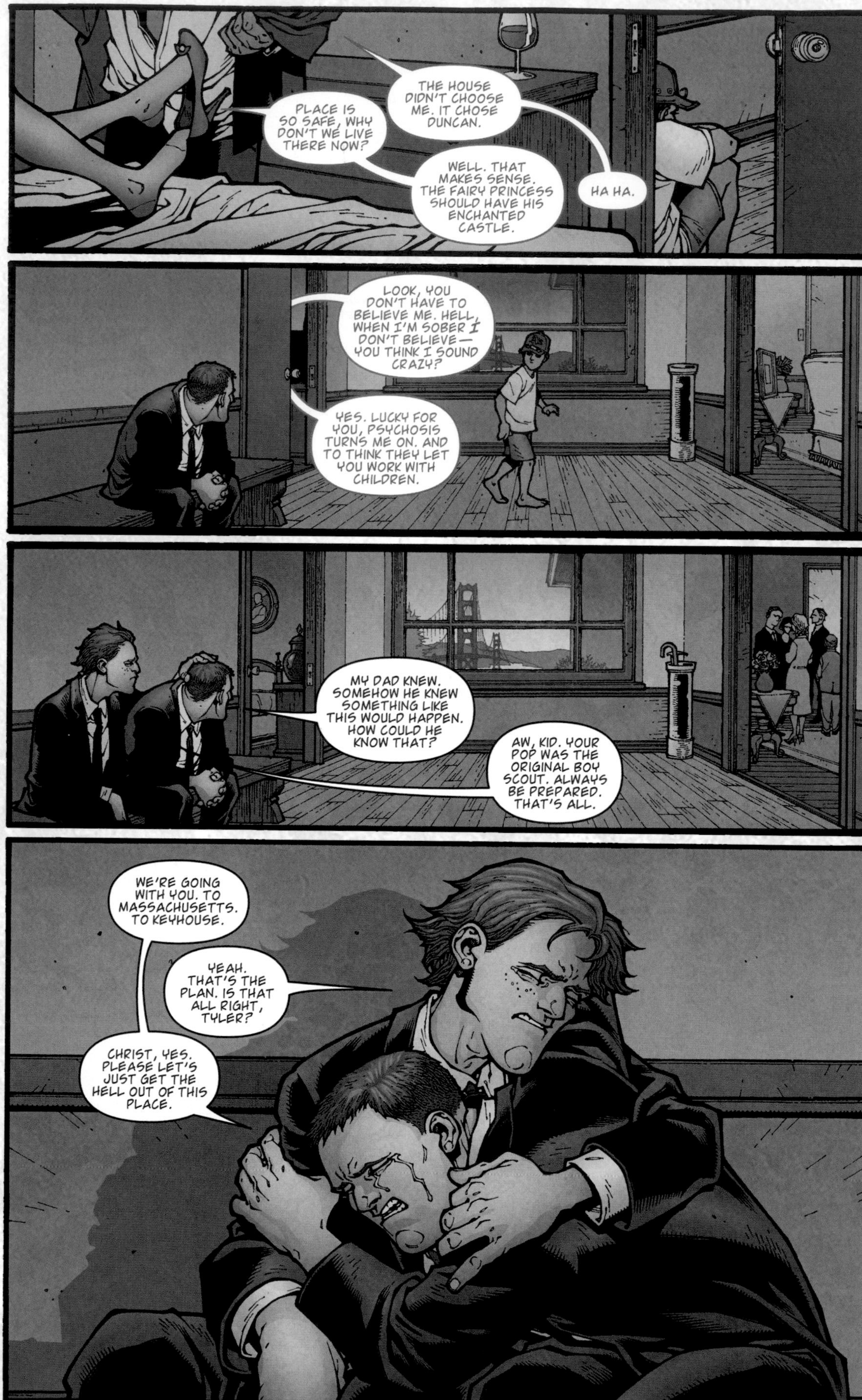

THE HOUSE DIDN'T CHOOSE ME. IT CHOSE DUNCAN.
PLACE IS SO SAFE, WHY DON'T WE LIVE THERE NOW?
WELL. THAT MAKES SENSE. THE FAIRY PRINCESS SHOULD HAVE HIS ENCHANTED CASTLE.
HA HA.
LOOK, YOU DON'T HAVE TO BELIEVE ME. HELL, WHEN I'M SOBER I DON'T BELIEVE— YOU THINK I SOUND CRAZY?
YES. LUCKY FOR YOU, PSYCHOSIS TURNS ME ON. AND TO THINK THEY LET YOU WORK WITH CHILDREN.
MY DAD KNEW. SOMEHOW HE KNEW SOMETHING LIKE THIS WOULD HAPPEN. HOW COULD HE KNOW THAT?
AW, KID. YOUR POP WAS THE ORIGINAL BOY SCOUT. ALWAYS BE PREPARED. THAT'S ALL.
WE'RE GOING WITH YOU. TO MASSACHUSETTS. TO KEYHOUSE.
YEAH. THAT'S THE PLAN. IS THAT ALL RIGHT, TYLER?
CHRIST, YES. PLEASE LET'S JUST GET THE HELL OUT OF THIS PLACE.

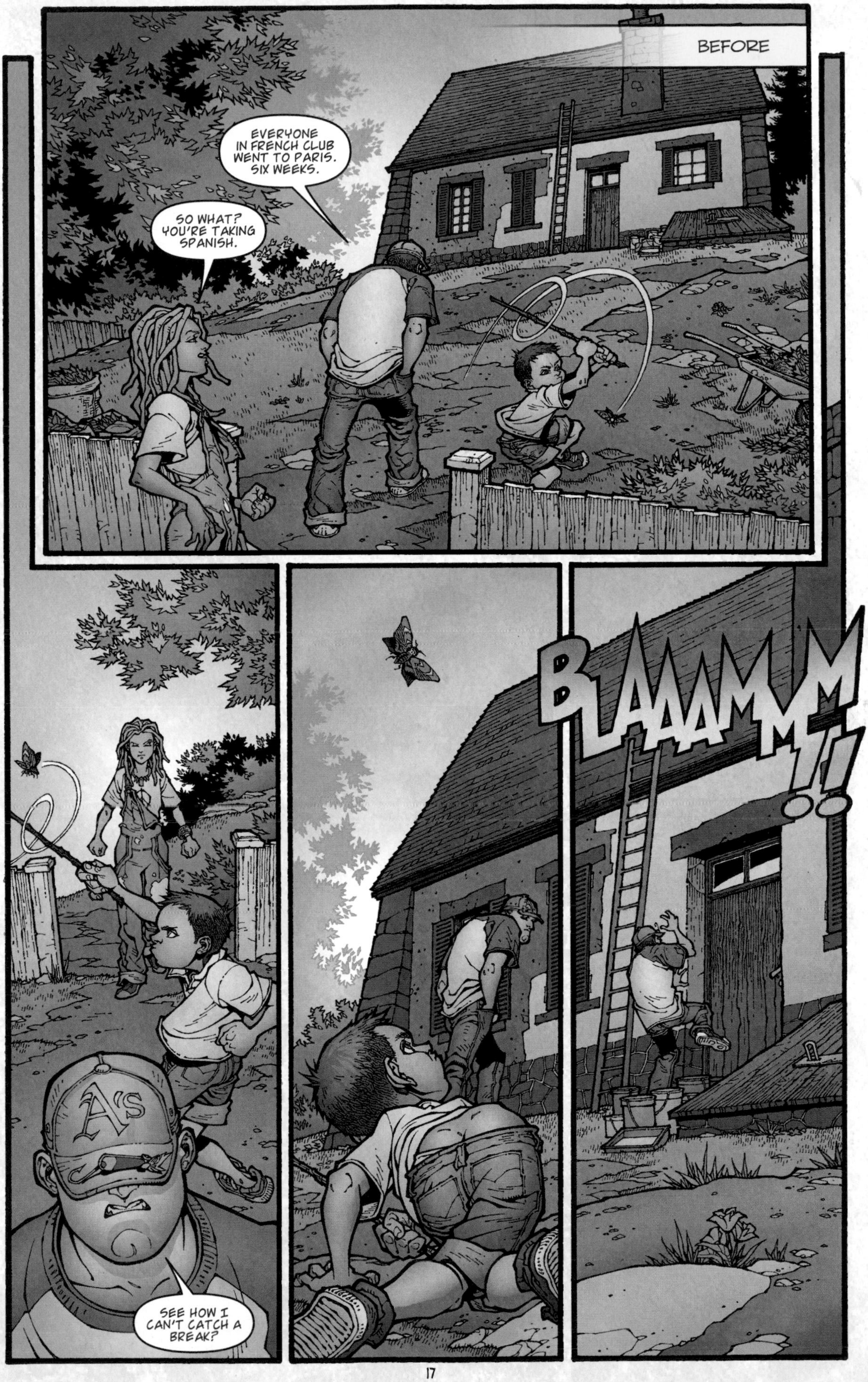
BEFORE
EVERYONE IN FRENCH CLUB WENT TO PARIS. SIX WEEKS.
SO WHAT? YOU'RE TAKING SPANISH.
A's
SEE HOW I CAN'T CATCH A BREAK?
BLAAAMMM!!

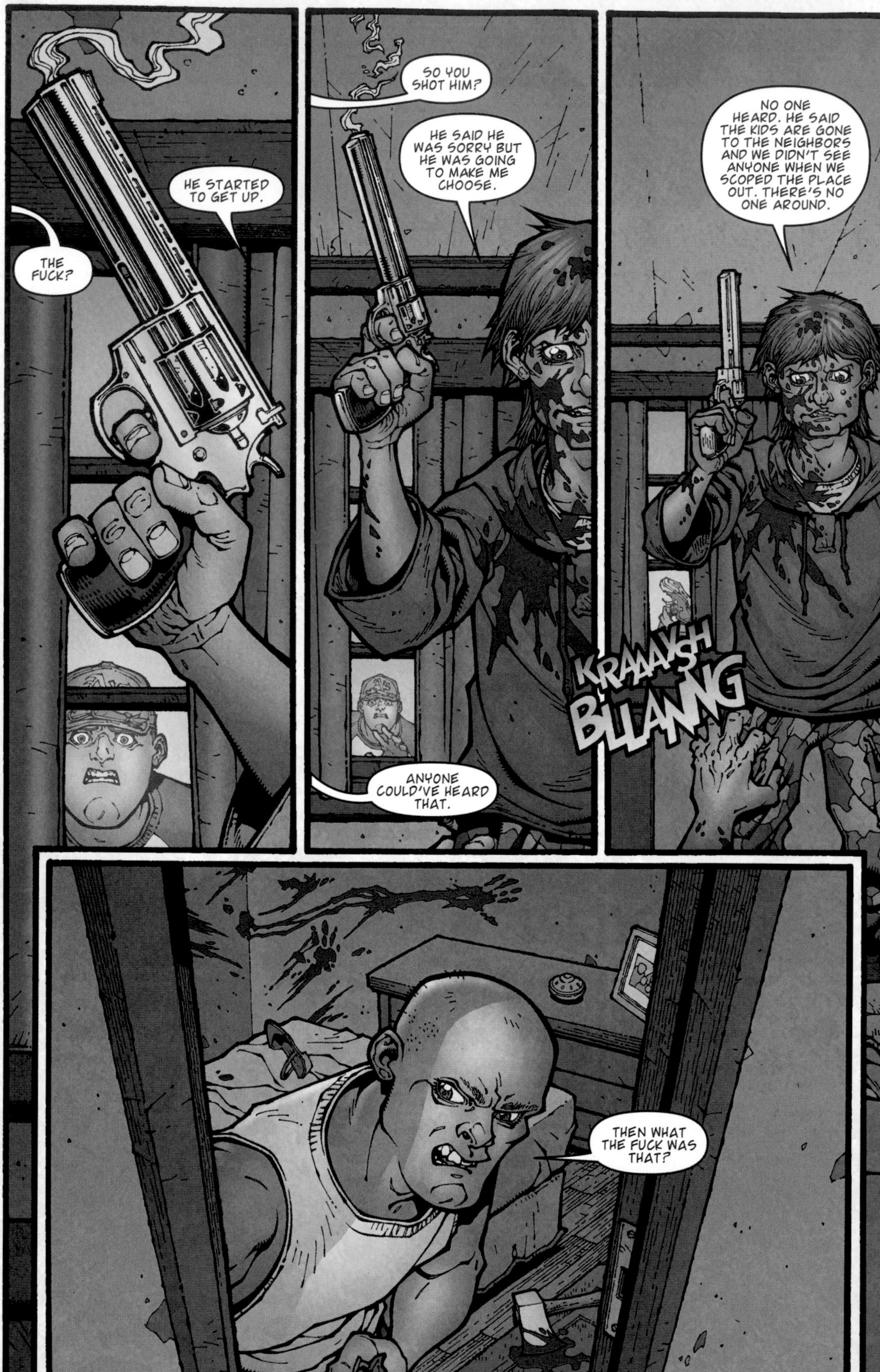
THE FUCK?
HE STARTED TO GET UP.
SO YOU SHOT HIM?
HE SAID HE WAS SORRY BUT HE WAS GOING TO MAKE ME CHOOSE.
ANYONE COULD'VE HEARD THAT.
NO ONE HEARD. HE SAID THE KIDS ARE GONE TO THE NEIGHBORS AND WE DIDN'T SEE ANYONE WHEN WE SCOPED THE PLACE OUT. THERE'S NO ONE AROUND.
KRAAAYSH
BLLANNG
THEN WHAT THE FUCK WAS THAT?

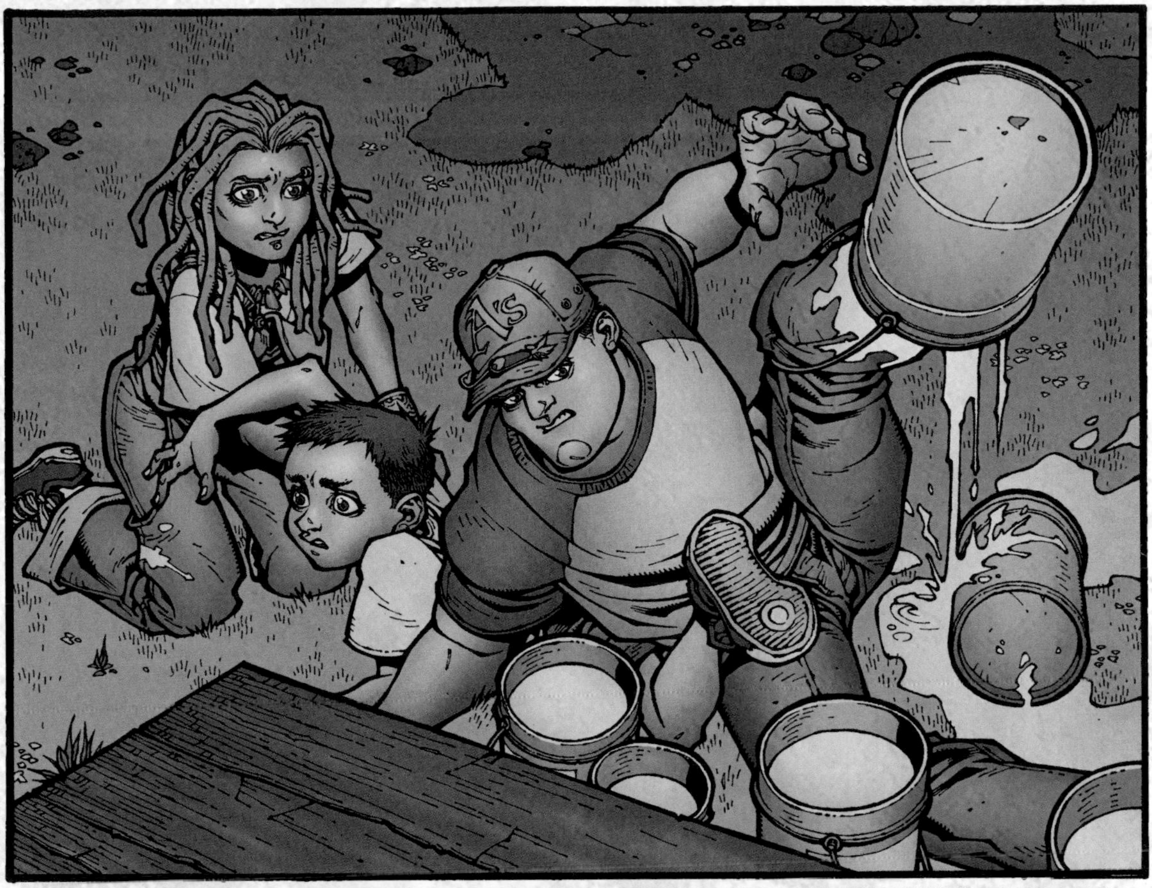

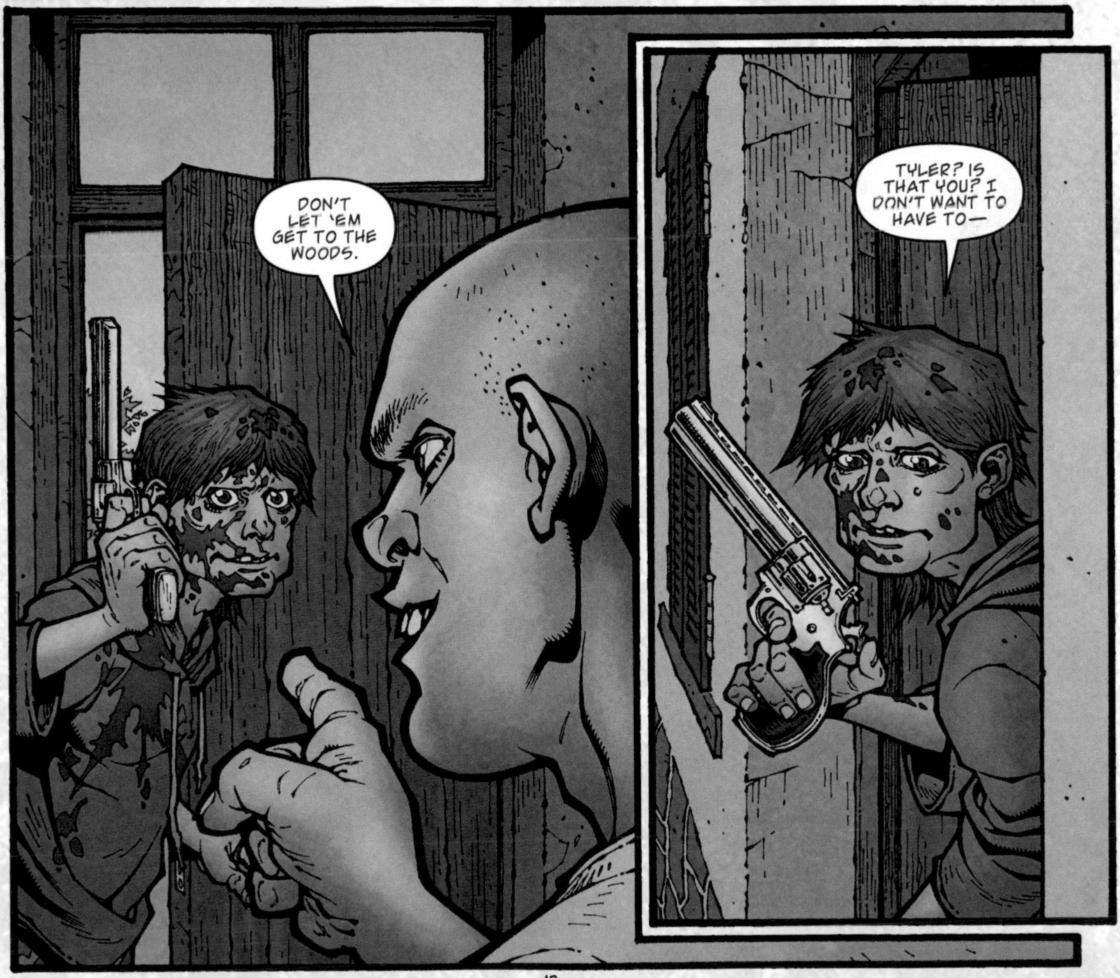
DON'T LET 'EM GET TO THE WOODS.
TYLER? IS THAT YOU? I DON'T WANT TO HAVE TO—

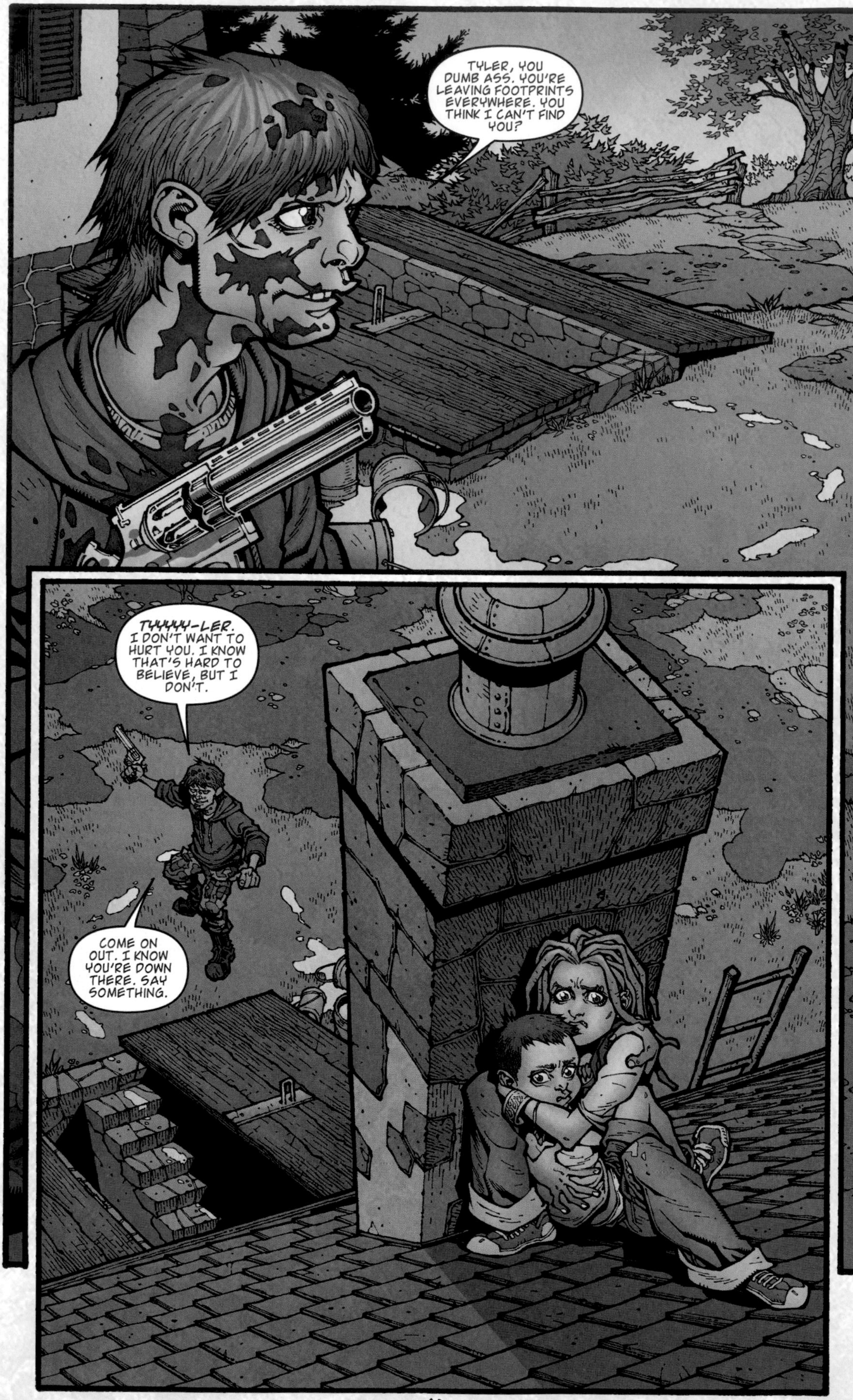

TYLER, YOU DUMB ASS. YOU'RE LEAVING FOOTPRINTS EVERYWHERE. YOU THINK I CAN'T FIND YOU?
TYYYYY-LER. I DON'T WANT TO HURT YOU. I KNOW THAT'S HARD TO BELIEVE, BUT I DON'T.
COME ON OUT. I KNOW YOU'RE DOWN THERE. SAY SOMETHING.

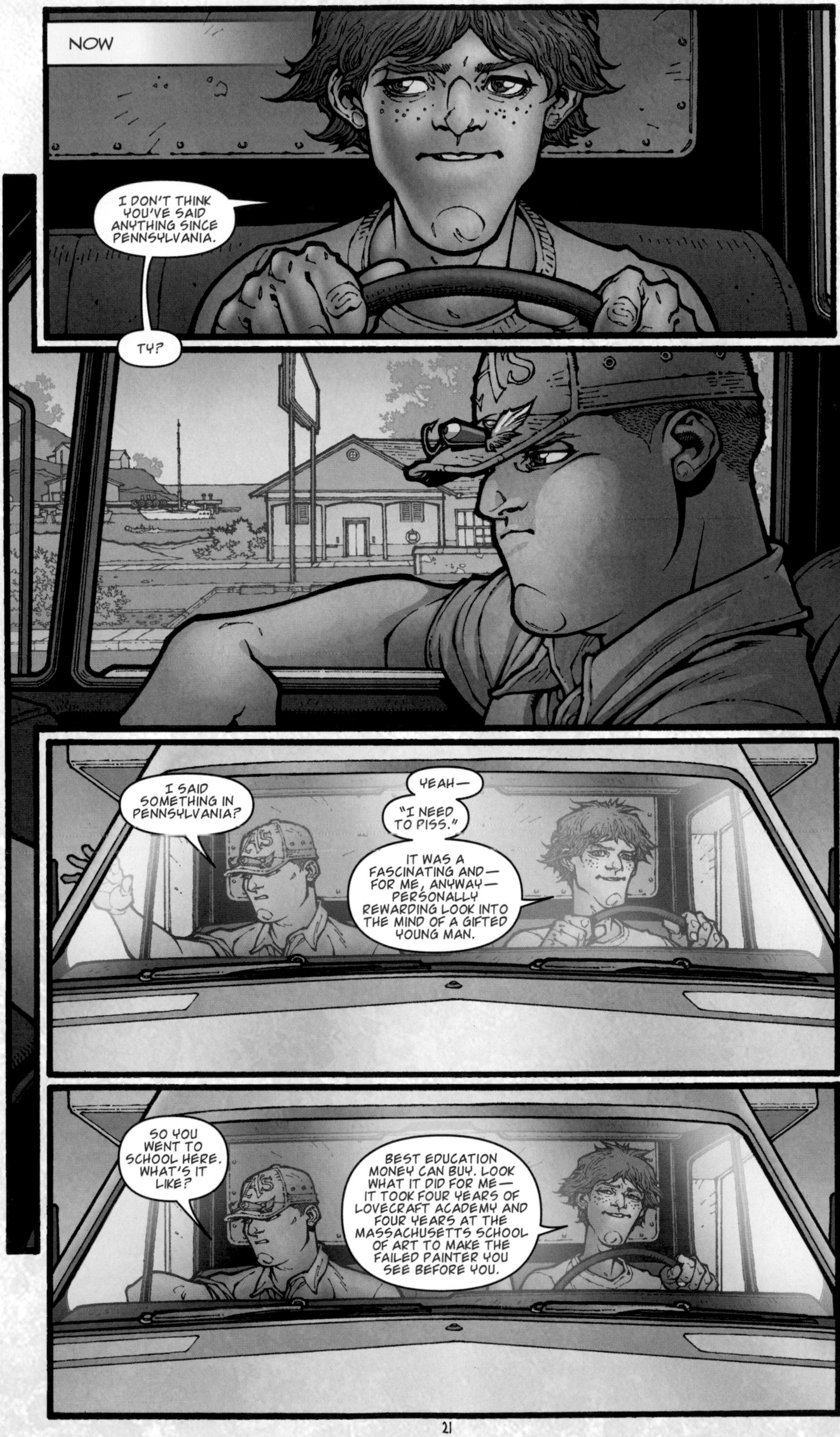
NOW
I DON'T THINK YOU'VE SAID ANYTHING SINCE PENNSYLVANIA.
TY?
I SAID SOMETHING IN PENNSYLVANIA?
YEAH—
"I NEED TO PISS."
IT WAS A FASCINATING AND—FOR ME, ANYWAY—PERSONALLY REWARDING LOOK INTO THE MIND OF A GIFTED YOUNG MAN.
SO YOU WENT TO SCHOOL HERE. WHAT'S IT LIKE?
BEST EDUCATION MONEY CAN BUY. LOOK WHAT IT DID FOR ME—IT TOOK FOUR YEARS OF LOVECRAFT ACADEMY AND FOUR YEARS AT THE MASSACHUSETTS SCHOOL OF ART TO MAKE THE FAILED PAINTER YOU SEE BEFORE YOU.

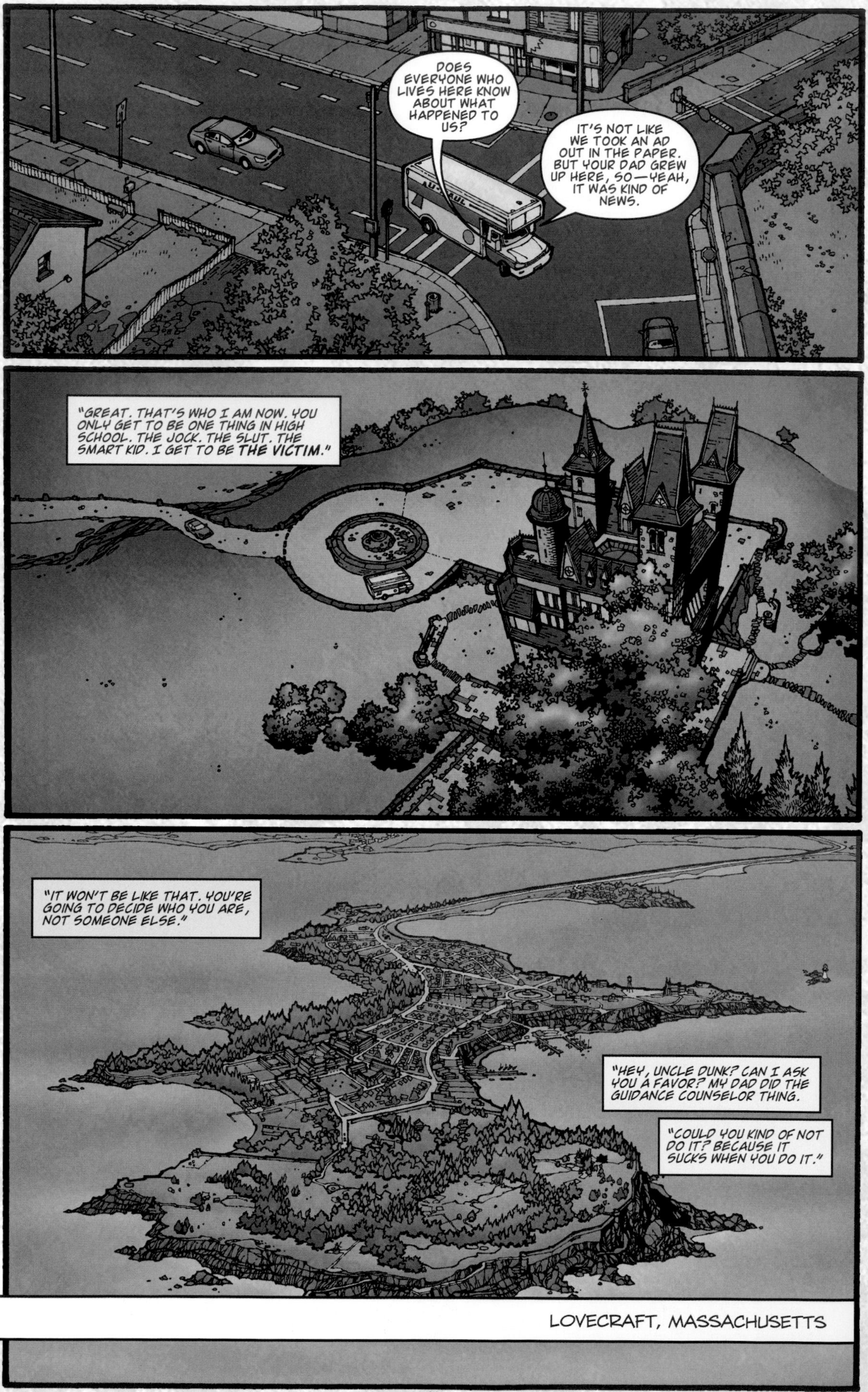
DOES EVERYONE WHO LIVES HERE KNOW ABOUT WHAT HAPPENED TO US?
IT'S NOT LIKE WE TOOK AN AD OUT IN THE PAPER. BUT YOUR DAD GREW UP HERE, SO—YEAH, IT WAS KIND OF NEWS.
"GREAT. THAT'S WHO I AM NOW. YOU ONLY GET TO BE ONE THING IN HIGH SCHOOL. THE JOCK. THE SLUT. THE SMART KID. I GET TO BE THE VICTIM."
"IT WON'T BE LIKE THAT. YOU'RE GOING TO DECIDE WHO YOU ARE, NOT SOMEONE ELSE."
"HEY, UNCLE DUNK? CAN I ASK YOU A FAVOR? MY DAD DID THE GUIDANCE COUNSELOR THING.
"COULD YOU KIND OF NOT DO IT? BECAUSE IT SUCKS WHEN YOU DO IT."
LOVECRAFT, MASSACHUSETTS

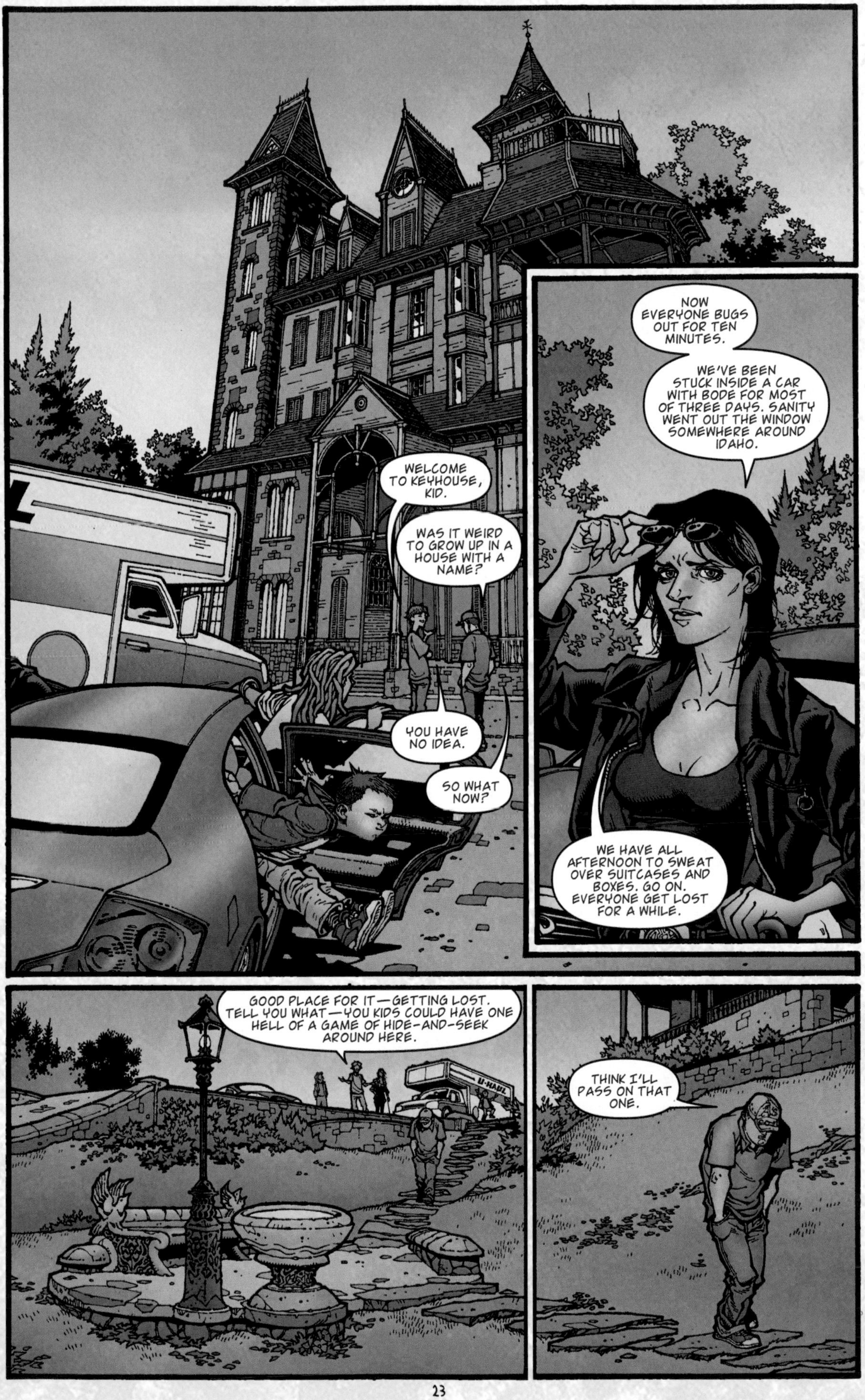
WELCOME TO KEYHOUSE, KID.
WAS IT WEIRD TO GROW UP IN A HOUSE WITH A NAME?
YOU HAVE NO IDEA.
SO WHAT NOW?
NOW EVERYONE BUGS OUT FOR TEN MINUTES.
WE'VE BEEN STUCK INSIDE A CAR WITH BODE FOR MOST OF THREE DAYS. SANITY WENT OUT THE WINDOW SOMEWHERE AROUND IDAHO.
WE HAVE ALL AFTERNOON TO SWEAT OVER SUITCASES AND BOXES. GO ON. EVERYONE GET LOST FOR A WHILE.
GOOD PLACE FOR IT—GETTING LOST. TELL YOU WHAT—YOU KIDS COULD HAVE ONE HELL OF A GAME OF HIDE-AND-SEEK AROUND HERE.
U-HAUL
THINK I'LL PASS ON THAT ONE.

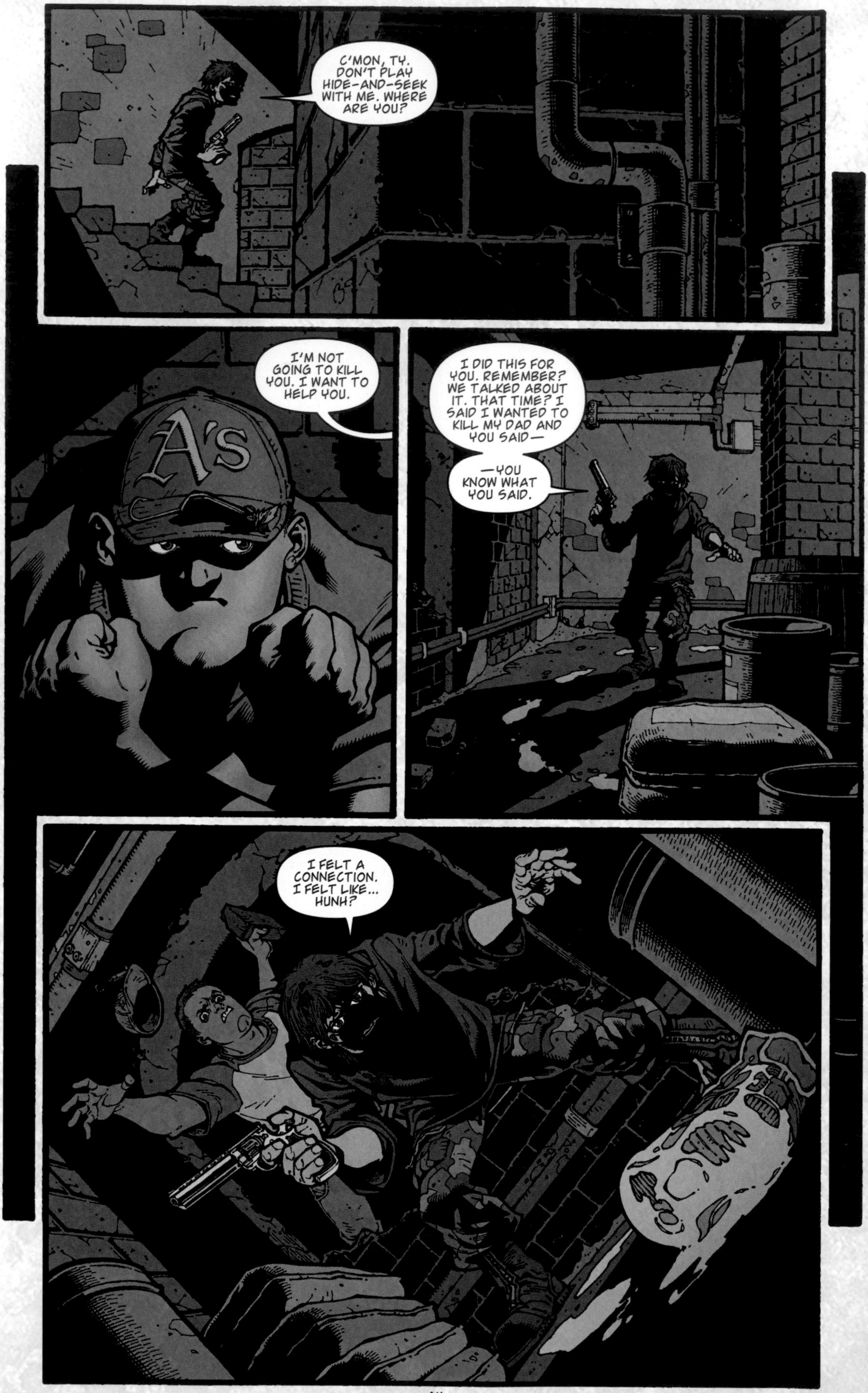
C'MON, TY. DON'T PLAY HIDE-AND-SEEK WITH ME. WHERE ARE YOU?
I'M NOT GOING TO KILL YOU. I WANT TO HELP YOU.
I DID THIS FOR YOU. REMEMBER? WE TALKED ABOUT IT. THAT TIME? I SAID I WANTED TO KILL MY DAD AND YOU SAID—
—YOU KNOW WHAT YOU SAID.
I FELT A CONNECTION. I FELT LIKE... HUNH?

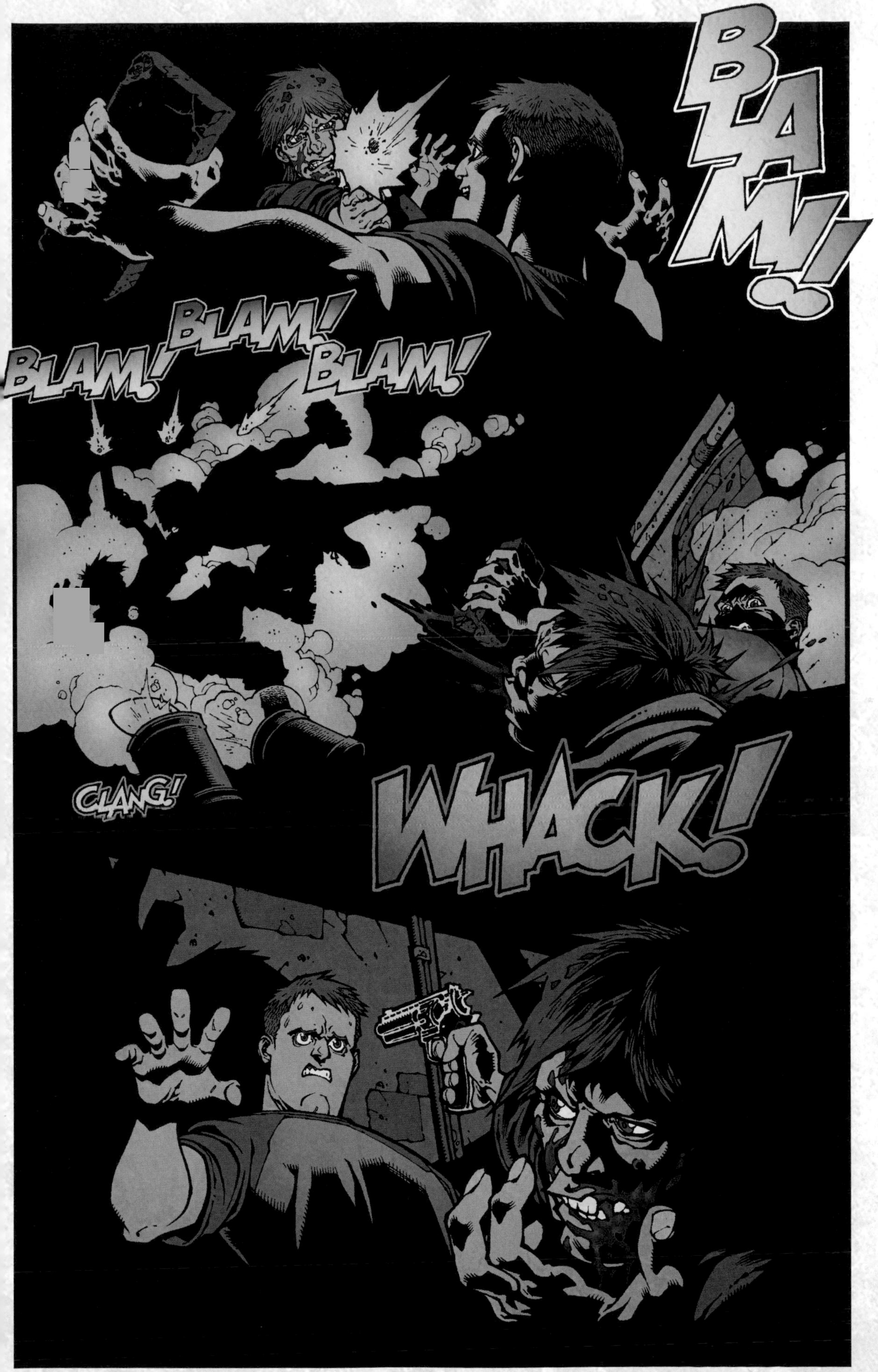
BLAM!
BLAM! BLAM! BLAM!
CLANG!
WHACK!

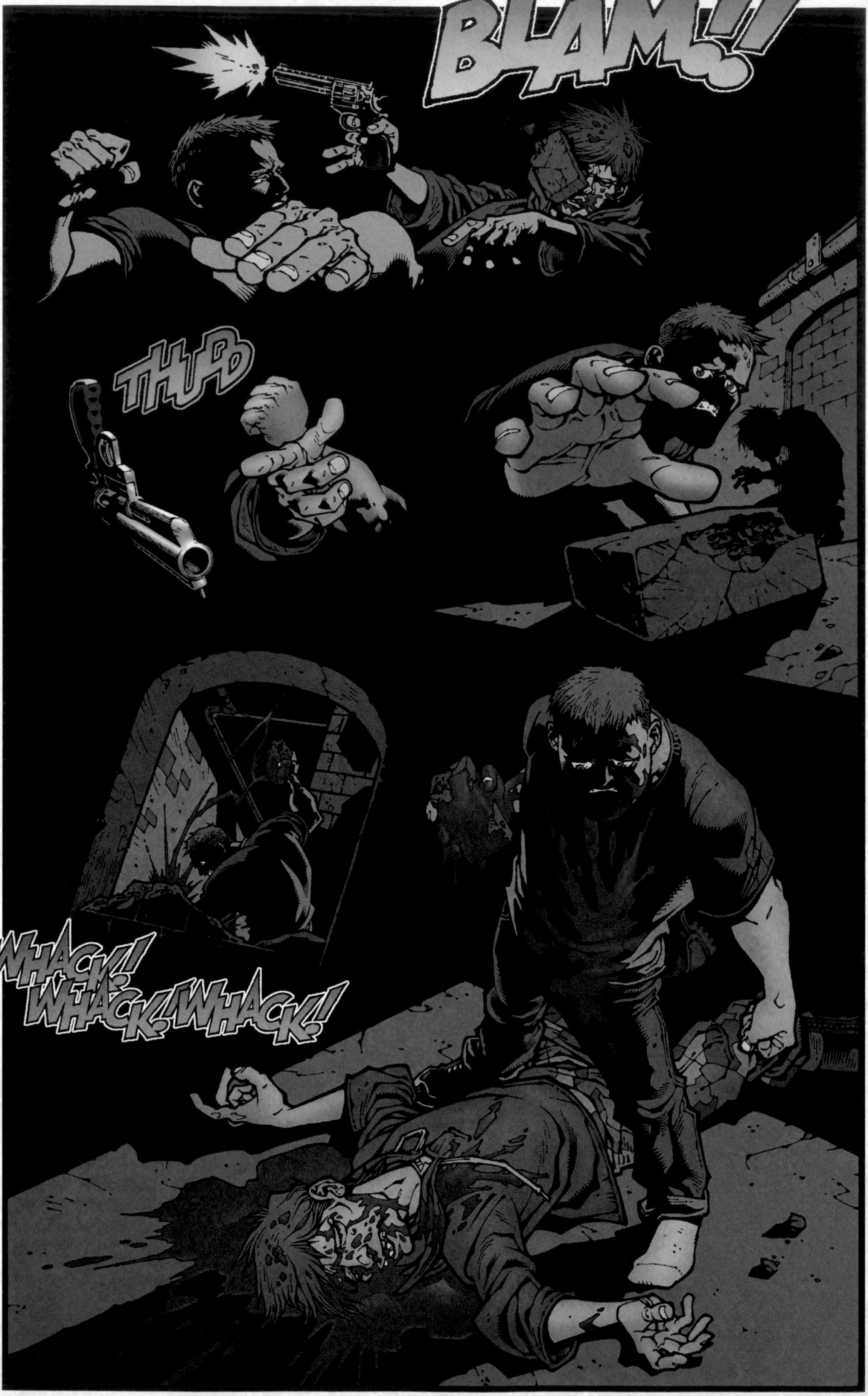
BLAM!!
THUD
WHACK!
WHACK! WHACK!

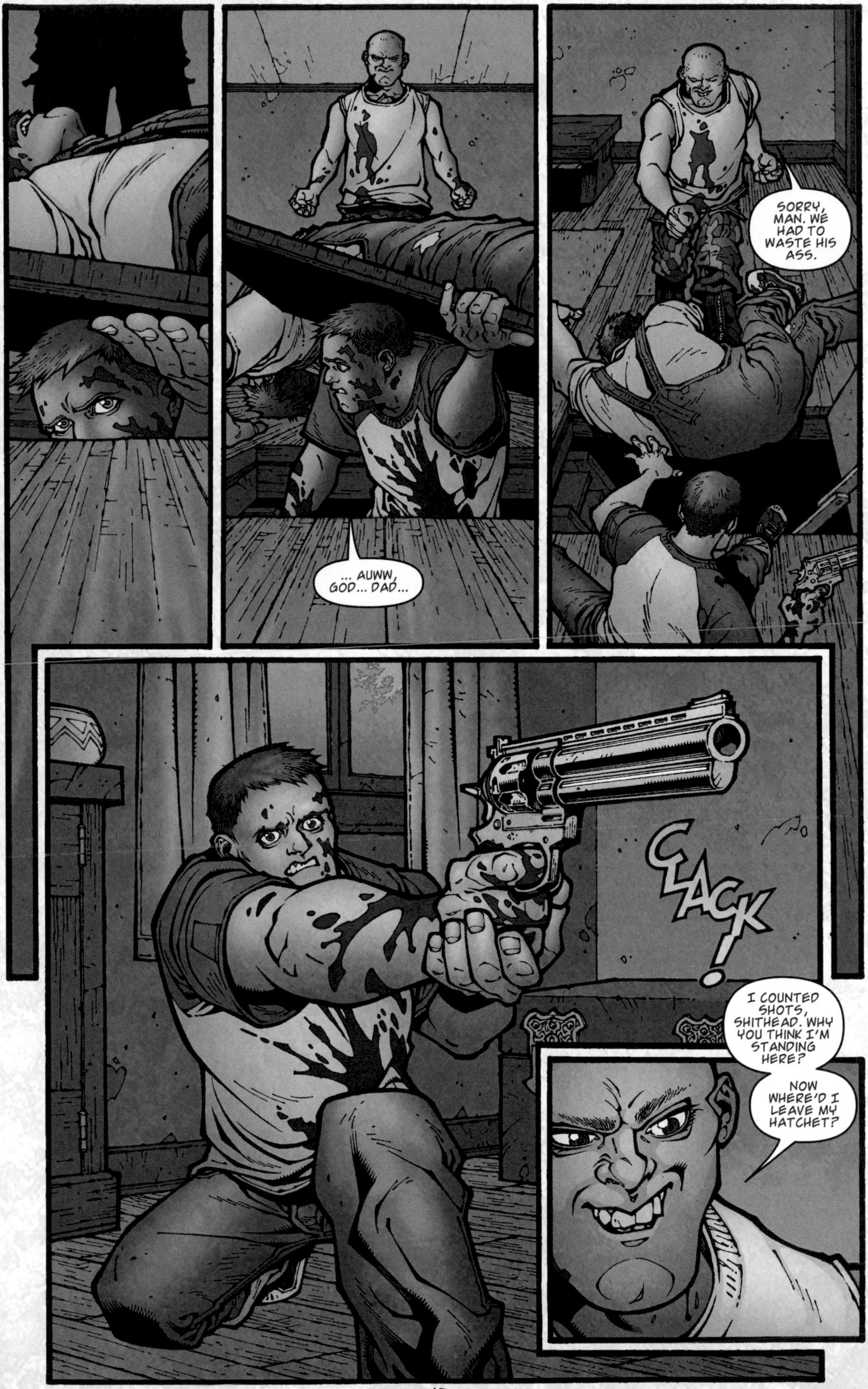
... AUWW, GOD... DAD...
SORRY, MAN. WE HAD TO WASTE HIS ASS.
CLACK!
I COUNTED SHOTS, SHITHEAD. WHY YOU THINK I'M STANDING HERE?
NOW WHERE'D I LEAVE MY HATCHET?

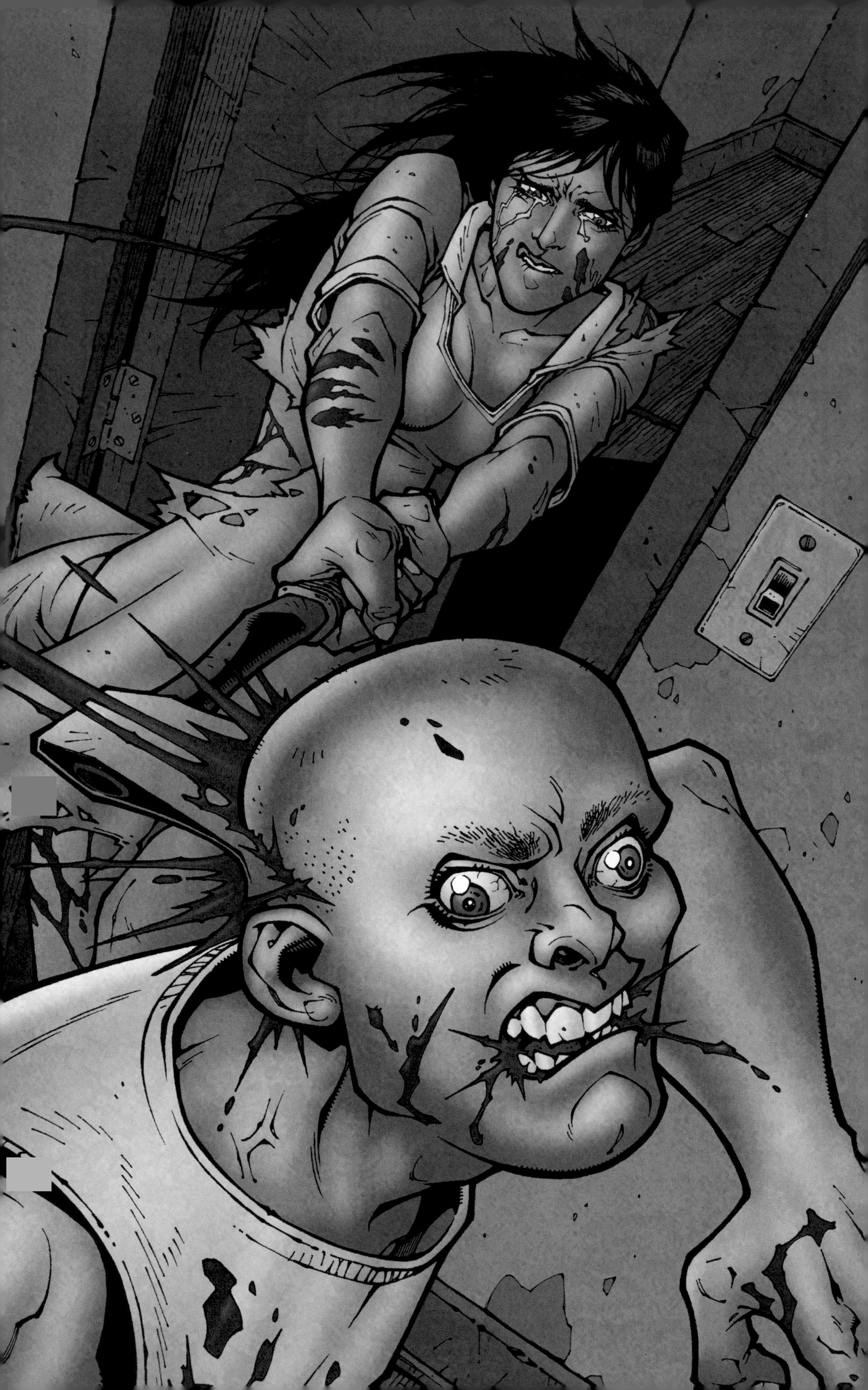

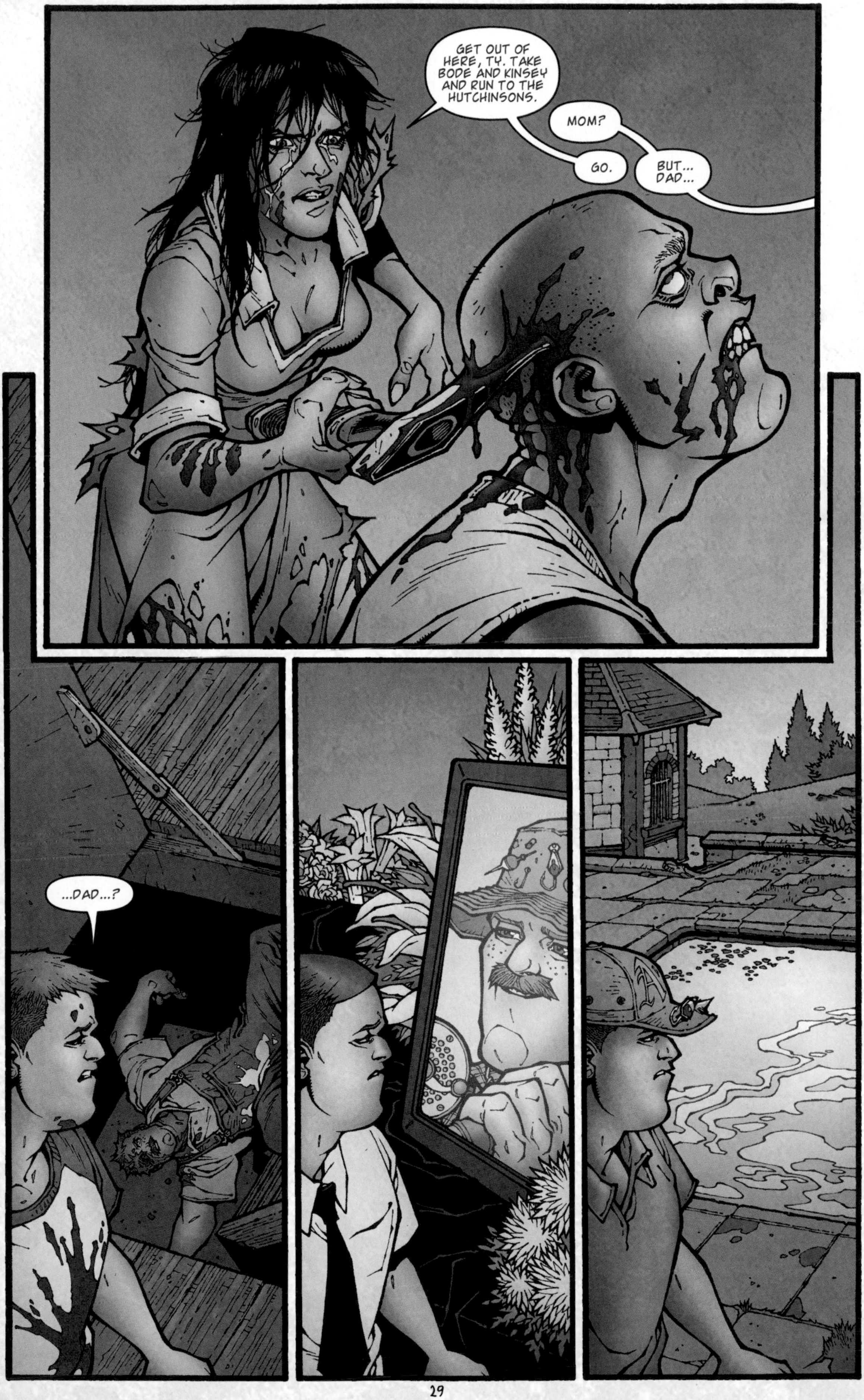
GET OUT OF HERE, TY. TAKE BODE AND KINSEY AND RUN TO THE HUTCHINSONS.
MOM?
GO.
BUT... DAD...
...DAD...?

WANT TO GO INSIDE AND LOOK AROUND? WE GET TO PICK OUR OWN BEDROOMS. YOU'RE OLDEST. YOU COULD PICK FIRST.

I'LL JUST THROW DOWN WHEREVER.

WHAT'S HOLDING YOU TOGETHER?

I MEAN, I'VE CRIED ABOUT A THOUSAND TIMES. I KNOW YOU AND DAD BUTTED HEADS A LOT, BUT YOU WERE LIKE—CHRIST— LIKE HIS FAVORITE OR SOMETHING...

...AW, SHIT. HERE I GO AGAIN.

WHATEVER I WAS TO HIM—I WASN'T WORTH IT.

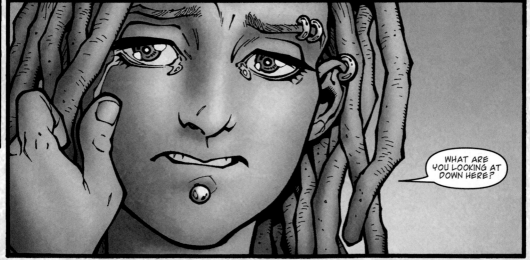

WHAT ARE YOU LOOKING AT DOWN HERE?

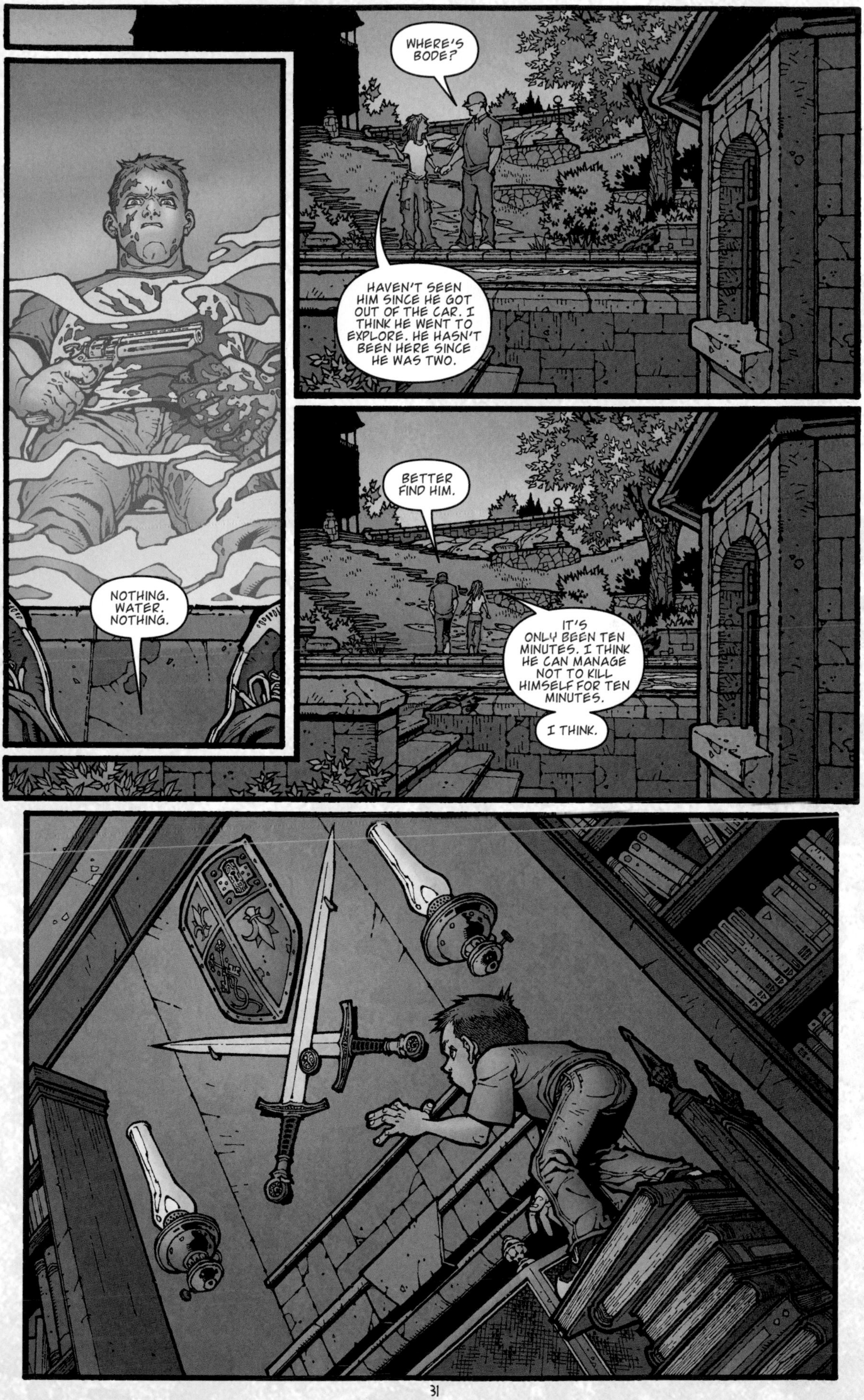
NOTHING. WATER. NOTHING.
WHERE'S BODE?
HAVEN'T SEEN HIM SINCE HE GOT OUT OF THE CAR. I THINK HE WENT TO EXPLORE. HE HASN'T BEEN HERE SINCE HE WAS TWO.
BETTER FIND HIM.
IT'S ONLY BEEN TEN MINUTES. I THINK HE CAN MANAGE NOT TO KILL HIMSELF FOR TEN MINUTES.
I THINK.

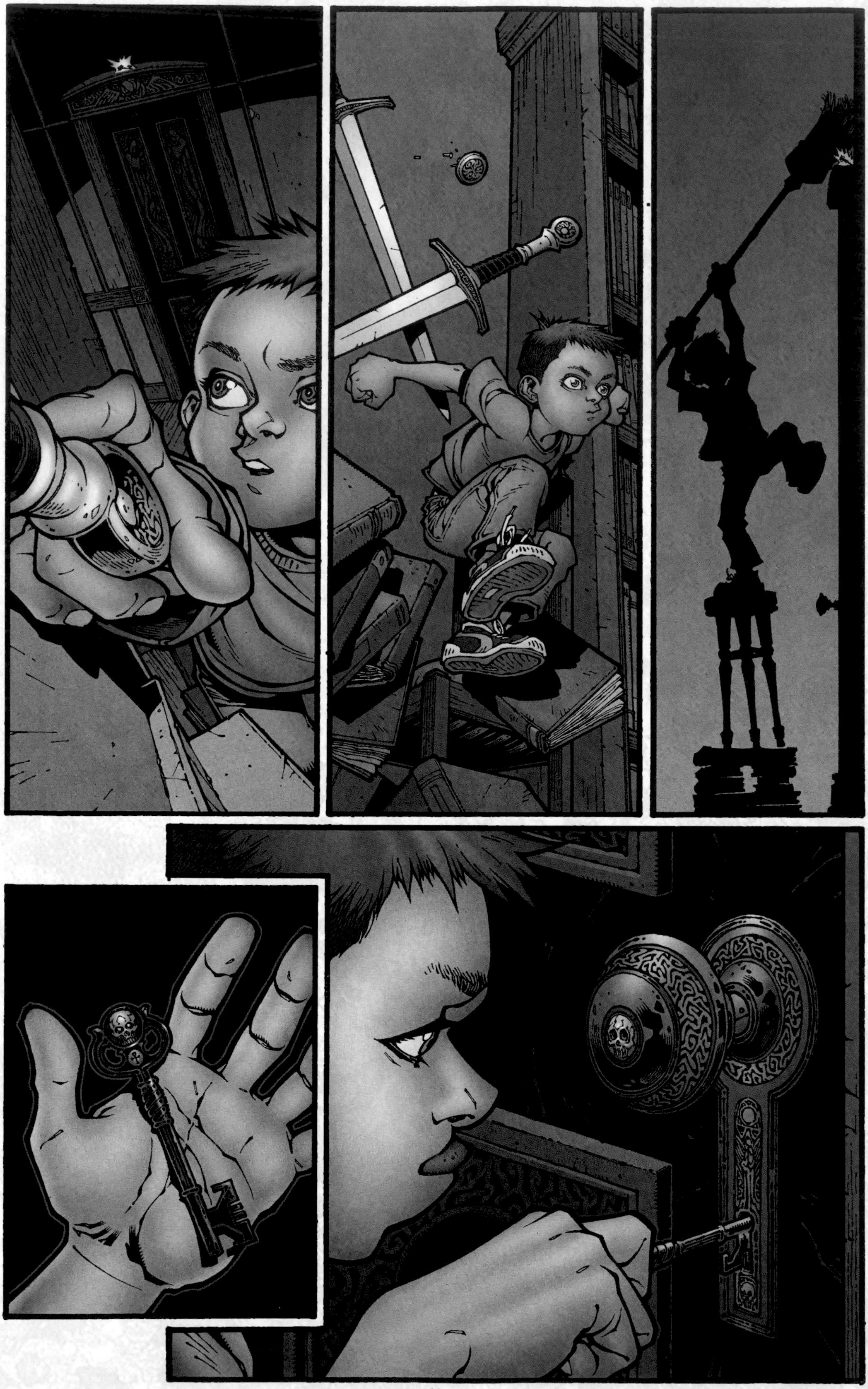

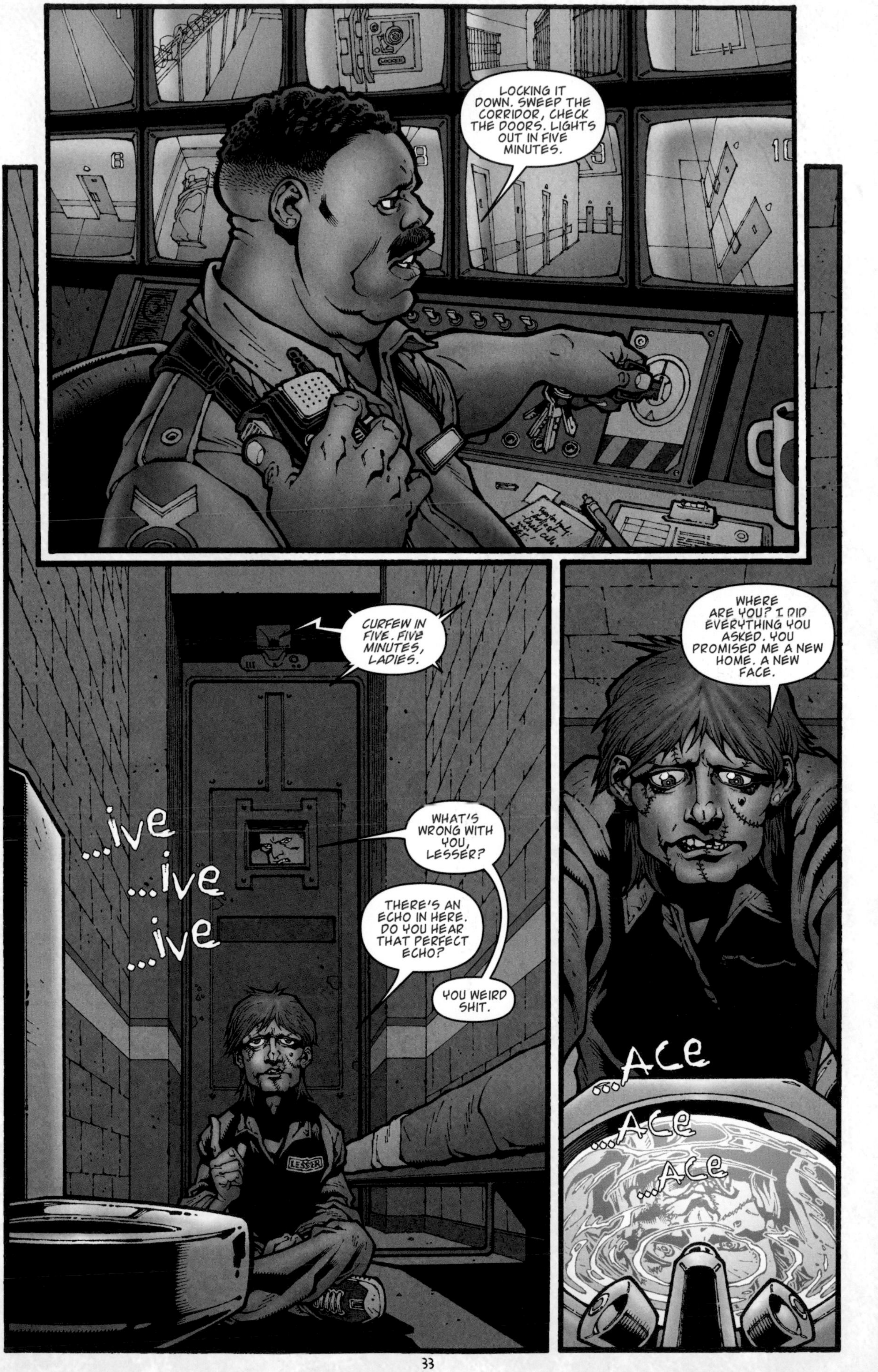

LOCKING IT DOWN. SWEEP THE CORRIDOR, CHECK THE DOORS. LIGHTS OUT IN FIVE MINUTES.
CURFEW IN FIVE. FIVE MINUTES, LADIES.
...ive
...ive
...ive
WHAT'S WRONG WITH YOU, LESSER?
THERE'S AN ECHO IN HERE. DO YOU HEAR THAT PERFECT ECHO?
YOU WEIRD SHIT.
WHERE ARE YOU? I DID EVERYTHING YOU ASKED. YOU PROMISED ME A NEW HOME. A NEW FACE.
...ACE
...ACE
...ACE

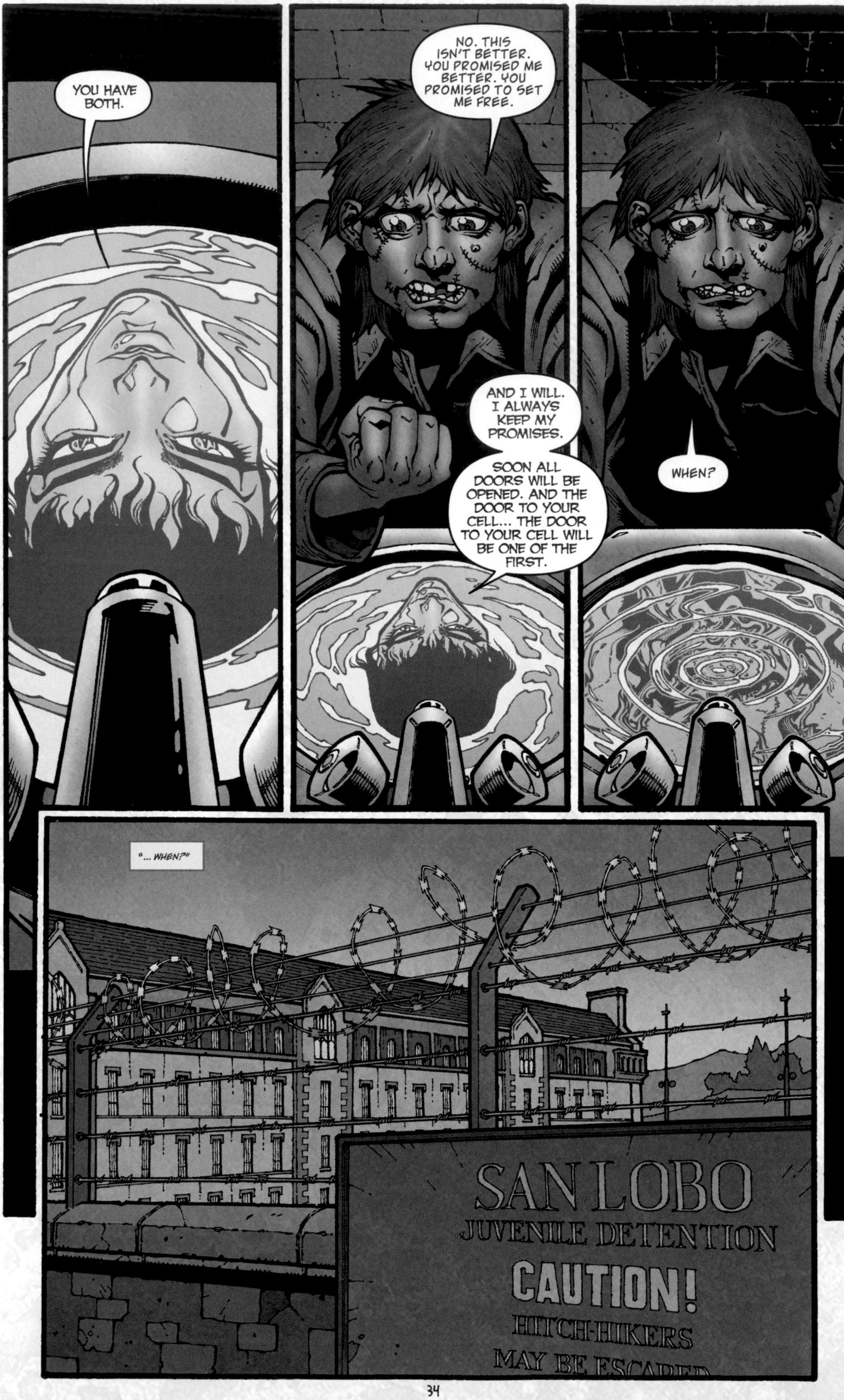

YOU HAVE BOTH.
NO. THIS ISN'T BETTER. YOU PROMISED ME BETTER. YOU PROMISED TO SET ME FREE.
AND I WILL. I ALWAYS KEEP MY PROMISES.
SOON ALL DOORS WILL BE OPENED. AND THE DOOR TO YOUR CELL... THE DOOR TO YOUR CELL WILL BE ONE OF THE FIRST.
WHEN?
"... WHEN?"
SAN LOBO
JUVENILE DETENTION
CAUTION!
HITCH-HIKERS

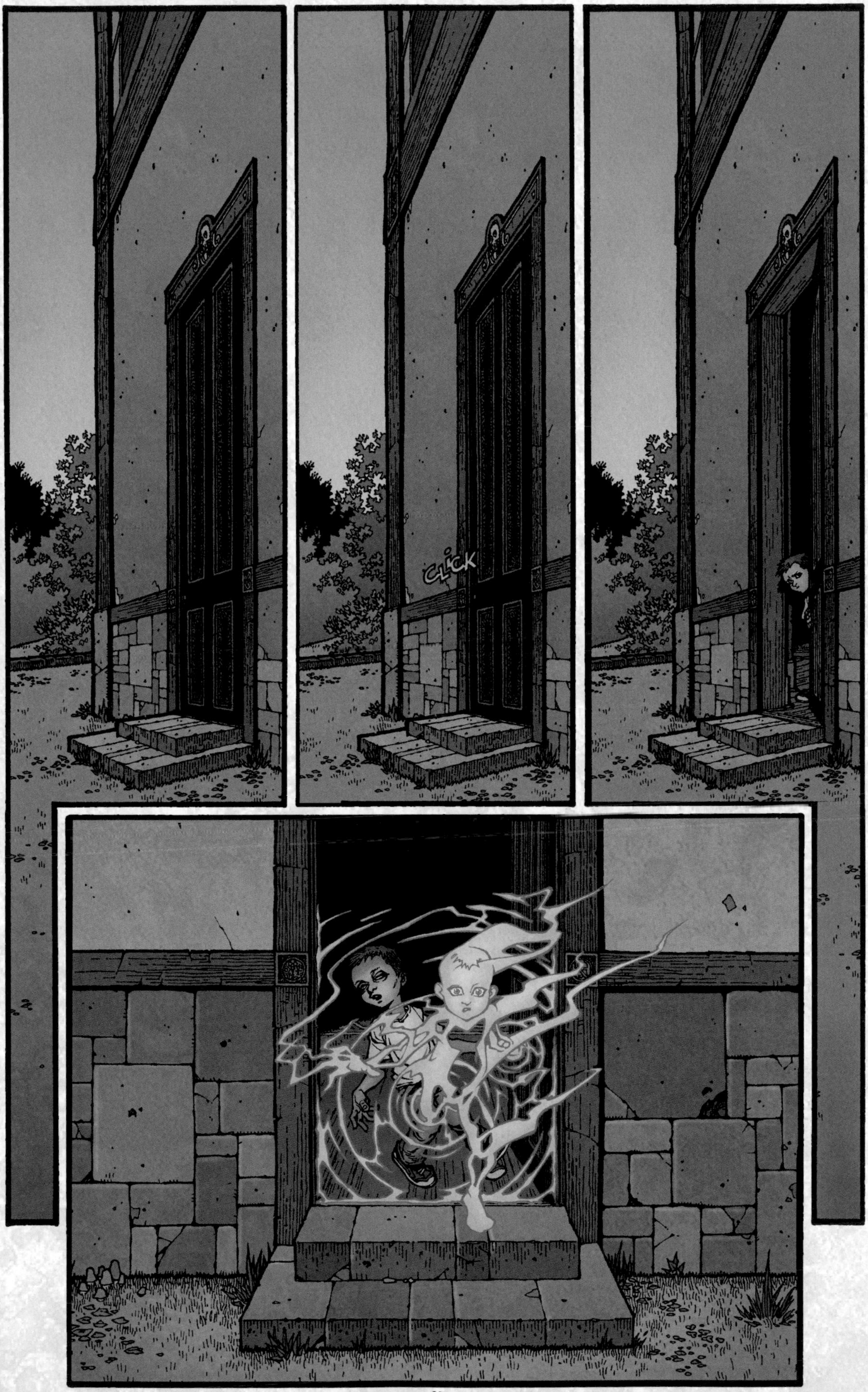
CLICK

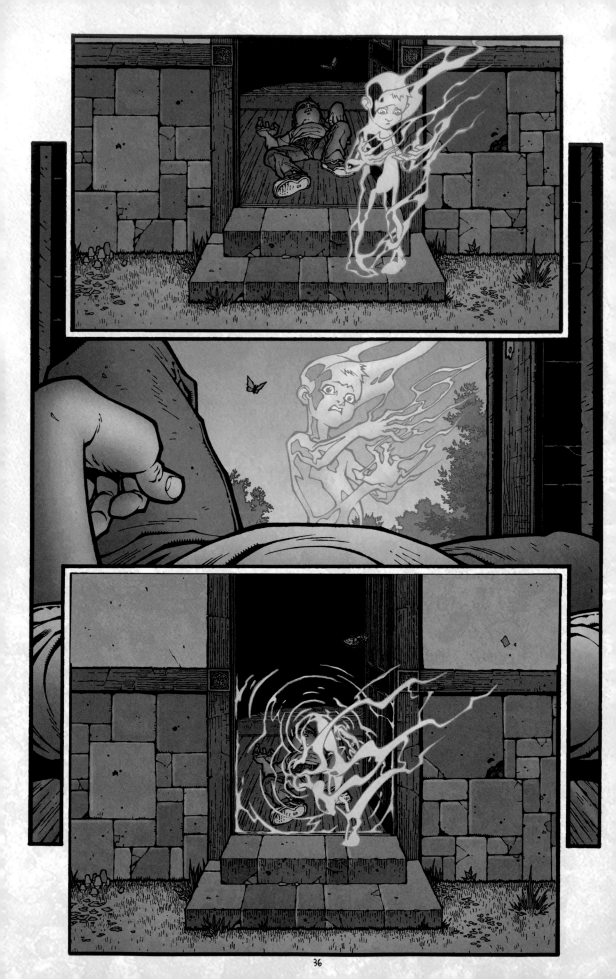

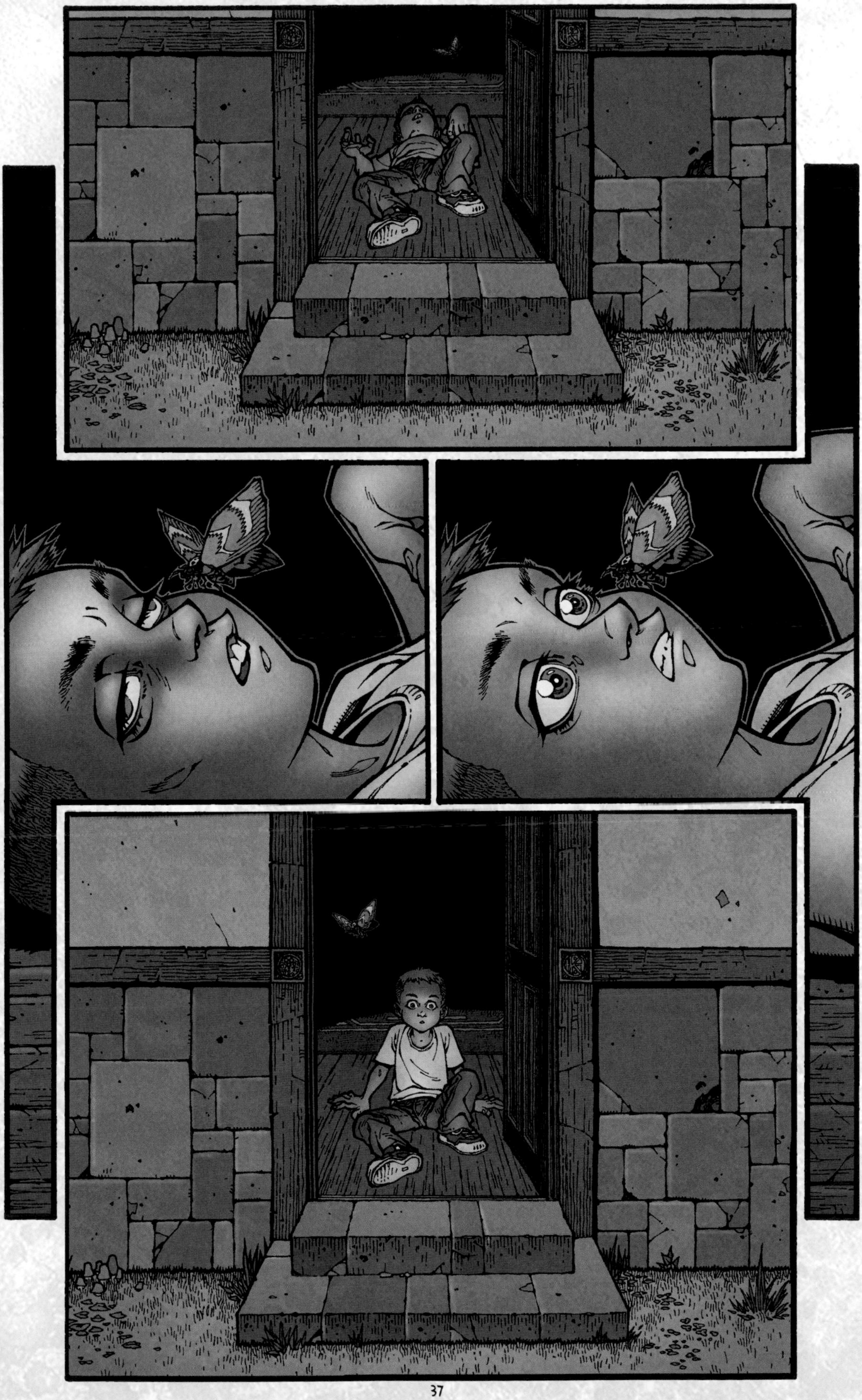

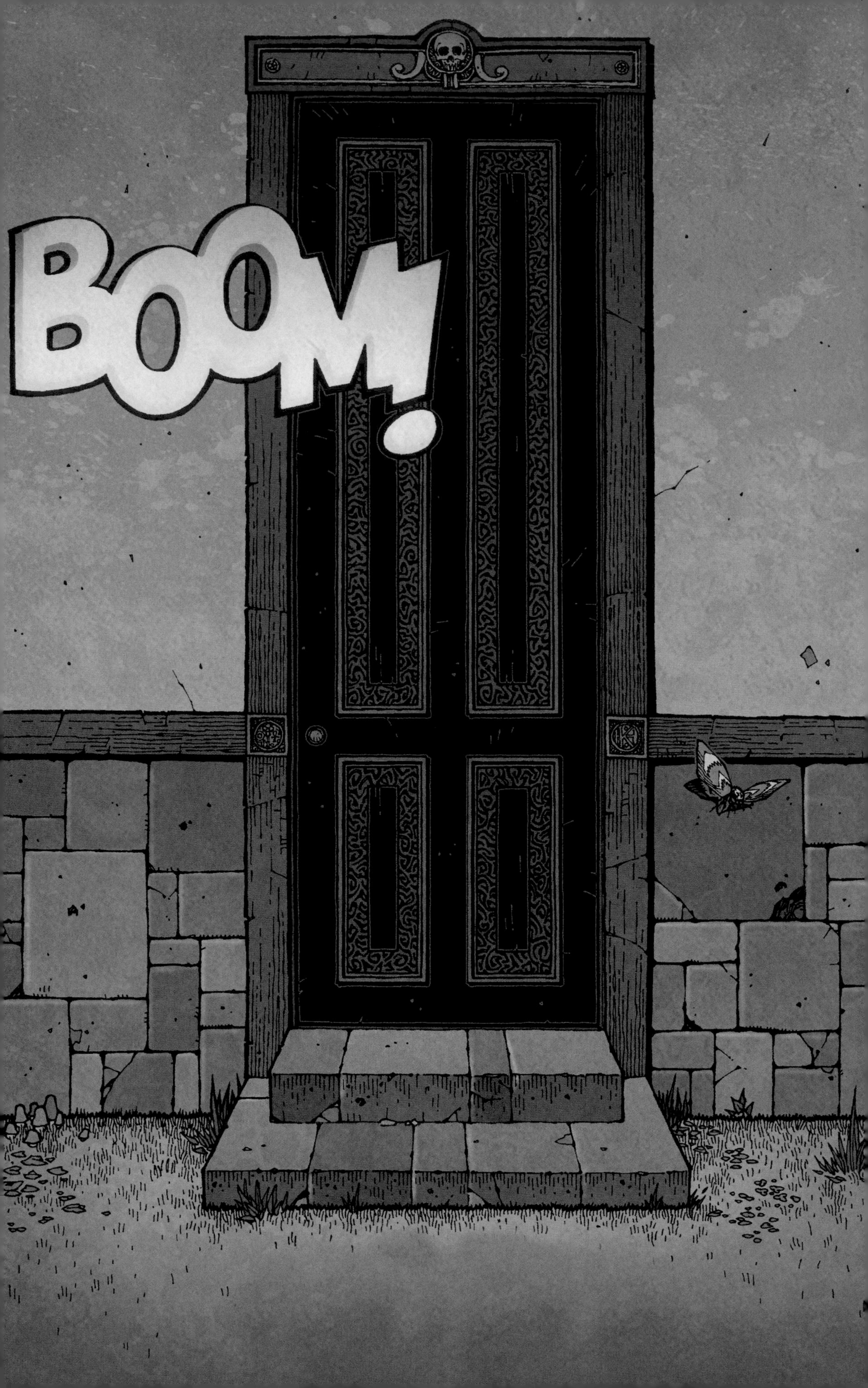
BOOM!

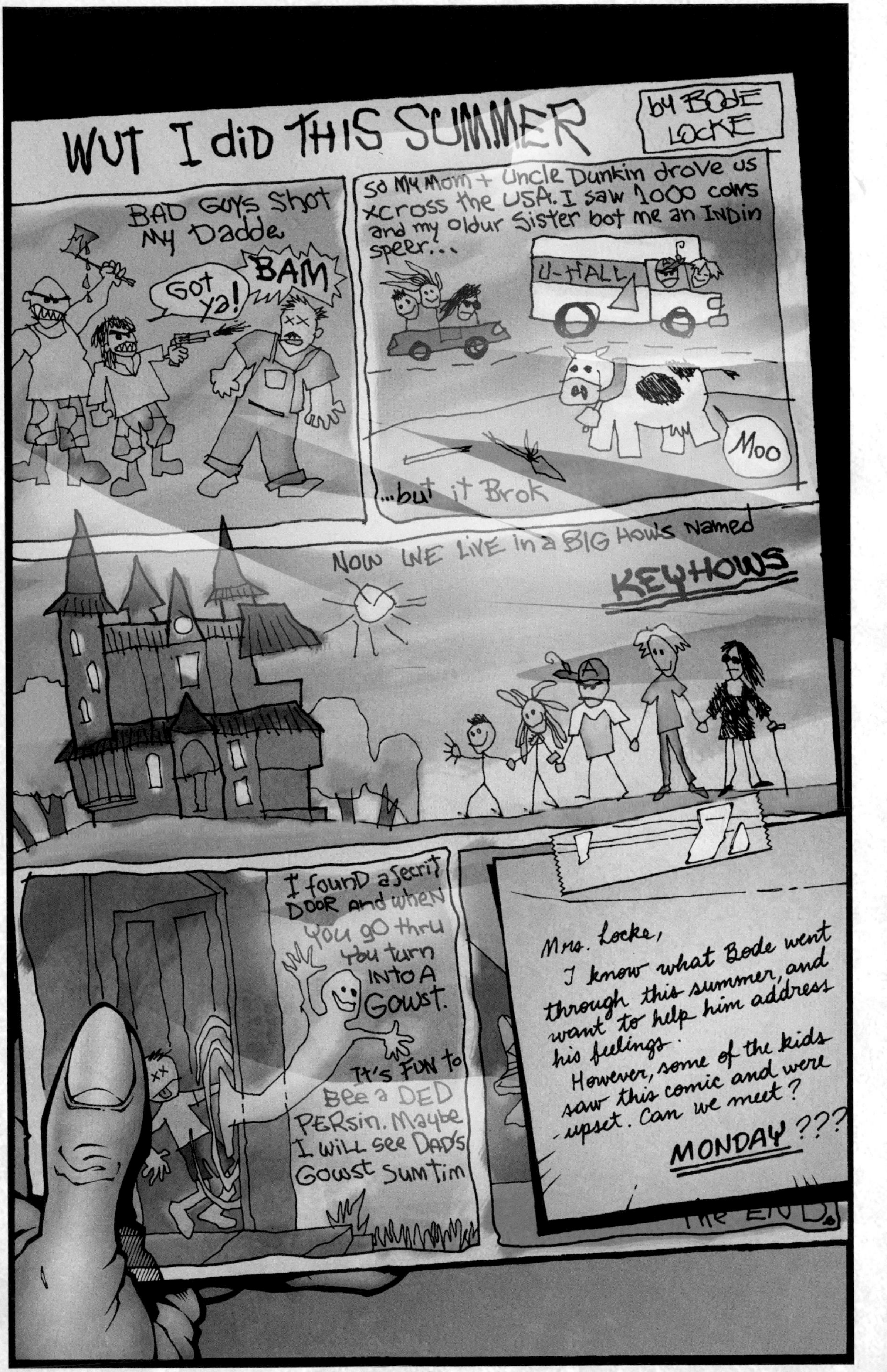
WUT I diD THIS SUMMER
by BODE LOCKE
BAD GUYS Shot My Dadde
Got ya!
BAM
So My Mom + Uncle Dunkin drove us xcross the USA. I saw 1000 cows and my oldur Sister bot me an INDin speer...
U-HALL
Moo
...but it Brok
NOW WE LIVE in a BIG Hows Named
KEYHOWS
I founD a Secrit DOOR And when You go thru You turn INTO A GOWST.
IT'S FUN to Bee a DED PERSin. Maybe I will see DAD's Gowst SumTim
Mrs. Locke,
I know what Bode went through this summer, and want to help him address his feelings.
However, some of the kids saw this comic and were upset. Can we meet?
MONDAY???

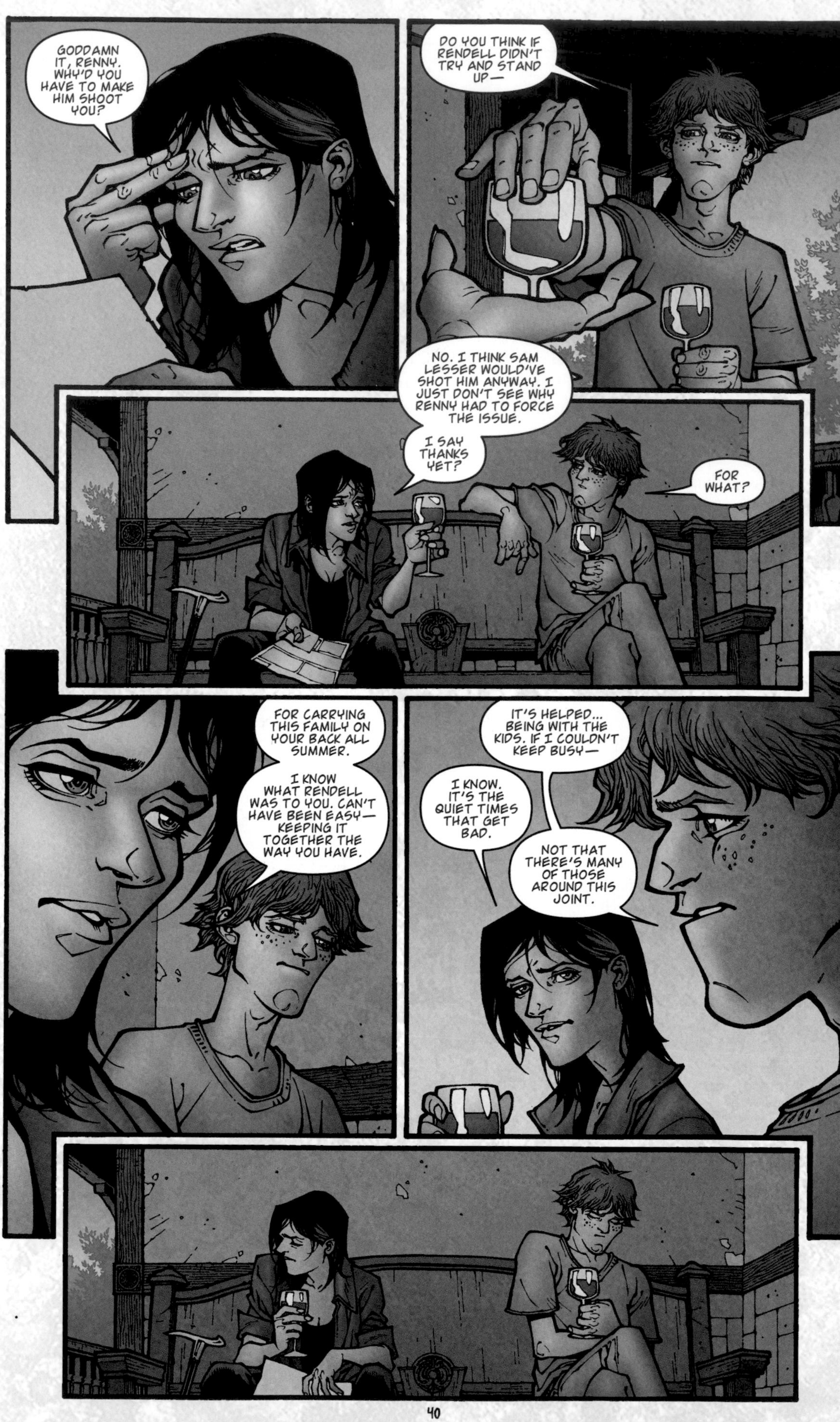

GODDAMN IT, RENNY. WHY'D YOU HAVE TO MAKE HIM SHOOT YOU?
DO YOU THINK IF RENDELL DIDN'T TRY AND STAND UP—
NO. I THINK SAM LESSER WOULD'VE SHOT HIM ANYWAY. I JUST DON'T SEE WHY RENNY HAD TO FORCE THE ISSUE.
I SAY THANKS YET?
FOR WHAT?
FOR CARRYING THIS FAMILY ON YOUR BACK ALL SUMMER.
I KNOW WHAT RENDELL WAS TO YOU. CAN'T HAVE BEEN EASY— KEEPING IT TOGETHER THE WAY YOU HAVE.
IT'S HELPED... BEING WITH THE KIDS. IF I COULDN'T KEEP BUSY—
I KNOW. IT'S THE QUIET TIMES THAT GET BAD.
NOT THAT THERE'S MANY OF THOSE AROUND THIS JOINT.

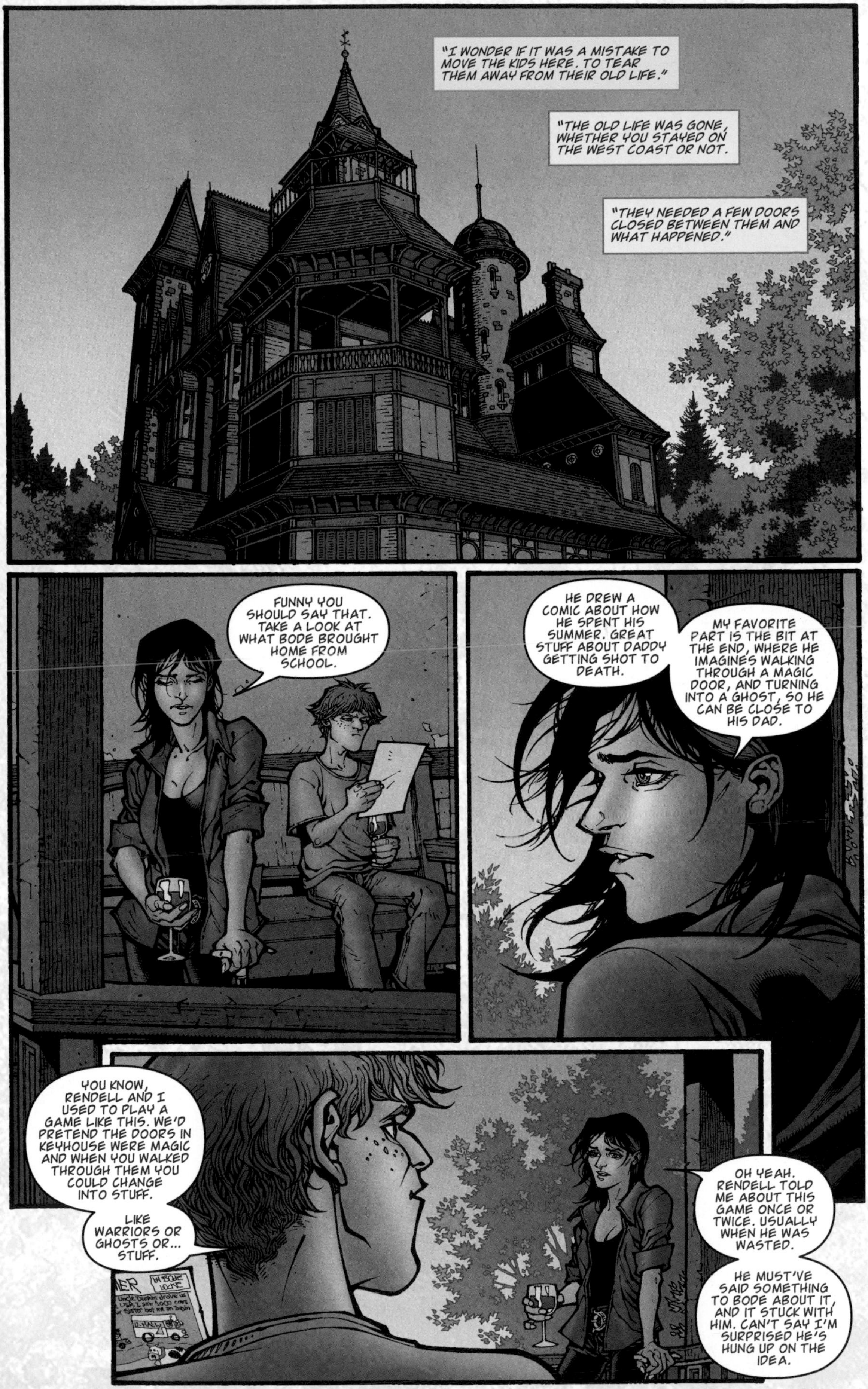
"I WONDER IF IT WAS A MISTAKE TO MOVE THE KIDS HERE. TO TEAR THEM AWAY FROM THEIR OLD LIFE."
"THE OLD LIFE WAS GONE, WHETHER YOU STAYED ON THE WEST COAST OR NOT.
"THEY NEEDED A FEW DOORS CLOSED BETWEEN THEM AND WHAT HAPPENED."
FUNNY YOU SHOULD SAY THAT. TAKE A LOOK AT WHAT BODE BROUGHT HOME FROM SCHOOL.
HE DREW A COMIC ABOUT HOW HE SPENT HIS SUMMER. GREAT STUFF ABOUT DADDY GETTING SHOT TO DEATH.
MY FAVORITE PART IS THE BIT AT THE END, WHERE HE IMAGINES WALKING THROUGH A MAGIC DOOR, AND TURNING INTO A GHOST, SO HE CAN BE CLOSE TO HIS DAD.
YOU KNOW, RENDELL AND I USED TO PLAY A GAME LIKE THIS. WE'D PRETEND THE DOORS IN KEYHOUSE WERE MAGIC AND WHEN YOU WALKED THROUGH THEM YOU COULD CHANGE INTO STUFF.
LIKE WARRIORS OR GHOSTS OR... STUFF.
OH YEAH. RENDELL TOLD ME ABOUT THIS GAME ONCE OR TWICE. USUALLY WHEN HE WAS WASTED.
HE MUST'VE SAID SOMETHING TO BODE ABOUT IT, AND IT STUCK WITH HIM. CAN'T SAY I'M SURPRISED HE'S HUNG UP ON THE IDEA.

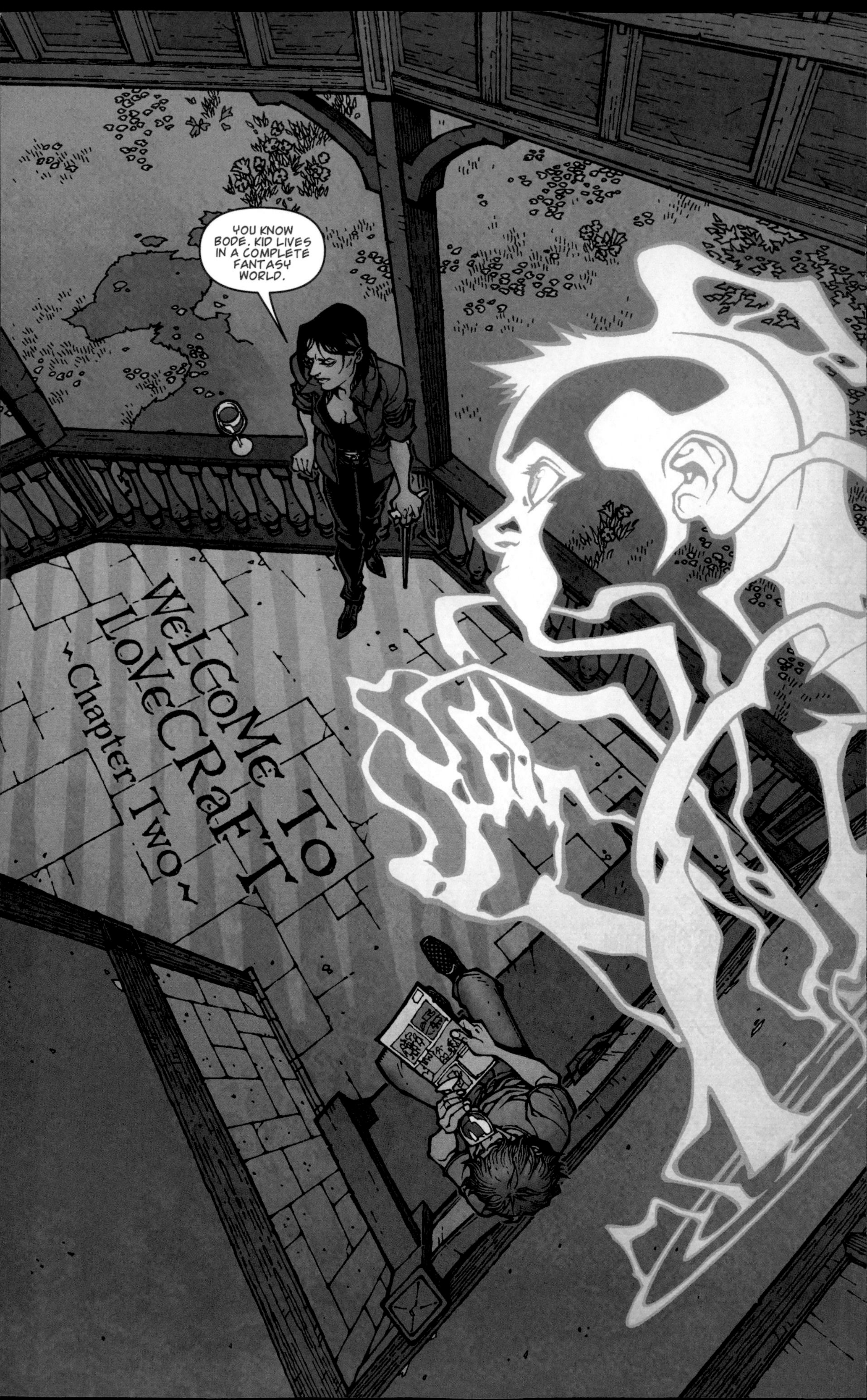
YOU KNOW BODE. KID LIVES IN A COMPLETE FANTASY WORLD.
WELCOME TO LOVECRAFT
~Chapter Two~

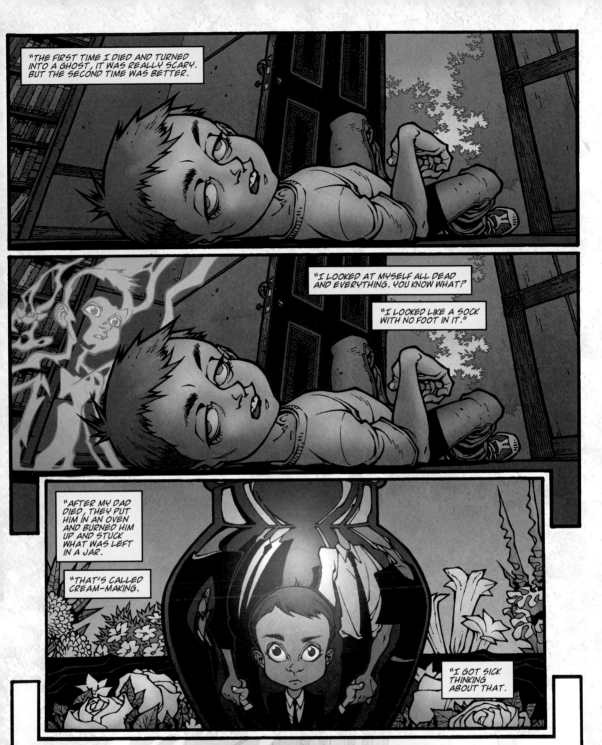

"THE FIRST TIME I DIED AND TURNED INTO A GHOST, IT WAS REALLY SCARY. BUT THE SECOND TIME WAS BETTER.

"I LOOKED AT MYSELF ALL DEAD AND EVERYTHING. YOU KNOW WHAT?

"I LOOKED LIKE A SOCK WITH NO FOOT IN IT."

"AFTER MY DAD DIED, THEY PUT HIM IN AN OVEN AND BURNED HIM UP AND STUCK WHAT WAS LEFT IN A JAR.

"THAT'S CALLED CREAM-MAKING.

"I GOT SICK THINKING ABOUT THAT.

"BUT MY BROTHER TYLER SAID DAD COULDN'T FEEL IT. MY BROTHER SAID HE WASN'T IN HIS BODY WHEN HE BURNED UP.

"I DIDN'T UNDERSTAND TYLER THEN, BUT I DO NOW. IT'S LIKE WE BURNED AN EMPTY SOCK."

"TYLER.

"WHEN YOU'RE DEAD, YOU GO PLACES IN BRIGHT FLASHES.

"SOMETIMES YOU GO TO SOMEONE JUST 'CAUSE YOU WERE THINKING ABOUT THEM.

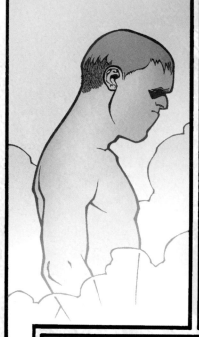

"TY'S TAKING ANOTHER SHOWER.

"WE USED TO PLAY FUN STUFF LIKE TORTURE AND MURDERBLANKET AND BURIED ALIVE AND WHACK-A-BODE, BUT NOW HE NEVER WANTS TO PLAY AND HE'S ALWAYS OFF BY HIMSELF LIKE IN THE SHOWER OR SOMETHING.

"I BET IT'S REALLY BAD FOR HIS SKIN. YOU GET WRINKLY WHEN YOU'RE IN THE WATER TOO LONG AND IF HE DOESN'T WATCH OUT, HE'LL GET ALL OLD AND WRINKLY FOR GOOD.

"WHEN YOU'RE A GHOST, YOU'RE SERIOUSLY COLD."

GA-ZAAAAAAH!

"OTHER TIMES, THINGS GET ALL BRIGHT AND YOU GO SEE SOMEONE BECAUSE THEY WERE THINKING ABOUT YOU."

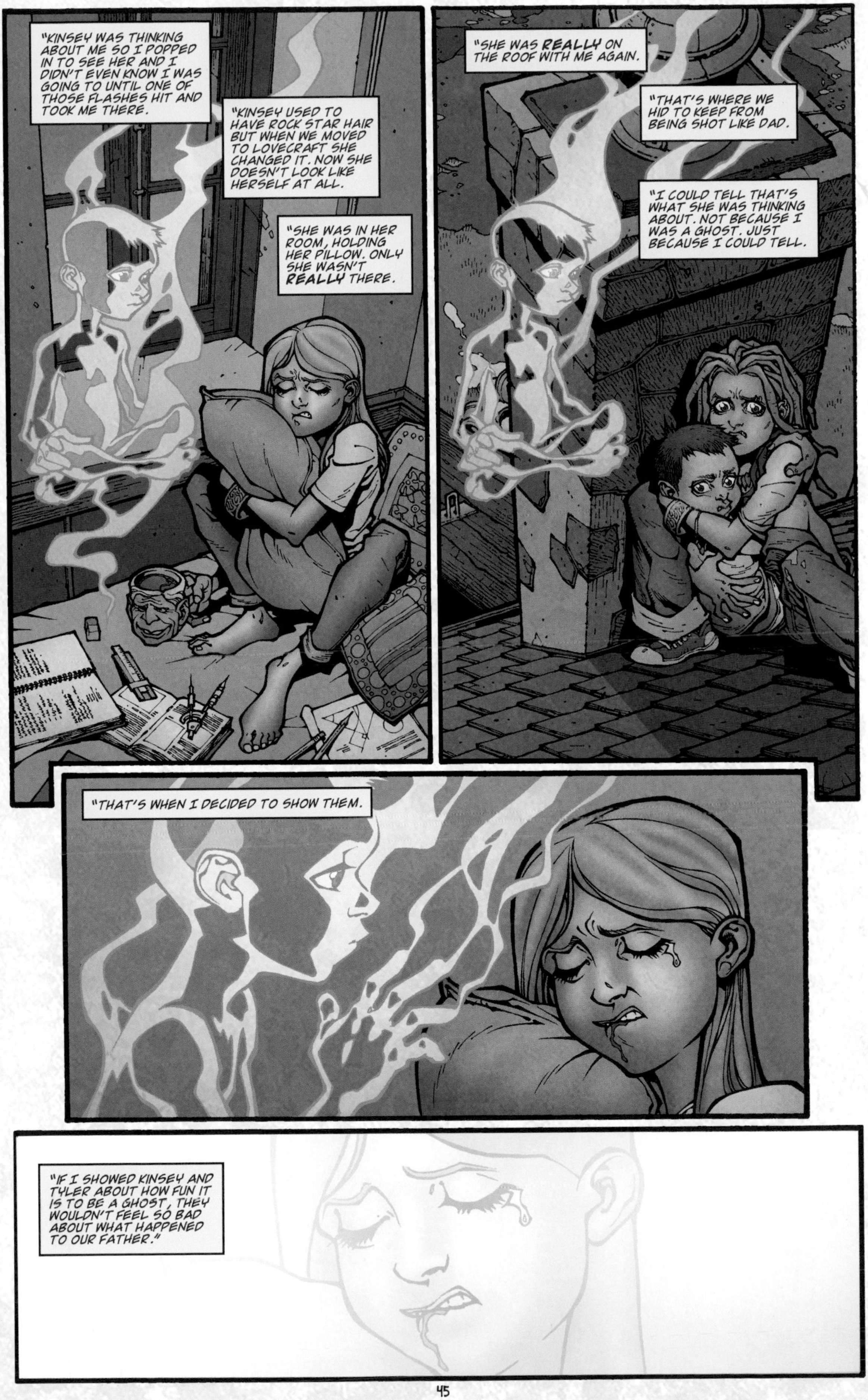
"KINSEY WAS THINKING ABOUT ME SO I POPPED IN TO SEE HER AND I DIDN'T EVEN KNOW I WAS GOING TO UNTIL ONE OF THOSE FLASHES HIT AND TOOK ME THERE.
"KINSEY USED TO HAVE ROCK STAR HAIR BUT WHEN WE MOVED TO LOVECRAFT SHE CHANGED IT. NOW SHE DOESN'T LOOK LIKE HERSELF AT ALL.
"SHE WAS IN HER ROOM, HOLDING HER PILLOW. ONLY SHE WASN'T **REALLY** THERE.
"SHE WAS **REALLY** ON THE ROOF WITH ME AGAIN.
"THAT'S WHERE WE HID TO KEEP FROM BEING SHOT LIKE DAD.
"I COULD TELL THAT'S WHAT SHE WAS THINKING ABOUT. NOT BECAUSE I WAS A GHOST. JUST BECAUSE I COULD TELL.
"THAT'S WHEN I DECIDED TO SHOW THEM.
"IF I SHOWED KINSEY AND TYLER ABOUT HOW FUN IT IS TO BE A GHOST, THEY WOULDN'T FEEL SO BAD ABOUT WHAT HAPPENED TO OUR FATHER."

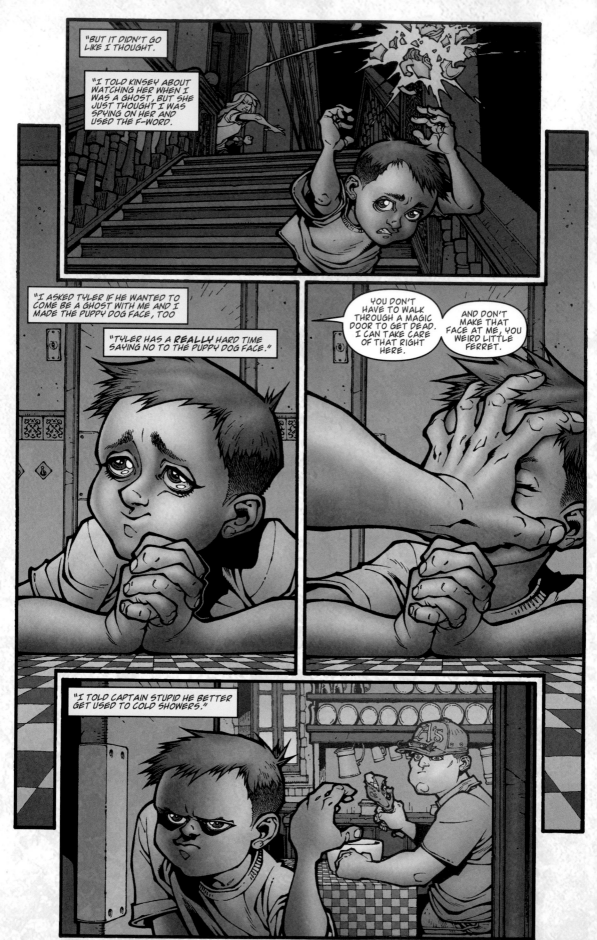

"BUT IT DIDN'T GO LIKE I THOUGHT.

"I TOLD KINSEY ABOUT WATCHING HER WHEN I WAS A GHOST, BUT SHE JUST THOUGHT I WAS SPYING ON HER AND USED THE F-WORD.

"I ASKED TYLER IF HE WANTED TO COME BE A GHOST WITH ME AND I MADE THE PUPPY DOG FACE, TOO

"TYLER HAS A **REALLY** HARD TIME SAYING NO TO THE PUPPY DOG FACE."

YOU DON'T HAVE TO WALK THROUGH A MAGIC DOOR TO GET DEAD. I CAN TAKE CARE OF THAT RIGHT HERE.

AND DON'T MAKE THAT FACE AT ME, YOU WEIRD LITTLE FERRET.

"I TOLD CAPTAIN STUPID HE BETTER GET USED TO COLD SHOWERS."

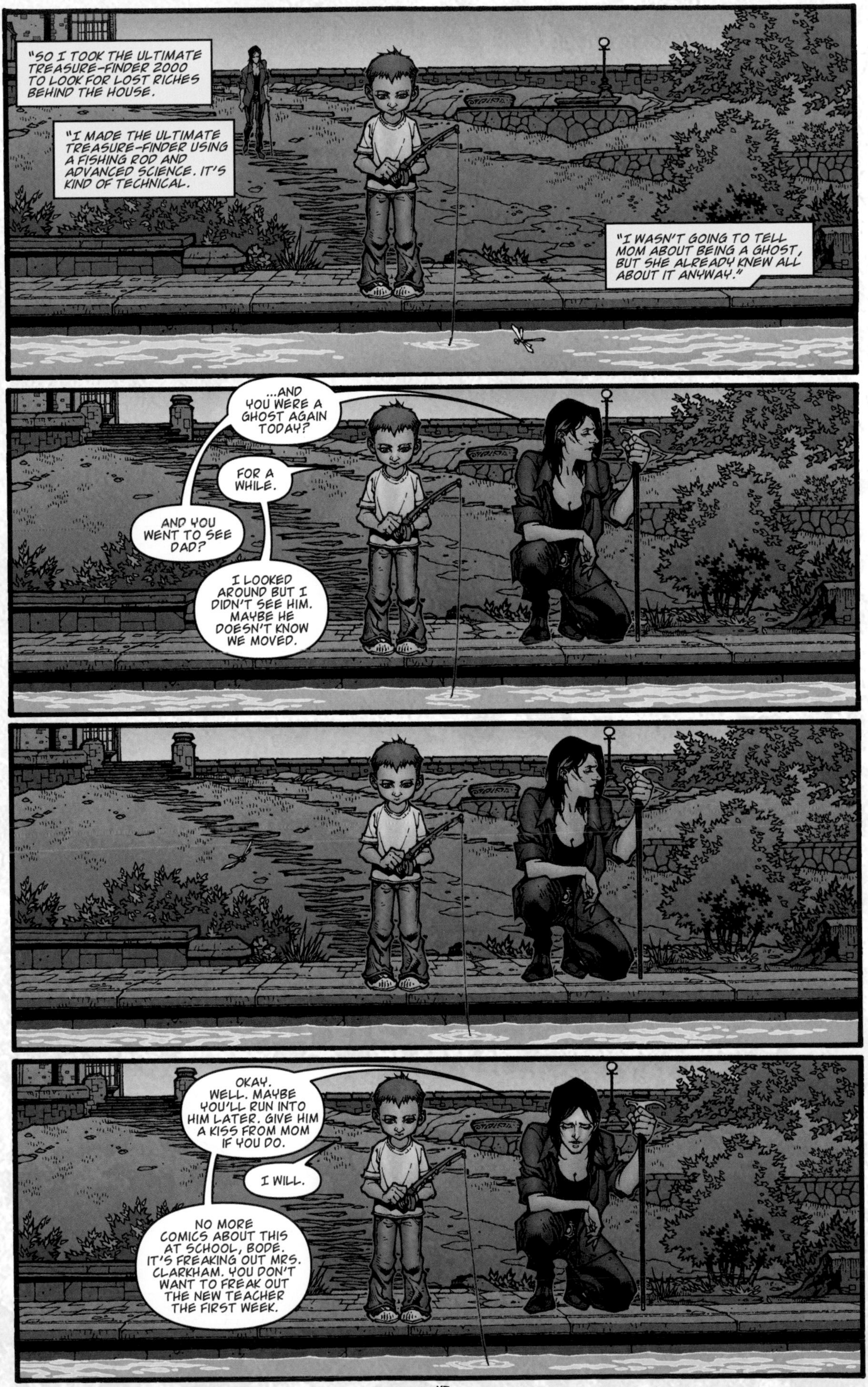
"SO I TOOK THE ULTIMATE TREASURE-FINDER 2000 TO LOOK FOR LOST RICHES BEHIND THE HOUSE.
"I MADE THE ULTIMATE TREASURE-FINDER USING A FISHING ROD AND ADVANCED SCIENCE. IT'S KIND OF TECHNICAL.
"I WASN'T GOING TO TELL MOM ABOUT BEING A GHOST, BUT SHE ALREADY KNEW ALL ABOUT IT ANYWAY."
...AND YOU WERE A GHOST AGAIN TODAY?
FOR A WHILE.
AND YOU WENT TO SEE DAD?
I LOOKED AROUND BUT I DIDN'T SEE HIM. MAYBE HE DOESN'T KNOW WE MOVED.
OKAY. WELL. MAYBE YOU'LL RUN INTO HIM LATER. GIVE HIM A KISS FROM MOM IF YOU DO.
I WILL.
NO MORE COMICS ABOUT THIS AT SCHOOL, BODE. IT'S FREAKING OUT MRS. CLARKHAM. YOU DON'T WANT TO FREAK OUT THE NEW TEACHER THE FIRST WEEK.

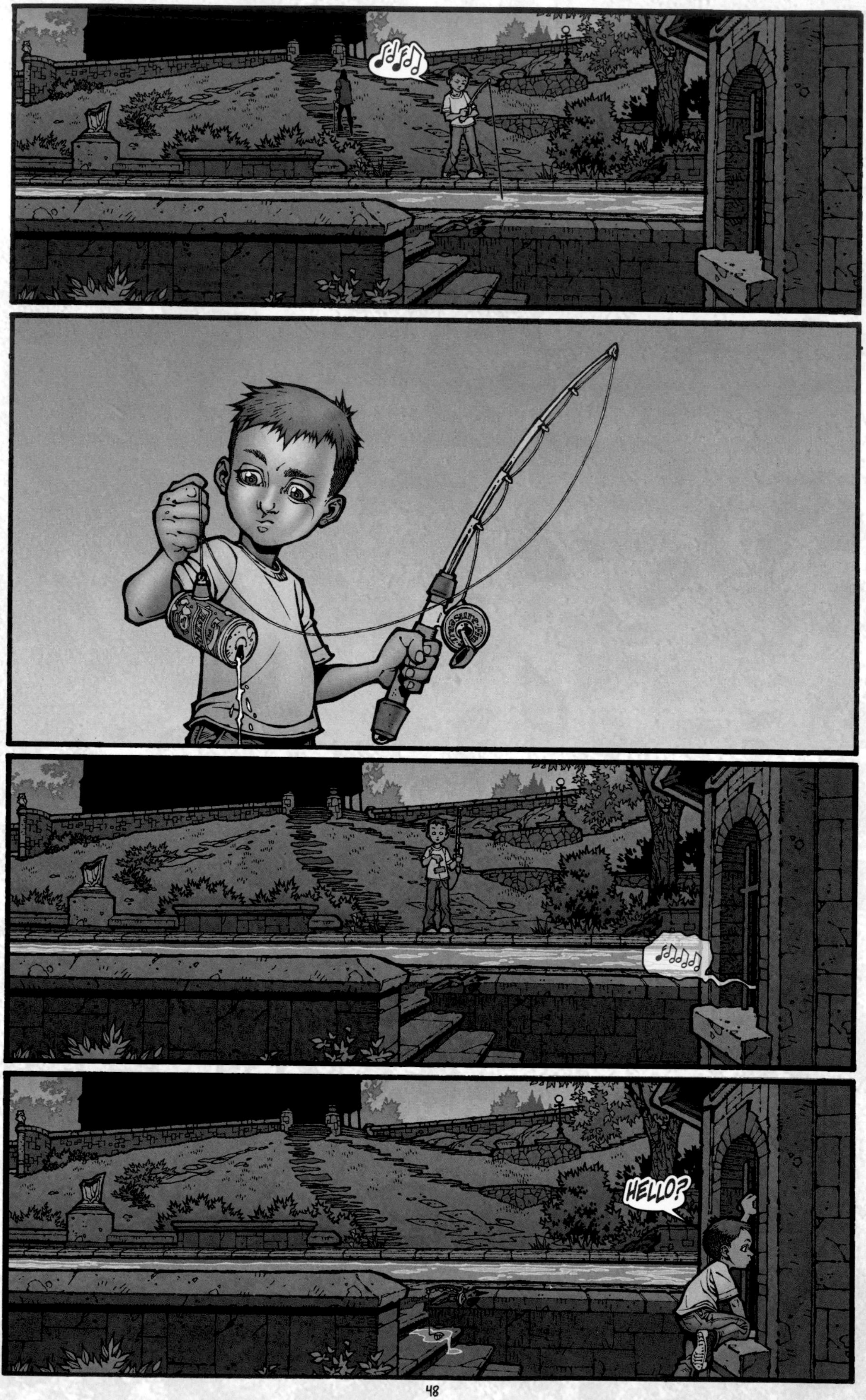
HELLO?

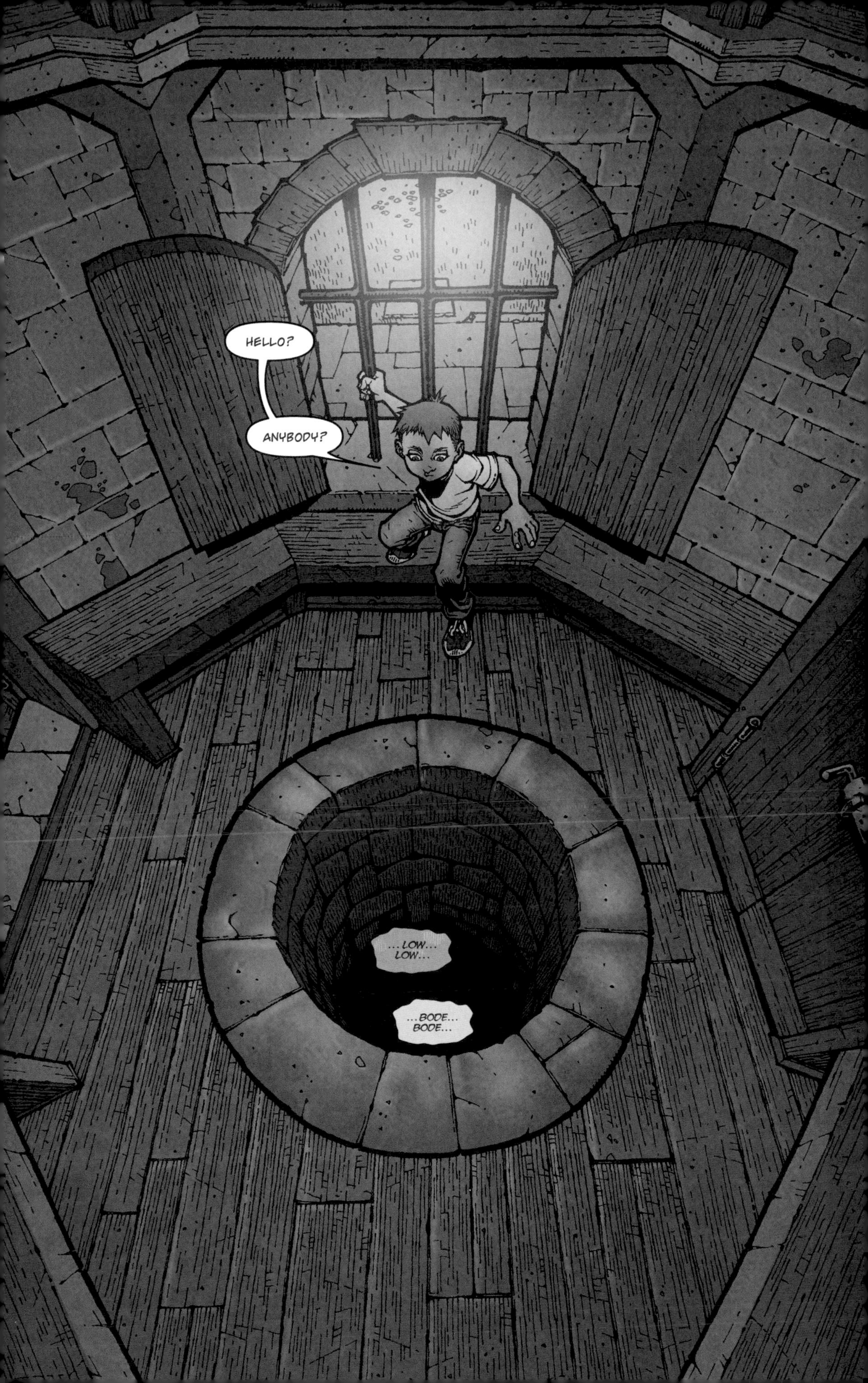
HELLO?
ANYBODY?
...LOW... LOW...
...BODE... BODE...

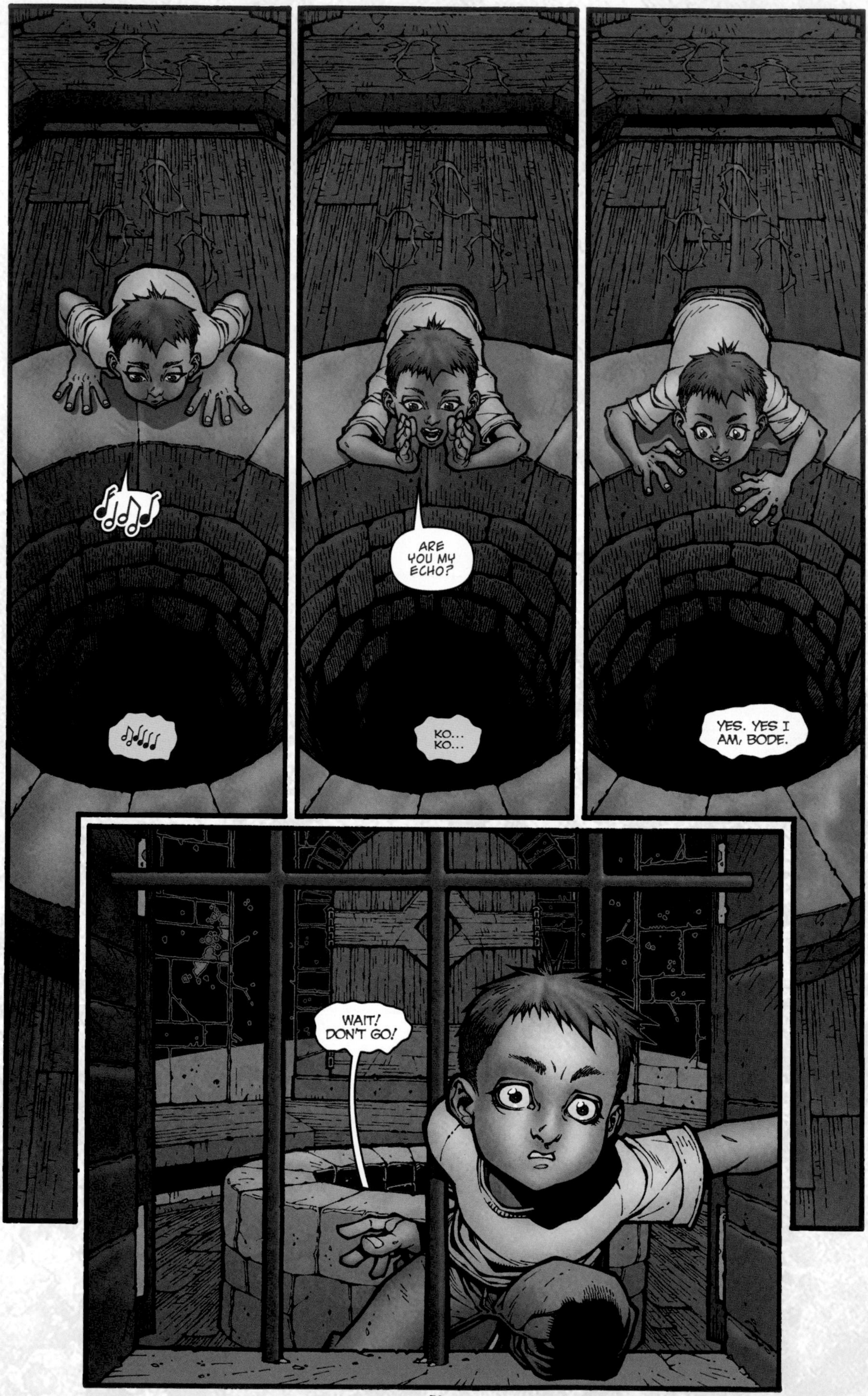

ARE YOU MY ECHO?
KO... KO...
YES. YES I AM, BODE.
WAIT! DON'T GO!

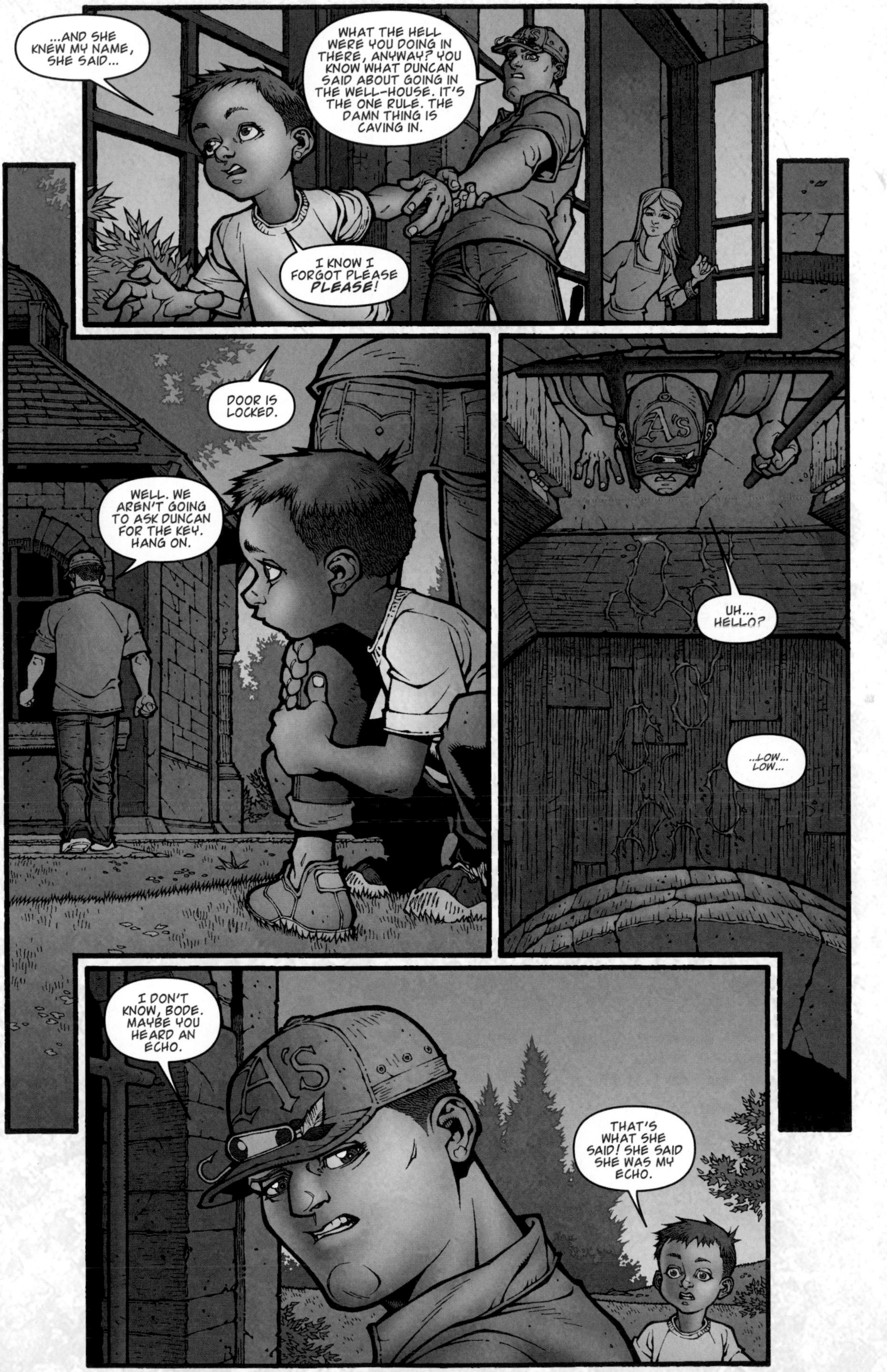
...AND SHE KNEW MY NAME, SHE SAID...
WHAT THE HELL WERE YOU DOING IN THERE, ANYWAY? YOU KNOW WHAT DUNCAN SAID ABOUT GOING IN THE WELL-HOUSE. IT'S THE ONE RULE. THE DAMN THING IS CAVING IN.
I KNOW I FORGOT PLEASE PLEASE!
DOOR IS LOCKED.
WELL. WE AREN'T GOING TO ASK DUNCAN FOR THE KEY. HANG ON.
UH... HELLO?
...LOW... LOW...
I DON'T KNOW, BODE. MAYBE YOU HEARD AN ECHO.
THAT'S WHAT SHE SAID! SHE SAID SHE WAS MY ECHO.

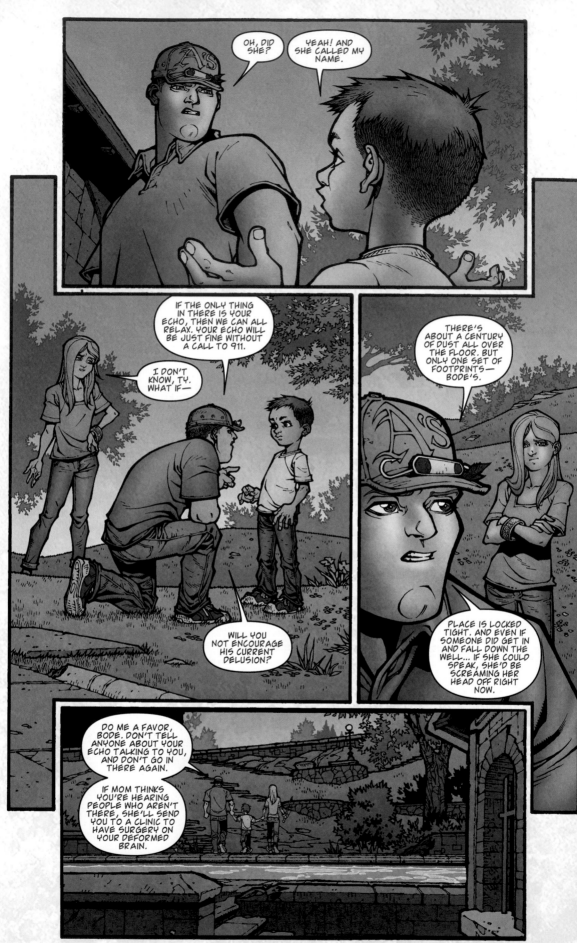

OH, DID SHE?

YEAH! AND SHE CALLED MY NAME.

IF THE ONLY THING IN THERE IS YOUR ECHO, THEN WE CAN ALL RELAX. YOUR ECHO WILL BE JUST FINE WITHOUT A CALL TO 911.

I DON'T KNOW, TY. WHAT IF—

WILL YOU NOT ENCOURAGE HIS CURRENT DELUSION?

THERE'S ABOUT A CENTURY OF DUST ALL OVER THE FLOOR. BUT ONLY ONE SET OF FOOTPRINTS— BODE'S.

PLACE IS LOCKED TIGHT. AND EVEN IF SOMEONE DID GET IN AND FALL DOWN THE WELL... IF SHE COULD SPEAK, SHE'D BE SCREAMING HER HEAD OFF RIGHT NOW.

DO ME A FAVOR, BODE. DON'T TELL ANYONE ABOUT YOUR ECHO TALKING TO YOU, AND DON'T GO IN THERE AGAIN.

IF MOM THINKS YOU'RE HEARING PEOPLE WHO AREN'T THERE, SHE'LL SEND YOU TO A CLINIC TO HAVE SURGERY ON YOUR DEFORMED BRAIN.

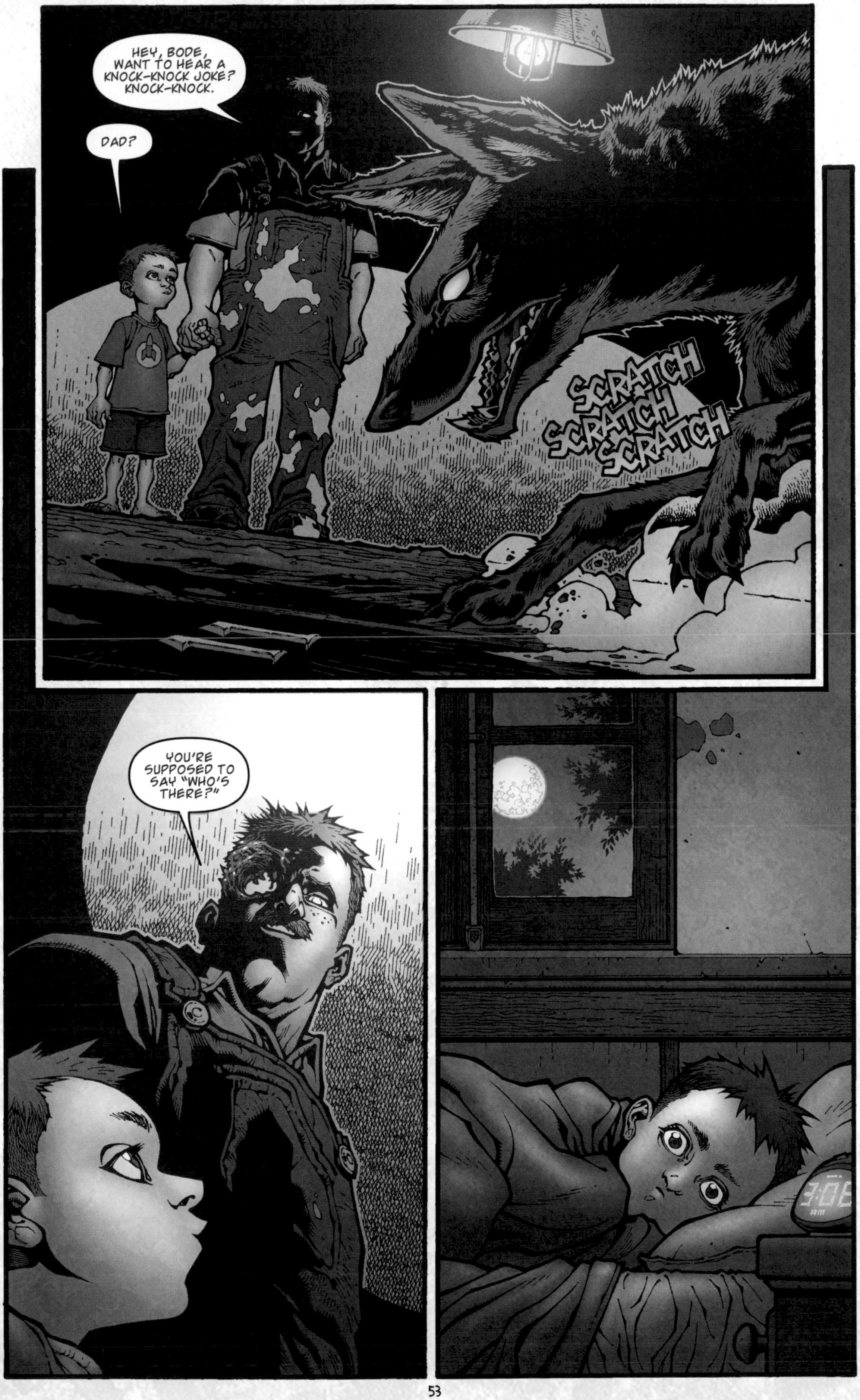
HEY, BODE, WANT TO HEAR A KNOCK-KNOCK JOKE? KNOCK-KNOCK.
DAD?
SCRATCH SCRATCH SCRATCH
YOU'RE SUPPOSED TO SAY "WHO'S THERE?"

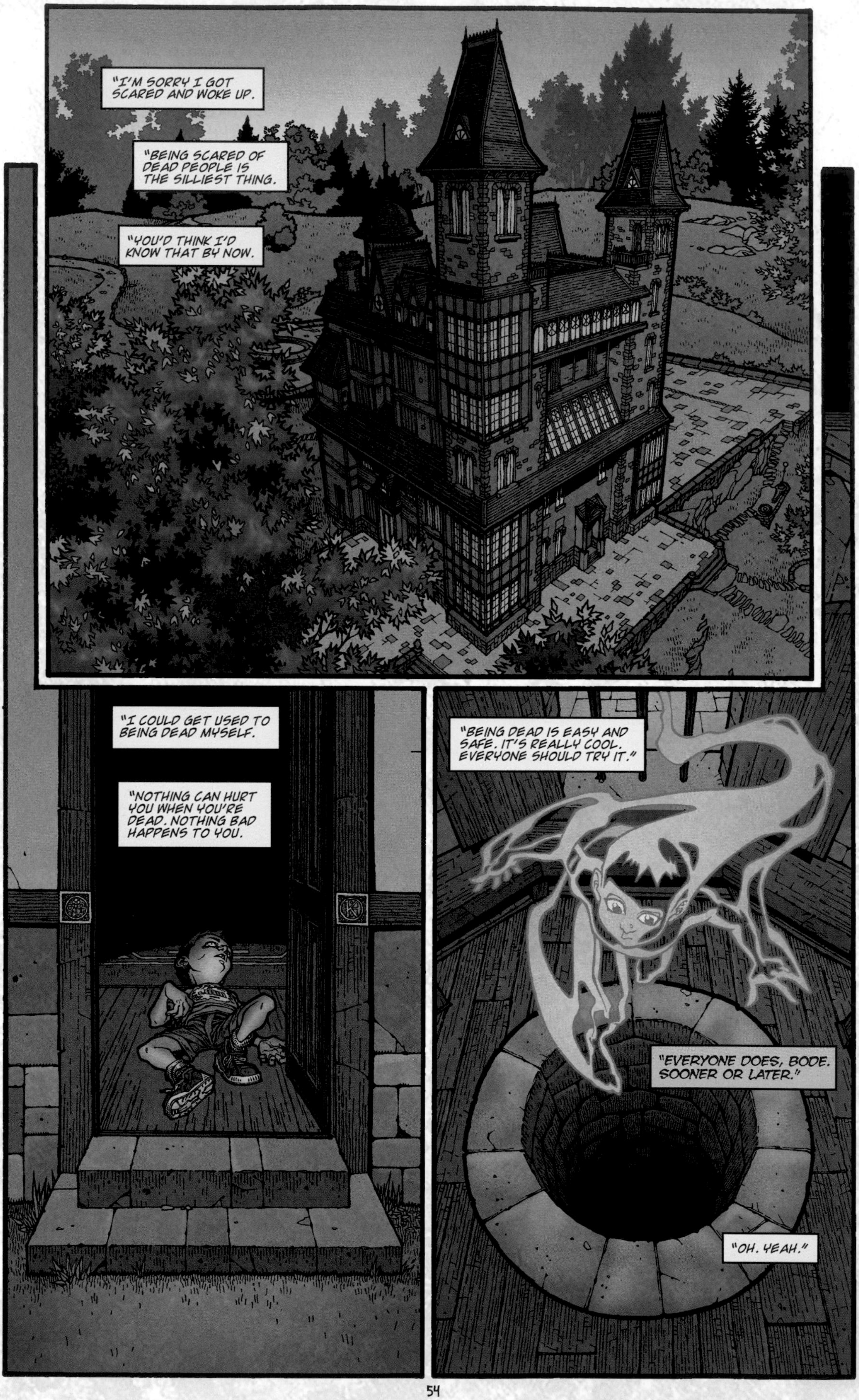
"I'M SORRY I GOT SCARED AND WOKE UP.
"BEING SCARED OF DEAD PEOPLE IS THE SILLIEST THING.
"YOU'D THINK I'D KNOW THAT BY NOW.
"I COULD GET USED TO BEING DEAD MYSELF.
"NOTHING CAN HURT YOU WHEN YOU'RE DEAD. NOTHING BAD HAPPENS TO YOU.
"BEING DEAD IS EASY AND SAFE. IT'S REALLY COOL. EVERYONE SHOULD TRY IT."
"EVERYONE DOES, BODE. SOONER OR LATER."
"OH. YEAH."

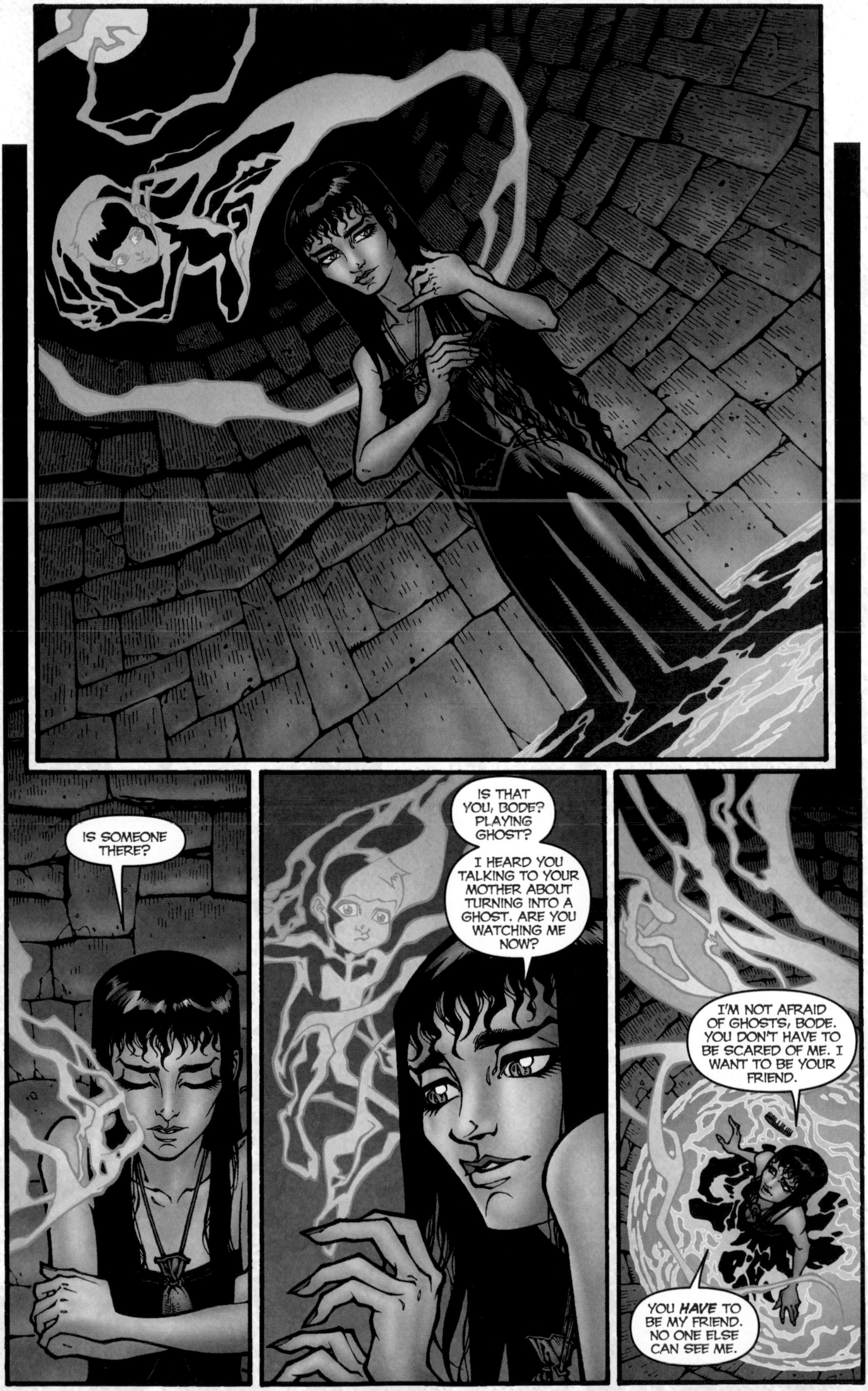
IS SOMEONE THERE?
IS THAT YOU, BODE? PLAYING GHOST?
I HEARD YOU TALKING TO YOUR MOTHER ABOUT TURNING INTO A GHOST. ARE YOU WATCHING ME NOW?
I'M NOT AFRAID OF GHOSTS, BODE. YOU DON'T HAVE TO BE SCARED OF ME. I WANT TO BE YOUR FRIEND.
YOU *HAVE* TO BE MY FRIEND. NO ONE ELSE CAN SEE ME.

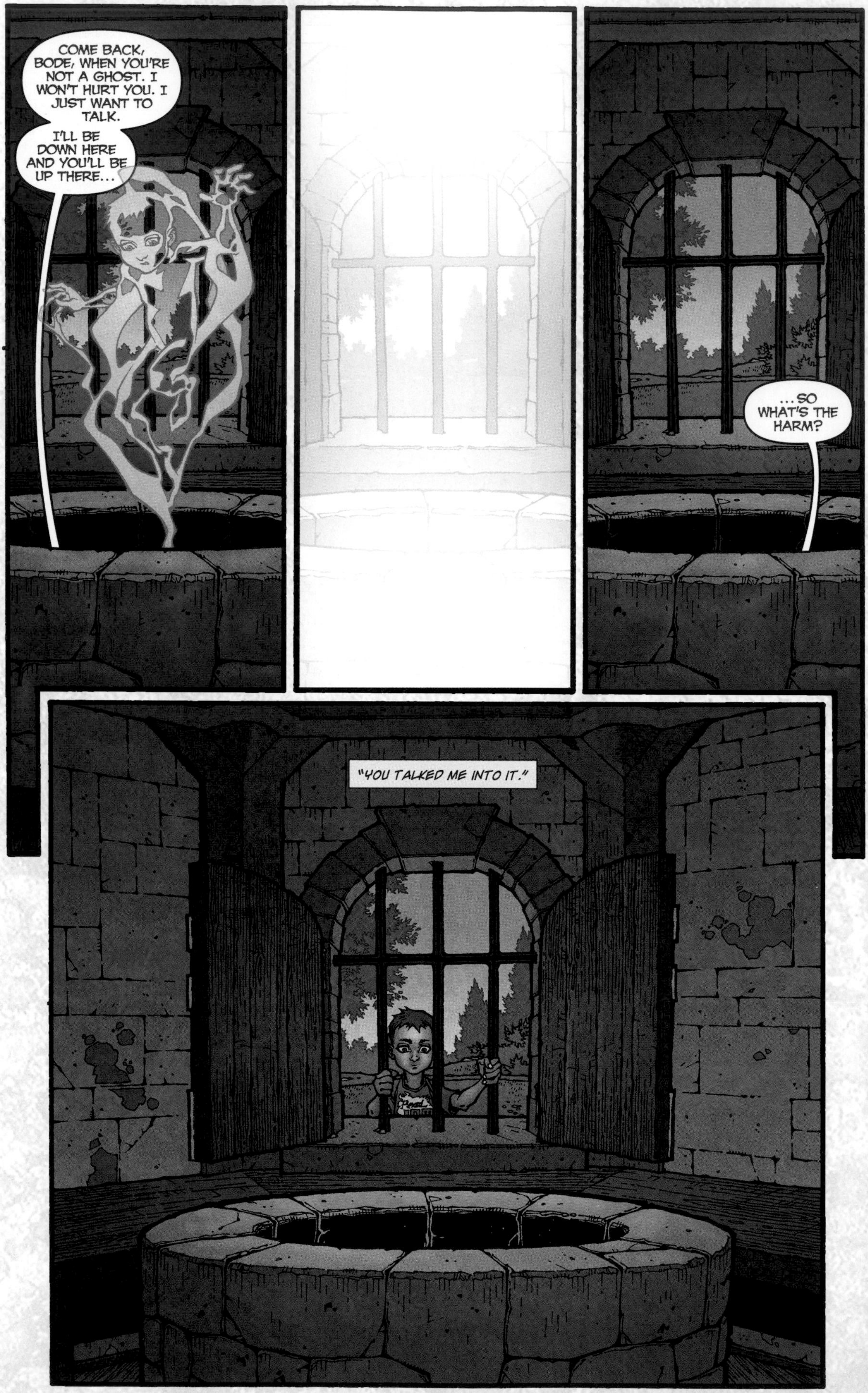
COME BACK, BODE, WHEN YOU'RE NOT A GHOST. I WON'T HURT YOU. I JUST WANT TO TALK.
I'LL BE DOWN HERE AND YOU'LL BE UP THERE...
...SO WHAT'S THE HARM?
"YOU TALKED ME INTO IT."

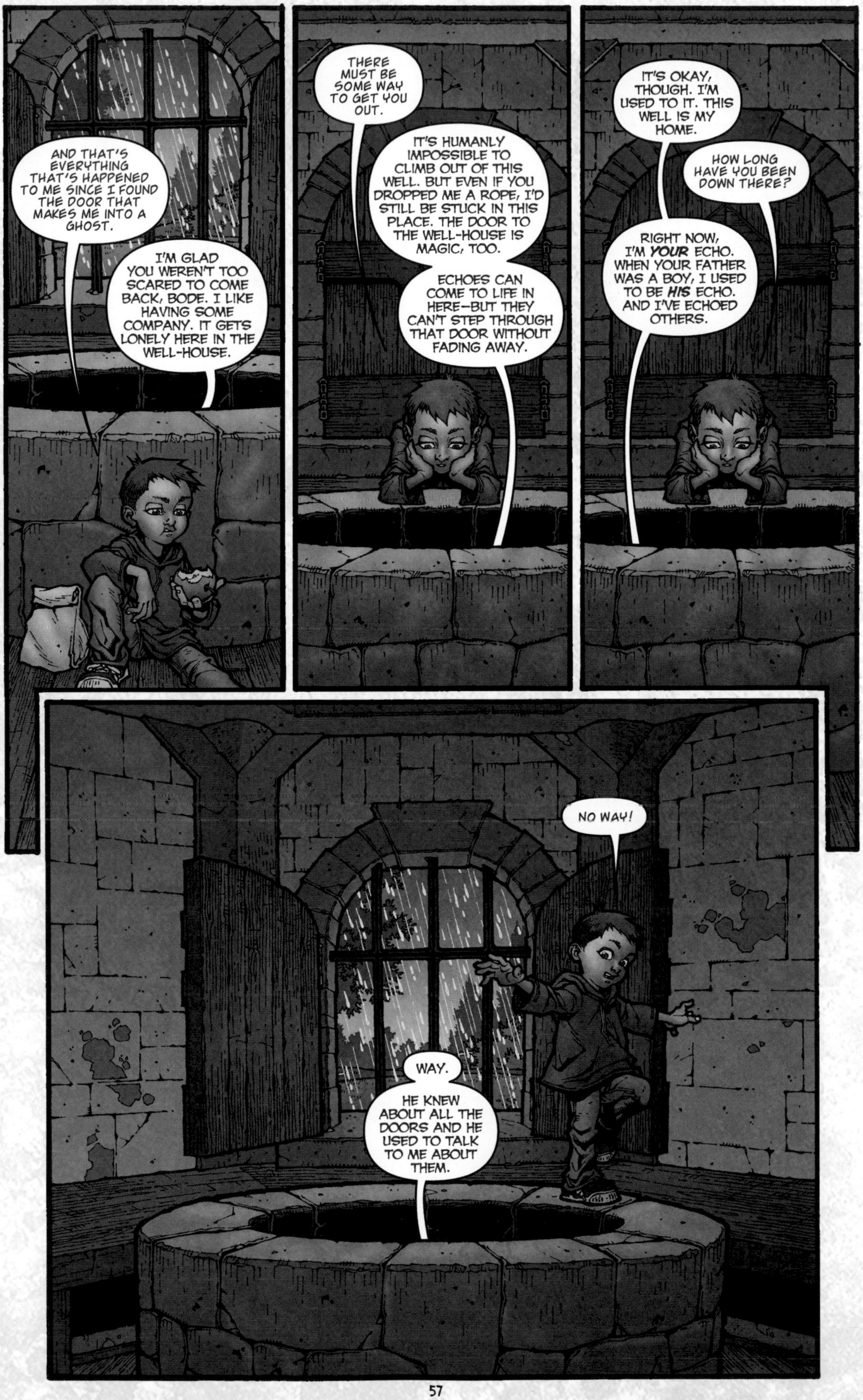
AND THAT'S EVERYTHING THAT'S HAPPENED TO ME SINCE I FOUND THE DOOR THAT MAKES ME INTO A GHOST.
I'M GLAD YOU WEREN'T TOO SCARED TO COME BACK, BODE. I LIKE HAVING SOME COMPANY. IT GETS LONELY HERE IN THE WELL-HOUSE.
THERE MUST BE SOME WAY TO GET YOU OUT.
IT'S HUMANLY IMPOSSIBLE TO CLIMB OUT OF THIS WELL. BUT EVEN IF YOU DROPPED ME A ROPE, I'D STILL BE STUCK IN THIS PLACE. THE DOOR TO THE WELL-HOUSE IS MAGIC, TOO.
ECHOES CAN COME TO LIFE IN HERE—BUT THEY CAN'T STEP THROUGH THAT DOOR WITHOUT FADING AWAY.
IT'S OKAY, THOUGH. I'M USED TO IT. THIS WELL IS MY HOME.
HOW LONG HAVE YOU BEEN DOWN THERE?
RIGHT NOW, I'M **YOUR** ECHO. WHEN YOUR FATHER WAS A BOY, I USED TO BE **HIS** ECHO. AND I'VE ECHOED OTHERS.
NO WAY!
WAY.
HE KNEW ABOUT ALL THE DOORS AND HE USED TO TALK TO ME ABOUT THEM.

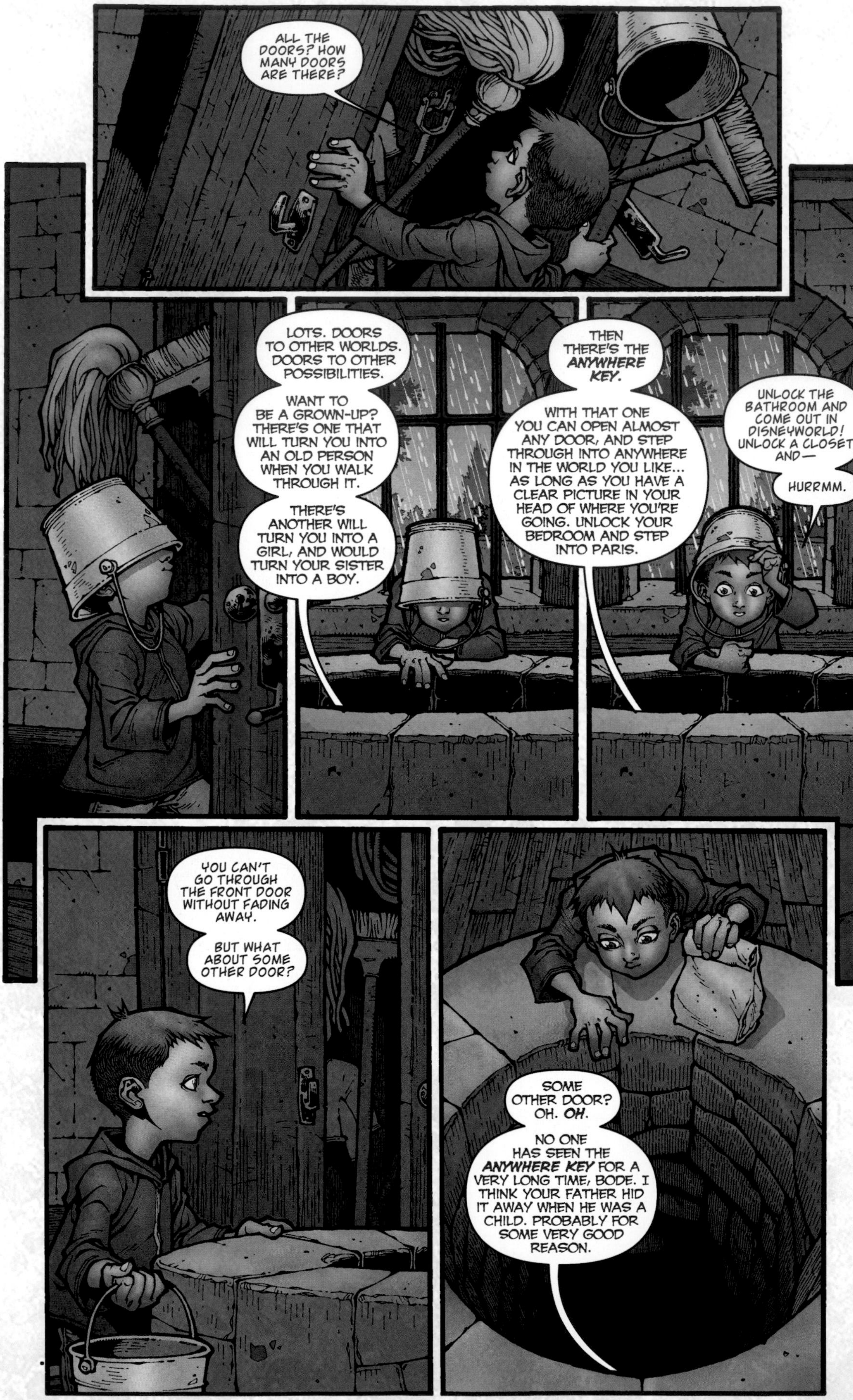
ALL THE DOORS? HOW MANY DOORS ARE THERE?
LOTS. DOORS TO OTHER WORLDS. DOORS TO OTHER POSSIBILITIES.
WANT TO BE A GROWN-UP? THERE'S ONE THAT WILL TURN YOU INTO AN OLD PERSON WHEN YOU WALK THROUGH IT.
THERE'S ANOTHER WILL TURN YOU INTO A GIRL, AND WOULD TURN YOUR SISTER INTO A BOY.
THEN THERE'S THE ANYWHERE KEY.
WITH THAT ONE YOU CAN OPEN ALMOST ANY DOOR, AND STEP THROUGH INTO ANYWHERE IN THE WORLD YOU LIKE... AS LONG AS YOU HAVE A CLEAR PICTURE IN YOUR HEAD OF WHERE YOU'RE GOING. UNLOCK YOUR BEDROOM AND STEP INTO PARIS.
UNLOCK THE BATHROOM AND COME OUT IN DISNEYWORLD! UNLOCK A CLOSET AND—
HURRMM.
YOU CAN'T GO THROUGH THE FRONT DOOR WITHOUT FADING AWAY.
BUT WHAT ABOUT SOME OTHER DOOR?
SOME OTHER DOOR? OH. OH.
NO ONE HAS SEEN THE ANYWHERE KEY FOR A VERY LONG TIME, BODE. I THINK YOUR FATHER HID IT AWAY WHEN HE WAS A CHILD. PROBABLY FOR SOME VERY GOOD REASON.

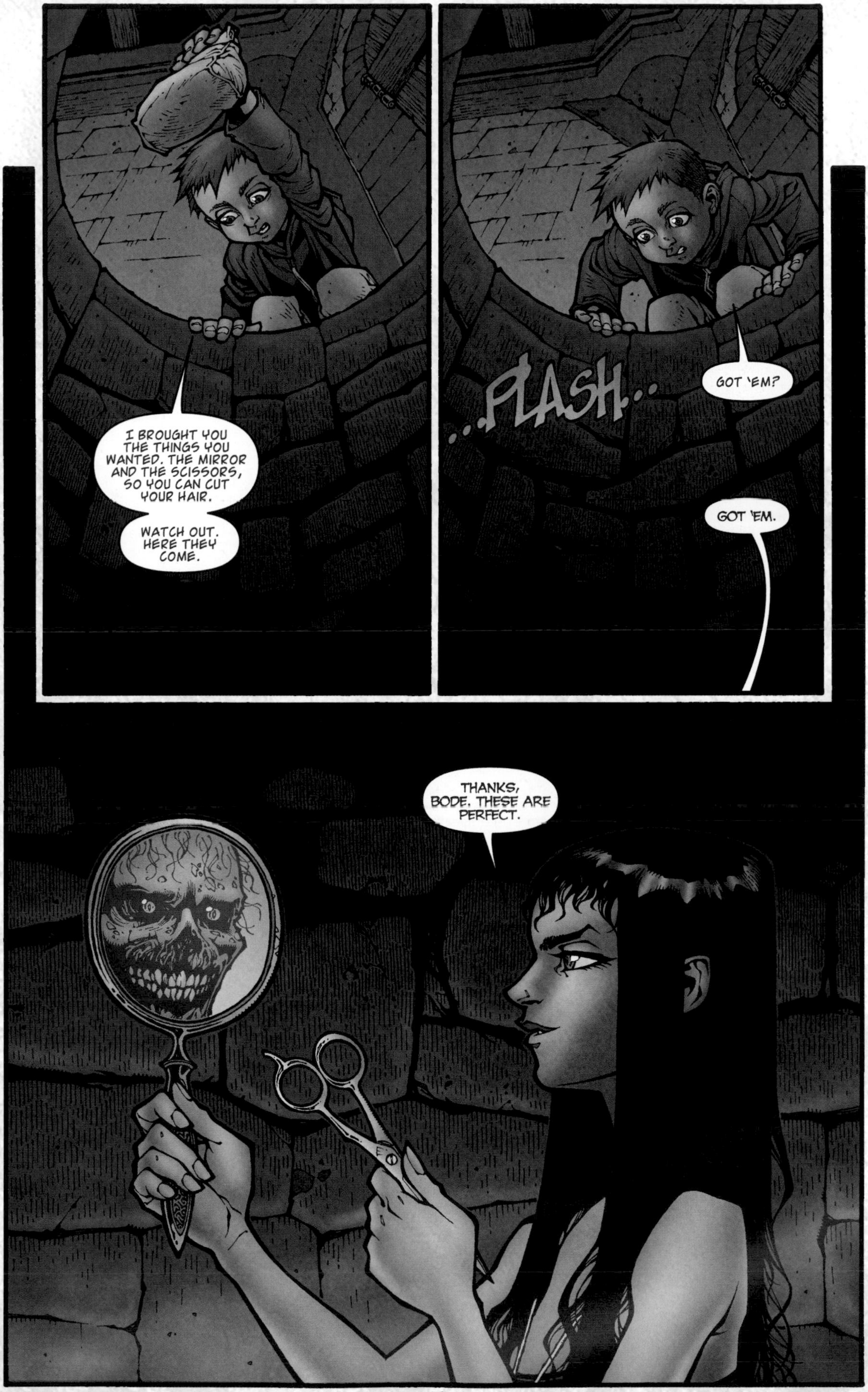
I BROUGHT YOU THE THINGS YOU WANTED. THE MIRROR AND THE SCISSORS, SO YOU CAN CUT YOUR HAIR.
WATCH OUT. HERE THEY COME.
...FLASH...
GOT 'EM?
GOT 'EM.
THANKS, BODE. THESE ARE PERFECT.

SAN LOBO
JUVENILE DETENTION
CAUTION!
~~HIGH VOLTAGE~~

SAM. I'VE GOT SOMETHING FOR YOU, SOMETHING I PROMISED.

WHAT ARE YOU TALKING ABOUT? I DIDN'T ASK FOR THIS.

YES, YOU DID, SAM. YES, YOU DID.

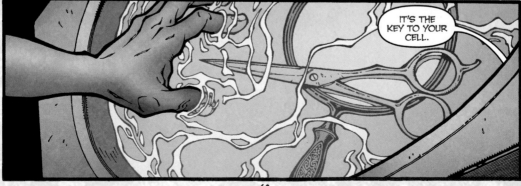

IT'S THE KEY TO YOUR CELL.

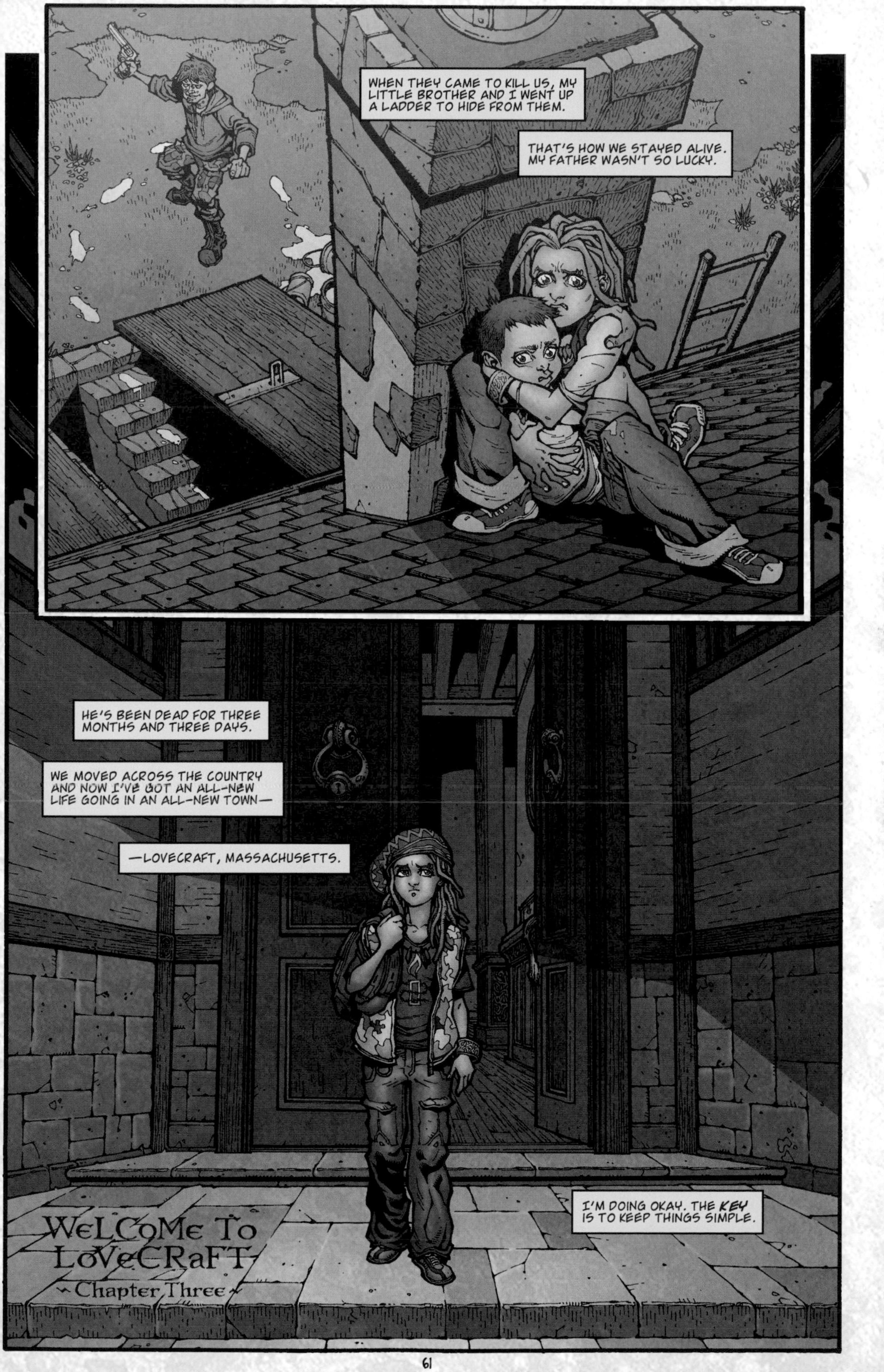
WHEN THEY CAME TO KILL US, MY LITTLE BROTHER AND I WENT UP A LADDER TO HIDE FROM THEM.
THAT'S HOW WE STAYED ALIVE. MY FATHER WASN'T SO LUCKY.
HE'S BEEN DEAD FOR THREE MONTHS AND THREE DAYS.
WE MOVED ACROSS THE COUNTRY AND NOW I'VE GOT AN ALL-NEW LIFE GOING IN AN ALL-NEW TOWN—
—LOVECRAFT, MASSACHUSETTS.
I'M DOING OKAY. THE KEY IS TO KEEP THINGS SIMPLE.
WELCOME TO LOVECRAFT
Chapter Three

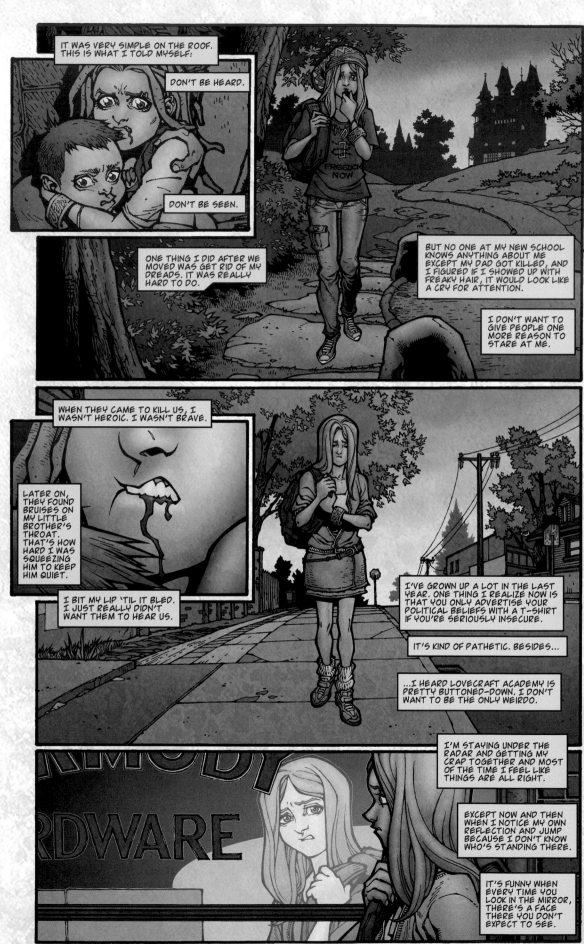

IT WAS VERY SIMPLE ON THE ROOF. THIS IS WHAT I TOLD MYSELF:

DON'T BE HEARD.

DON'T BE SEEN.

ONE THING I DID AFTER WE MOVED WAS GET RID OF MY DREADS. IT WAS REALLY HARD TO DO.

BUT NO ONE AT MY NEW SCHOOL KNOWS ANYTHING ABOUT ME EXCEPT MY DAD GOT KILLED, AND I FIGURED IF I SHOWED UP WITH FREAKY HAIR, IT WOULD LOOK LIKE A CRY FOR ATTENTION.

I DON'T WANT TO GIVE PEOPLE ONE MORE REASON TO STARE AT ME.

WHEN THEY CAME TO KILL US, I WASN'T HEROIC. I WASN'T BRAVE.

LATER ON, THEY FOUND BRUISES ON MY LITTLE BROTHER'S THROAT. THAT'S HOW HARD I WAS SQUEEZING HIM TO KEEP HIM QUIET.

I BIT MY LIP 'TIL IT BLED. I JUST REALLY DIDN'T WANT THEM TO HEAR US.

I'VE GROWN UP A LOT IN THE LAST YEAR. ONE THING I REALIZE NOW IS THAT YOU ONLY ADVERTISE YOUR POLITICAL BELIEFS WITH A T-SHIRT IF YOU'RE SERIOUSLY INSECURE.

IT'S KIND OF PATHETIC. BESIDES...

...I HEARD LOVECRAFT ACADEMY IS PRETTY BUTTONED-DOWN. I DON'T WANT TO BE THE ONLY WEIRDO.

I'M STAYING UNDER THE RADAR AND GETTING MY CRAP TOGETHER AND MOST OF THE TIME I FEEL LIKE THINGS ARE ALL RIGHT.

EXCEPT NOW AND THEN WHEN I NOTICE MY OWN REFLECTION AND JUMP BECAUSE I DON'T KNOW WHO'S STANDING THERE.

IT'S FUNNY WHEN EVERY TIME YOU LOOK IN THE MIRROR, THERE'S A FACE THERE YOU DON'T EXPECT TO SEE.

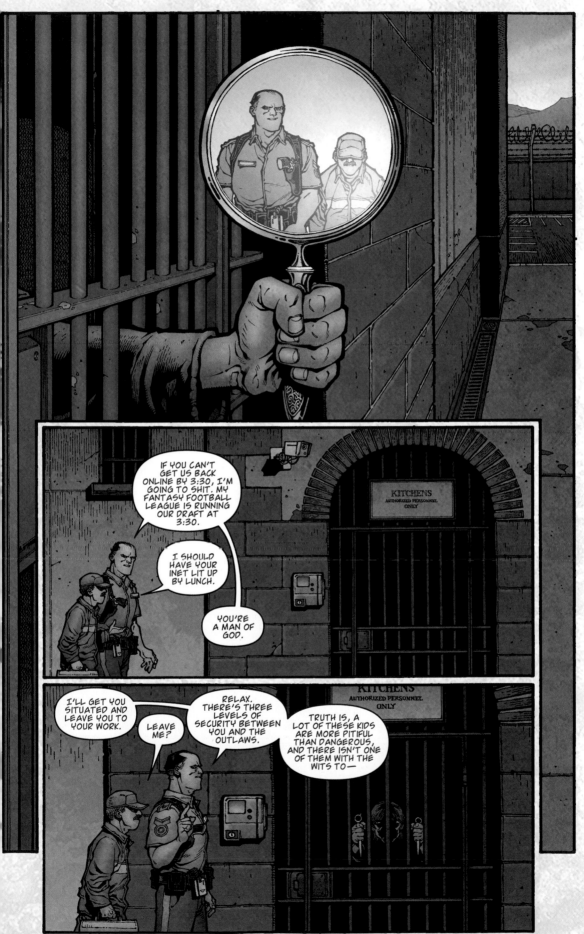

IF YOU CAN'T GET US BACK ONLINE BY 3:30, I'M GOING TO SHIT. MY FANTASY FOOTBALL LEAGUE IS RUNNING OUR DRAFT AT 3:30.

I SHOULD HAVE YOUR INET LIT UP BY LUNCH.

YOU'RE A MAN OF GOD.

KITCHENS
AUTHORIZED PERSONNEL ONLY

I'LL GET YOU SITUATED AND LEAVE YOU TO YOUR WORK.

LEAVE ME?

RELAX. THERE'S THREE LEVELS OF SECURITY BETWEEN YOU AND THE OUTLAWS.

TRUTH IS, A LOT OF THESE KIDS ARE MORE PITIFUL THAN DANGEROUS, AND THERE ISN'T ONE OF THEM WITH THE WITS TO—

KITCHENS
AUTHORIZED PERSONNEL ONLY

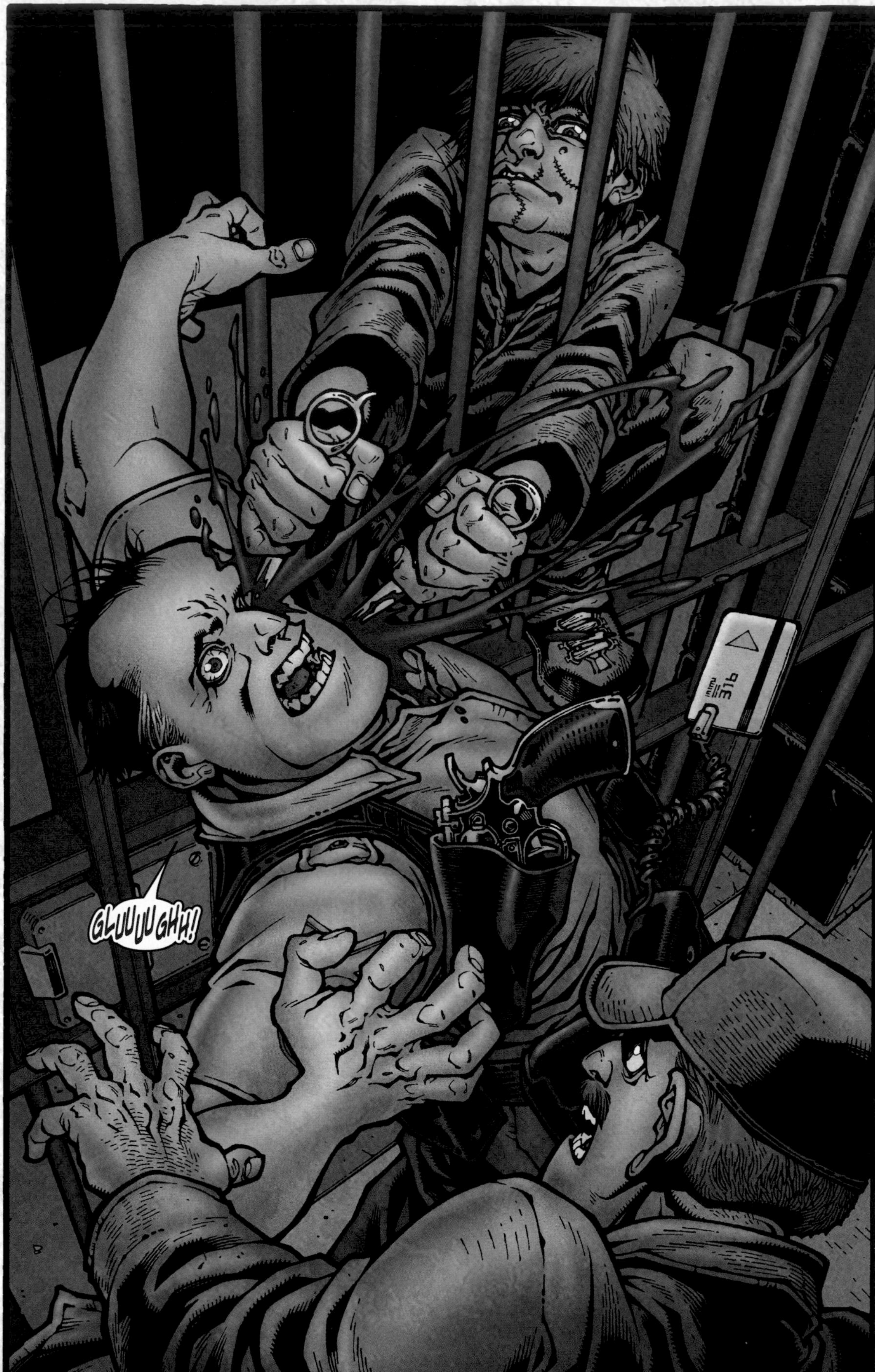
GLUUUUGHH!

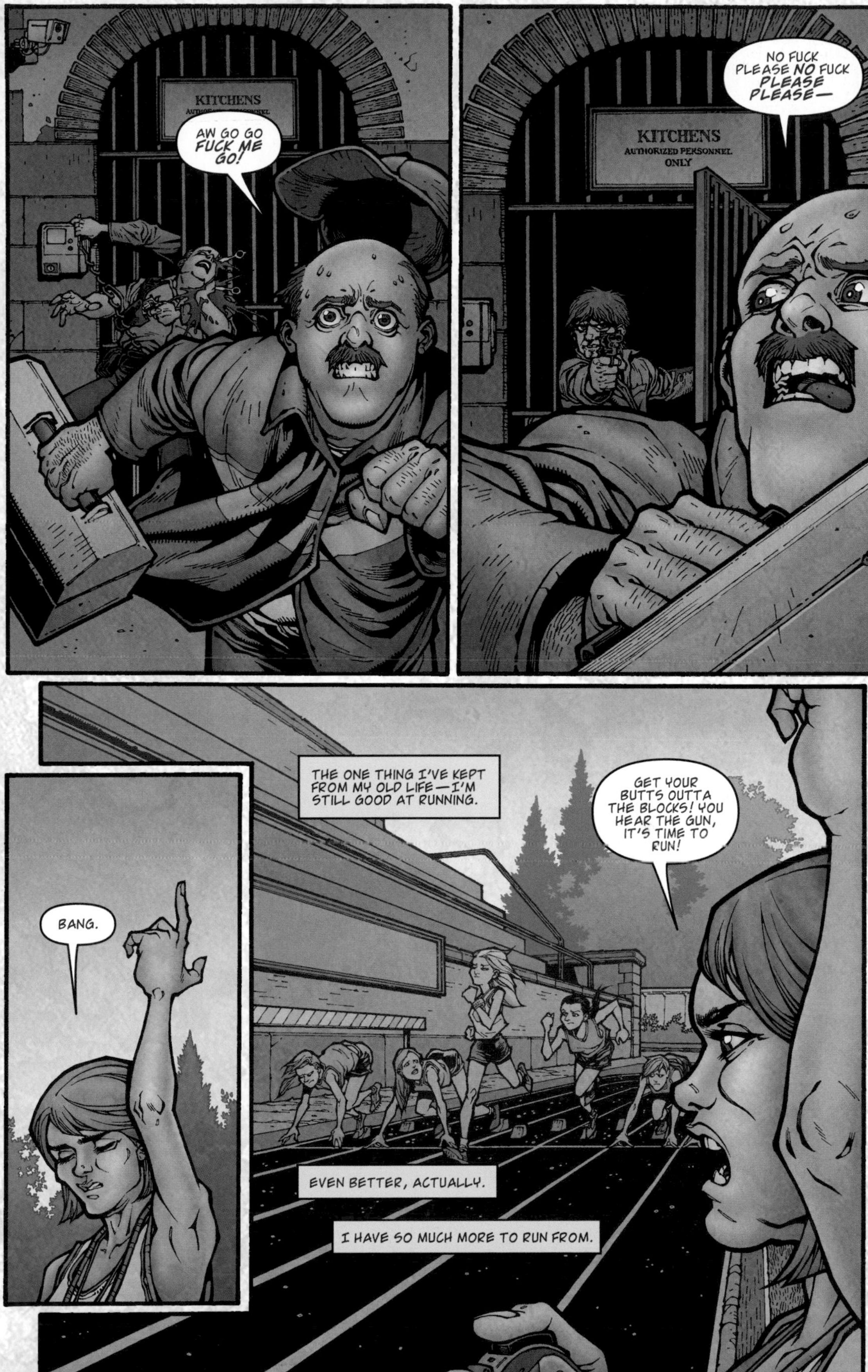
KITCHENS
AW GO GO FUCK ME GO!
NO FUCK PLEASE NO FUCK PLEASE PLEASE—
KITCHENS
AUTHORIZED PERSONNEL ONLY
THE ONE THING I'VE KEPT FROM MY OLD LIFE—I'M STILL GOOD AT RUNNING.
GET YOUR BUTTS OUTTA THE BLOCKS! YOU HEAR THE GUN, IT'S TIME TO RUN!
BANG.
EVEN BETTER, ACTUALLY.
I HAVE SO MUCH MORE TO RUN FROM.

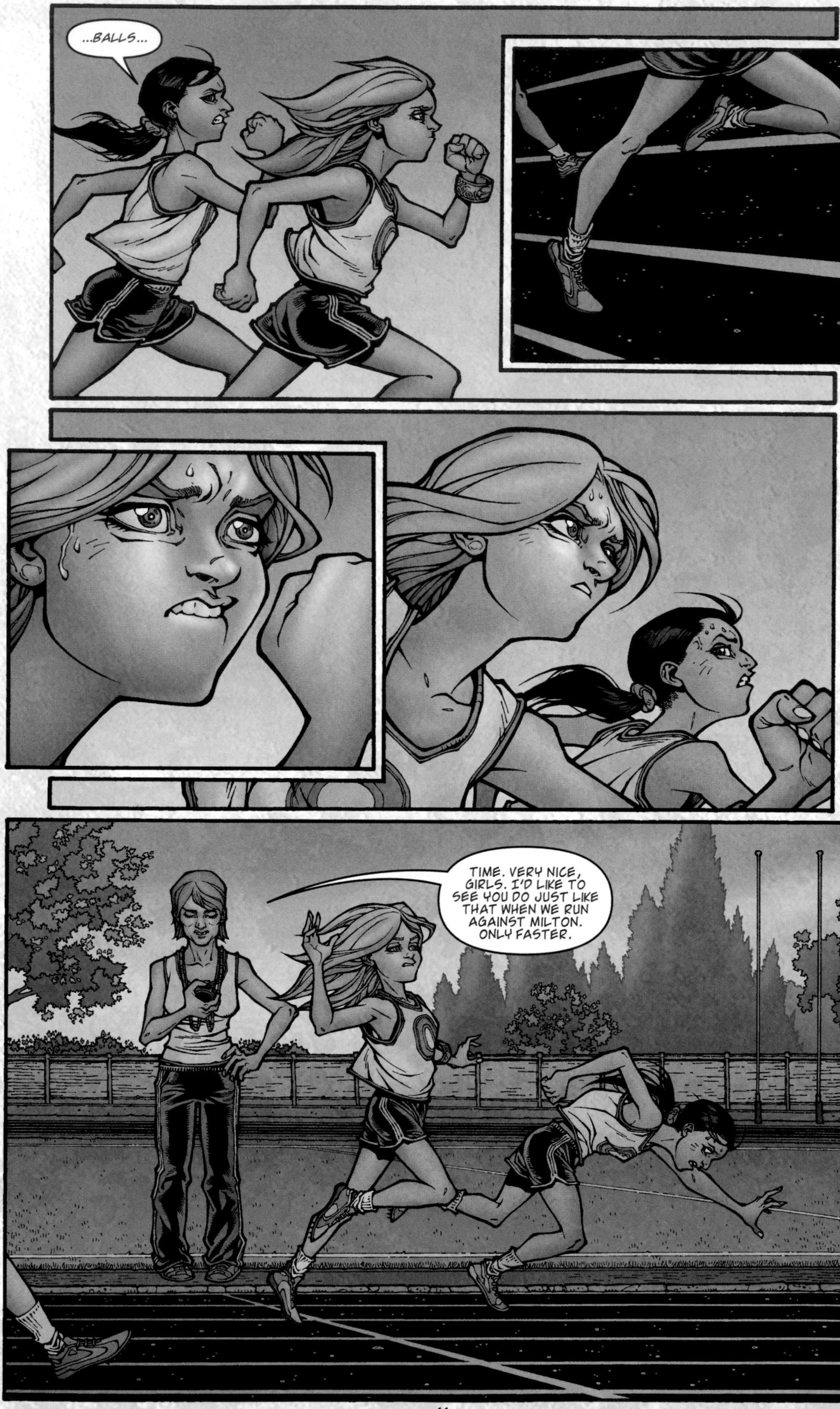
...BALLS...
TIME. VERY NICE, GIRLS. I'D LIKE TO SEE YOU DO JUST LIKE THAT WHEN WE RUN AGAINST MILTON. ONLY FASTER.

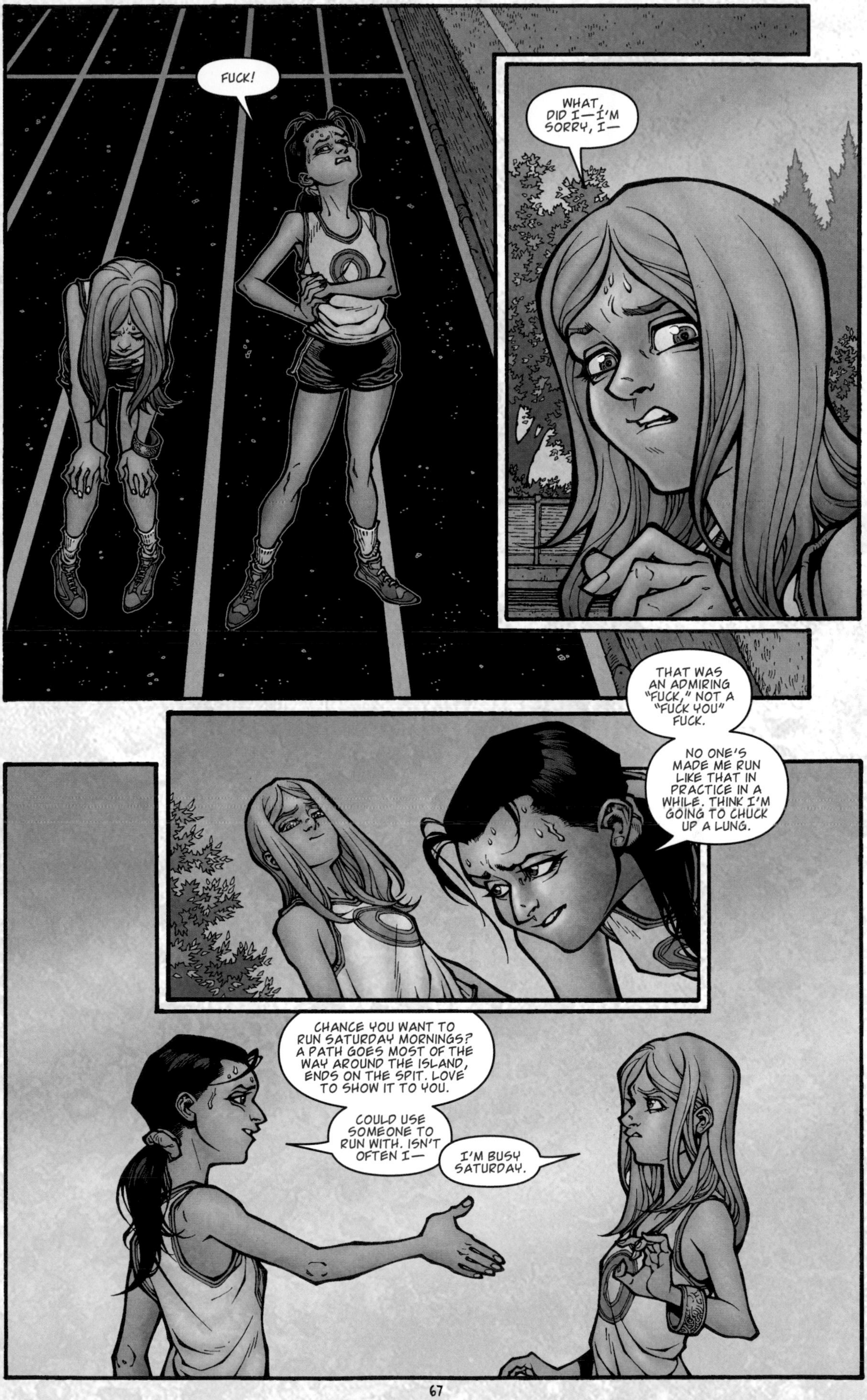
FUCK!
WHAT, DID I—I'M SORRY, I—
THAT WAS AN ADMIRING "FUCK," NOT A "FUCK YOU" FUCK.
NO ONE'S MADE ME RUN LIKE THAT IN PRACTICE IN A WHILE. THINK I'M GOING TO CHUCK UP A LUNG.
CHANCE YOU WANT TO RUN SATURDAY MORNINGS? A PATH GOES MOST OF THE WAY AROUND THE ISLAND, ENDS ON THE SPIT. LOVE TO SHOW IT TO YOU.
COULD USE SOMEONE TO RUN WITH. ISN'T OFTEN I—
I'M BUSY SATURDAY.

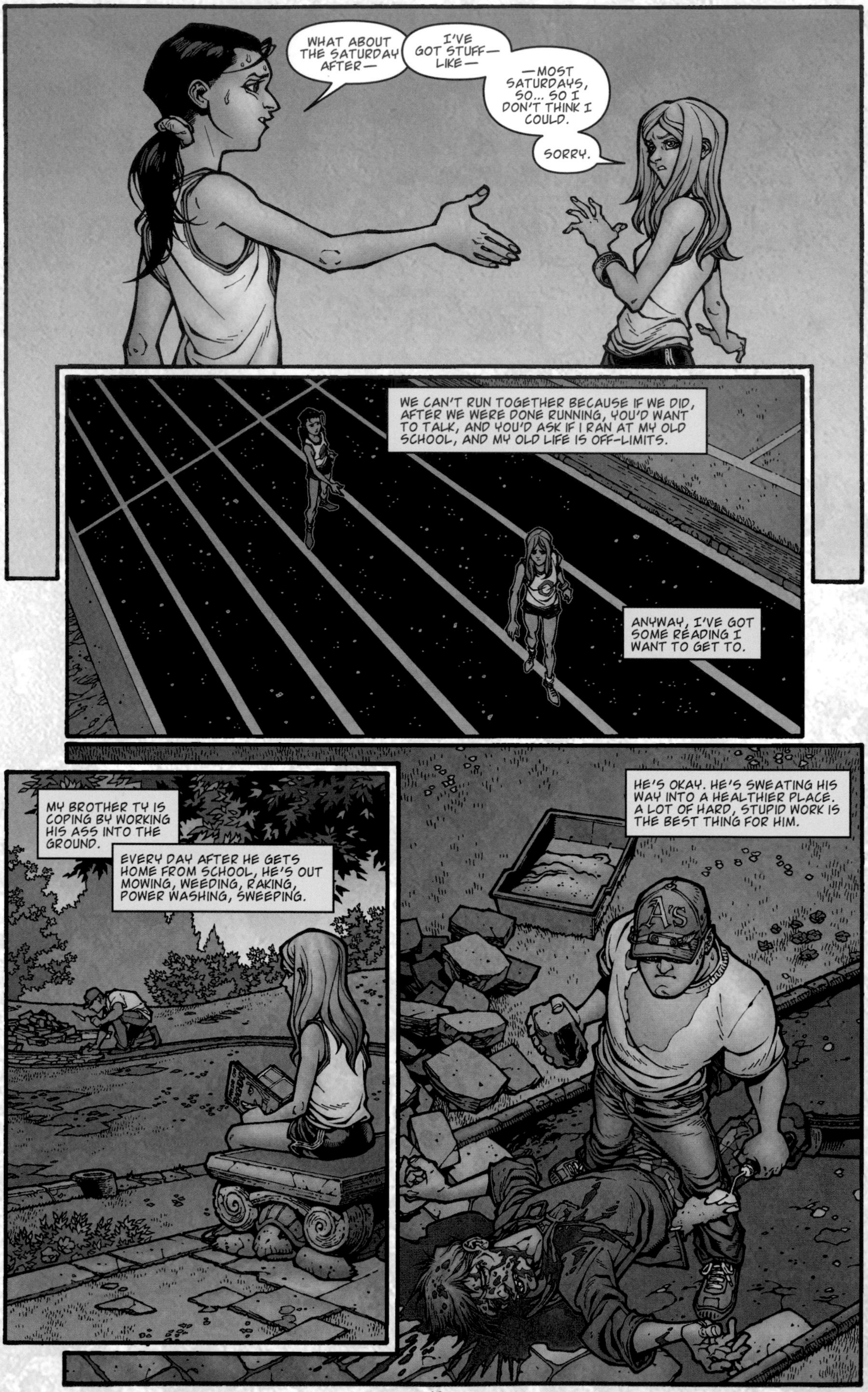
WHAT ABOUT THE SATURDAY AFTER—
I'VE GOT STUFF— LIKE—
—MOST SATURDAYS, SO... SO I DON'T THINK I COULD.
SORRY.
WE CAN'T RUN TOGETHER BECAUSE IF WE DID, AFTER WE WERE DONE RUNNING, YOU'D WANT TO TALK, AND YOU'D ASK IF I RAN AT MY OLD SCHOOL, AND MY OLD LIFE IS OFF-LIMITS.
ANYWAY, I'VE GOT SOME READING I WANT TO GET TO.
MY BROTHER TY IS COPING BY WORKING HIS ASS INTO THE GROUND.
EVERY DAY AFTER HE GETS HOME FROM SCHOOL, HE'S OUT MOWING, WEEDING, RAKING, POWER WASHING, SWEEPING.
HE'S OKAY. HE'S SWEATING HIS WAY INTO A HEALTHIER PLACE. A LOT OF HARD, STUPID WORK IS THE BEST THING FOR HIM.
A'S

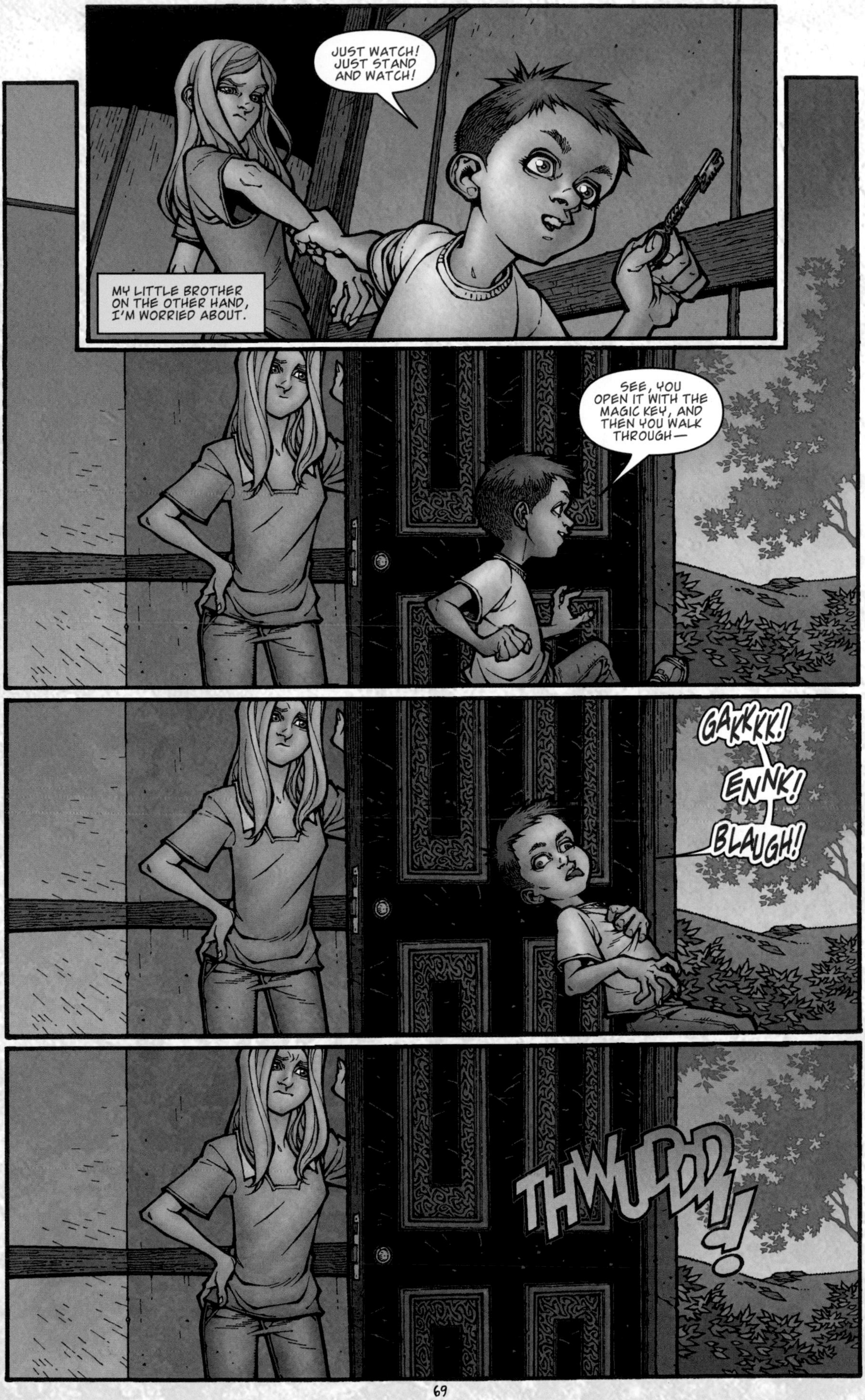
JUST WATCH! JUST STAND AND WATCH!
MY LITTLE BROTHER ON THE OTHER HAND, I'M WORRIED ABOUT.
SEE, YOU OPEN IT WITH THE MAGIC KEY, AND THEN YOU WALK THROUGH—
GAKKKK!
ENNK!
BLAUGH!
THWUDD!

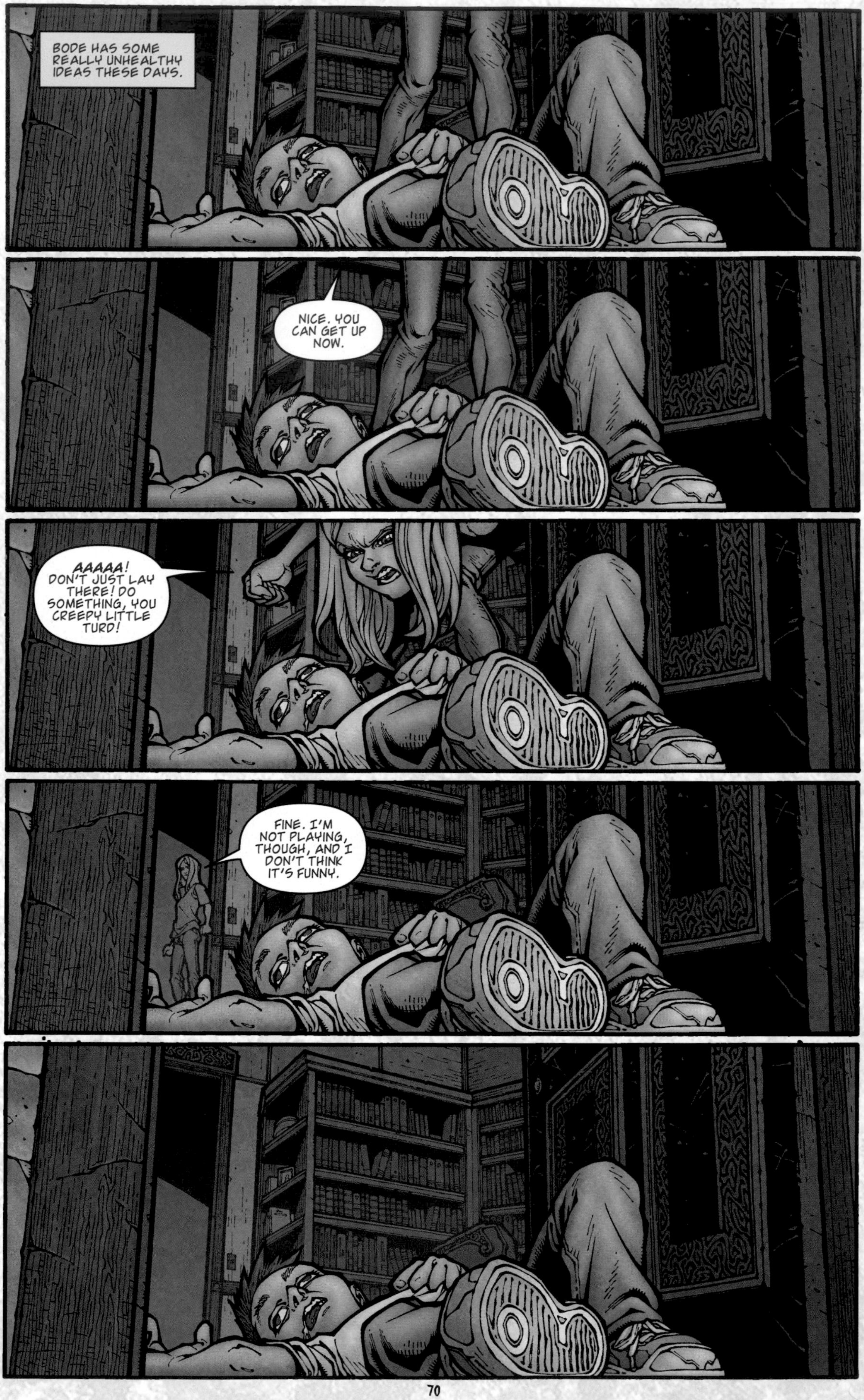

BODE HAS SOME REALLY UNHEALTHY IDEAS THESE DAYS.
NICE. YOU CAN GET UP NOW.
AAAAA! DON'T JUST LAY THERE! DO SOMETHING, YOU CREEPY LITTLE TURD!
FINE. I'M NOT PLAYING, THOUGH, AND I DON'T THINK IT'S FUNNY.

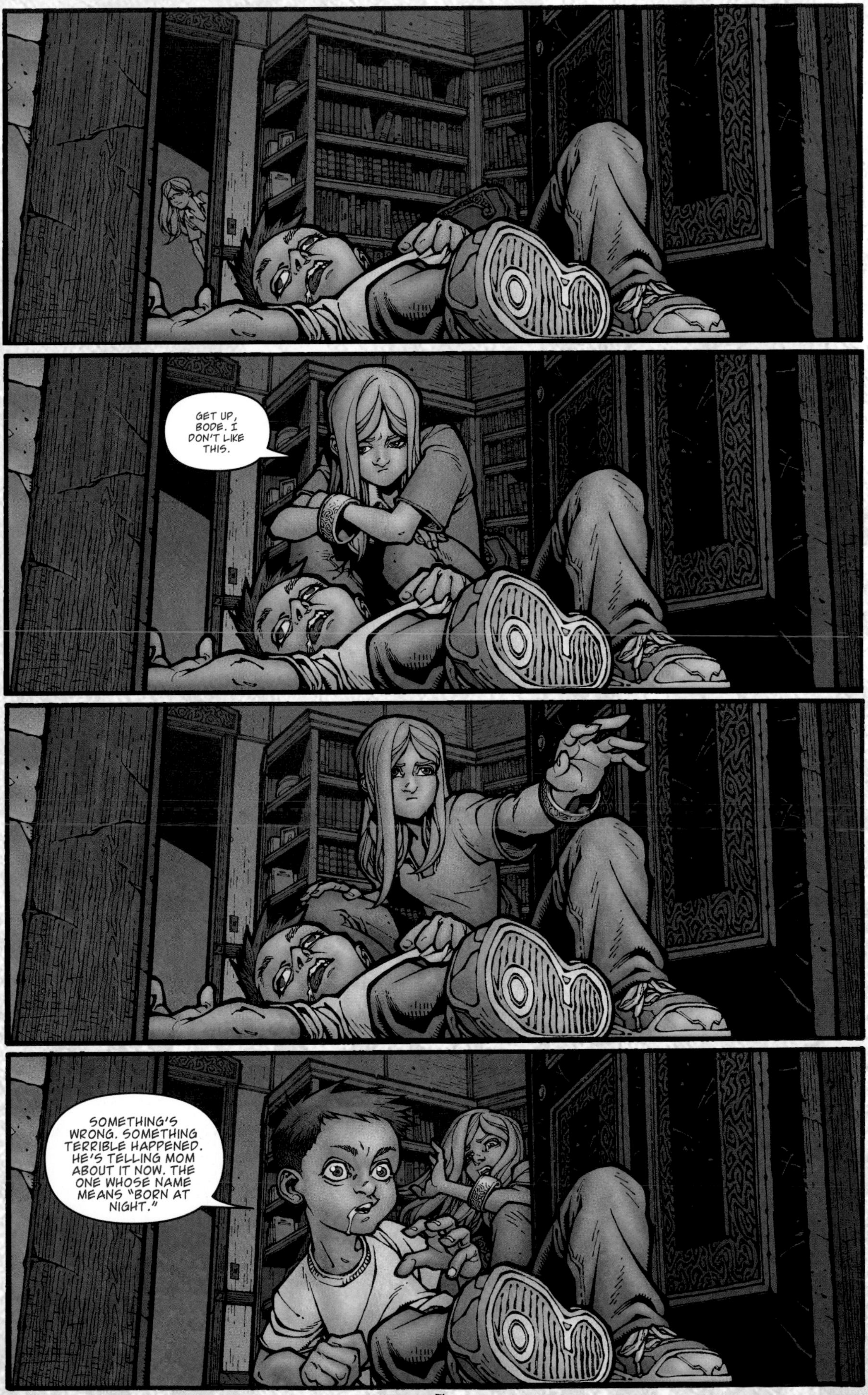
GET UP, BODE. I DON'T LIKE THIS.
SOMETHING'S WRONG. SOMETHING TERRIBLE HAPPENED. HE'S TELLING MOM ABOUT IT NOW. THE ONE WHOSE NAME MEANS "BORN AT NIGHT."

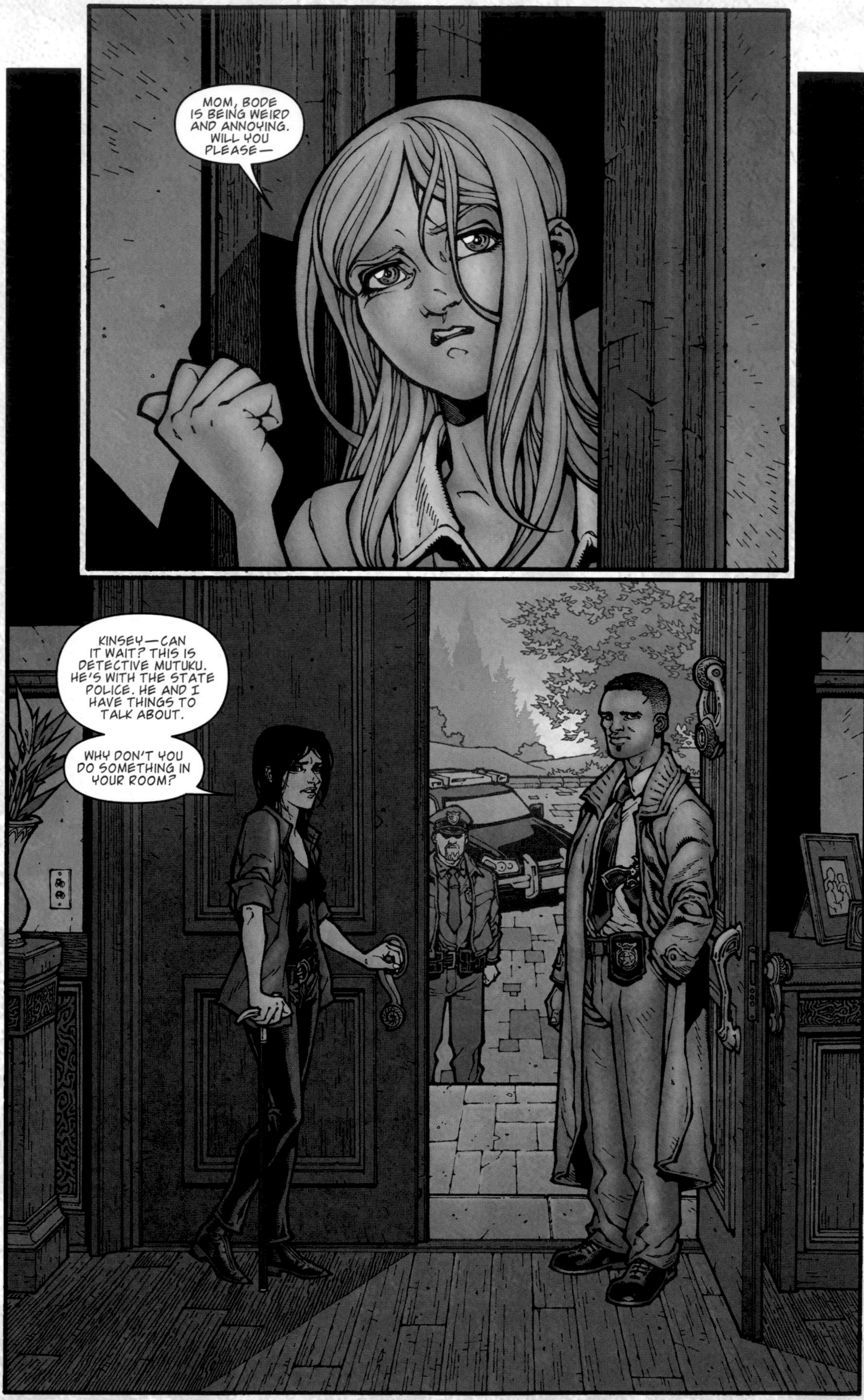
MOM, BODE IS BEING WEIRD AND ANNOYING. WILL YOU PLEASE—
KINSEY—CAN IT WAIT? THIS IS DETECTIVE MUTUKU. HE'S WITH THE STATE POLICE. HE AND I HAVE THINGS TO TALK ABOUT.
WHY DON'T YOU DO SOMETHING IN YOUR ROOM?

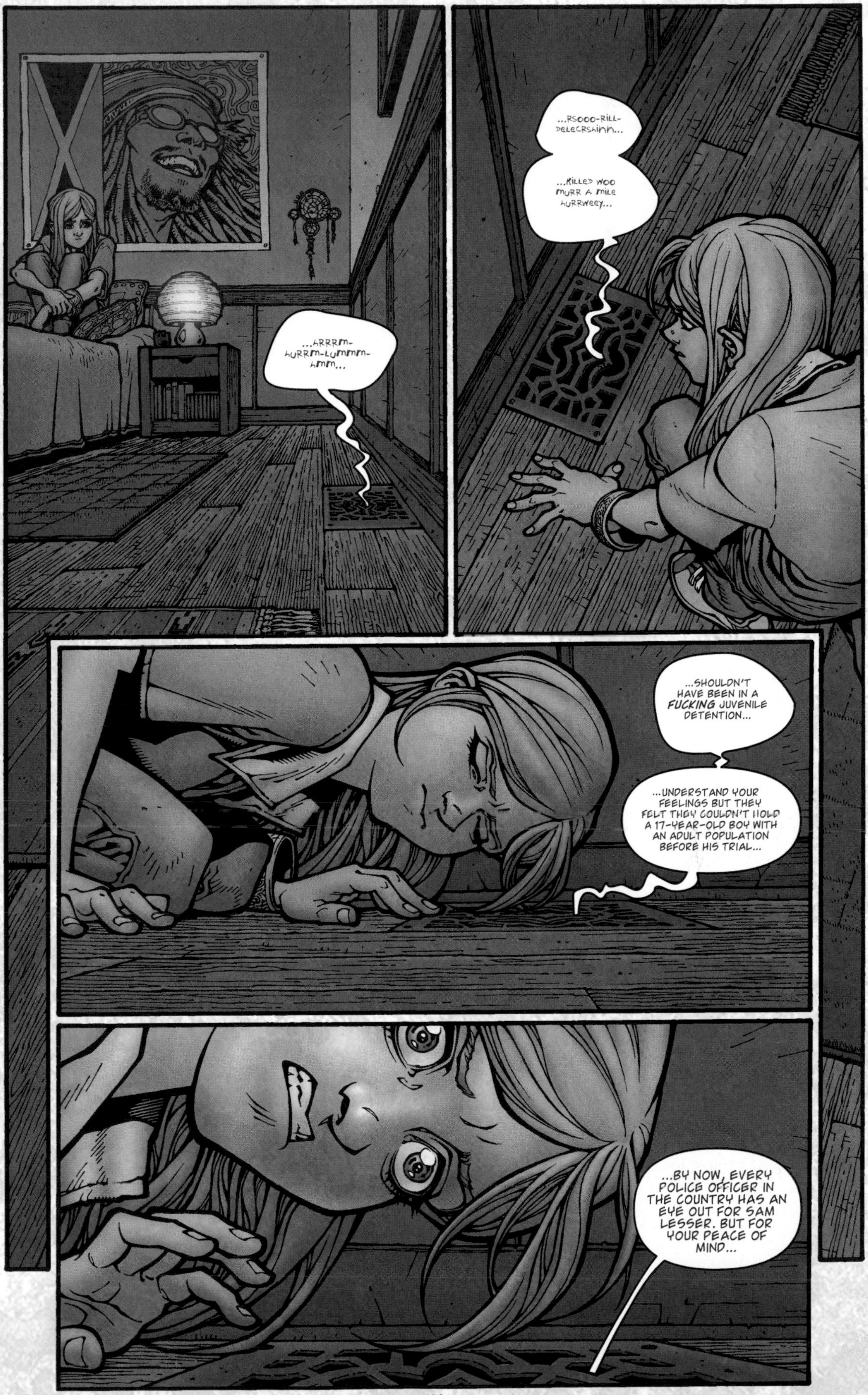
...ARRRM-HURRM-LUMMM-MMM...
...RSOOO-RILL-DELECRSHINN...
...KILLED WOO MURR A MILE HURRWEEY...
...SHOULDN'T HAVE BEEN IN A *FUCKING* JUVENILE DETENTION...
...UNDERSTAND YOUR FEELINGS BUT THEY FELT THEY COULDN'T HOLD A 17-YEAR-OLD BOY WITH AN ADULT POPULATION BEFORE HIS TRIAL...
...BY NOW, EVERY POLICE OFFICER IN THE COUNTRY HAS AN EYE OUT FOR SAM LESSER. BUT FOR YOUR PEACE OF MIND...

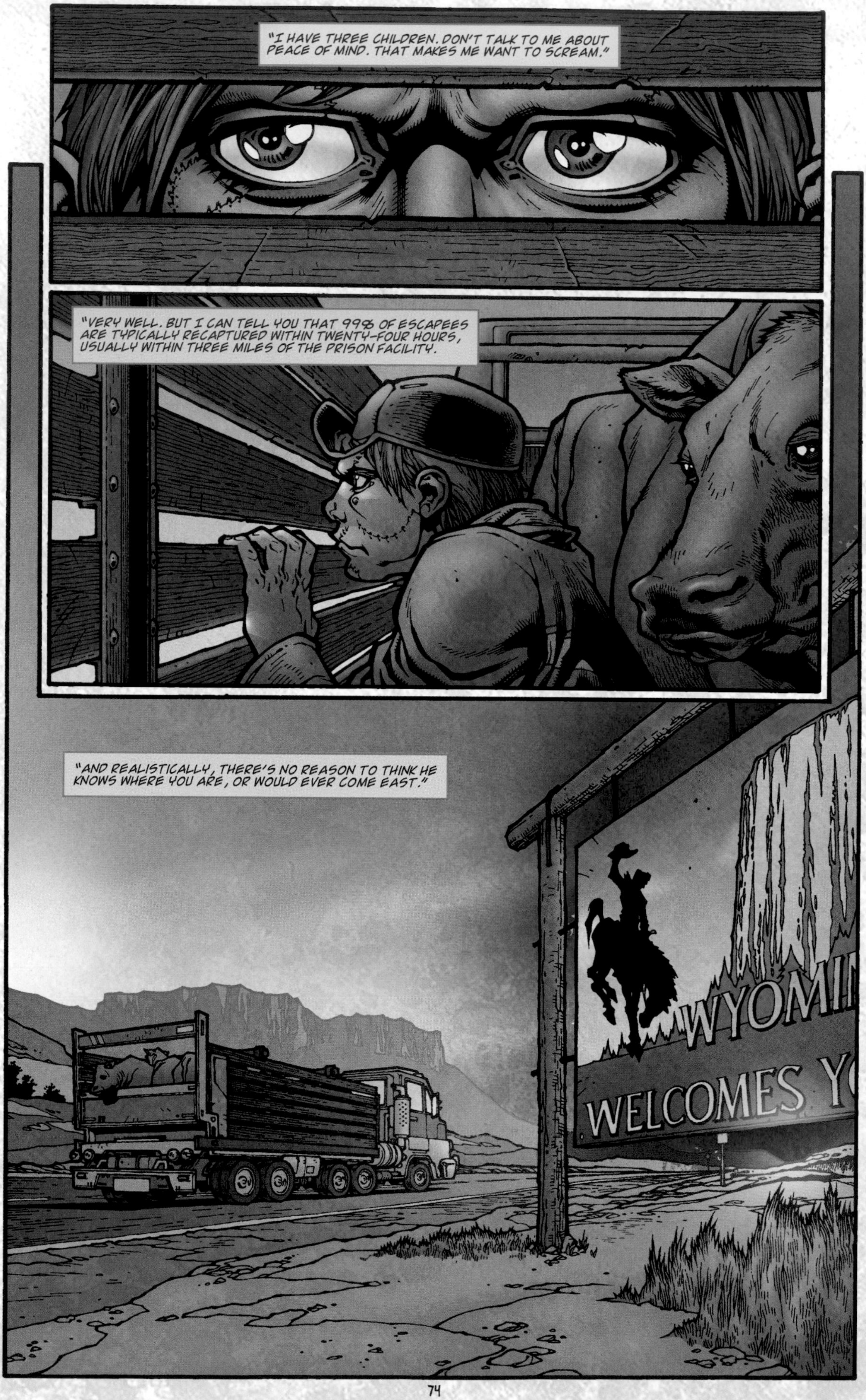
"I HAVE THREE CHILDREN. DON'T TALK TO ME ABOUT PEACE OF MIND. THAT MAKES ME WANT TO SCREAM."
"VERY WELL. BUT I CAN TELL YOU THAT 99% OF ESCAPEES ARE TYPICALLY RECAPTURED WITHIN TWENTY-FOUR HOURS, USUALLY WITHIN THREE MILES OF THE PRISON FACILITY.
"AND REALISTICALLY, THERE'S NO REASON TO THINK HE KNOWS WHERE YOU ARE, OR WOULD EVER COME EAST."
WYOMI
WELCOMES Y

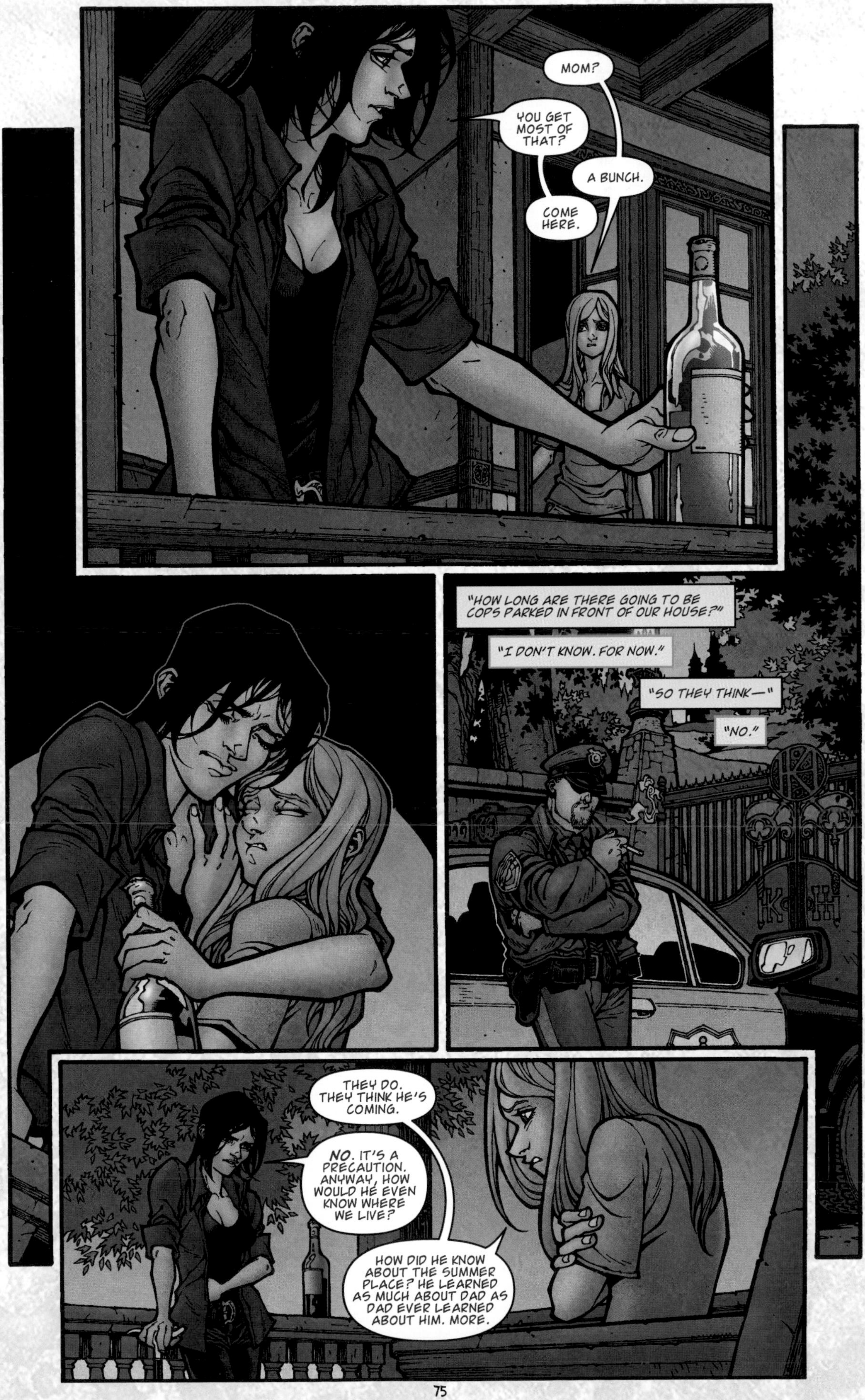
MOM?
YOU GET MOST OF THAT?
A BUNCH.
COME HERE.
"HOW LONG ARE THERE GOING TO BE COPS PARKED IN FRONT OF OUR HOUSE?"
"I DON'T KNOW. FOR NOW."
"SO THEY THINK—"
"NO."
THEY DO. THEY THINK HE'S COMING.
NO. IT'S A PRECAUTION. ANYWAY, HOW WOULD HE EVEN KNOW WHERE WE LIVE?
HOW DID HE KNOW ABOUT THE SUMMER PLACE? HE LEARNED AS MUCH ABOUT DAD AS DAD EVER LEARNED ABOUT HIM. MORE.

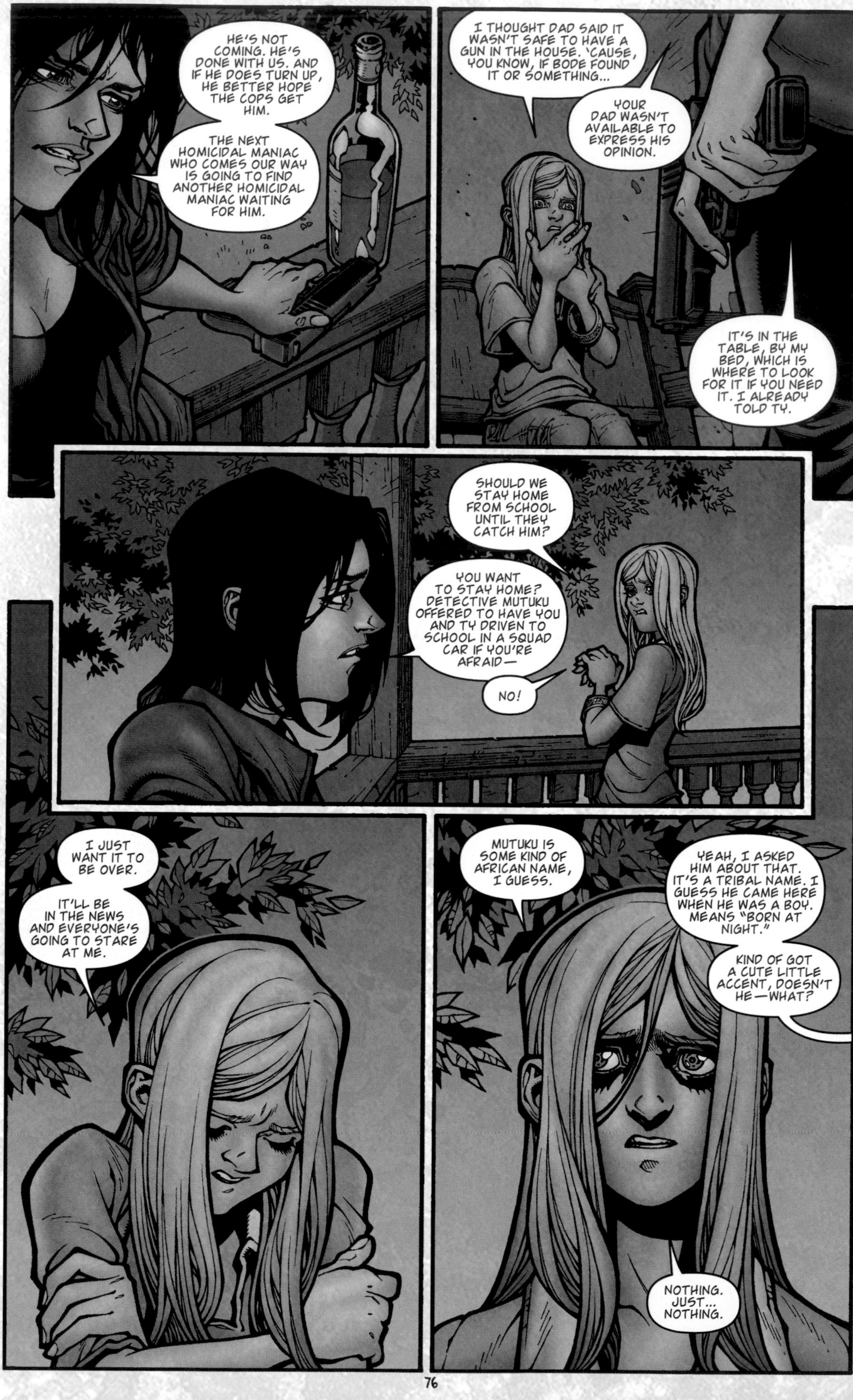
HE'S NOT COMING. HE'S DONE WITH US. AND IF HE DOES TURN UP, HE BETTER HOPE THE COPS GET HIM.
THE NEXT HOMICIDAL MANIAC WHO COMES OUR WAY IS GOING TO FIND ANOTHER HOMICIDAL MANIAC WAITING FOR HIM.
I THOUGHT DAD SAID IT WASN'T SAFE TO HAVE A GUN IN THE HOUSE. 'CAUSE, YOU KNOW, IF BODE FOUND IT OR SOMETHING...
YOUR DAD WASN'T AVAILABLE TO EXPRESS HIS OPINION.
IT'S IN THE TABLE, BY MY BED, WHICH IS WHERE TO LOOK FOR IT IF YOU NEED IT. I ALREADY TOLD TY.
SHOULD WE STAY HOME FROM SCHOOL UNTIL THEY CATCH HIM?
YOU WANT TO STAY HOME? DETECTIVE MUTUKU OFFERED TO HAVE YOU AND TY DRIVEN TO SCHOOL IN A SQUAD CAR IF YOU'RE AFRAID—
NO!
I JUST WANT IT TO BE OVER.
IT'LL BE IN THE NEWS AND EVERYONE'S GOING TO STARE AT ME.
MUTUKU IS SOME KIND OF AFRICAN NAME, I GUESS.
YEAH, I ASKED HIM ABOUT THAT. IT'S A TRIBAL NAME. I GUESS HE CAME HERE WHEN HE WAS A BOY. MEANS "BORN AT NIGHT."
KIND OF GOT A CUTE LITTLE ACCENT, DOESN'T HE—WHAT?
NOTHING. JUST... NOTHING.

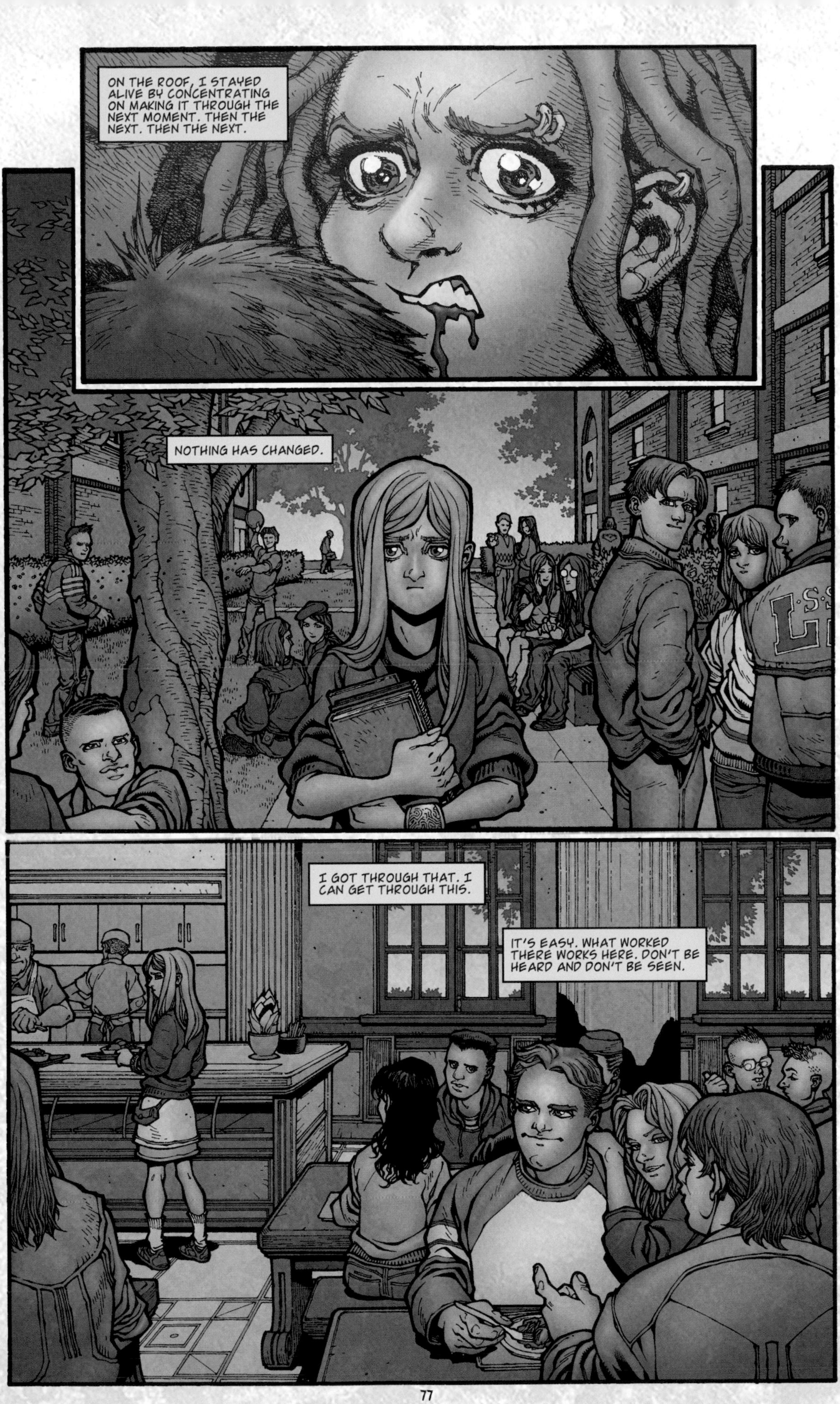
ON THE ROOF, I STAYED ALIVE BY CONCENTRATING ON MAKING IT THROUGH THE NEXT MOMENT. THEN THE NEXT. THEN THE NEXT.
NOTHING HAS CHANGED.
L·S·S
I GOT THROUGH THAT. I CAN GET THROUGH THIS.
IT'S EASY. WHAT WORKED THERE WORKS HERE. DON'T BE HEARD AND DON'T BE SEEN.

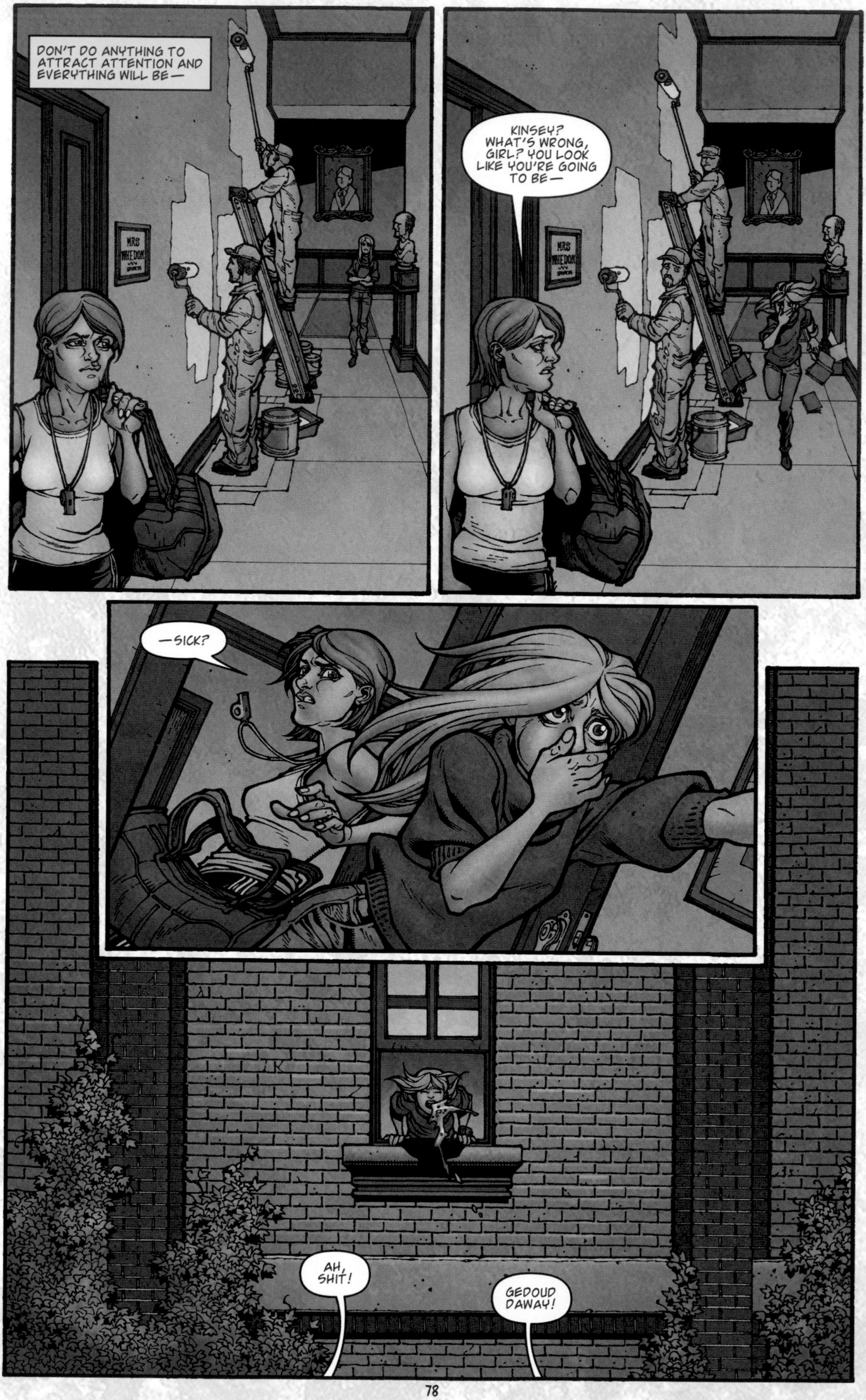
DON'T DO ANYTHING TO ATTRACT ATTENTION AND EVERYTHING WILL BE—
MRS WHEDON
KINSEY? WHAT'S WRONG, GIRL? YOU LOOK LIKE YOU'RE GOING TO BE—
—SICK?
AH, SHIT!
GEDOUD DAWAY!

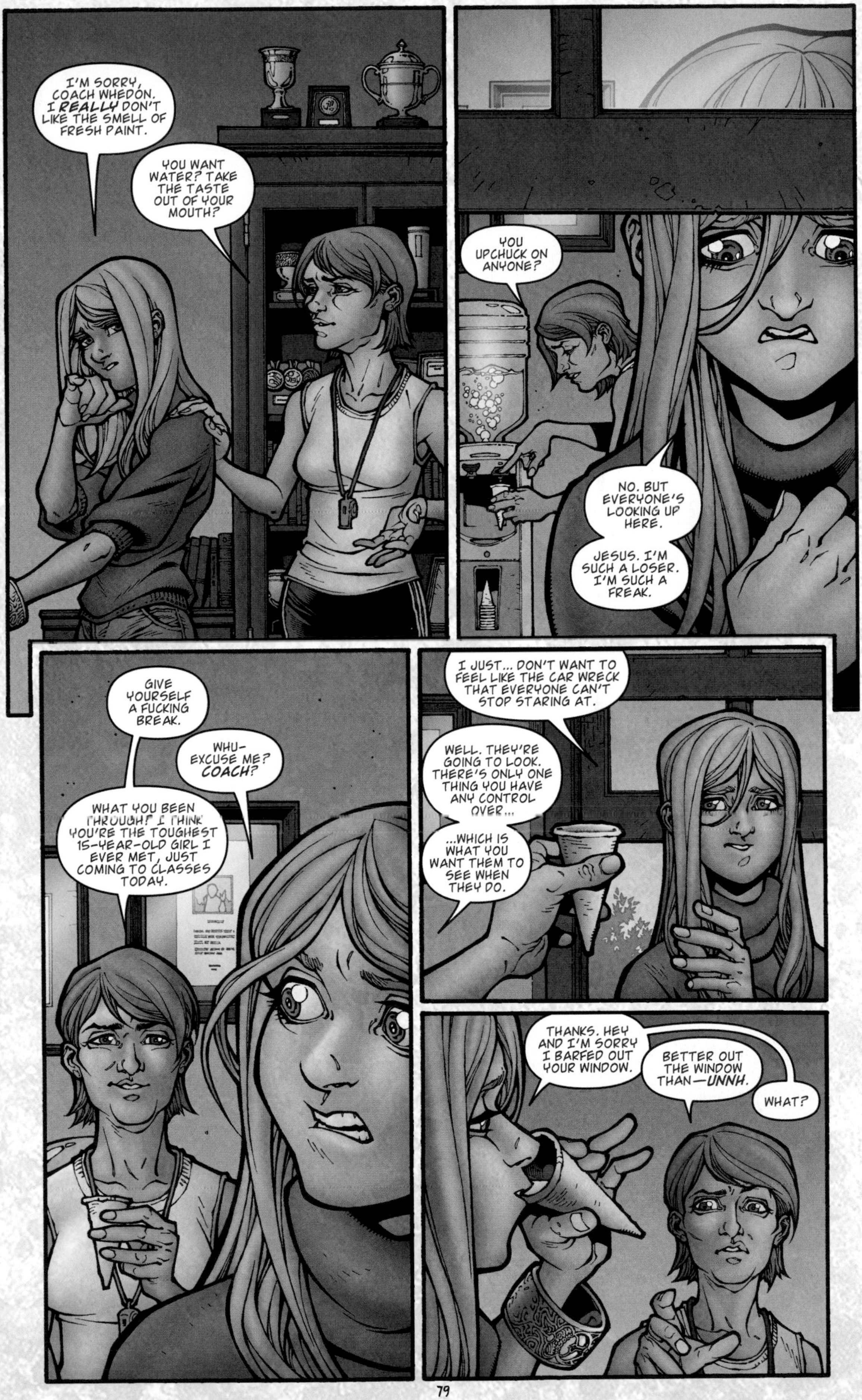
I'M SORRY, COACH WHEDON. I *REALLY* DON'T LIKE THE SMELL OF FRESH PAINT.
YOU WANT WATER? TAKE THE TASTE OUT OF YOUR MOUTH?
YOU UPCHUCK ON ANYONE?
NO. BUT EVERYONE'S LOOKING UP HERE.
JESUS. I'M SUCH A LOSER. I'M SUCH A FREAK.
GIVE YOURSELF A FUCKING BREAK.
WHU- EXCUSE ME? *COACH*?
WHAT YOU BEEN THROUGH? I THINK YOU'RE THE TOUGHEST 15-YEAR-OLD GIRL I EVER MET, JUST COMING TO CLASSES TODAY.
I JUST... DON'T WANT TO FEEL LIKE THE CAR WRECK THAT EVERYONE CAN'T STOP STARING AT.
WELL. THEY'RE GOING TO LOOK. THERE'S ONLY ONE THING YOU HAVE ANY CONTROL OVER...
...WHICH IS WHAT YOU WANT THEM TO SEE WHEN THEY DO.
THANKS. HEY AND I'M SORRY I BARFED OUT YOUR WINDOW.
BETTER OUT THE WINDOW THAN—*UNNH*.
WHAT?

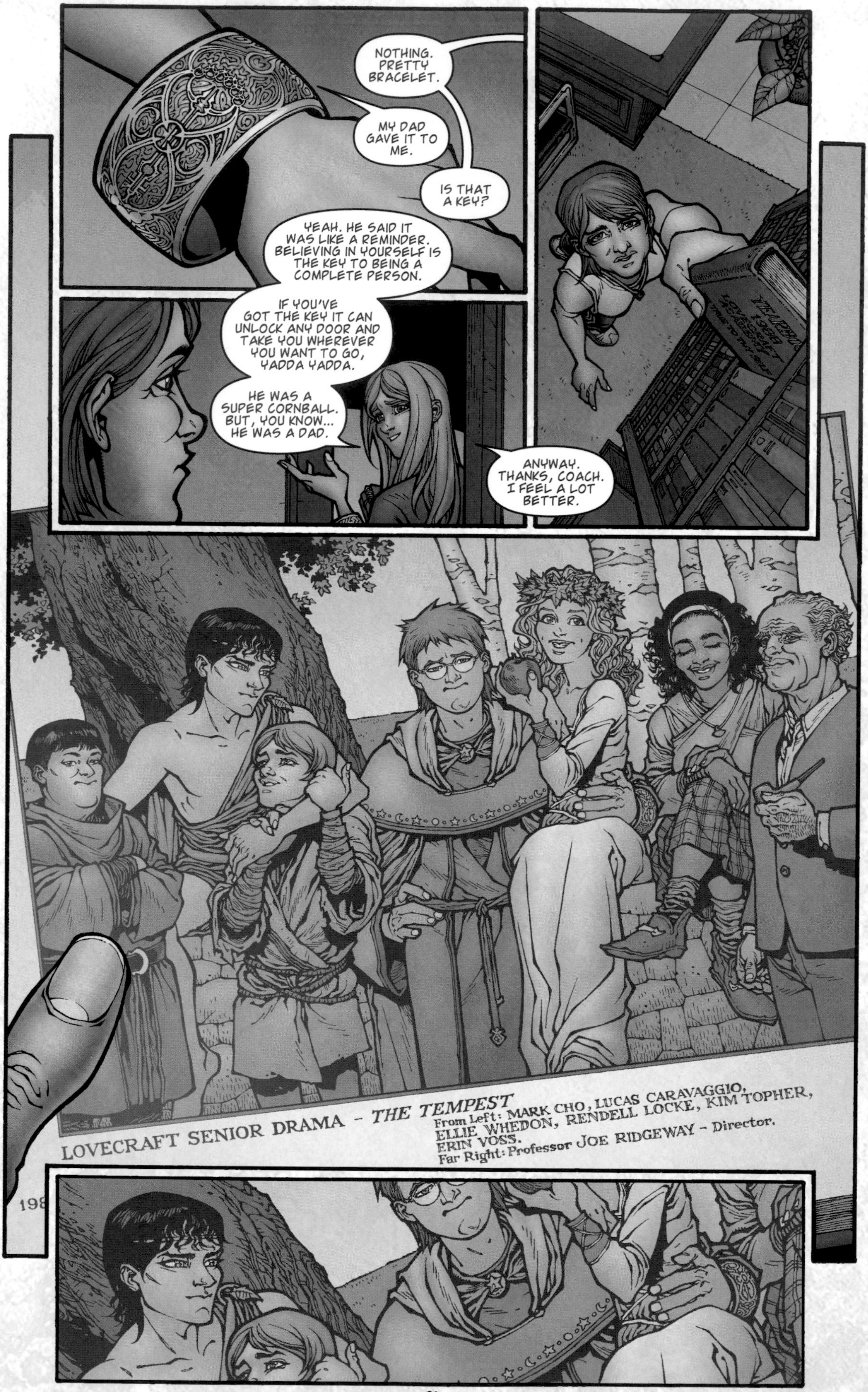
NOTHING. PRETTY BRACELET.
MY DAD GAVE IT TO ME.
IS THAT A KEY?
YEAH. HE SAID IT WAS LIKE A REMINDER. BELIEVING IN YOURSELF IS THE KEY TO BEING A COMPLETE PERSON.
IF YOU'VE GOT THE KEY IT CAN UNLOCK ANY DOOR AND TAKE YOU WHEREVER YOU WANT TO GO, YADDA YADDA.
HE WAS A SUPER CORNBALL. BUT, YOU KNOW... HE WAS A DAD.
ANYWAY. THANKS, COACH. I FEEL A LOT BETTER.
LOVECRAFT SENIOR DRAMA - THE TEMPEST
From Left: MARK CHO, LUCAS CARAVAGGIO, ELLIE WHEDON, RENDELL LOCKE, KIM TOPHER, ERIN VOSS.
Far Right: Professor JOE RIDGEWAY - Director.
198

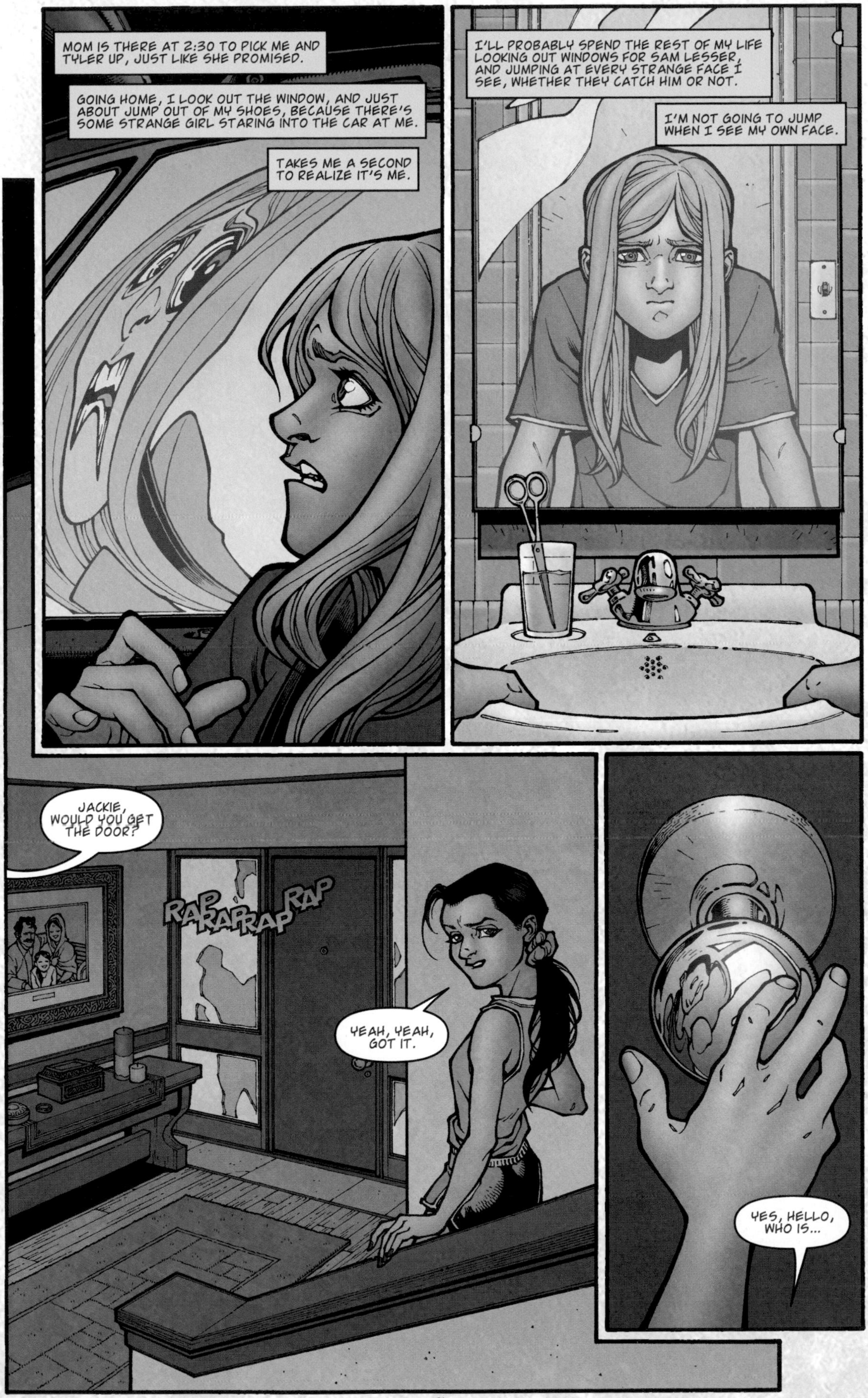
MOM IS THERE AT 2:30 TO PICK ME AND TYLER UP, JUST LIKE SHE PROMISED.
GOING HOME, I LOOK OUT THE WINDOW, AND JUST ABOUT JUMP OUT OF MY SHOES, BECAUSE THERE'S SOME STRANGE GIRL STARING INTO THE CAR AT ME.
TAKES ME A SECOND TO REALIZE IT'S ME.
I'LL PROBABLY SPEND THE REST OF MY LIFE LOOKING OUT WINDOWS FOR SAM LESSER, AND JUMPING AT EVERY STRANGE FACE I SEE, WHETHER THEY CATCH HIM OR NOT.
I'M NOT GOING TO JUMP WHEN I SEE MY OWN FACE.
JACKIE, WOULD YOU GET THE DOOR?
RAP RAP RAP RAP
YEAH, YEAH, GOT IT.
YES, HELLO, WHO IS...

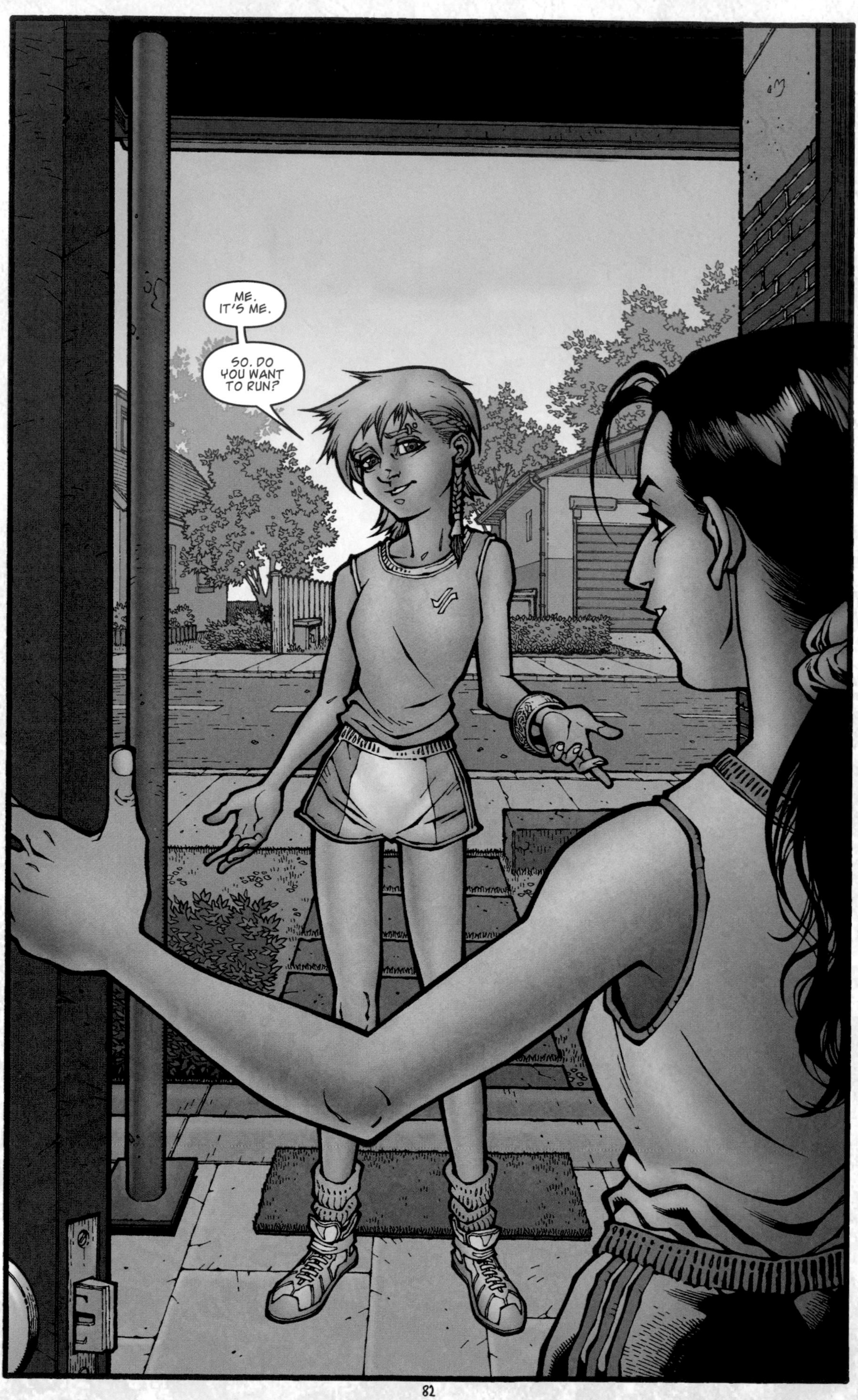
ME. IT'S ME.
SO. DO YOU WANT TO RUN?

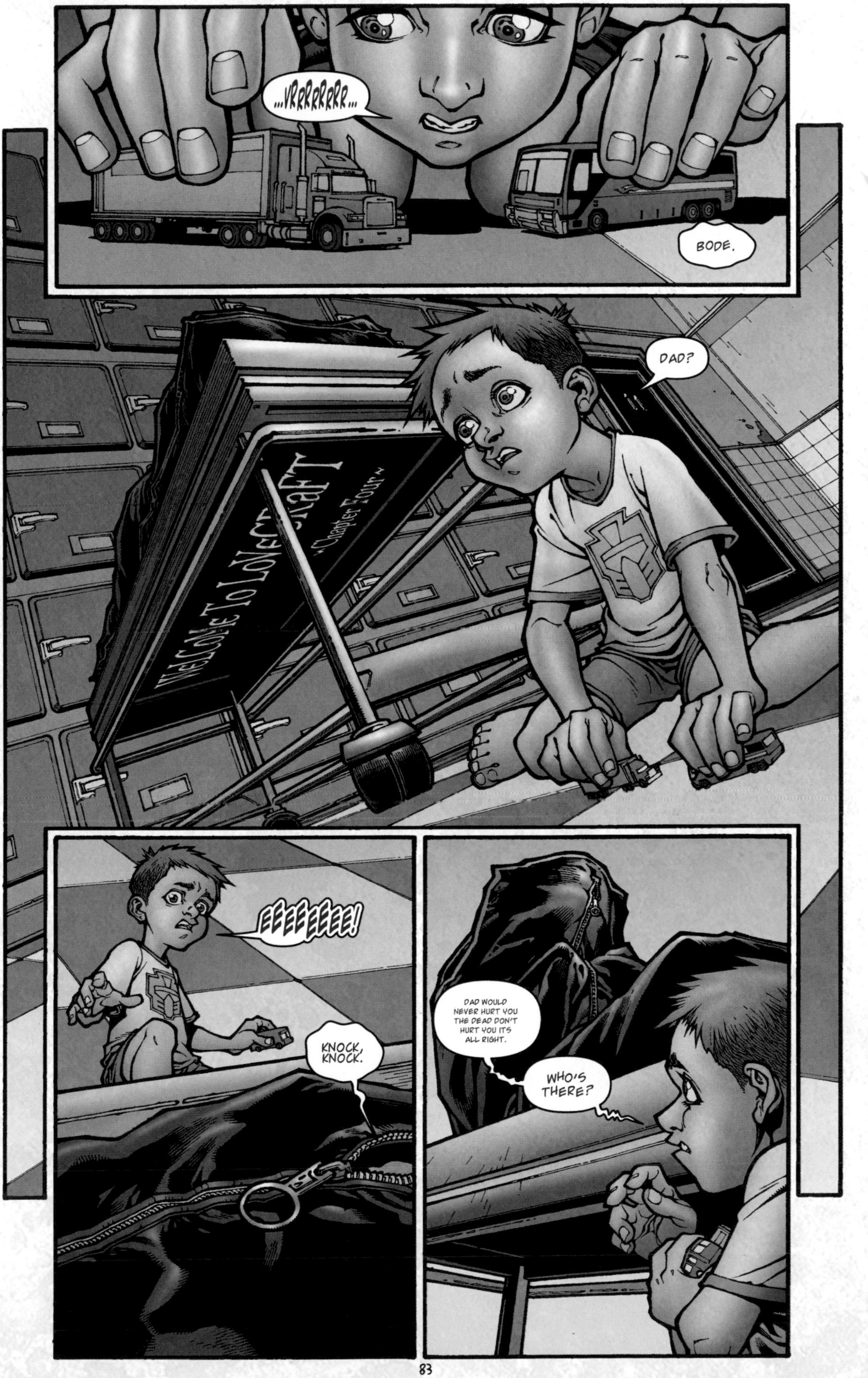
...VRRRRRRRR...
BODE.
DAD?
WELCOME TO LOVECRAFT
~Chapter Four~
EEEEEEEE!
KNOCK, KNOCK.
DAD WOULD NEVER HURT YOU THE DEAD DON'T HURT YOU ITS ALL RIGHT.
WHO'S THERE?

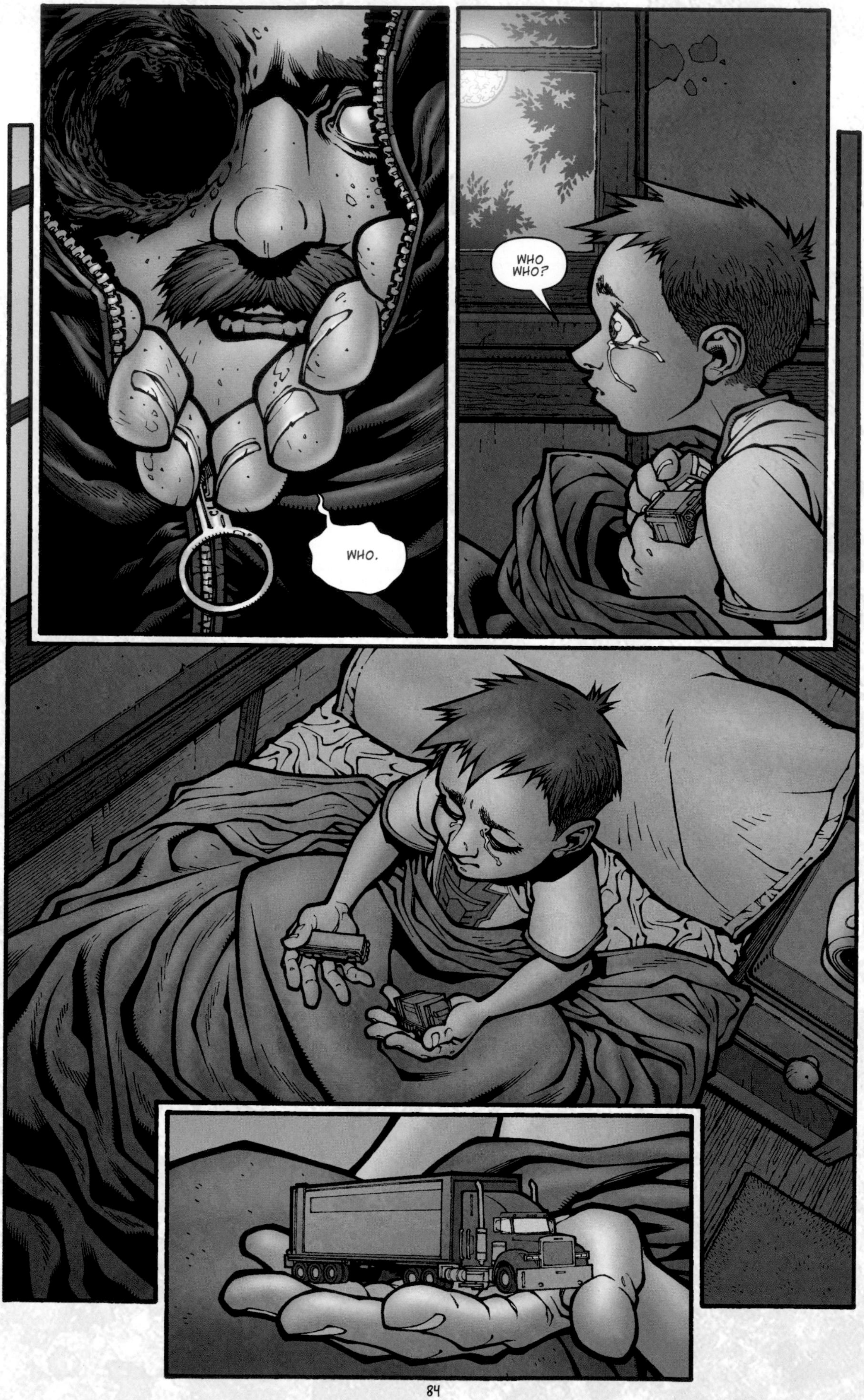
WHO.
WHO WHO?

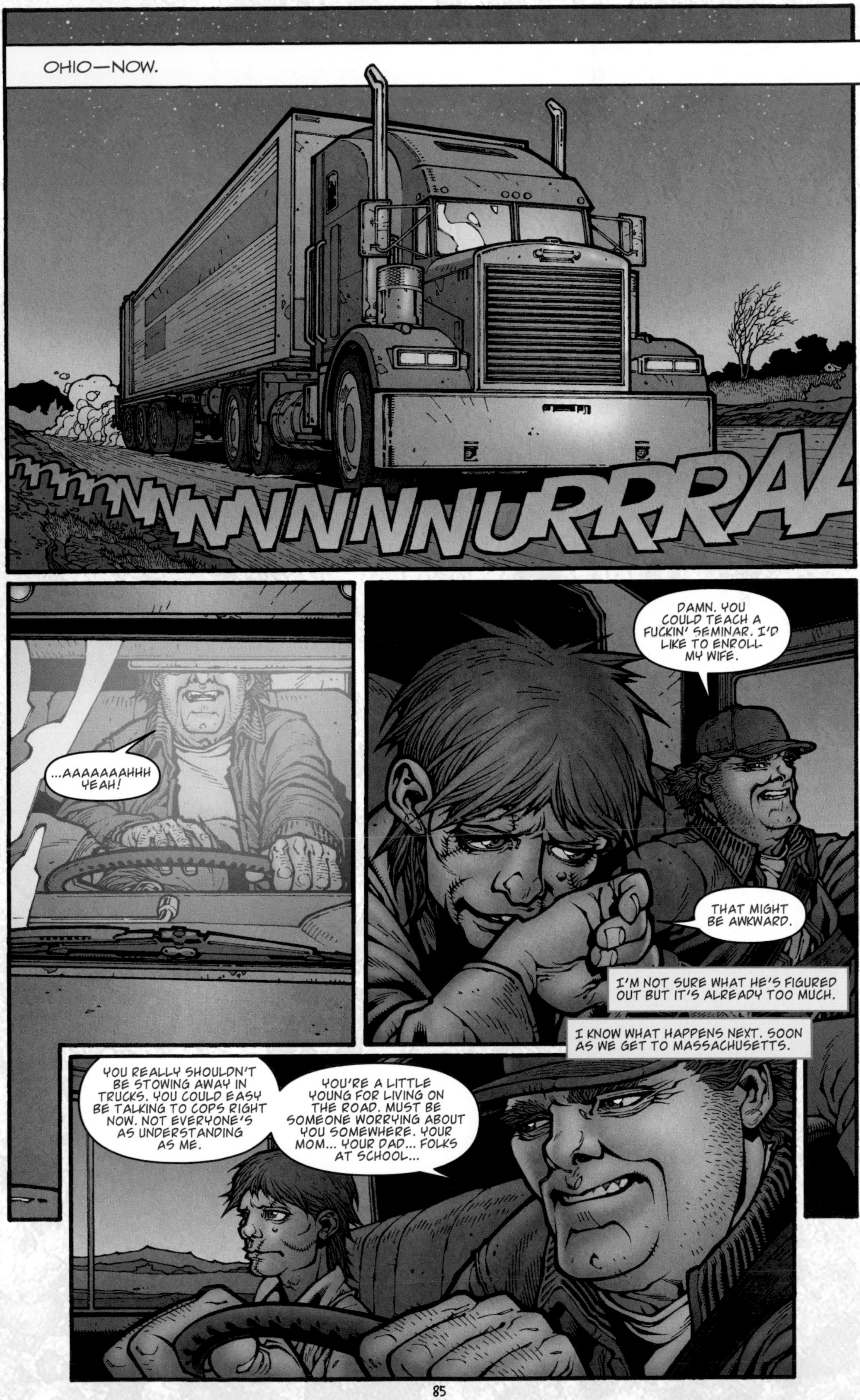
OHIO—NOW.
NNNNNNNNNNNURRRA
...AAAAAAAHHH YEAH!
DAMN. YOU COULD TEACH A FUCKIN' SEMINAR. I'D LIKE TO ENROLL MY WIFE.
THAT MIGHT BE AWKWARD.
I'M NOT SURE WHAT HE'S FIGURED OUT BUT IT'S ALREADY TOO MUCH.
I KNOW WHAT HAPPENS NEXT. SOON AS WE GET TO MASSACHUSETTS.
YOU REALLY SHOULDN'T BE STOWING AWAY IN TRUCKS. YOU COULD EASY BE TALKING TO COPS RIGHT NOW. NOT EVERYONE'S AS UNDERSTANDING AS ME.
YOU'RE A LITTLE YOUNG FOR LIVING ON THE ROAD. MUST BE SOMEONE WORRYING ABOUT YOU SOMEWHERE. YOUR MOM... YOUR DAD... FOLKS AT SCHOOL...

MOM? I GOT MY SATS. GUESS WHAT?

...SO I SAID, *BITCH*, YOU DON'T GO THERE WITH ME. AND SHE SAYS...

GUBBA! SLUB WHEE!

"NO... NOT REALLY."

MOM, REMEMBER WHEN YOU SAID IF I GOT 600S ON MY SATS, WE COULD TALK ABOUT COLLEGE...

YEAH, AND IF WE WIN THE LOTTERY. I'M GOIN' OUT TONIGHT. YOU AND THE BABY ARE STAYING AT DAD'S.

"I WAS REALLY CLOSE TO MY MOM."

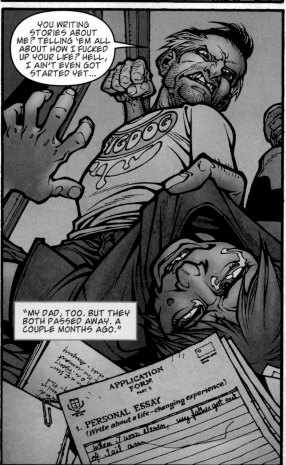

YOU WRITING STORIES ABOUT ME? TELLING 'EM ALL ABOUT HOW I FUCKED UP YOUR LIFE? HELL, I AIN'T EVEN GOT STARTED YET...

"MY DAD, TOO. BUT THEY BOTH PASSED AWAY. A COUPLE MONTHS AGO."

APPLICATION FORM
PART 3
1. PERSONAL ESSAY
(Write about a life-changing experience)
When I was eleven, my father got out of jail and...

DUDE, I FARTED. QUICK, PUT ON THE GAS MASK.

"AND I'M DONE WITH SCHOOL."

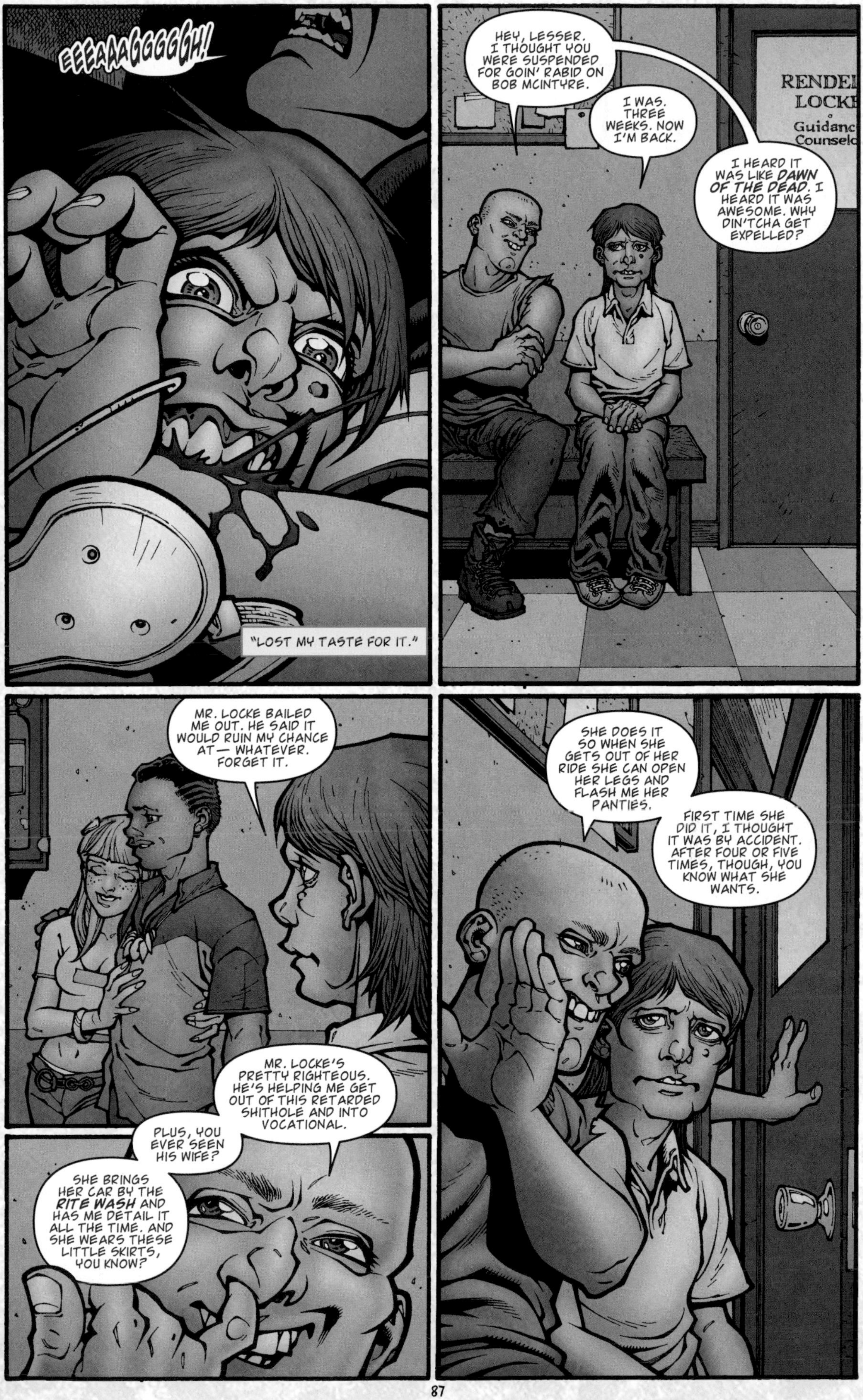
EEEAAAGGGGGH!
"LOST MY TASTE FOR IT."
HEY, LESSER. I THOUGHT YOU WERE SUSPENDED FOR GOIN' RABID ON BOB MCINTYRE.
I WAS. THREE WEEKS. NOW I'M BACK.
I HEARD IT WAS LIKE DAWN OF THE DEAD. I HEARD IT WAS AWESOME. WHY DIN'TCHA GET EXPELLED?
RENDEL
LOCKE
Guidanc
Counselo
MR. LOCKE BAILED ME OUT. HE SAID IT WOULD RUIN MY CHANCE AT— WHATEVER. FORGET IT.
MR. LOCKE'S PRETTY RIGHTEOUS. HE'S HELPING ME GET OUT OF THIS RETARDED SHITHOLE AND INTO VOCATIONAL.
PLUS, YOU EVER SEEN HIS WIFE?
SHE BRINGS HER CAR BY THE RITE WASH AND HAS ME DETAIL IT ALL THE TIME. AND SHE WEARS THESE LITTLE SKIRTS, YOU KNOW?
SHE DOES IT SO WHEN SHE GETS OUT OF HER RIDE SHE CAN OPEN HER LEGS AND FLASH ME HER PANTIES.
FIRST TIME SHE DID IT, I THOUGHT IT WAS BY ACCIDENT. AFTER FOUR OR FIVE TIMES, THOUGH, YOU KNOW WHAT SHE WANTS.

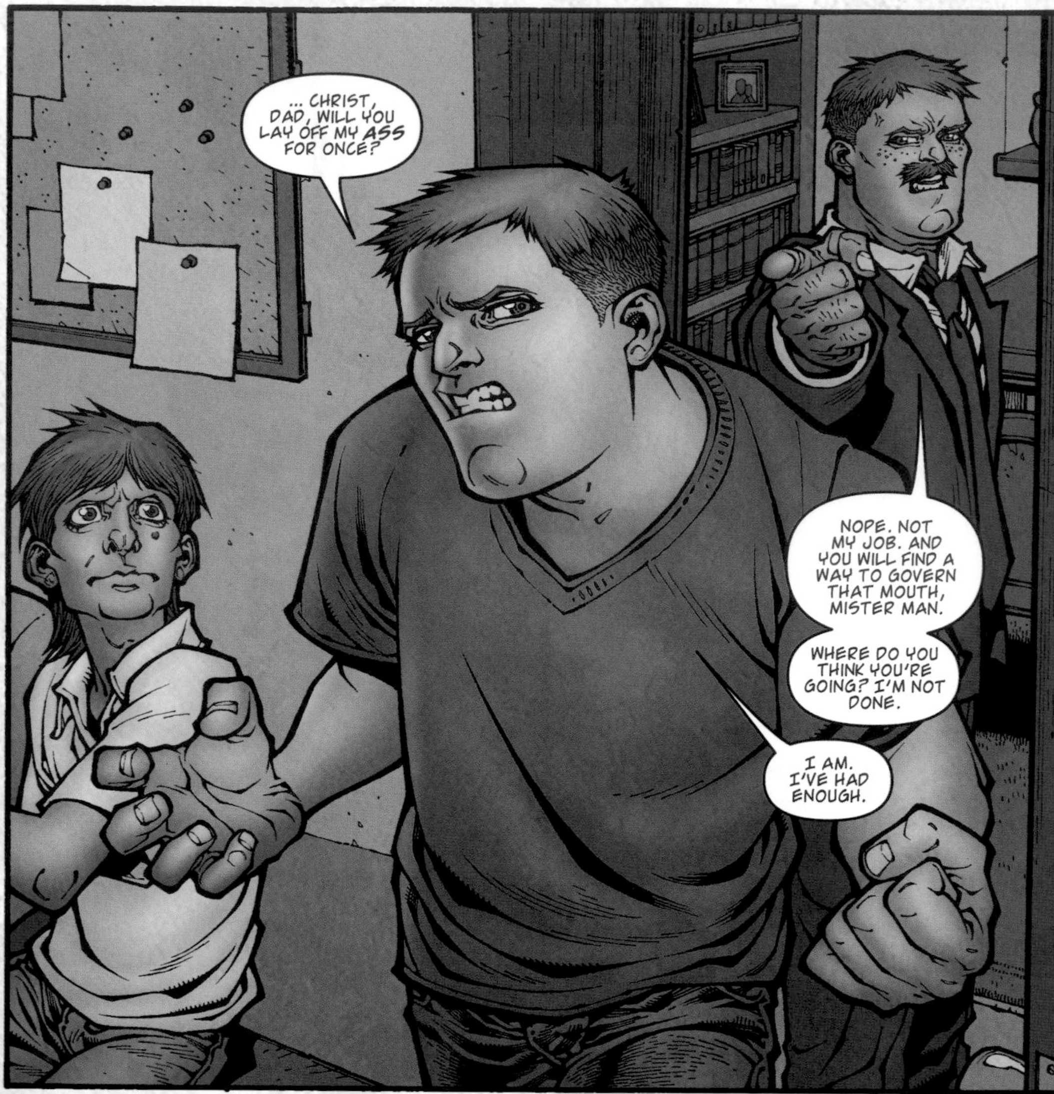
... CHRIST, DAD, WILL YOU LAY OFF MY ASS FOR ONCE?
NOPE. NOT MY JOB. AND YOU WILL FIND A WAY TO GOVERN THAT MOUTH, MISTER MAN.
WHERE DO YOU THINK YOU'RE GOING? I'M NOT DONE.
I AM. I'VE HAD ENOUGH.

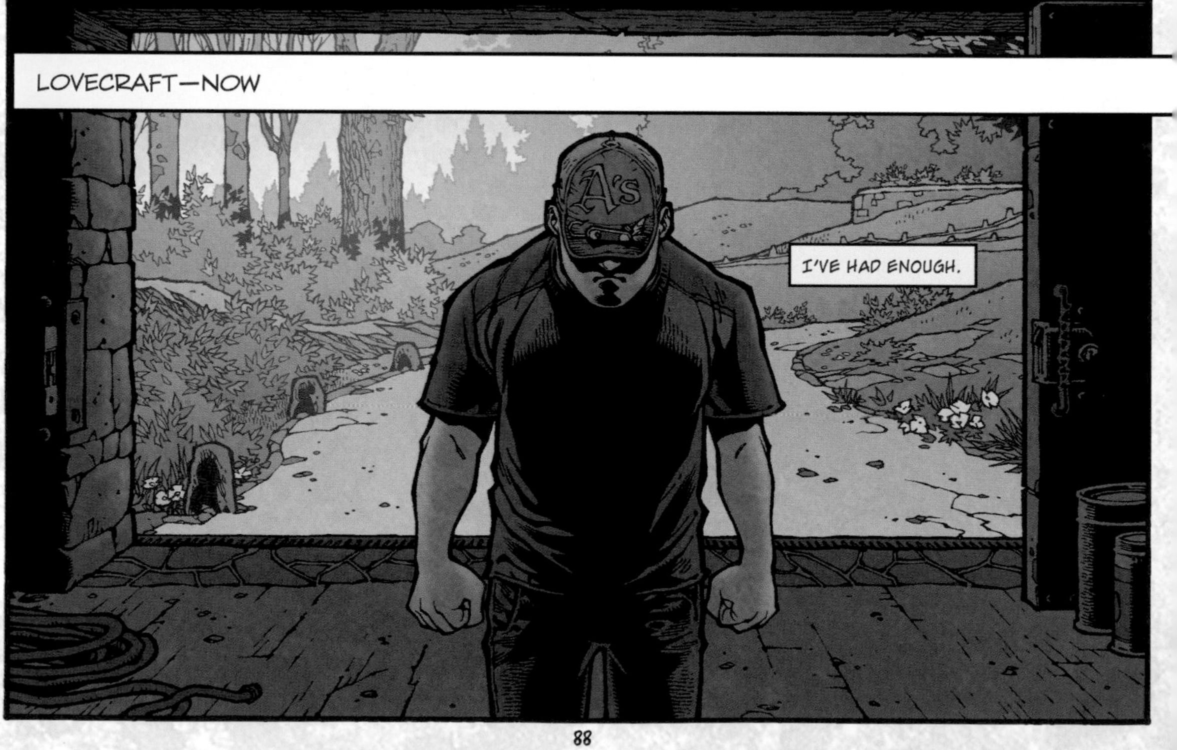
LOVECRAFT—NOW
A's
I'VE HAD ENOUGH.

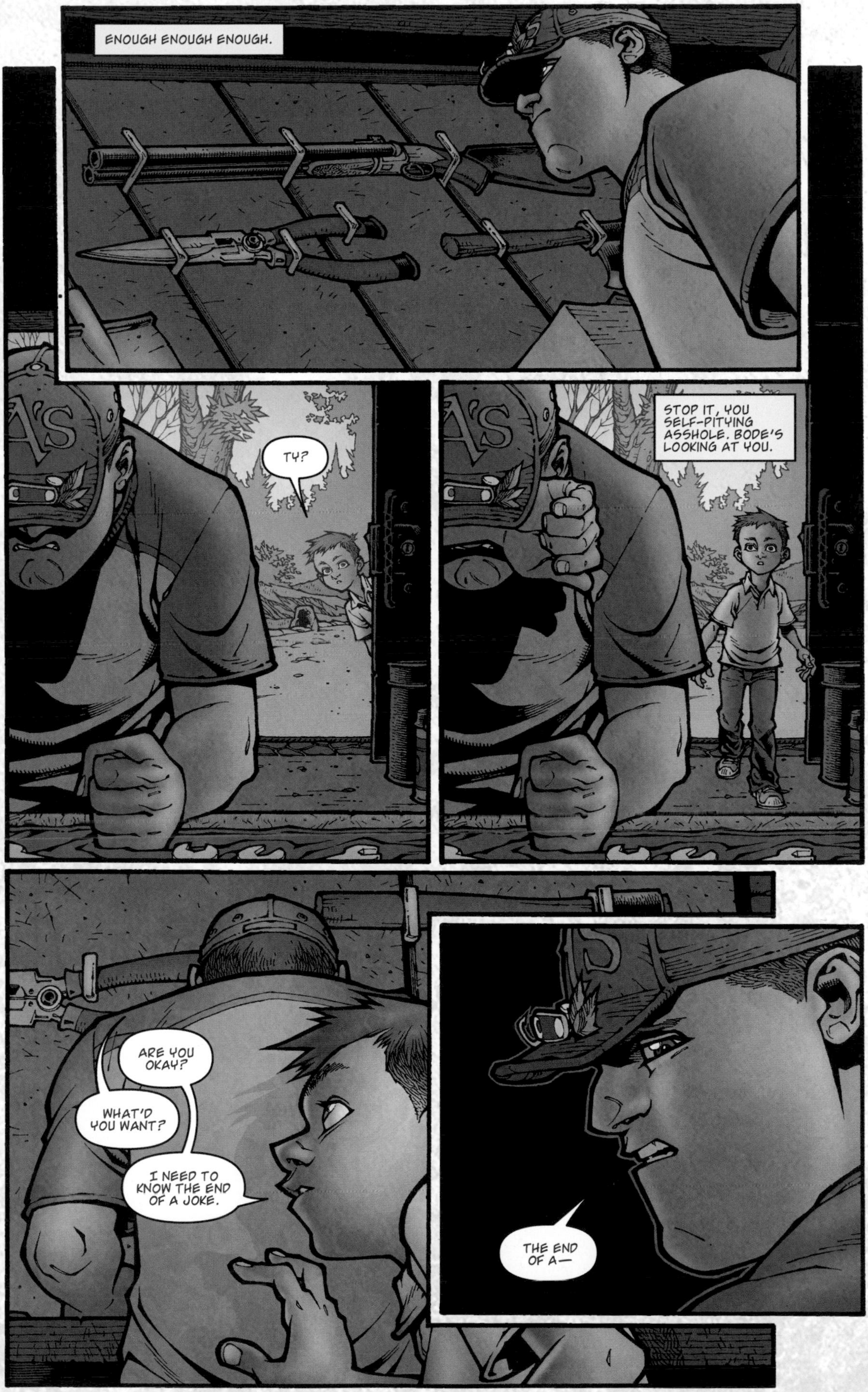
ENOUGH ENOUGH ENOUGH.
TY?
STOP IT, YOU SELF-PITYING ASSHOLE. BODE'S LOOKING AT YOU.
ARE YOU OKAY?
WHAT'D YOU WANT?
I NEED TO KNOW THE END OF A JOKE.
THE END OF A—

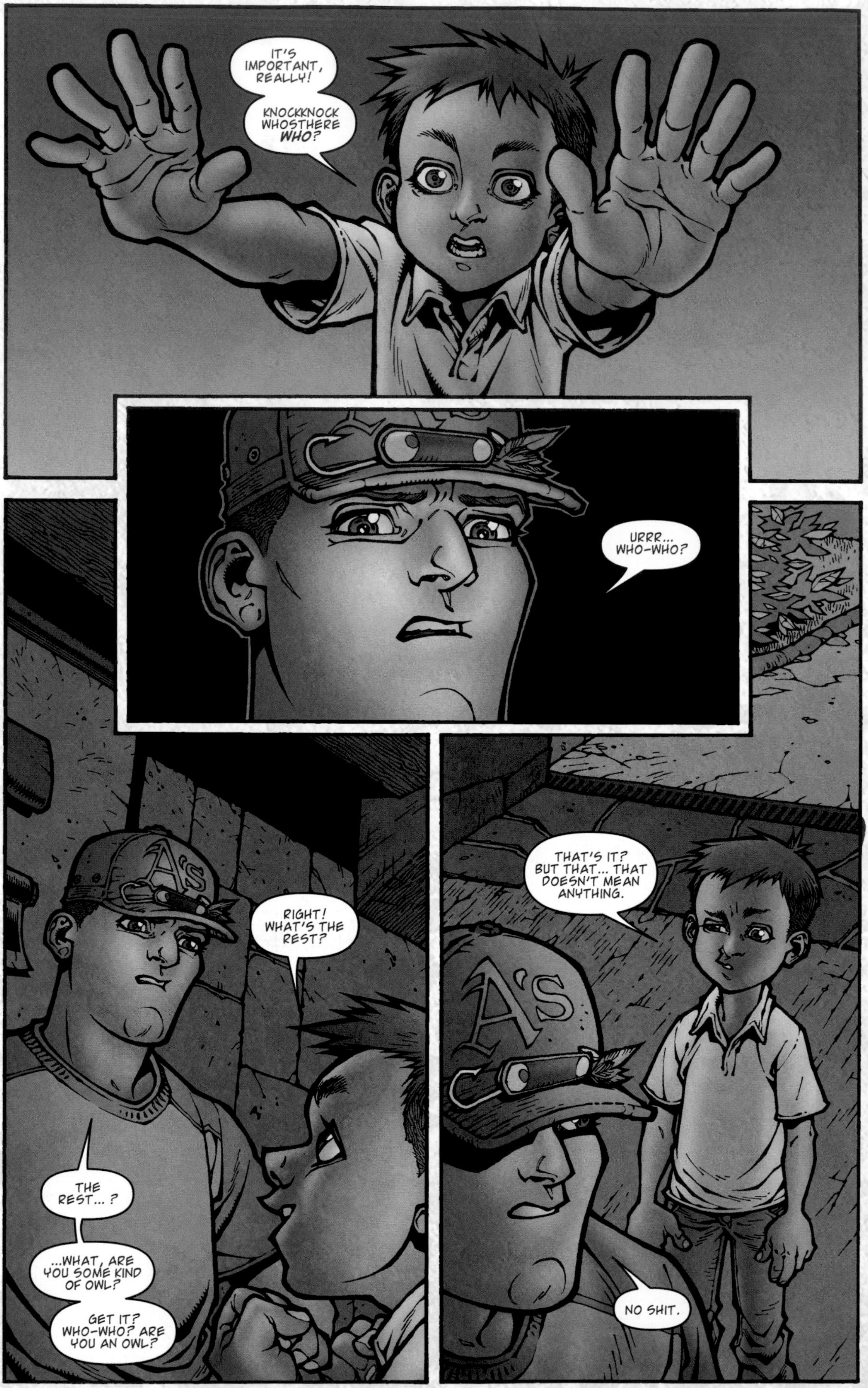
IT'S IMPORTANT, REALLY!
KNOCKKNOCK WHOSTHERE **WHO**?
URRR... WHO-WHO?
RIGHT! WHAT'S THE REST?
THE REST... ?
...WHAT, ARE YOU SOME KIND OF OWL?
GET IT? WHO-WHO? ARE YOU AN OWL?
THAT'S IT? BUT THAT... THAT DOESN'T MEAN ANYTHING.
NO SHIT.

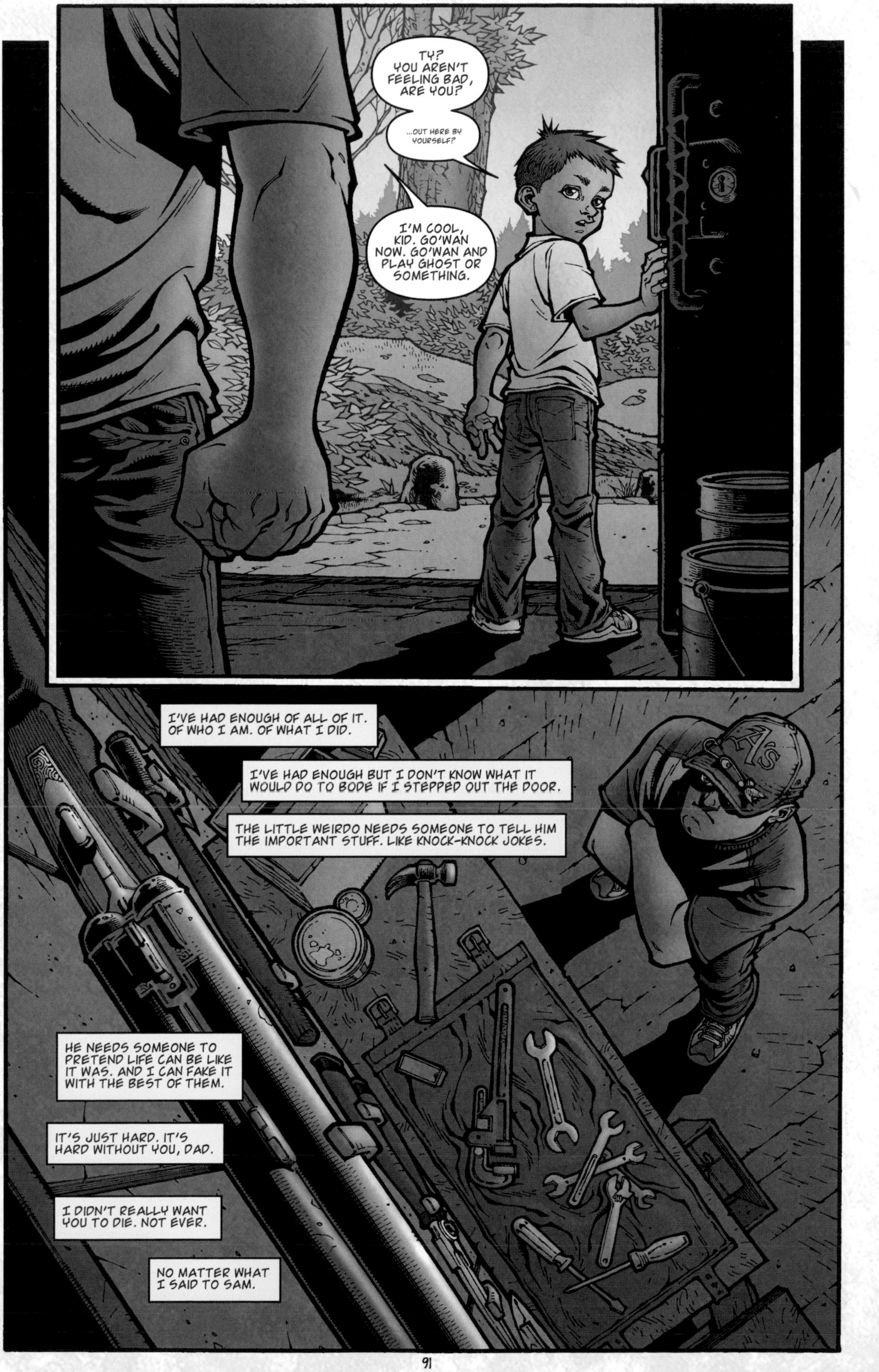

TY? YOU AREN'T FEELING BAD, ARE YOU?
...OUT HERE BY YOURSELF?
I'M COOL, KID. GO'WAN NOW. GO'WAN AND PLAY GHOST OR SOMETHING.
I'VE HAD ENOUGH OF ALL OF IT. OF WHO I AM. OF WHAT I DID.
I'VE HAD ENOUGH BUT I DON'T KNOW WHAT IT WOULD DO TO BODE IF I STEPPED OUT THE DOOR.
THE LITTLE WEIRDO NEEDS SOMEONE TO TELL HIM THE IMPORTANT STUFF. LIKE KNOCK-KNOCK JOKES.
HE NEEDS SOMEONE TO PRETEND LIFE CAN BE LIKE IT WAS. AND I CAN FAKE IT WITH THE BEST OF THEM.
IT'S JUST HARD. IT'S HARD WITHOUT YOU, DAD.
I DIDN'T REALLY WANT YOU TO DIE. NOT EVER.
NO MATTER WHAT I SAID TO SAM.

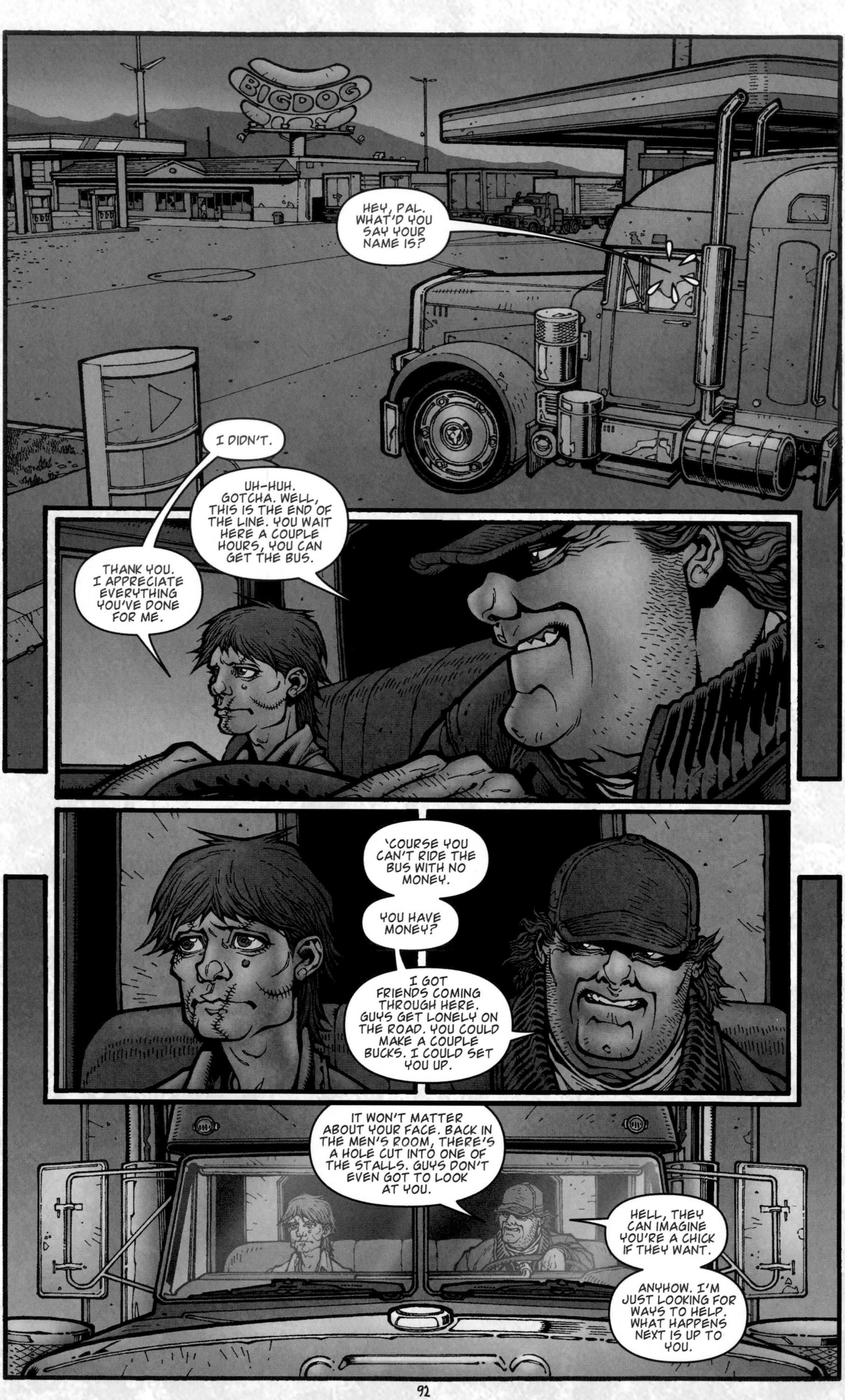
BIGDOG
HEY, PAL. WHAT'D YOU SAY YOUR NAME IS?
I DIDN'T.
UH-HUH. GOTCHA. WELL, THIS IS THE END OF THE LINE. YOU WAIT HERE A COUPLE HOURS, YOU CAN GET THE BUS.
THANK YOU. I APPRECIATE EVERYTHING YOU'VE DONE FOR ME.
'COURSE YOU CAN'T RIDE THE BUS WITH NO MONEY.
YOU HAVE MONEY?
I GOT FRIENDS COMING THROUGH HERE. GUYS GET LONELY ON THE ROAD. YOU COULD MAKE A COUPLE BUCKS. I COULD SET YOU UP.
IT WON'T MATTER ABOUT YOUR FACE. BACK IN THE MEN'S ROOM, THERE'S A HOLE CUT INTO ONE OF THE STALLS. GUYS DON'T EVEN GOT TO LOOK AT YOU.
HELL, THEY CAN IMAGINE YOU'RE A CHICK IF THEY WANT.
ANYHOW. I'M JUST LOOKING FOR WAYS TO HELP. WHAT HAPPENS NEXT IS UP TO YOU.

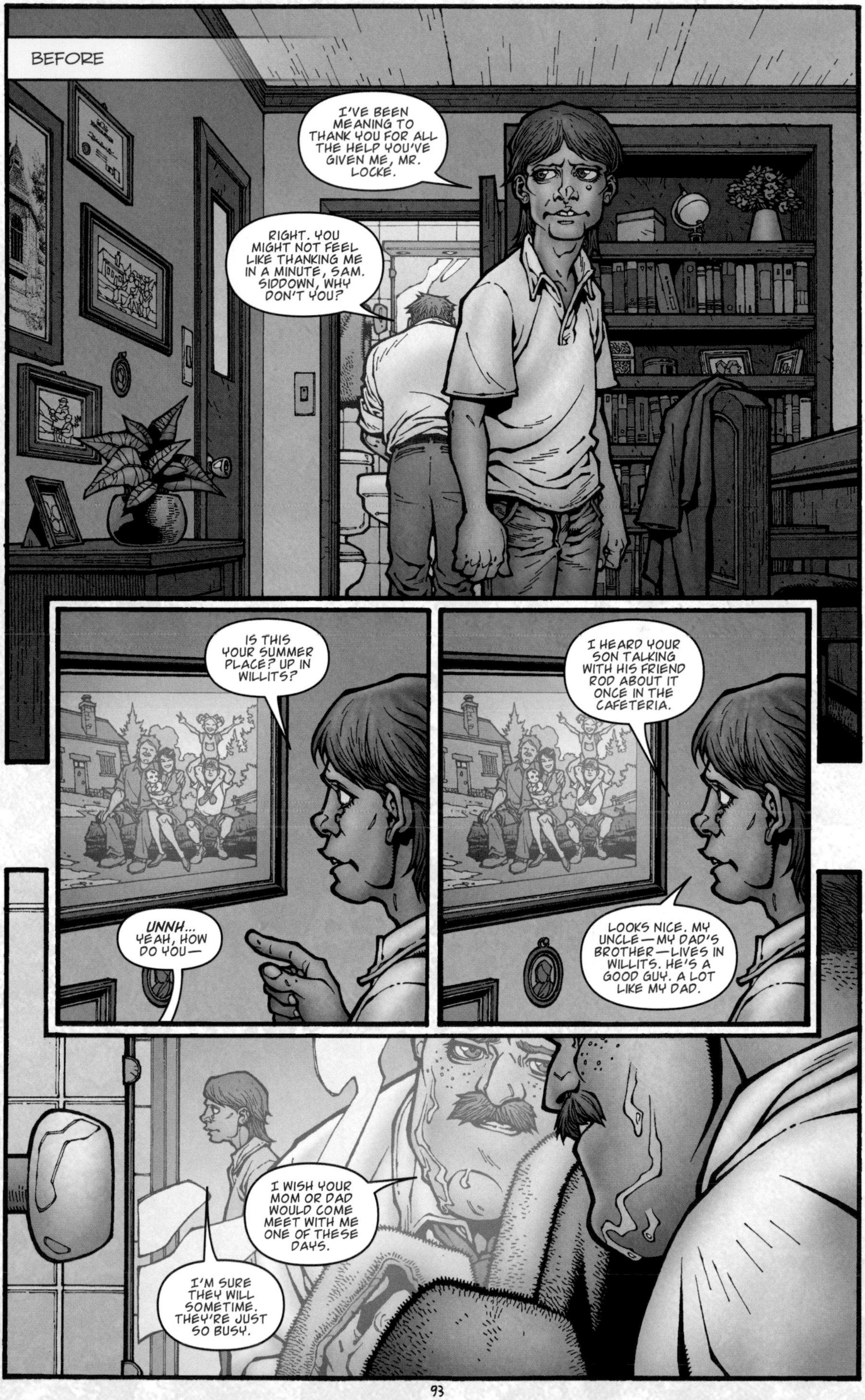
BEFORE
I'VE BEEN MEANING TO THANK YOU FOR ALL THE HELP YOU'VE GIVEN ME, MR. LOCKE.
RIGHT. YOU MIGHT NOT FEEL LIKE THANKING ME IN A MINUTE, SAM. SIDDOWN, WHY DON'T YOU?
IS THIS YOUR SUMMER PLACE? UP IN WILLITS?
UNNH... YEAH, HOW DO YOU—
I HEARD YOUR SON TALKING WITH HIS FRIEND ROD ABOUT IT ONCE IN THE CAFETERIA.
LOOKS NICE. MY UNCLE—MY DAD'S BROTHER—LIVES IN WILLITS. HE'S A GOOD GUY. A LOT LIKE MY DAD.
I WISH YOUR MOM OR DAD WOULD COME MEET WITH ME ONE OF THESE DAYS.
I'M SURE THEY WILL SOMETIME. THEY'RE JUST SO BUSY.

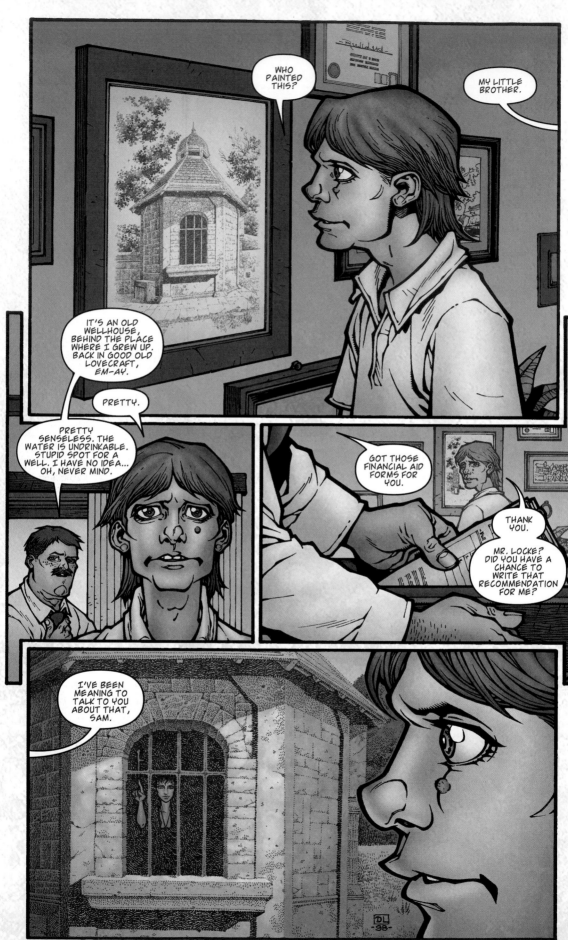

WHO PAINTED THIS?

MY LITTLE BROTHER.

IT'S AN OLD WELLHOUSE, BEHIND THE PLACE WHERE I GREW UP. BACK IN GOOD OLD LOVECRAFT, EM—AY.

PRETTY.

PRETTY SENSELESS. THE WATER IS UNDRINKABLE. STUPID SPOT FOR A WELL. I HAVE NO IDEA... OH, NEVER MIND.

GOT THOSE FINANCIAL AID FORMS FOR YOU.

THANK YOU.

MR. LOCKE? DID YOU HAVE A CHANCE TO WRITE THAT RECOMMENDATION FOR ME?

I'VE BEEN MEANING TO TALK TO YOU ABOUT THAT, SAM.

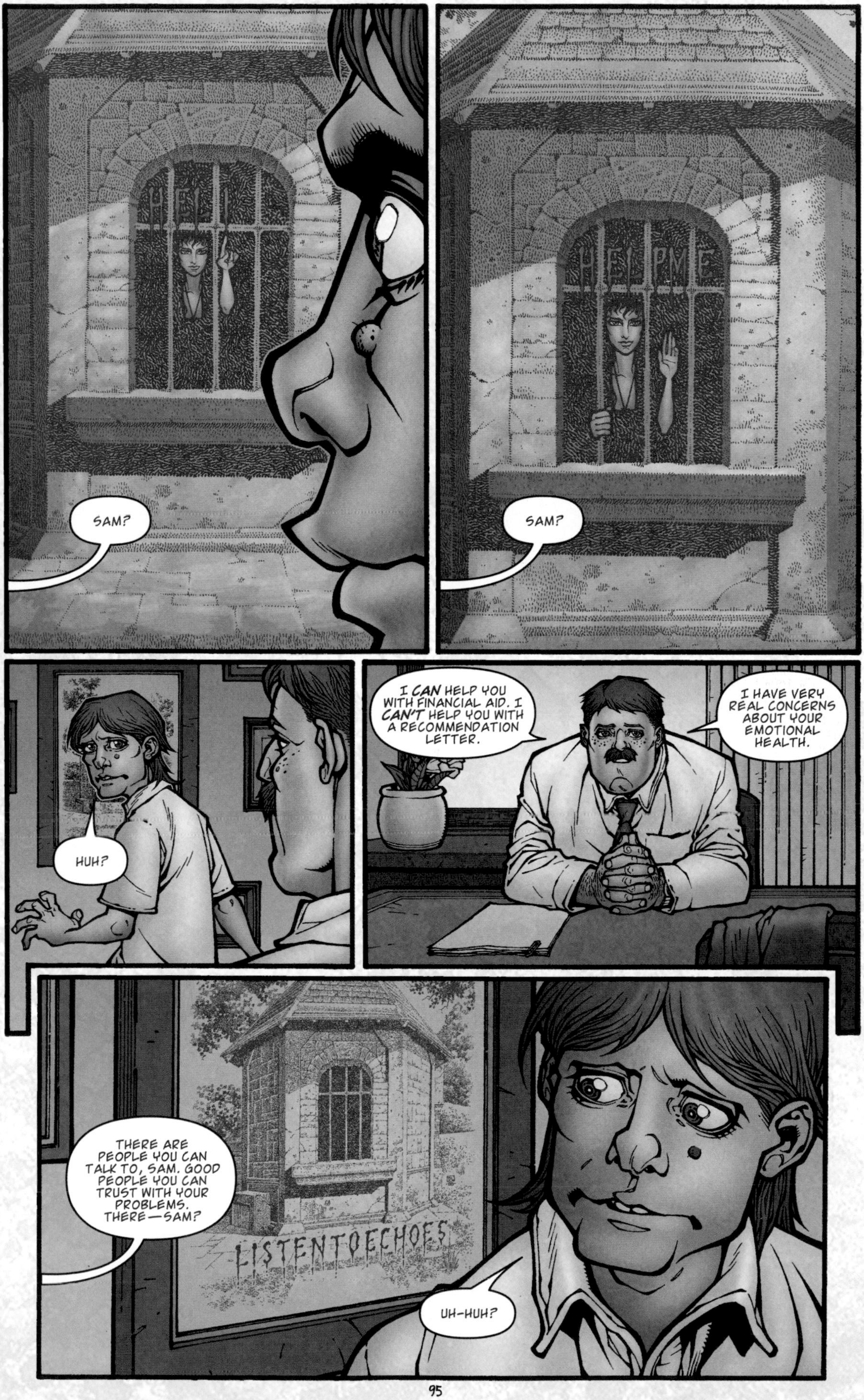
SAM?
HELPME
SAM?
HUH?
I CAN HELP YOU WITH FINANCIAL AID. I CAN'T HELP YOU WITH A RECOMMENDATION LETTER.
I HAVE VERY REAL CONCERNS ABOUT YOUR EMOTIONAL HEALTH.
THERE ARE PEOPLE YOU CAN TALK TO, SAM. GOOD PEOPLE YOU CAN TRUST WITH YOUR PROBLEMS. THERE—SAM?
LISTENTOECHOES
UH-HUH?

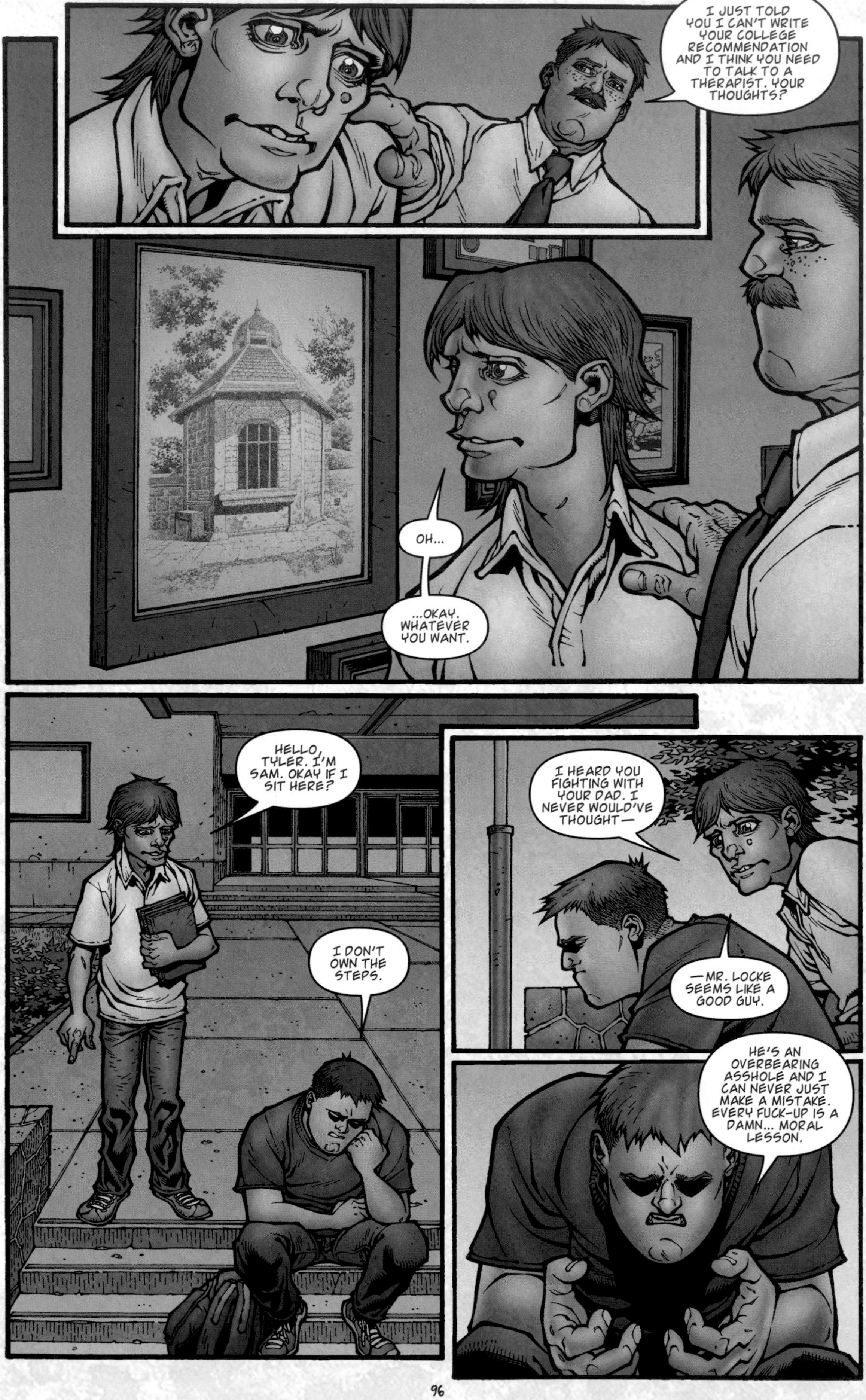
I JUST TOLD YOU I CAN'T WRITE YOUR COLLEGE RECOMMENDATION AND I THINK YOU NEED TO TALK TO A THERAPIST. YOUR THOUGHTS?
OH...
...OKAY. WHATEVER YOU WANT.
HELLO, TYLER. I'M SAM. OKAY IF I SIT HERE?
I DON'T OWN THE STEPS.
I HEARD YOU FIGHTING WITH YOUR DAD. I NEVER WOULD'VE THOUGHT—
—MR. LOCKE SEEMS LIKE A GOOD GUY.
HE'S AN OVERBEARING ASSHOLE AND I CAN NEVER JUST MAKE A MISTAKE. EVERY FUCK-UP IS A DAMN... MORAL LESSON.

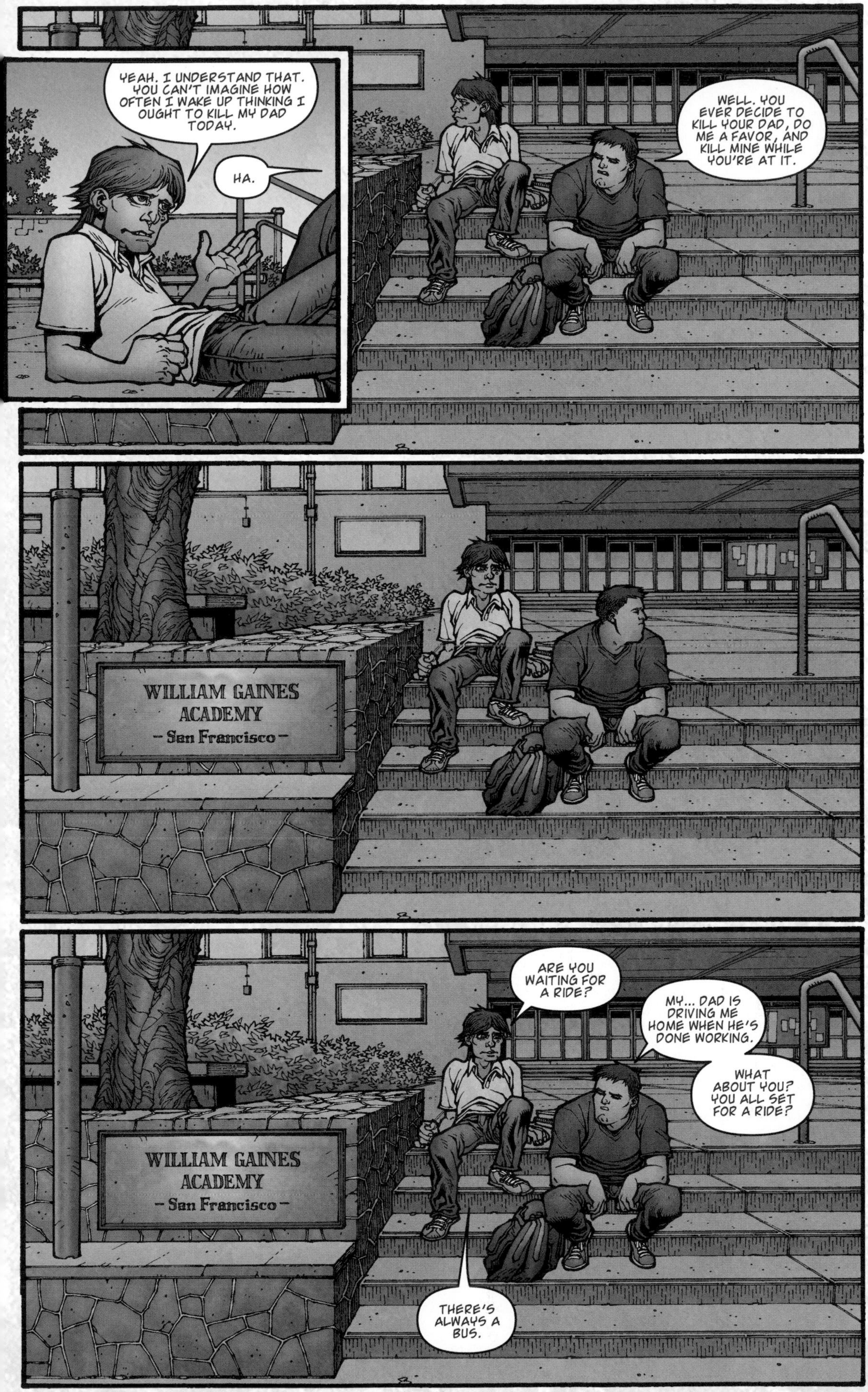
YEAH. I UNDERSTAND THAT. YOU CAN'T IMAGINE HOW OFTEN I WAKE UP THINKING I OUGHT TO KILL MY DAD TODAY.
HA.
WELL. YOU EVER DECIDE TO KILL YOUR DAD, DO ME A FAVOR, AND KILL MINE WHILE YOU'RE AT IT.
WILLIAM GAINES ACADEMY
– San Francisco –
WILLIAM GAINES ACADEMY
– San Francisco –
ARE YOU WAITING FOR A RIDE?
MY... DAD IS DRIVING ME HOME WHEN HE'S DONE WORKING.
WHAT ABOUT YOU? YOU ALL SET FOR A RIDE?
THERE'S ALWAYS A BUS.

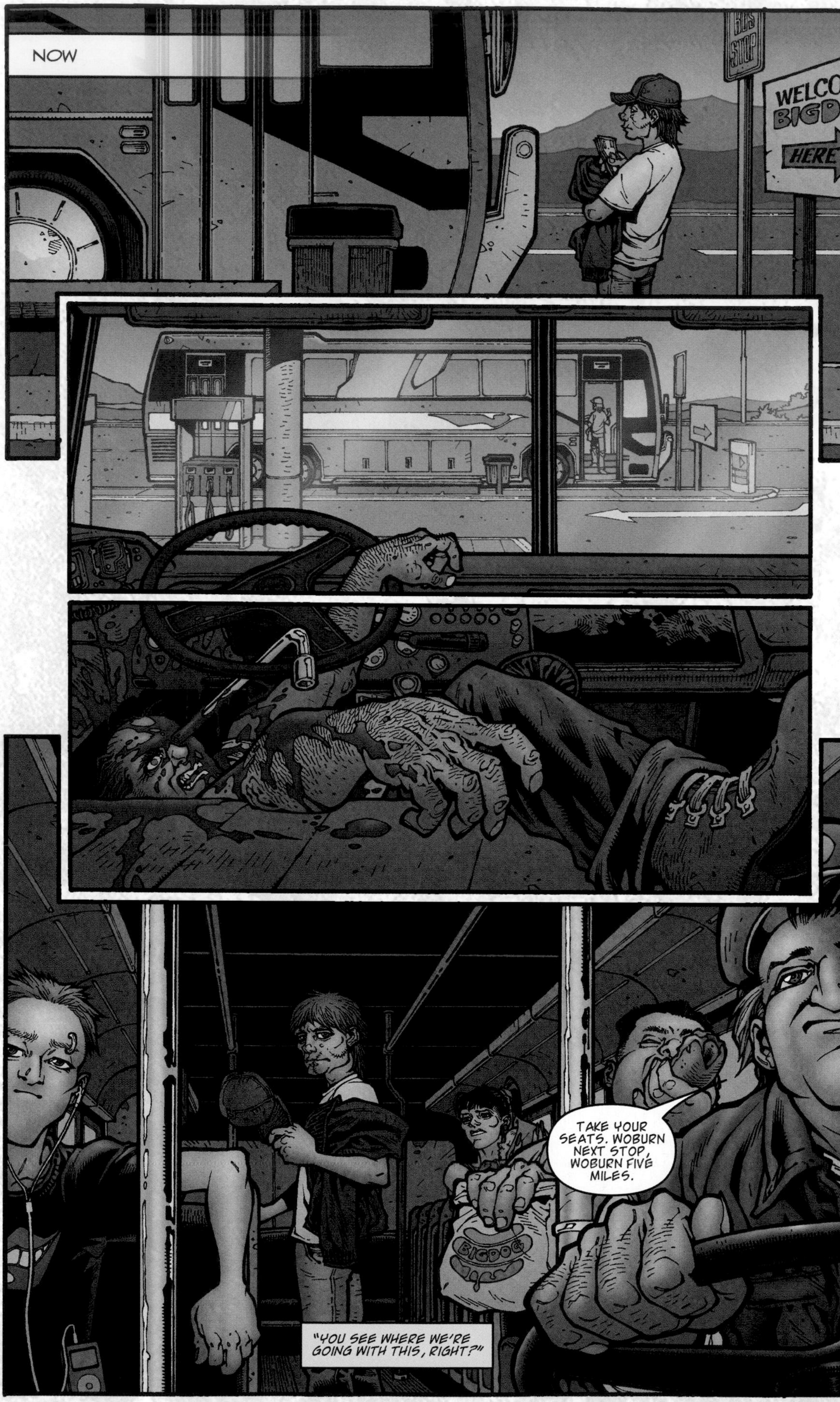
NOW
WELCOME
BIGDOG
HERE
TAKE YOUR SEATS. WOBURN NEXT STOP, WOBURN FIVE MILES.
BIGDOG
"YOU SEE WHERE WE'RE GOING WITH THIS, RIGHT?"

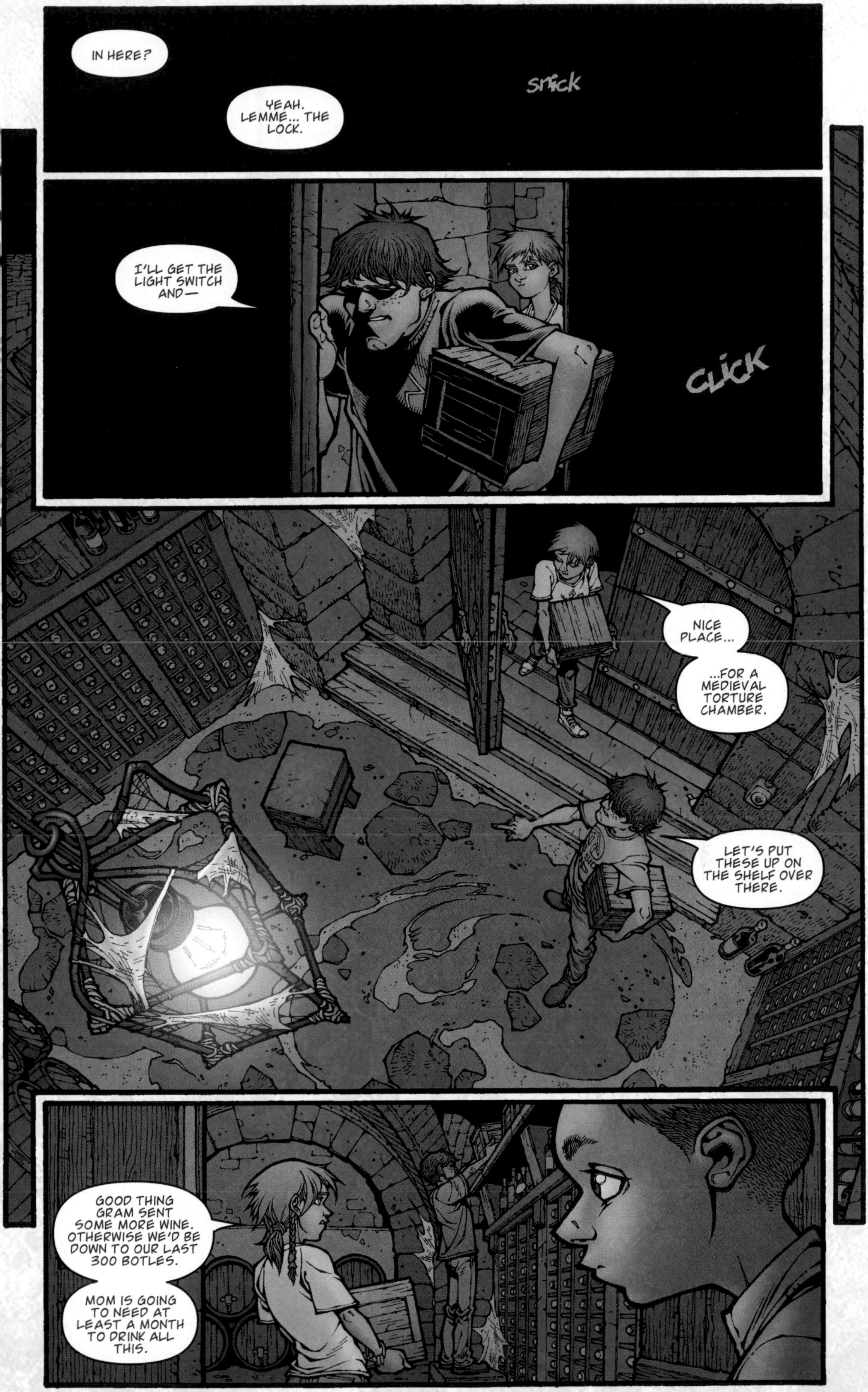

IN HERE?
YEAH. LEMME... THE LOCK.
snick
I'LL GET THE LIGHT SWITCH AND—
CLICK
NICE PLACE...
...FOR A MEDIEVAL TORTURE CHAMBER.
LET'S PUT THESE UP ON THE SHELF OVER THERE.
GOOD THING GRAM SENT SOME MORE WINE. OTHERWISE WE'D BE DOWN TO OUR LAST 300 BOTLES.
MOM IS GOING TO NEED AT LEAST A MONTH TO DRINK ALL THIS.

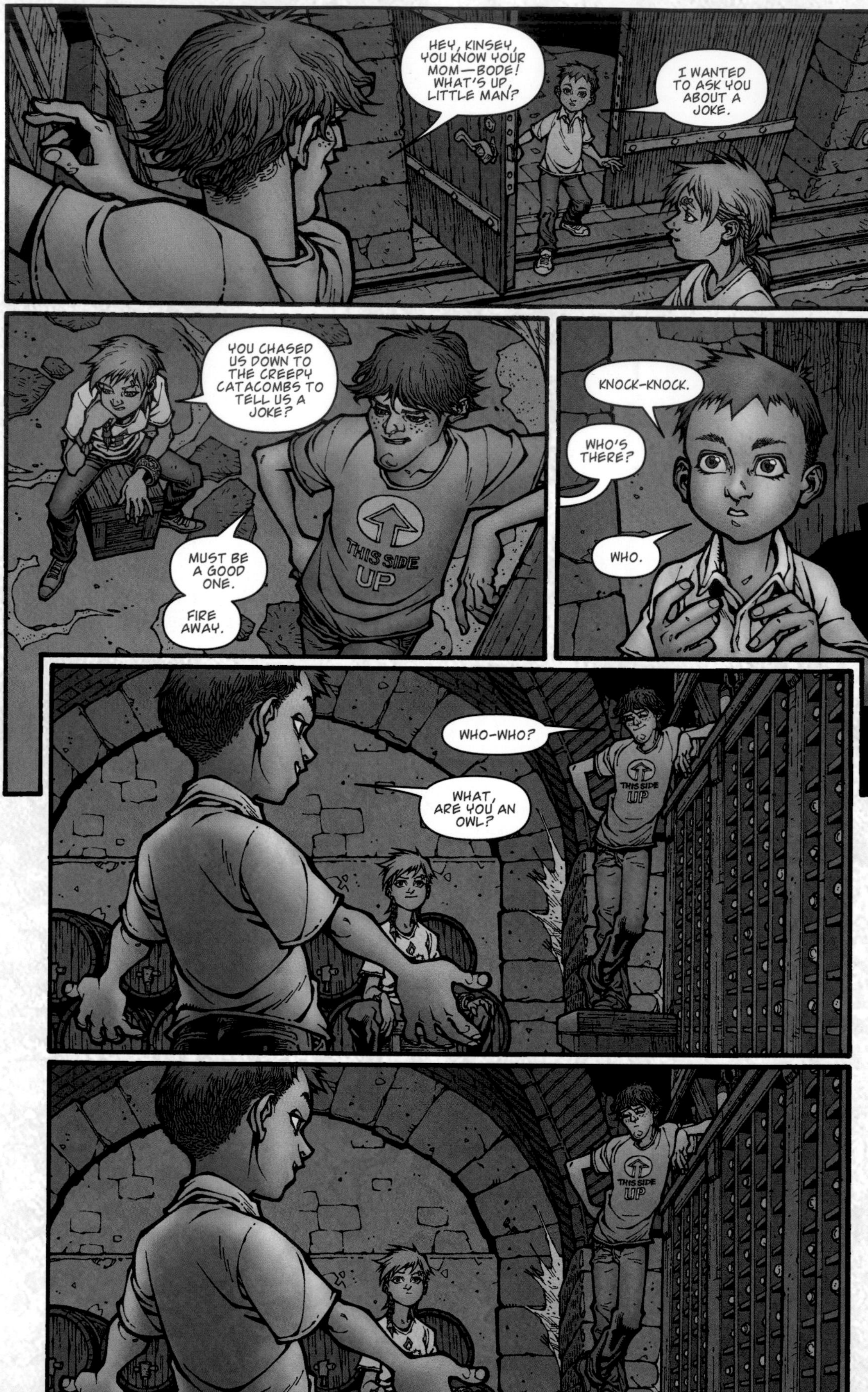
HEY, KINSEY, YOU KNOW YOUR MOM—BODE! WHAT'S UP, LITTLE MAN?
I WANTED TO ASK YOU ABOUT A JOKE.
YOU CHASED US DOWN TO THE CREEPY CATACOMBS TO TELL US A JOKE?
MUST BE A GOOD ONE.
FIRE AWAY.
THIS SIDE UP
KNOCK-KNOCK.
WHO'S THERE?
WHO.
WHO-WHO?
WHAT, ARE YOU AN OWL?
THIS SIDE UP
THIS SIDE UP

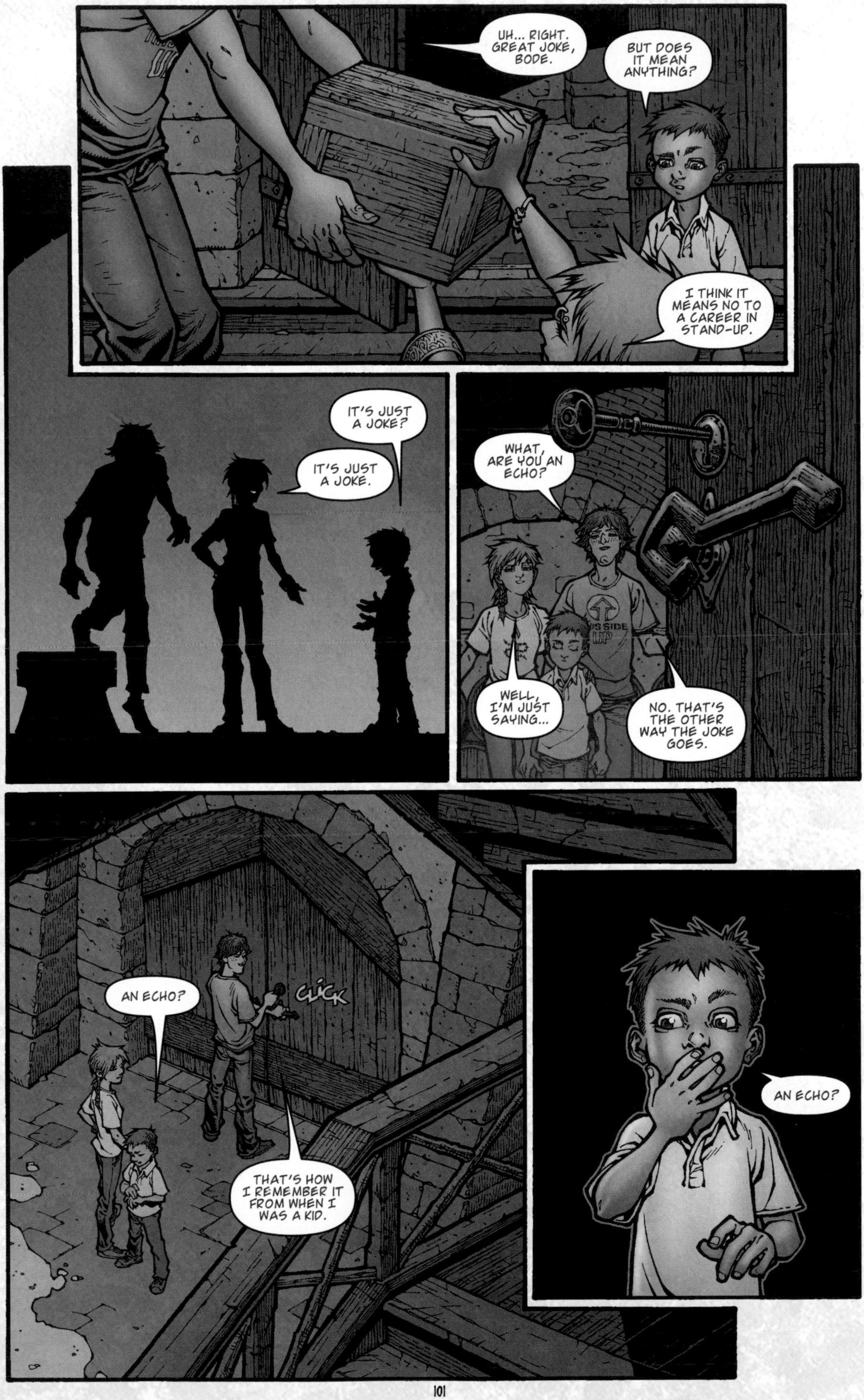
UH... RIGHT. GREAT JOKE, BODE.
BUT DOES IT MEAN ANYTHING?
I THINK IT MEANS NO TO A CAREER IN STAND-UP.
IT'S JUST A JOKE?
IT'S JUST A JOKE.
WHAT, ARE YOU AN ECHO?
WELL, I'M JUST SAYING...
NO. THAT'S THE OTHER WAY THE JOKE GOES.
AN ECHO?
CLICK
THAT'S HOW I REMEMBER IT FROM WHEN I WAS A KID.
AN ECHO?

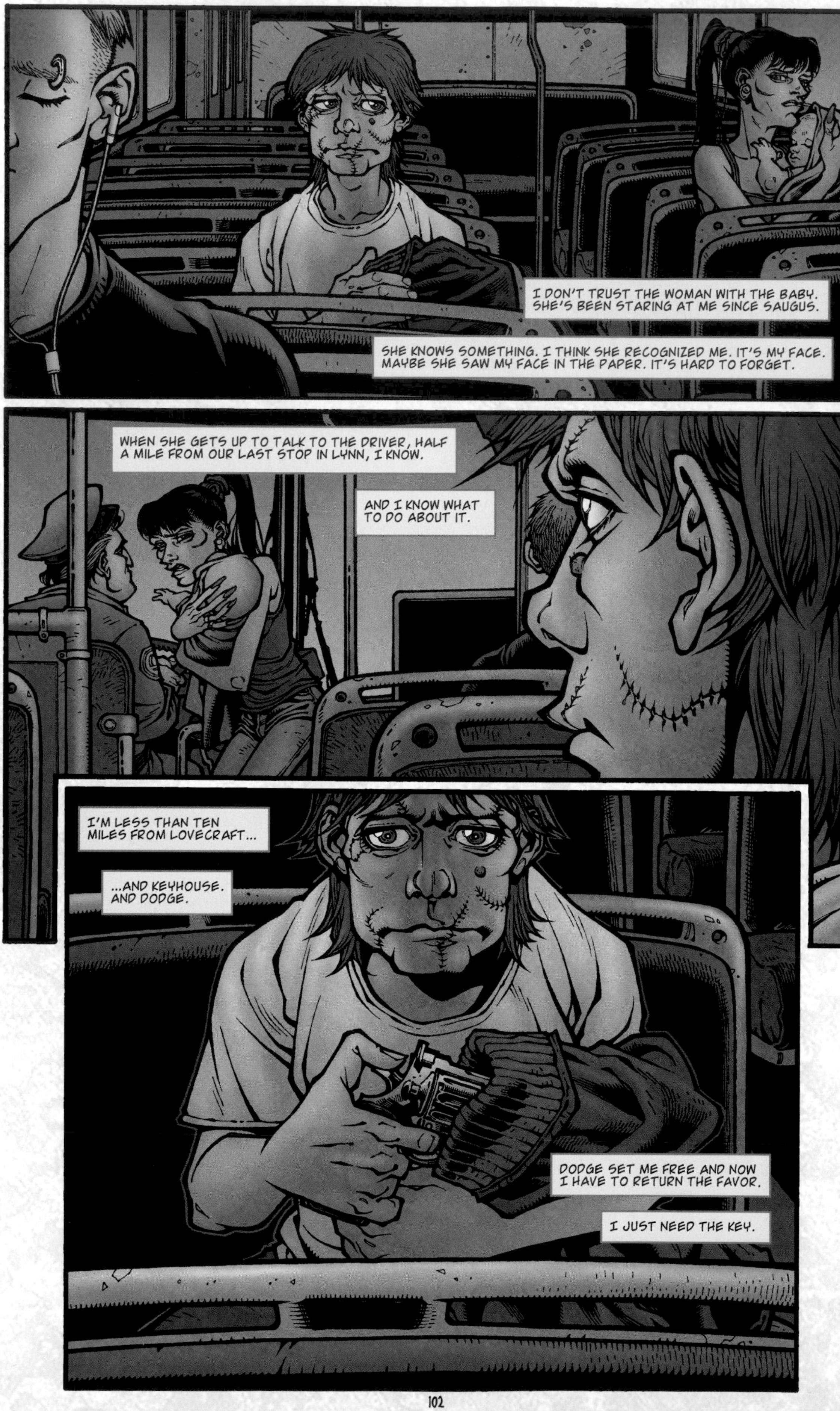
I DON'T TRUST THE WOMAN WITH THE BABY. SHE'S BEEN STARING AT ME SINCE SAUGUS.
SHE KNOWS SOMETHING. I THINK SHE RECOGNIZED ME. IT'S MY FACE. MAYBE SHE SAW MY FACE IN THE PAPER. IT'S HARD TO FORGET.
WHEN SHE GETS UP TO TALK TO THE DRIVER, HALF A MILE FROM OUR LAST STOP IN LYNN, I KNOW.
AND I KNOW WHAT TO DO ABOUT IT.
I'M LESS THAN TEN MILES FROM LOVECRAFT...
...AND KEYHOUSE. AND DODGE.
DODGE SET ME FREE AND NOW I HAVE TO RETURN THE FAVOR.
I JUST NEED THE KEY.

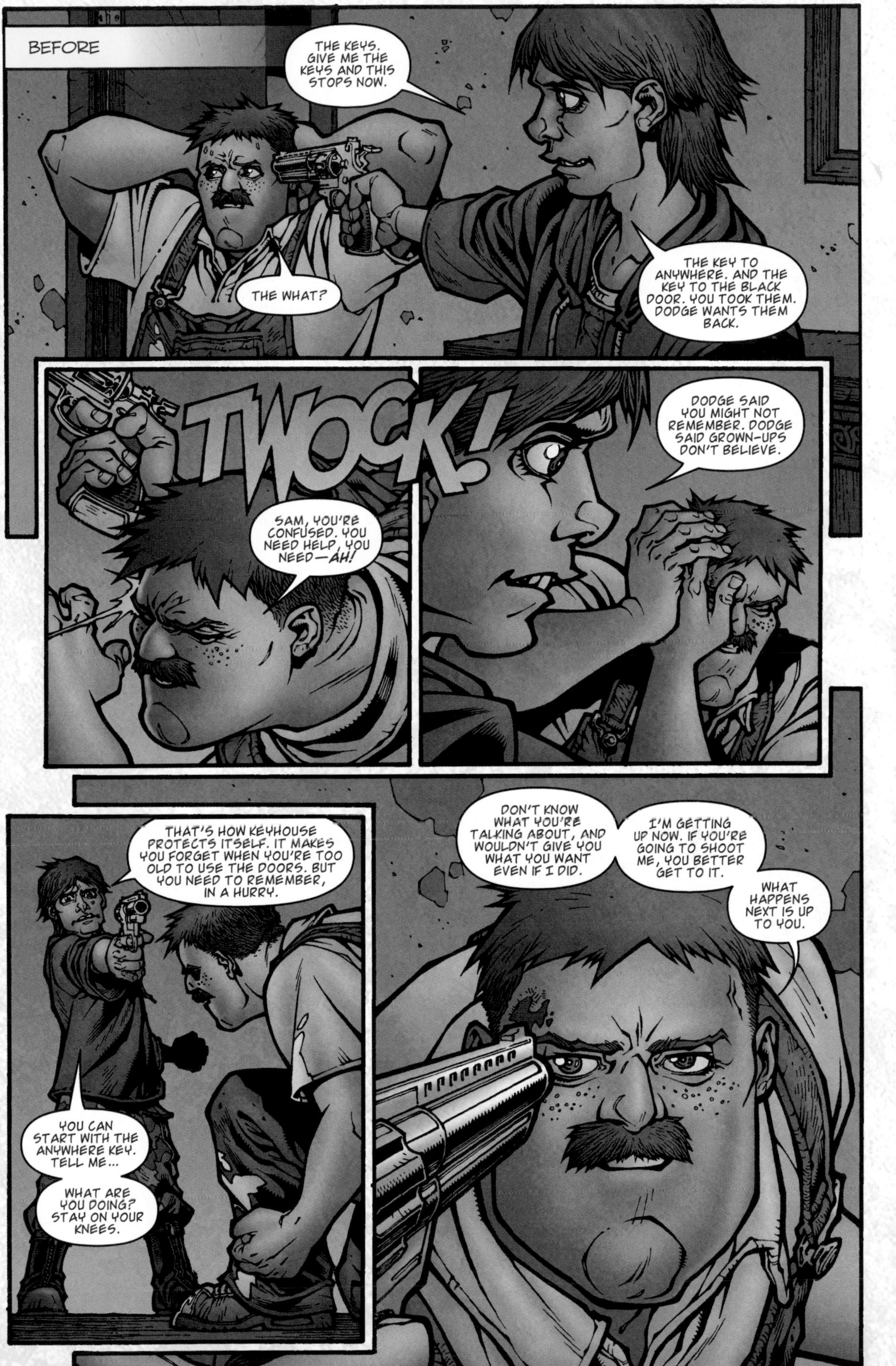
BEFORE
THE KEYS. GIVE ME THE KEYS AND THIS STOPS NOW.
THE WHAT?
THE KEY TO ANYWHERE. AND THE KEY TO THE BLACK DOOR. YOU TOOK THEM. DODGE WANTS THEM BACK.
TWOCK!
SAM, YOU'RE CONFUSED. YOU NEED HELP, YOU NEED—AH!
DODGE SAID YOU MIGHT NOT REMEMBER. DODGE SAID GROWN-UPS DON'T BELIEVE.
THAT'S HOW KEYHOUSE PROTECTS ITSELF. IT MAKES YOU FORGET WHEN YOU'RE TOO OLD TO USE THE DOORS. BUT YOU NEED TO REMEMBER, IN A HURRY.
YOU CAN START WITH THE ANYWHERE KEY. TELL ME...
WHAT ARE YOU DOING? STAY ON YOUR KNEES.
DON'T KNOW WHAT YOU'RE TALKING ABOUT, AND WOULDN'T GIVE YOU WHAT YOU WANT EVEN IF I DID.
I'M GETTING UP NOW. IF YOU'RE GOING TO SHOOT ME, YOU BETTER GET TO IT.
WHAT HAPPENS NEXT IS UP TO YOU.

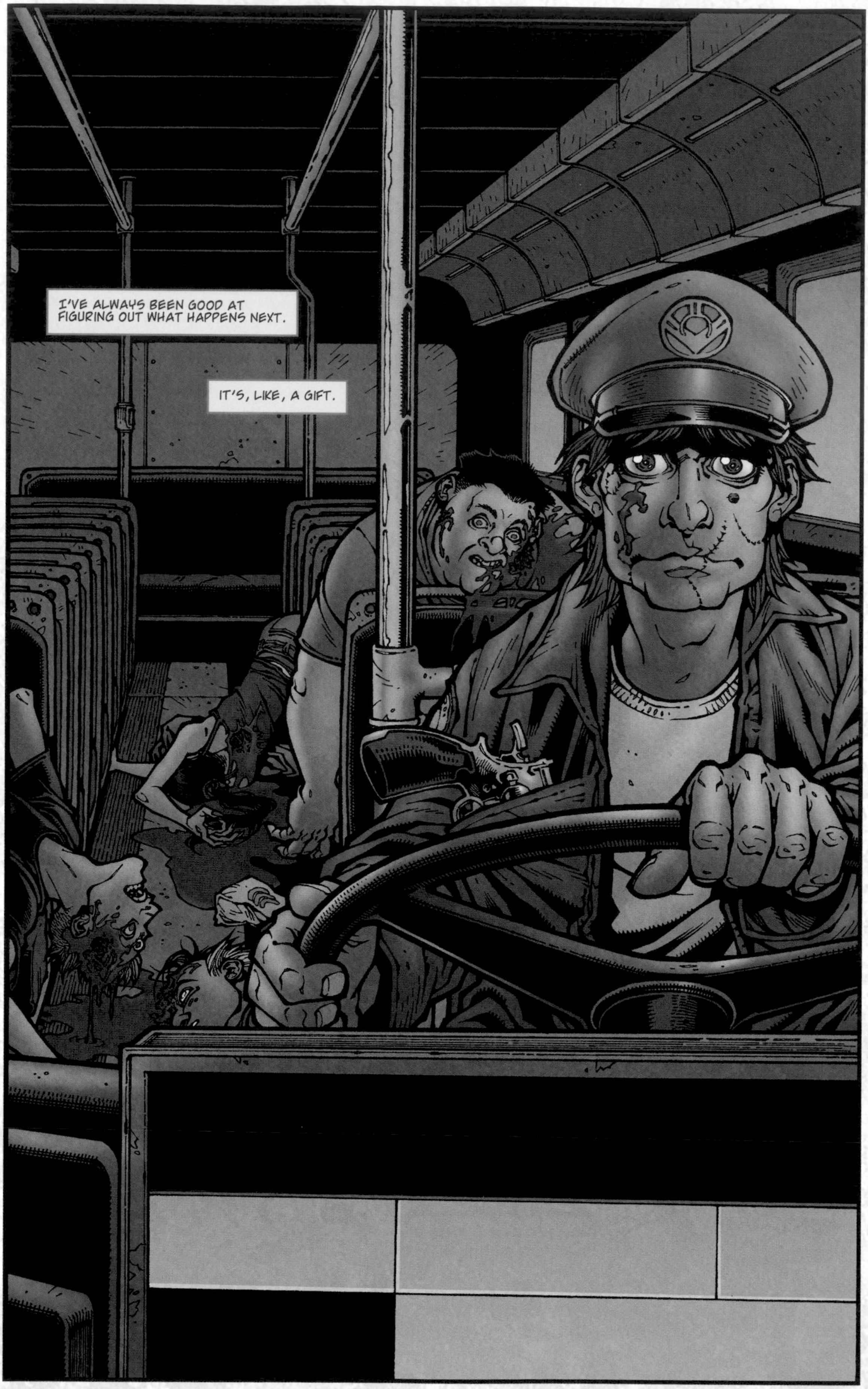
I'VE ALWAYS BEEN GOOD AT FIGURING OUT WHAT HAPPENS NEXT.
IT'S, LIKE, A GIFT.

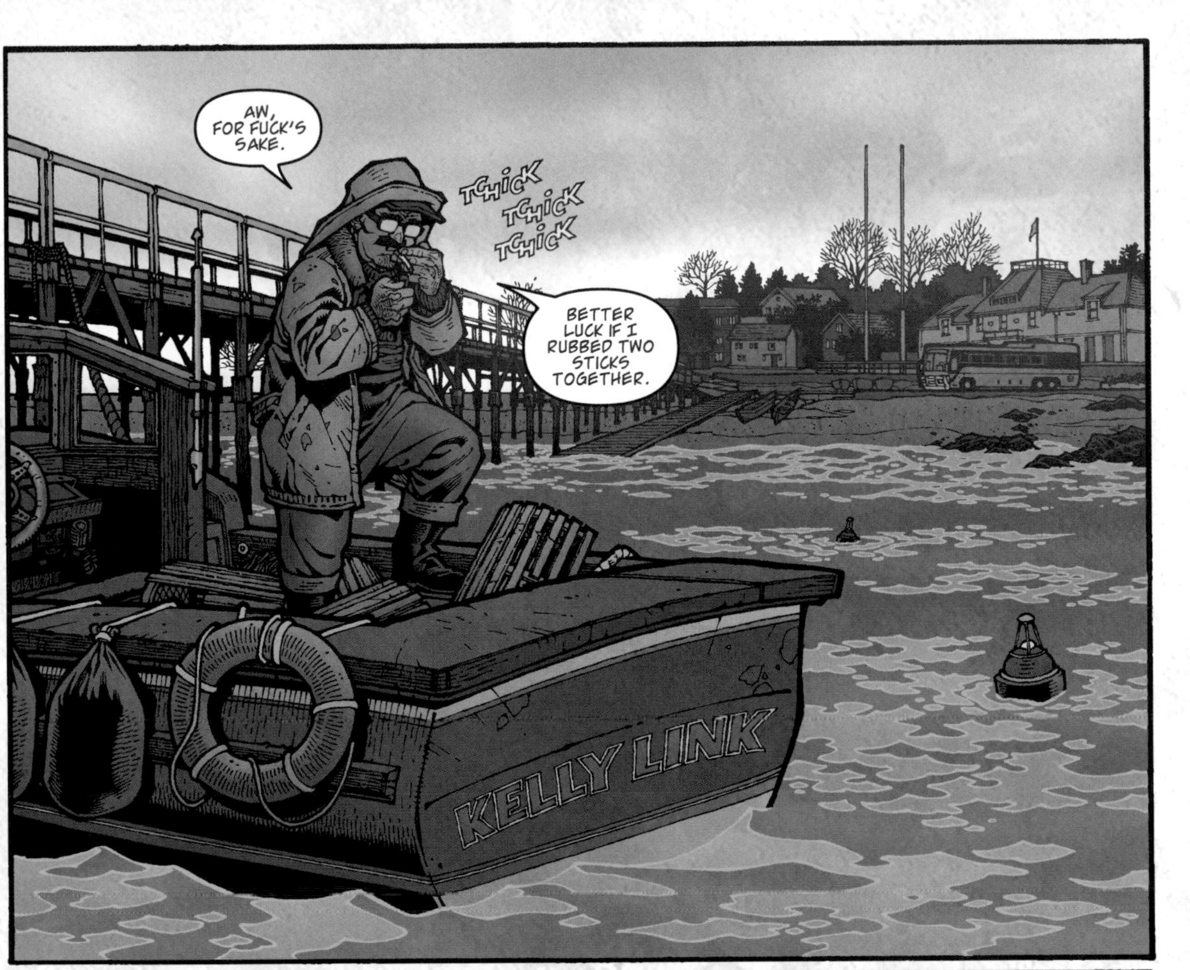
AW, FOR FUCK'S SAKE.
TCHICK TCHICK TCHICK
BETTER LUCK IF I RUBBED TWO STICKS TOGETHER.
KELLY LINK

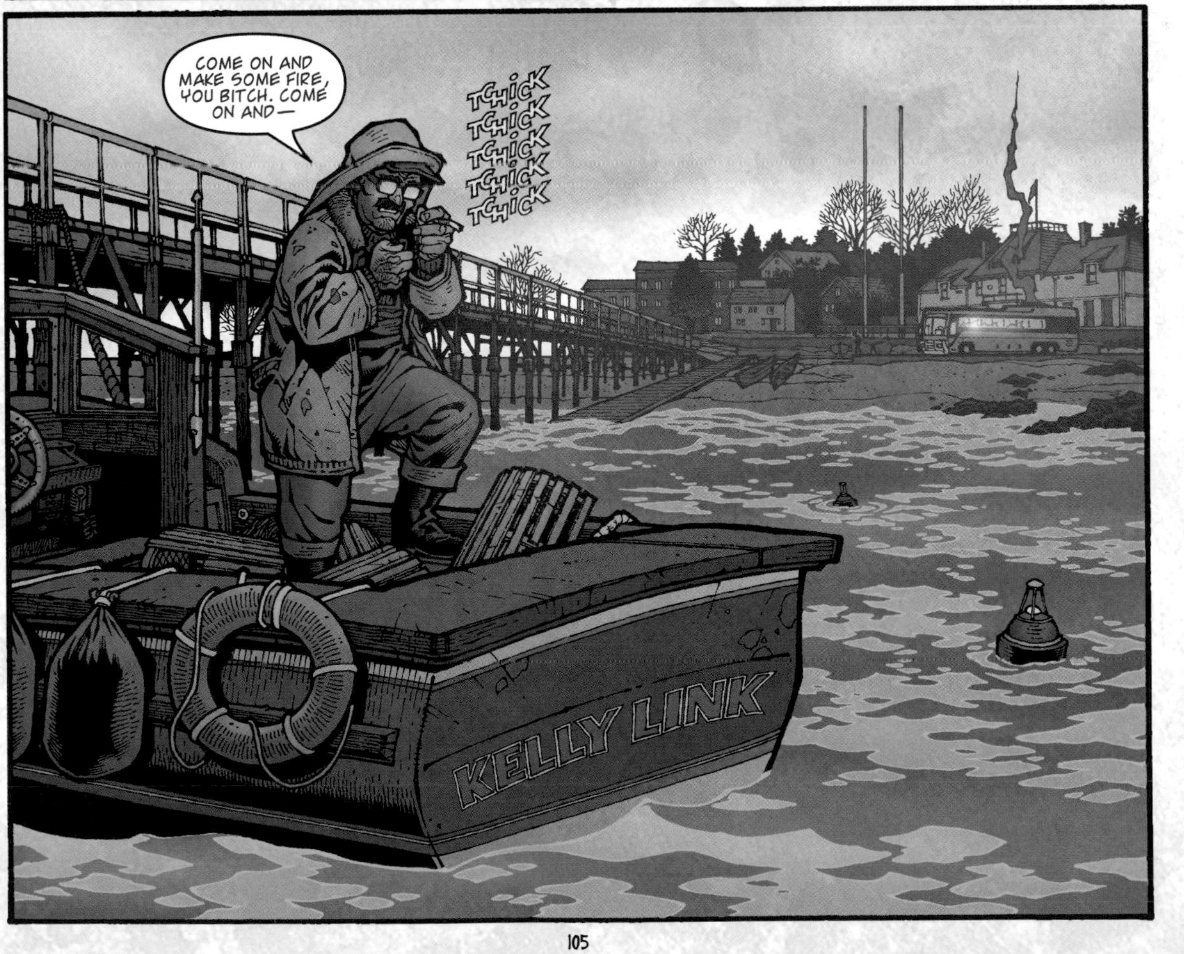
COME ON AND MAKE SOME FIRE, YOU BITCH. COME ON AND—
TCHICK TCHICK TCHICK TCHICK TCHICK
KELLY LINK

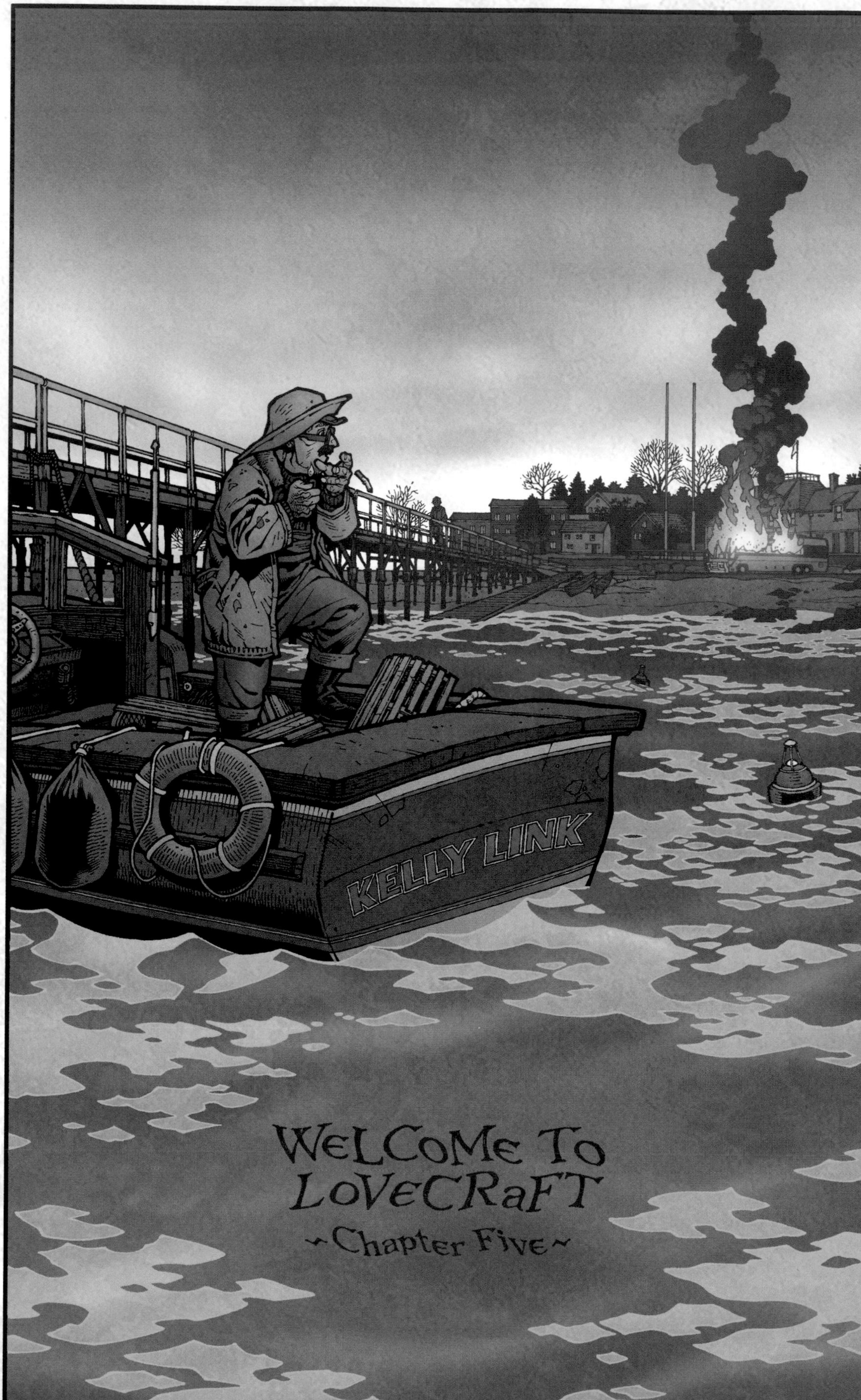
KELLY LINK
WELCOME TO LOVECRAFT
~Chapter Five~

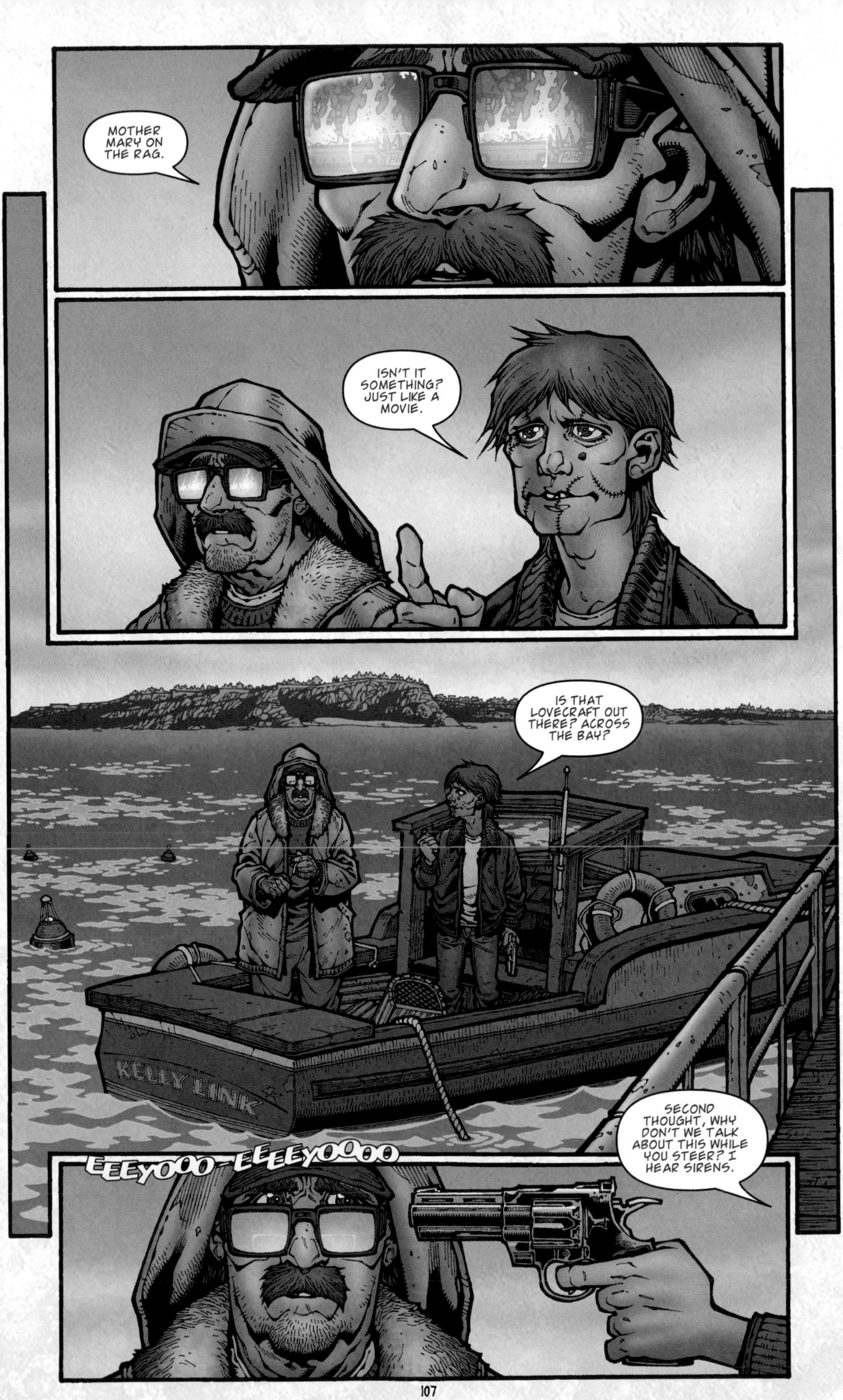
MOTHER MARY ON THE RAG.
ISN'T IT SOMETHING? JUST LIKE A MOVIE.
IS THAT LOVECRAFT OUT THERE? ACROSS THE BAY?
KELLY LINK
SECOND THOUGHT, WHY DON'T WE TALK ABOUT THIS WHILE YOU STEER? I HEAR SIRENS.
EEEYOOO-EEEEYOOOO

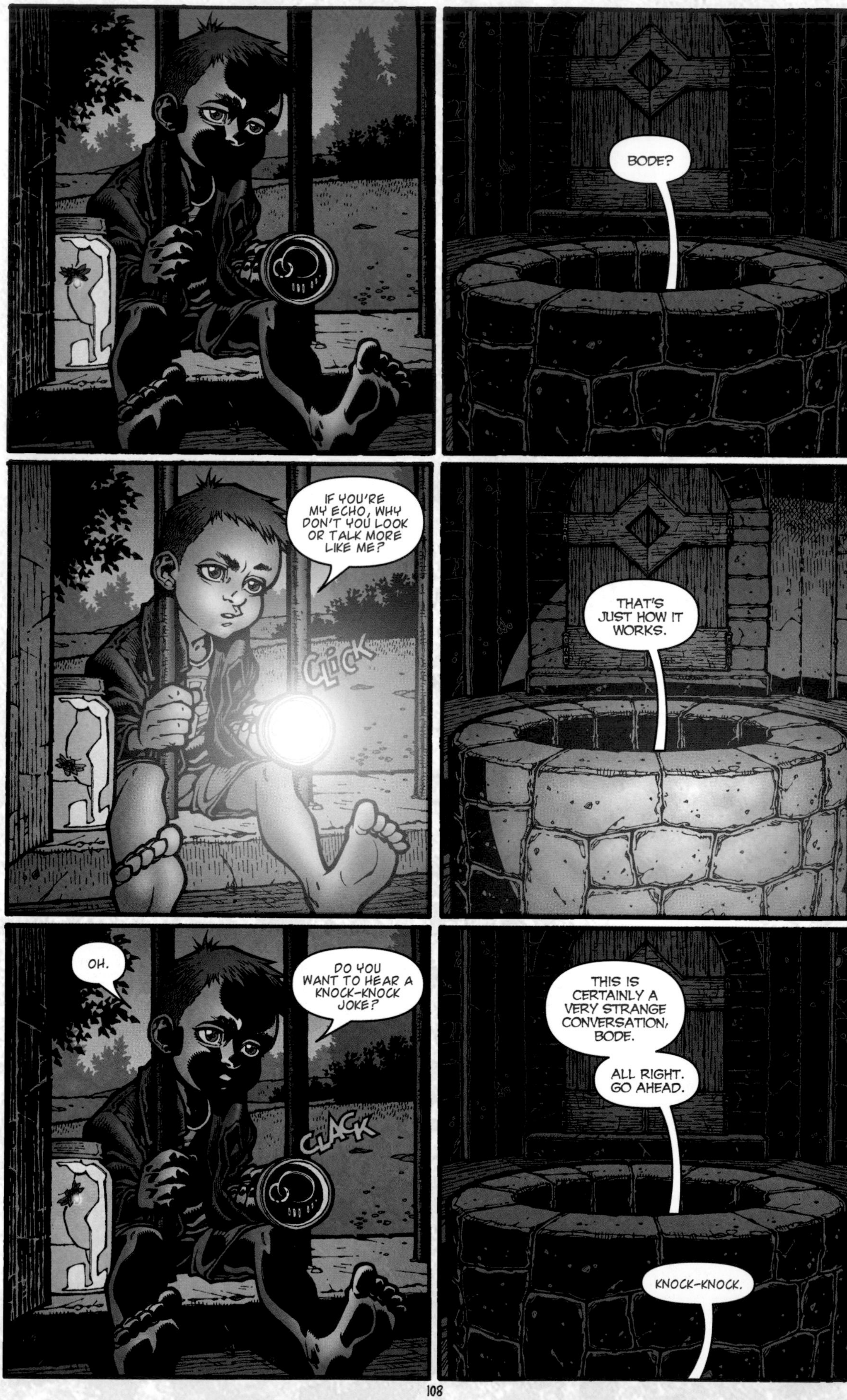

BODE?
IF YOU'RE MY ECHO, WHY DON'T YOU LOOK OR TALK MORE LIKE ME?
CLICK
THAT'S JUST HOW IT WORKS.
OH.
DO YOU WANT TO HEAR A KNOCK-KNOCK JOKE?
CLACK
THIS IS CERTAINLY A VERY STRANGE CONVERSATION, BODE.
ALL RIGHT. GO AHEAD.
KNOCK-KNOCK.

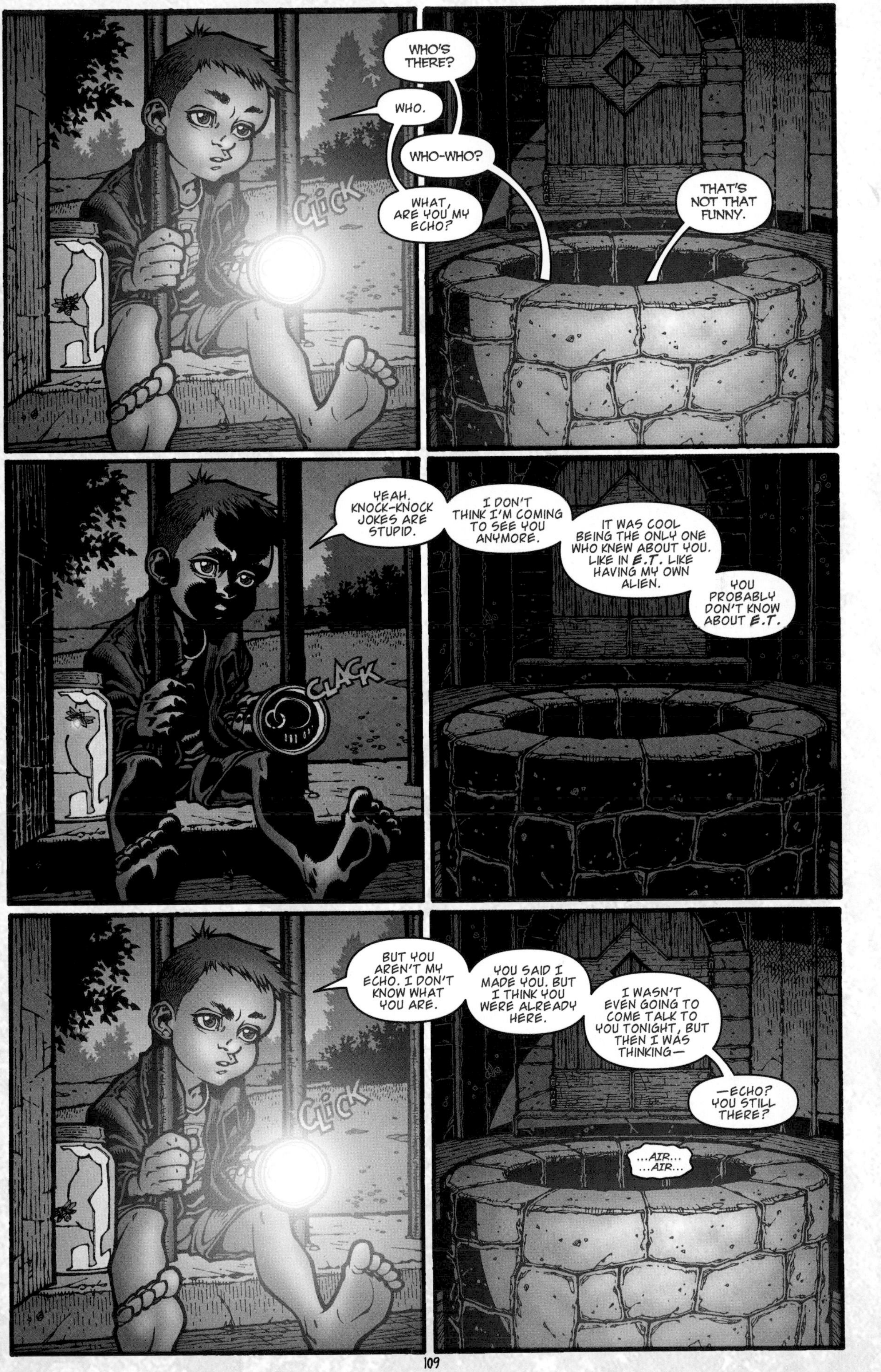
WHO'S THERE?
WHO.
WHO-WHO?
WHAT, ARE YOU MY ECHO?
CLICK
THAT'S NOT THAT FUNNY.
YEAH. KNOCK-KNOCK JOKES ARE STUPID.
I DON'T THINK I'M COMING TO SEE YOU ANYMORE.
CLACK
IT WAS COOL BEING THE ONLY ONE WHO KNEW ABOUT YOU. LIKE IN E.T. LIKE HAVING MY OWN ALIEN.
YOU PROBABLY DON'T KNOW ABOUT E.T.
BUT YOU AREN'T MY ECHO. I DON'T KNOW WHAT YOU ARE.
YOU SAID I MADE YOU. BUT I THINK YOU WERE ALREADY HERE.
CLICK
I WASN'T EVEN GOING TO COME TALK TO YOU TONIGHT, BUT THEN I WAS THINKING—
—ECHO? YOU STILL THERE?
...AIR... ...AIR...

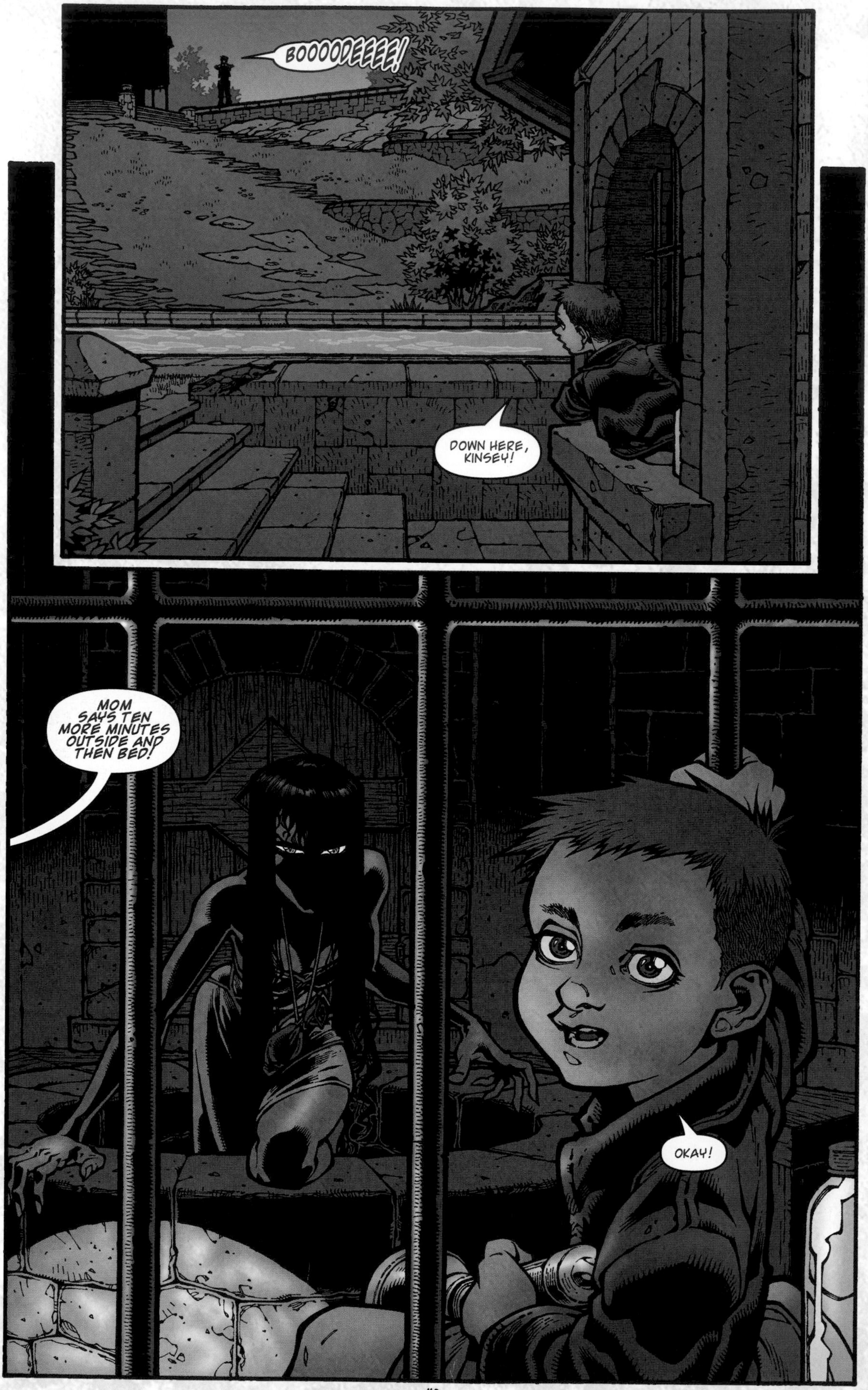
BOOOODEEEE!
DOWN HERE, KINSEY!
MOM SAYS TEN MORE MINUTES OUTSIDE AND THEN BED!
OKAY!

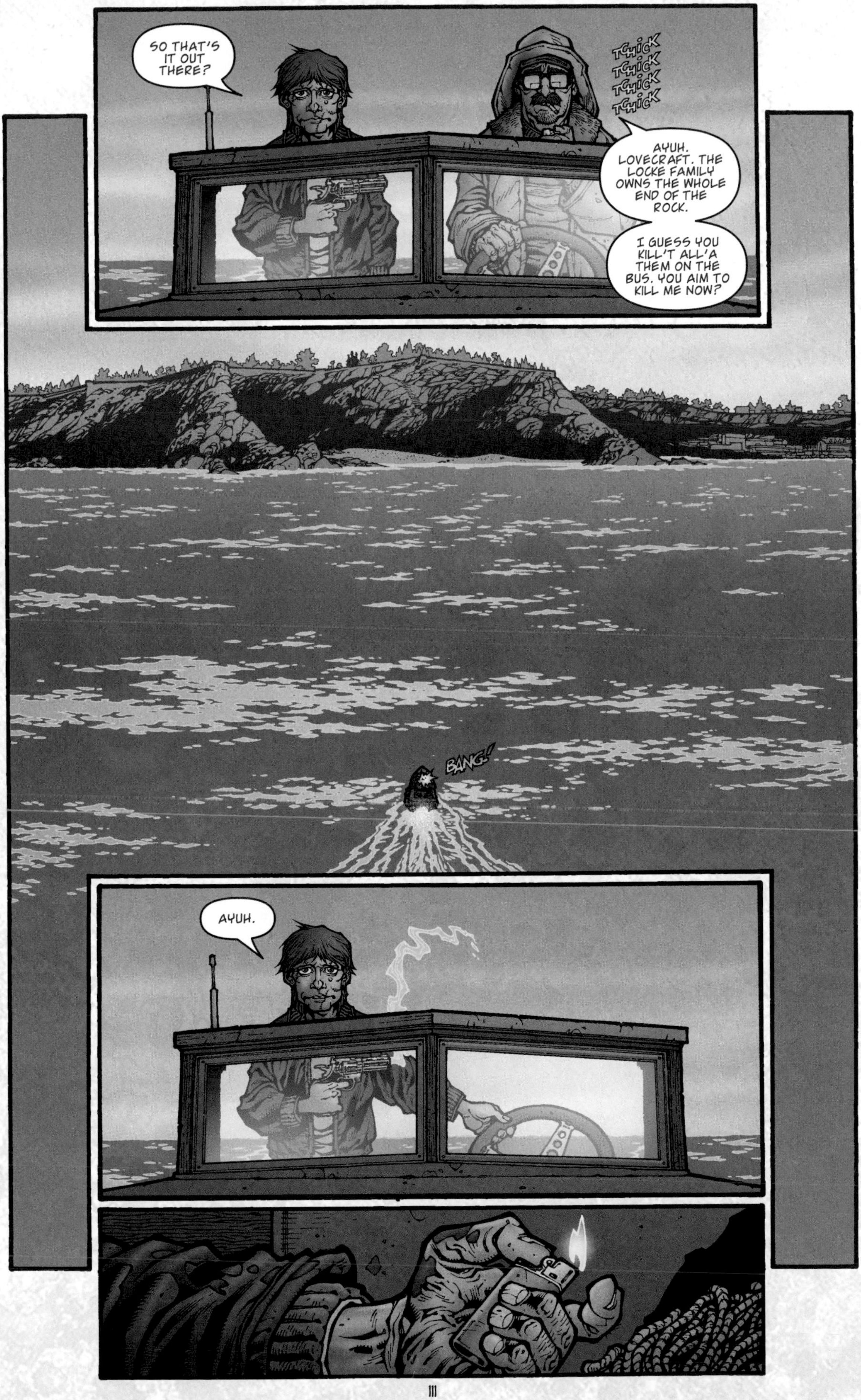
SO THAT'S IT OUT THERE?
TCHICK TCHICK TCHICK TCHICK
AYUH. LOVECRAFT. THE LOCKE FAMILY OWNS THE WHOLE END OF THE ROCK.
I GUESS YOU KILL'T ALL'A THEM ON THE BUS. YOU AIM TO KILL ME NOW?
BANG!
AYUH.

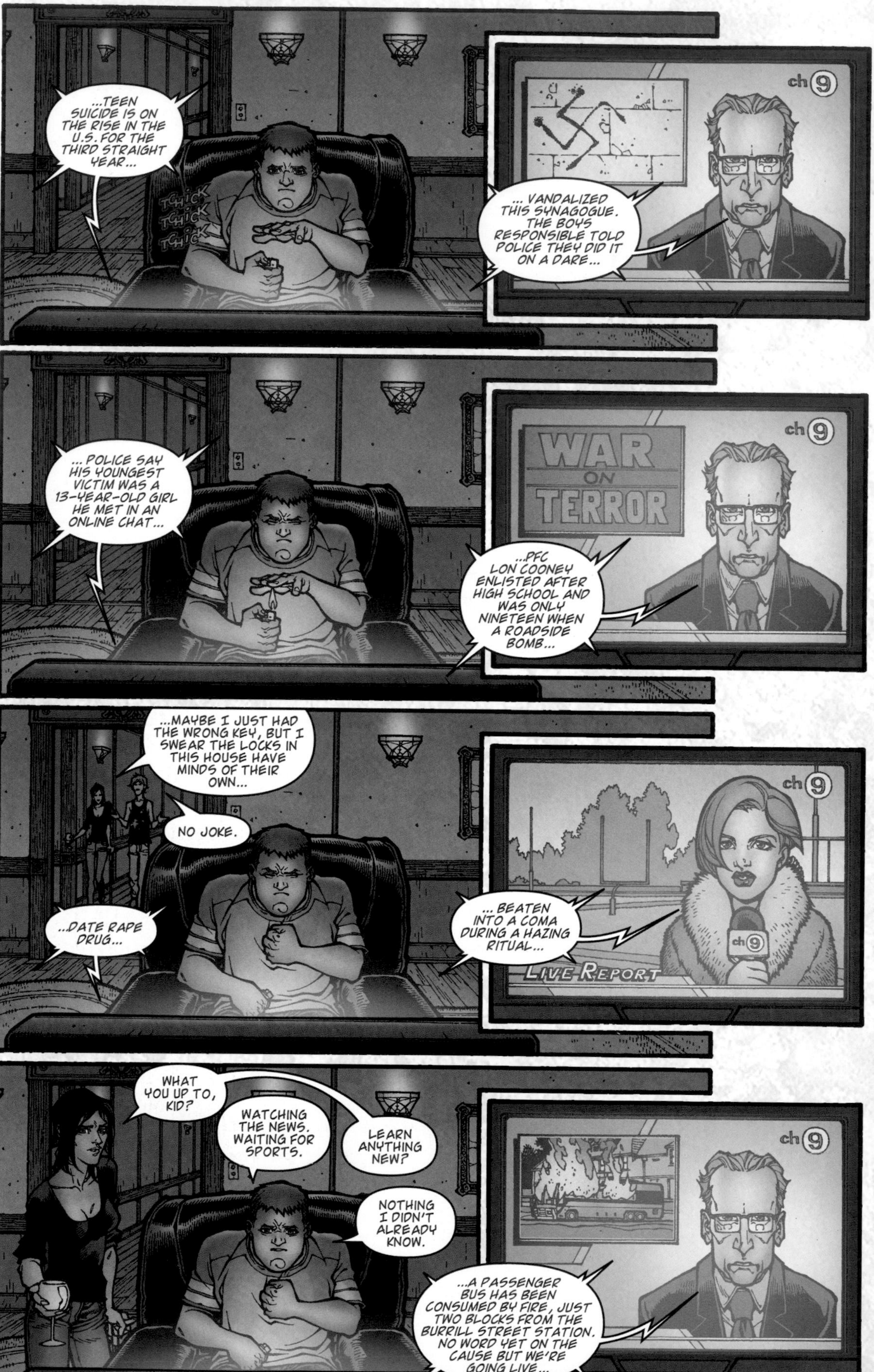
...TEEN SUICIDE IS ON THE RISE IN THE U.S. FOR THE THIRD STRAIGHT YEAR...
TCHICK TCHICK TCHICK
ch 9
... VANDALIZED THIS SYNAGOGUE. THE BOYS RESPONSIBLE TOLD POLICE THEY DID IT ON A DARE...
... POLICE SAY HIS YOUNGEST VICTIM WAS A 13-YEAR-OLD GIRL HE MET IN AN ONLINE CHAT...
WAR ON TERROR
ch 9
...PFC LON COONEY ENLISTED AFTER HIGH SCHOOL AND WAS ONLY NINETEEN WHEN A ROADSIDE BOMB...
...MAYBE I JUST HAD THE WRONG KEY, BUT I SWEAR THE LOCKS IN THIS HOUSE HAVE MINDS OF THEIR OWN...
NO JOKE.
...DATE RAPE DRUG...
ch 9
... BEATEN INTO A COMA DURING A HAZING RITUAL...
LIVE REPORT
WHAT YOU UP TO, KID?
WATCHING THE NEWS. WAITING FOR SPORTS.
LEARN ANYTHING NEW?
NOTHING I DIDN'T ALREADY KNOW.
ch 9
...A PASSENGER BUS HAS BEEN CONSUMED BY FIRE, JUST TWO BLOCKS FROM THE BURRILL STREET STATION. NO WORD YET ON THE CAUSE BUT WE'RE GOING LIVE...

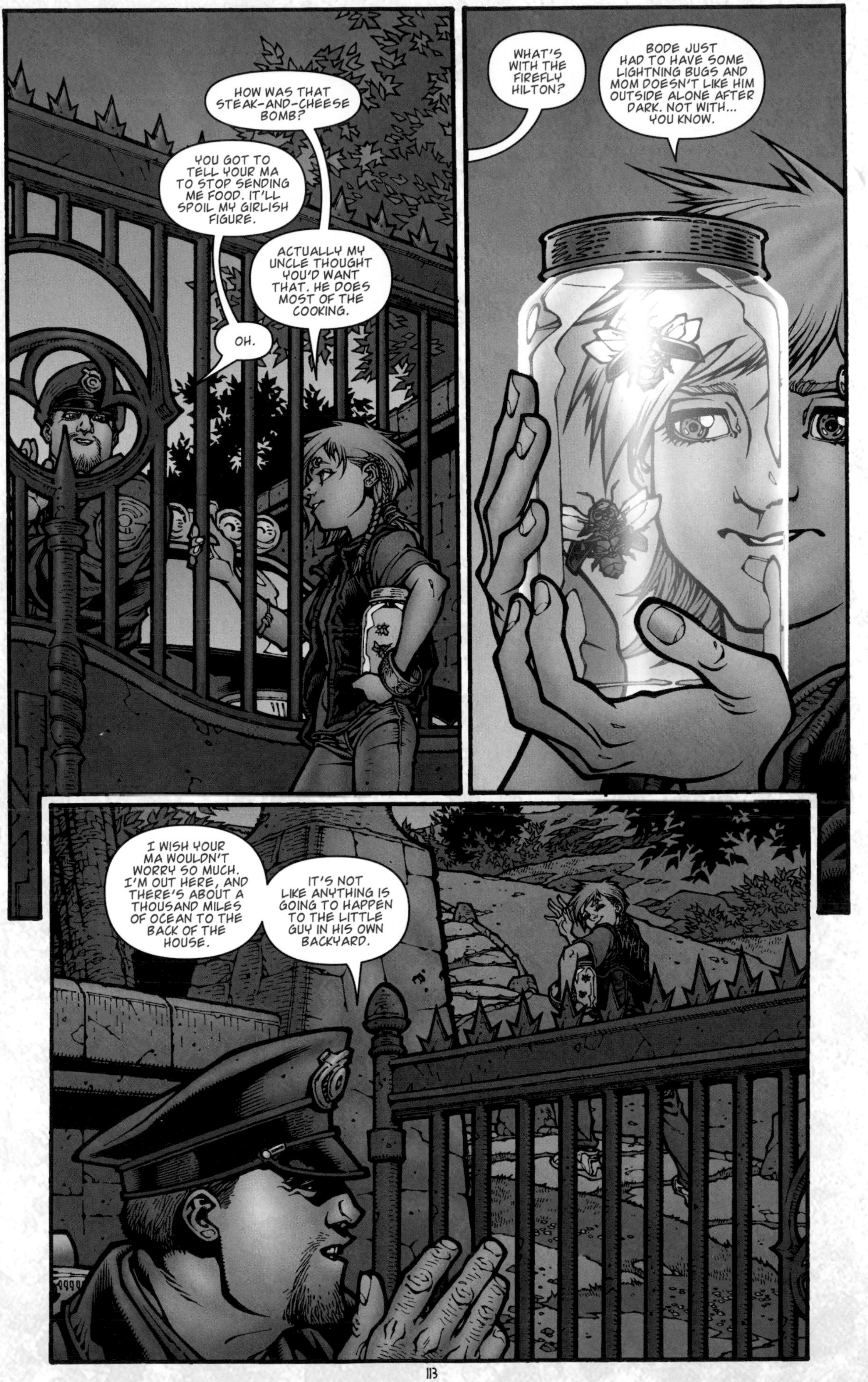
HOW WAS THAT STEAK-AND-CHEESE BOMB?
YOU GOT TO TELL YOUR MA TO STOP SENDING ME FOOD. IT'LL SPOIL MY GIRLISH FIGURE.
ACTUALLY MY UNCLE THOUGHT YOU'D WANT THAT. HE DOES MOST OF THE COOKING.
OH.
WHAT'S WITH THE FIREFLY HILTON?
BODE JUST HAD TO HAVE SOME LIGHTNING BUGS AND MOM DOESN'T LIKE HIM OUTSIDE ALONE AFTER DARK. NOT WITH... YOU KNOW.
I WISH YOUR MA WOULDN'T WORRY SO MUCH. I'M OUT HERE, AND THERE'S ABOUT A THOUSAND MILES OF OCEAN TO THE BACK OF THE HOUSE.
IT'S NOT LIKE ANYTHING IS GOING TO HAPPEN TO THE LITTLE GUY IN HIS OWN BACKYARD.

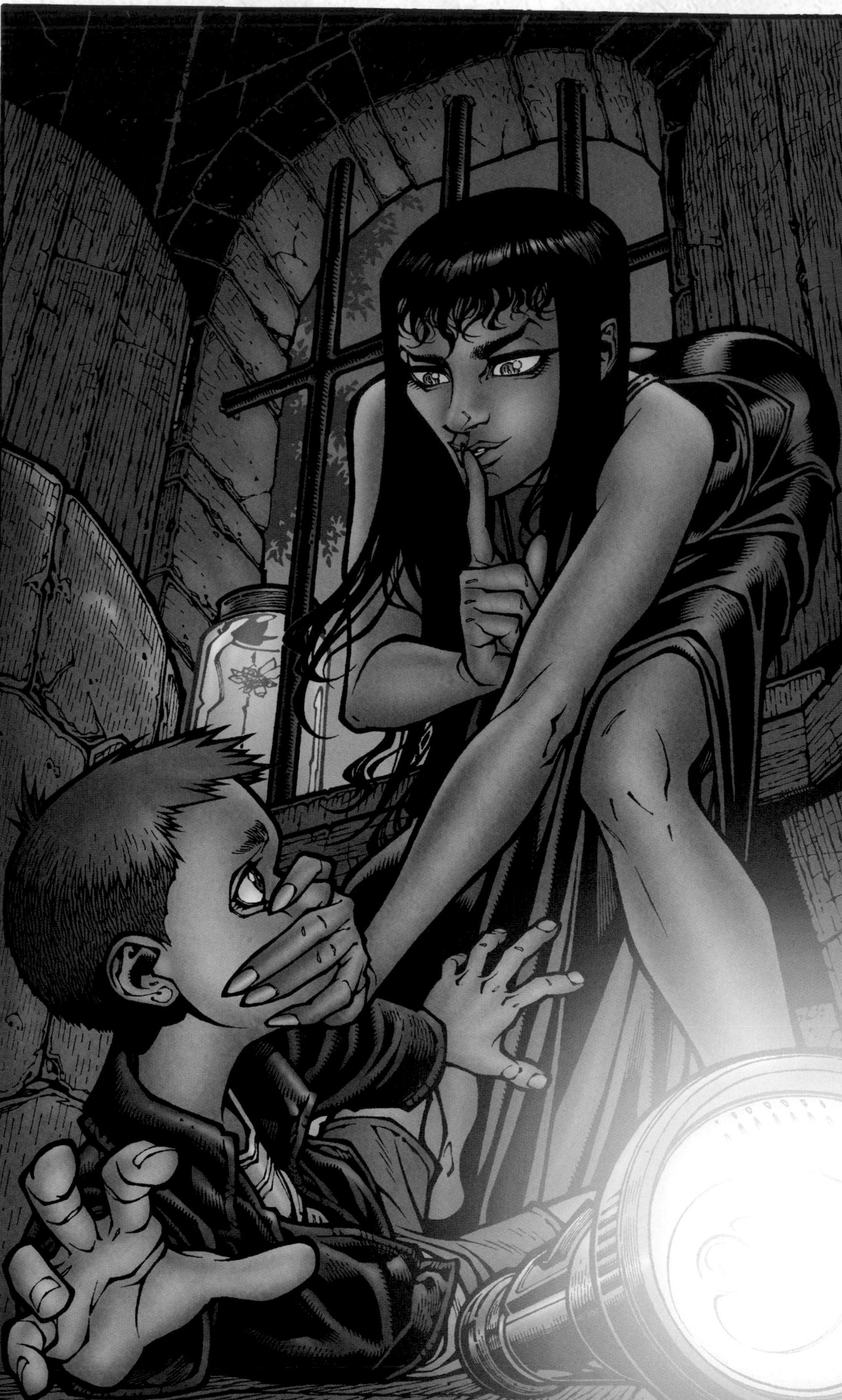

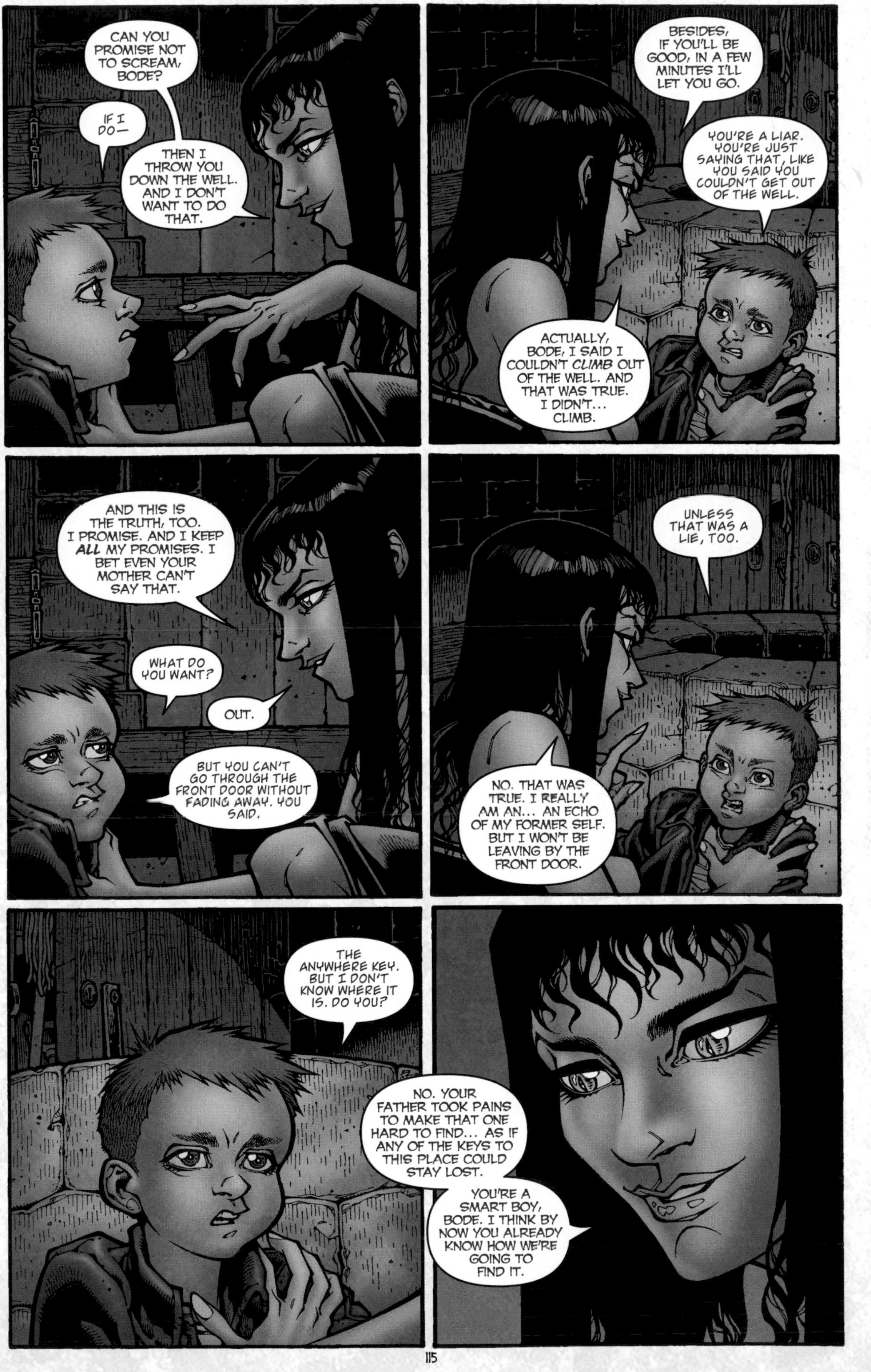
CAN YOU PROMISE NOT TO SCREAM, BODE?
IF I DO—
THEN I THROW YOU DOWN THE WELL. AND I DON'T WANT TO DO THAT.
BESIDES, IF YOU'LL BE GOOD, IN A FEW MINUTES I'LL LET YOU GO.
YOU'RE A LIAR. YOU'RE JUST SAYING THAT, LIKE YOU SAID YOU COULDN'T GET OUT OF THE WELL.
ACTUALLY, BODE, I SAID I COULDN'T CLIMB OUT OF THE WELL. AND THAT WAS TRUE. I DIDN'T... CLIMB.
AND THIS IS THE TRUTH, TOO. I PROMISE. AND I KEEP ALL MY PROMISES. I BET EVEN YOUR MOTHER CAN'T SAY THAT.
WHAT DO YOU WANT?
OUT.
BUT YOU CAN'T GO THROUGH THE FRONT DOOR WITHOUT FADING AWAY. YOU SAID.
UNLESS THAT WAS A LIE, TOO.
NO. THAT WAS TRUE. I REALLY AM AN... AN ECHO OF MY FORMER SELF. BUT I WON'T BE LEAVING BY THE FRONT DOOR.
THE ANYWHERE KEY. BUT I DON'T KNOW WHERE IT IS. DO YOU?
NO. YOUR FATHER TOOK PAINS TO MAKE THAT ONE HARD TO FIND... AS IF ANY OF THE KEYS TO THIS PLACE COULD STAY LOST.
YOU'RE A SMART BOY, BODE. I THINK BY NOW YOU ALREADY KNOW HOW WE'RE GOING TO FIND IT.

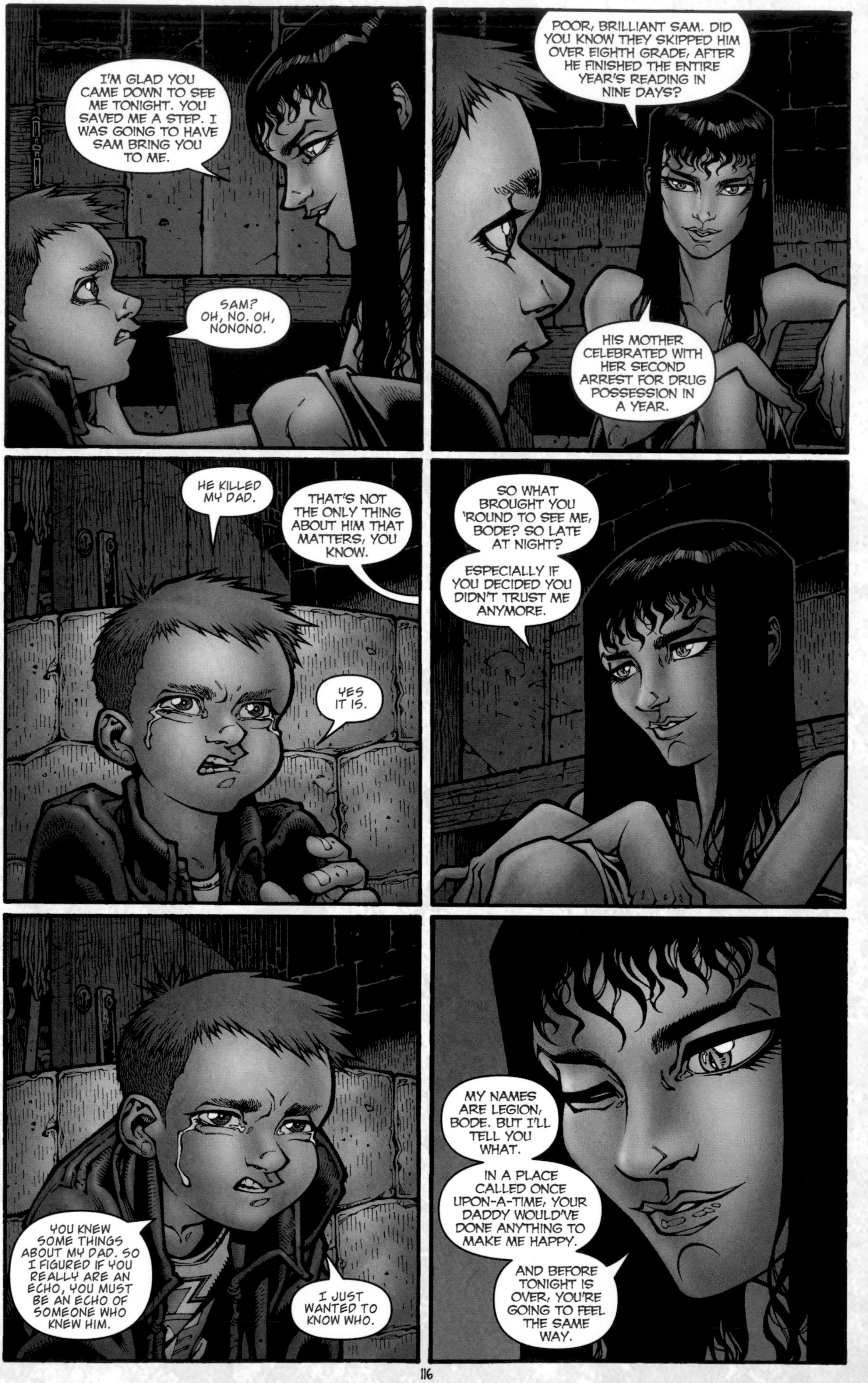
I'M GLAD YOU CAME DOWN TO SEE ME TONIGHT. YOU SAVED ME A STEP. I WAS GOING TO HAVE SAM BRING YOU TO ME.
SAM? OH, NO. OH, NONONO.
POOR, BRILLIANT SAM. DID YOU KNOW THEY SKIPPED HIM OVER EIGHTH GRADE, AFTER HE FINISHED THE ENTIRE YEAR'S READING IN NINE DAYS?
HIS MOTHER CELEBRATED WITH HER SECOND ARREST FOR DRUG POSSESSION IN A YEAR.
HE KILLED MY DAD.
THAT'S NOT THE ONLY THING ABOUT HIM THAT MATTERS, YOU KNOW.
YES IT IS.
SO WHAT BROUGHT YOU 'ROUND TO SEE ME, BODE? SO LATE AT NIGHT?
ESPECIALLY IF YOU DECIDED YOU DIDN'T TRUST ME ANYMORE.
YOU KNEW SOME THINGS ABOUT MY DAD. SO I FIGURED IF YOU REALLY ARE AN ECHO, YOU MUST BE AN ECHO OF SOMEONE WHO KNEW HIM.
I JUST WANTED TO KNOW WHO.
MY NAMES ARE LEGION, BODE. BUT I'LL TELL YOU WHAT.
IN A PLACE CALLED ONCE UPON-A-TIME, YOUR DADDY WOULD'VE DONE ANYTHING TO MAKE ME HAPPY.
AND BEFORE TONIGHT IS OVER, YOU'RE GOING TO FEEL THE SAME WAY.

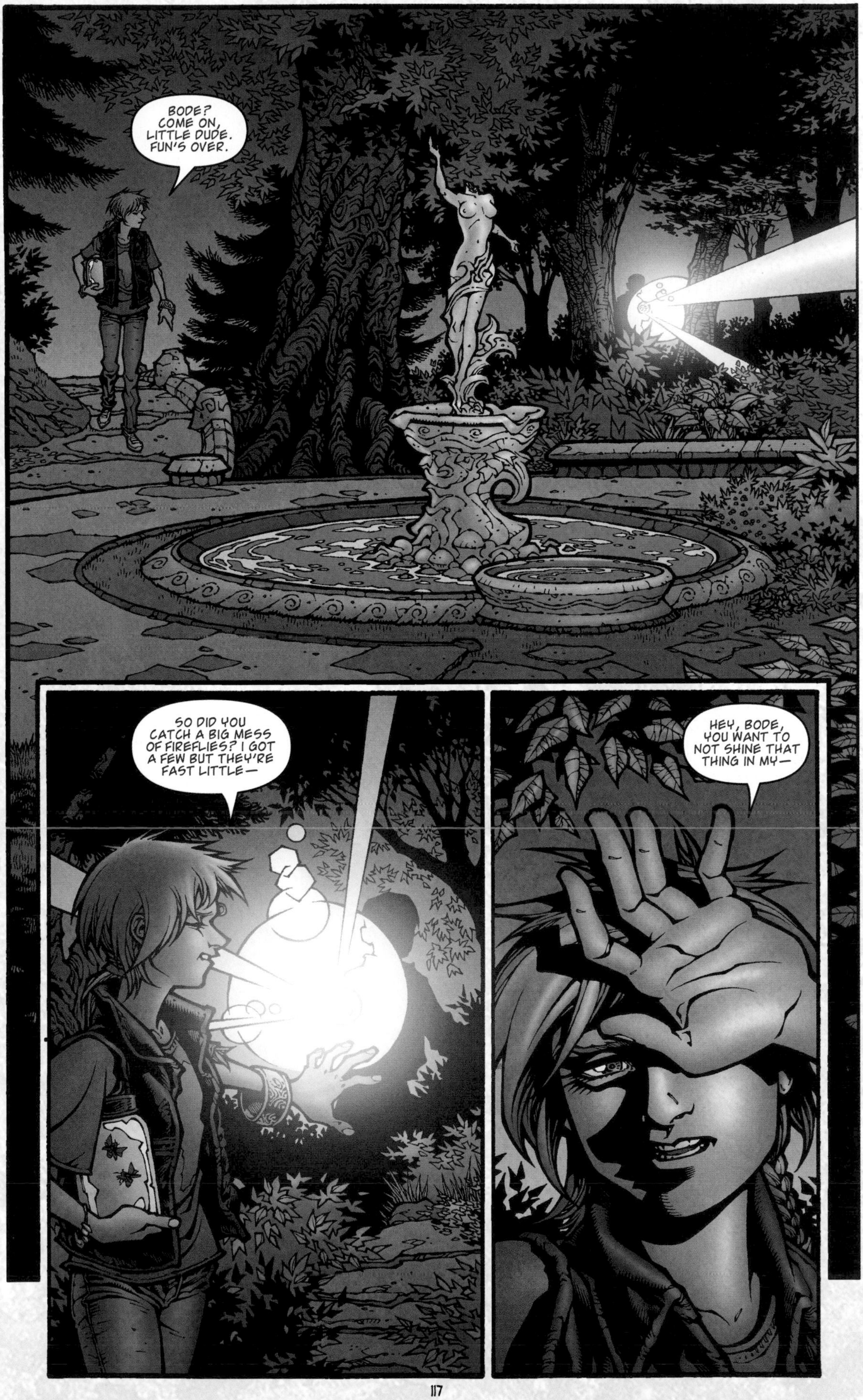
BODE? COME ON, LITTLE DUDE. FUN'S OVER.
SO DID YOU CATCH A BIG MESS OF FIREFLIES? I GOT A FEW BUT THEY'RE FAST LITTLE—
HEY, BODE, YOU WANT TO NOT SHINE THAT THING IN MY—

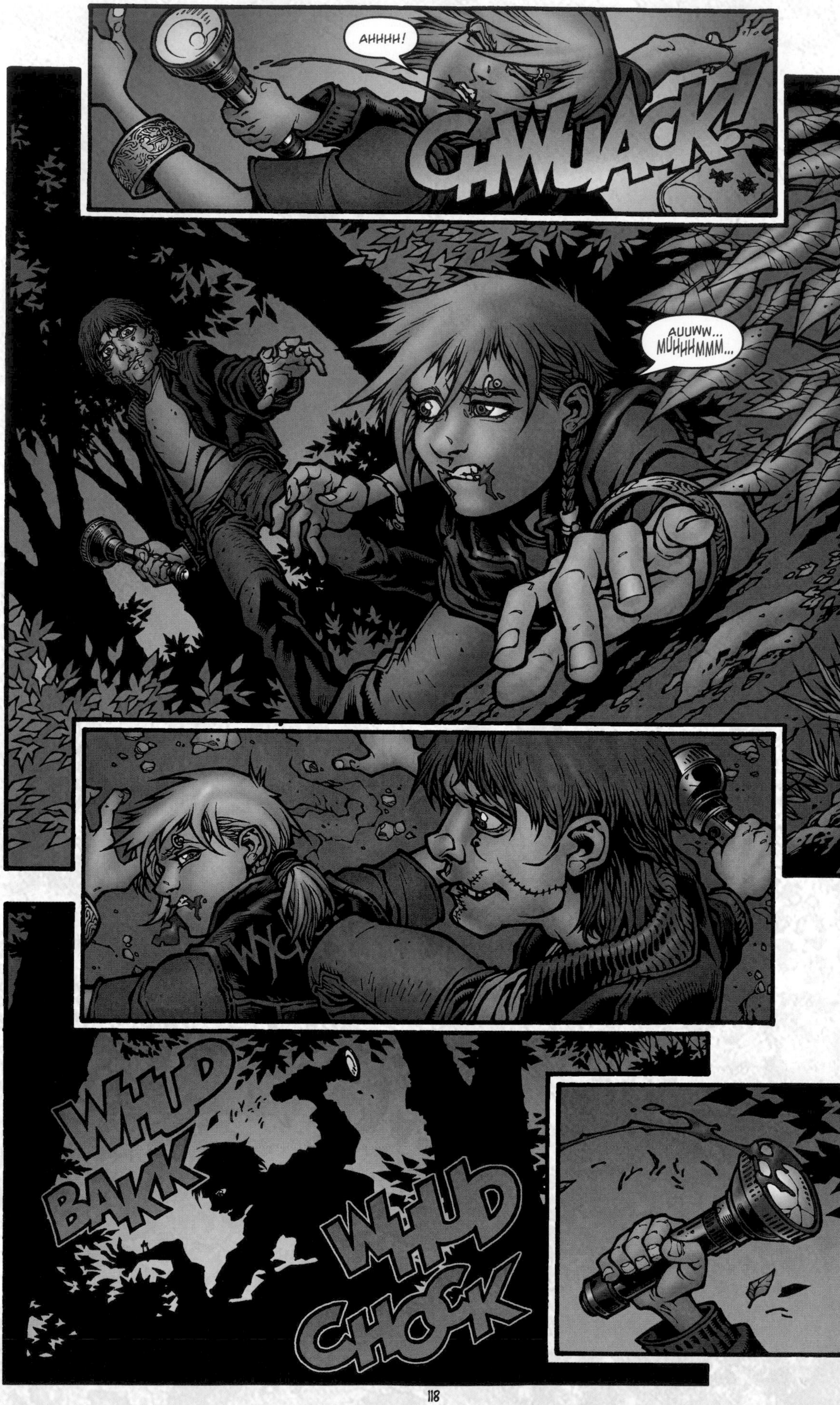
AHHHH!
CHWUACK!
AUUWW... MUHHHMMM...
WHUD
BAKK
WHUD
CHOCK

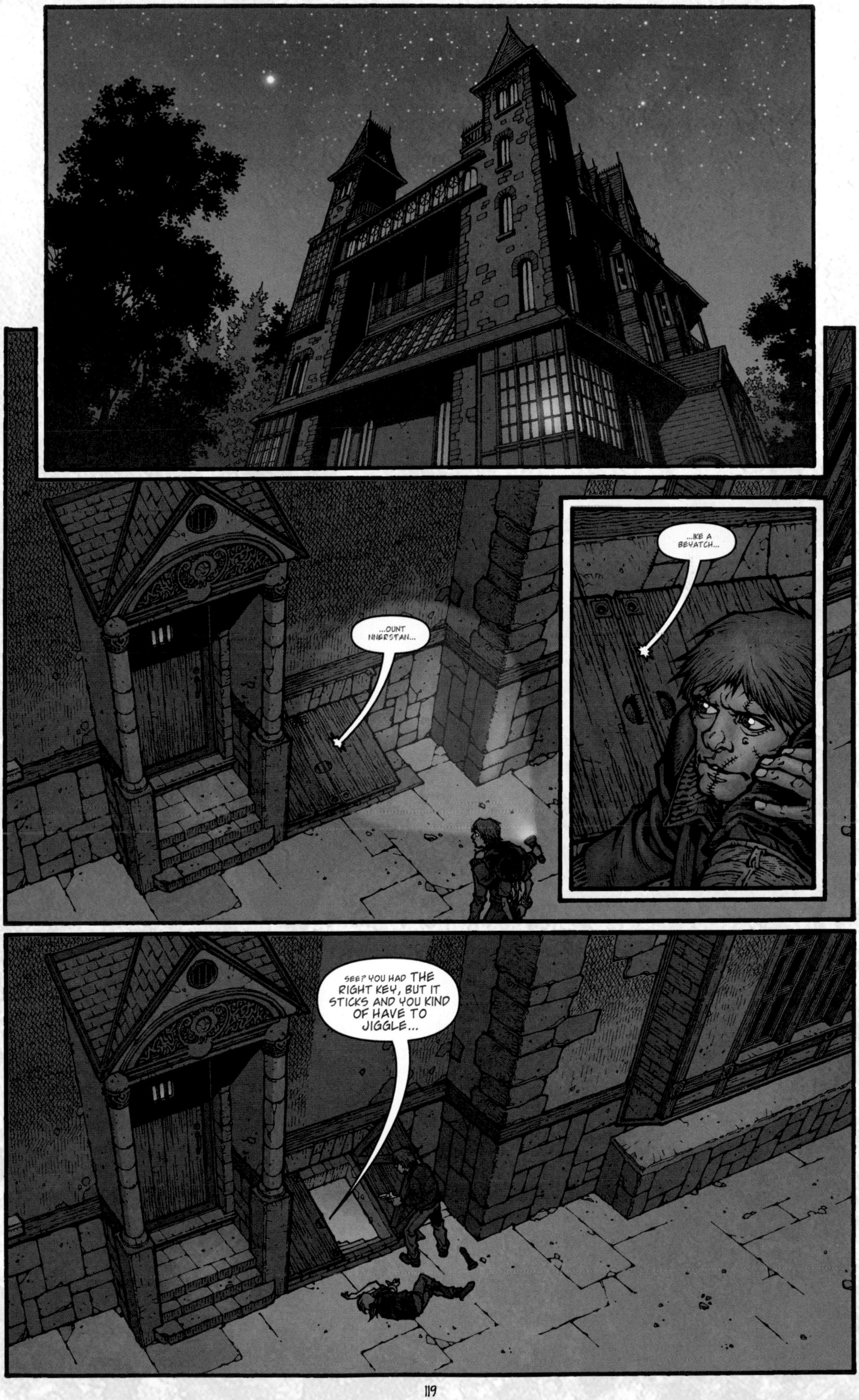
...OUNT
NNERSTAN...
...IKE A
BEYATCH...
SEE? YOU HAD THE RIGHT KEY, BUT IT STICKS AND YOU KIND OF HAVE TO JIGGLE...

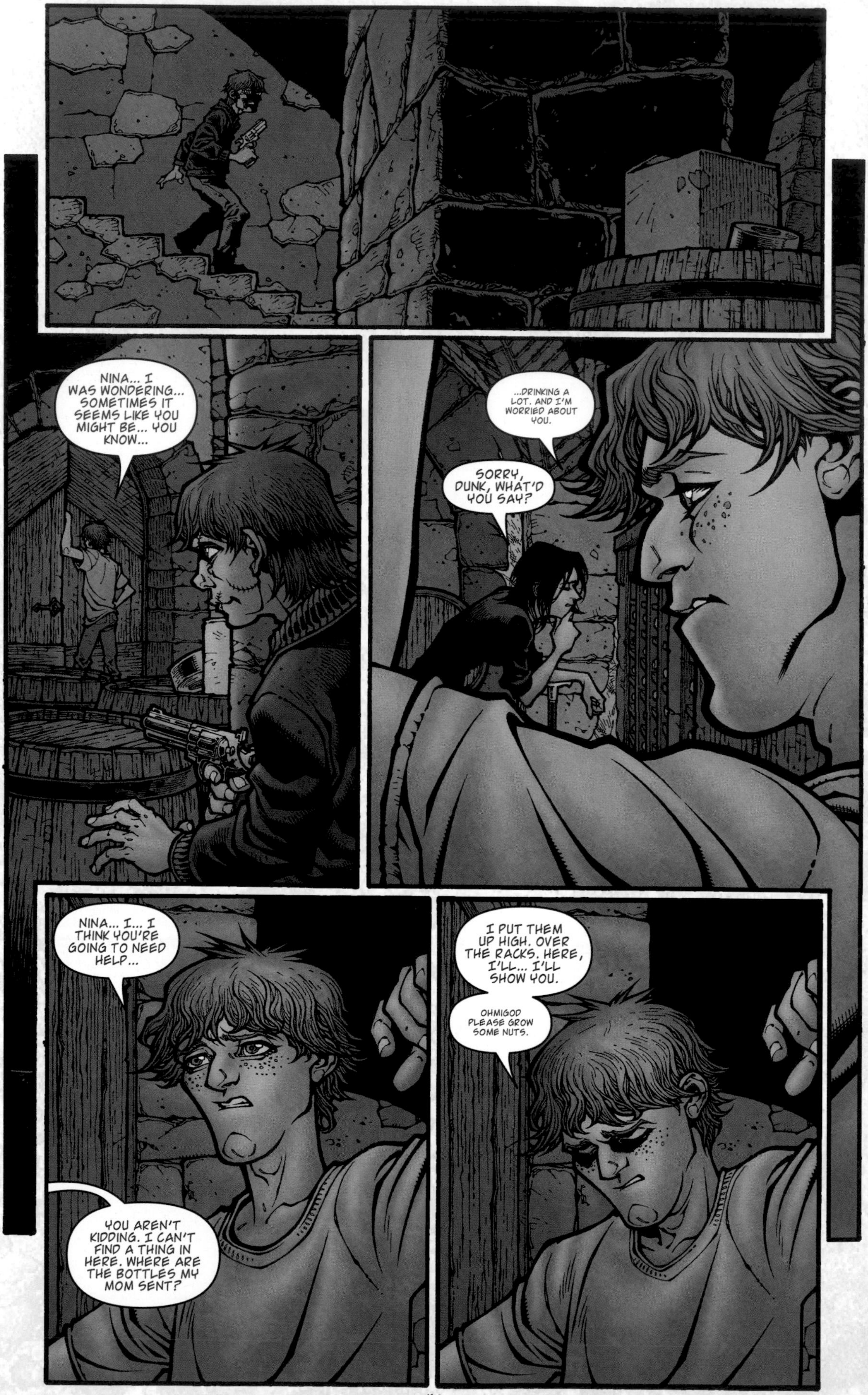
NINA... I WAS WONDERING... SOMETIMES IT SEEMS LIKE YOU MIGHT BE... YOU KNOW...
...DRINKING A LOT. AND I'M WORRIED ABOUT YOU.
SORRY, DUNK, WHAT'D YOU SAY?
NINA... I... I THINK YOU'RE GOING TO NEED HELP...
YOU AREN'T KIDDING. I CAN'T FIND A THING IN HERE. WHERE ARE THE BOTTLES MY MOM SENT?
I PUT THEM UP HIGH. OVER THE RACKS. HERE, I'LL... I'LL SHOW YOU.
OHMIGOD PLEASE GROW SOME NUTS.

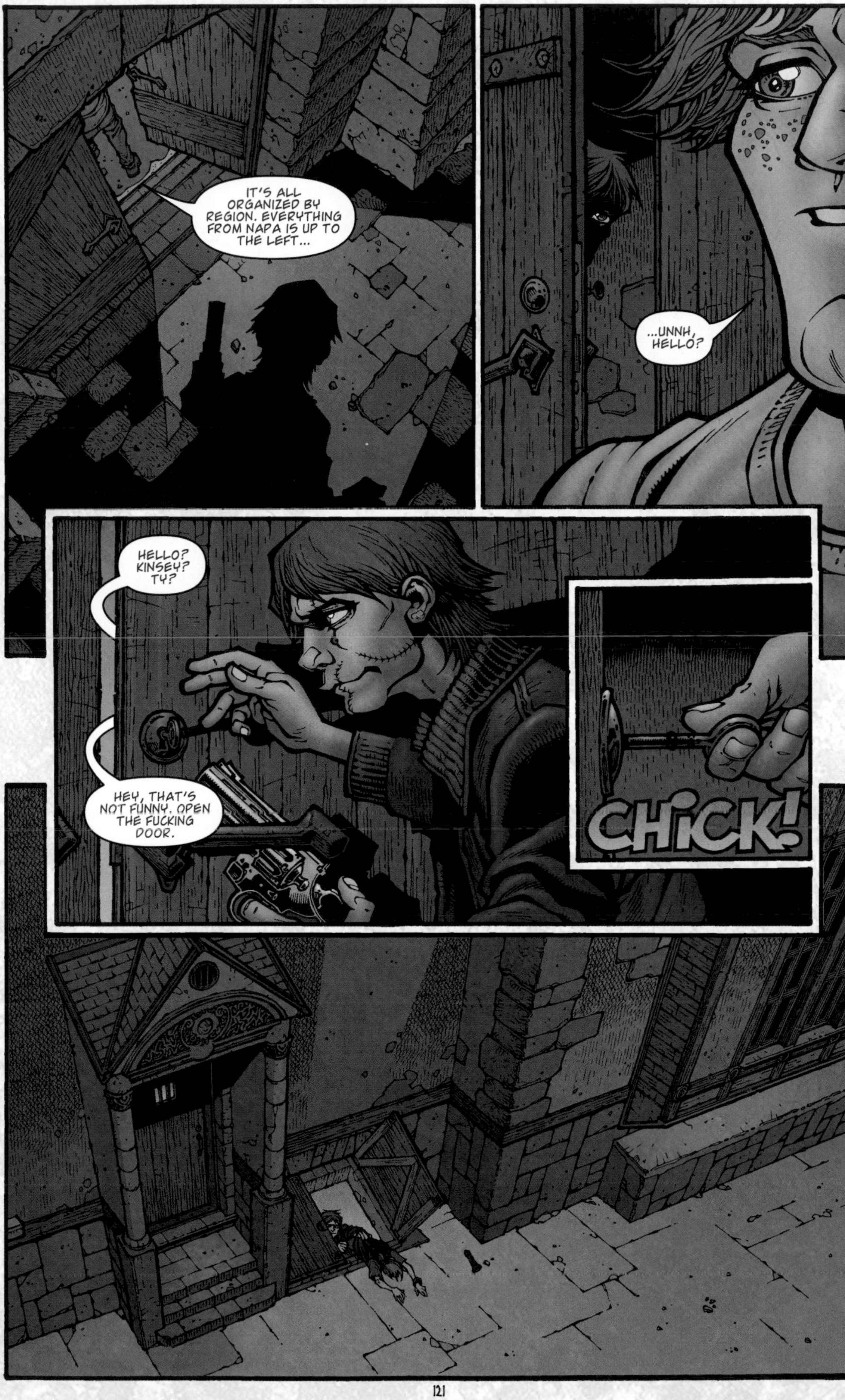
IT'S ALL ORGANIZED BY REGION. EVERYTHING FROM NAPA IS UP TO THE LEFT...
...UNNH, HELLO?
HELLO? KINSEY? TY?
HEY, THAT'S NOT FUNNY. OPEN THE FUCKING DOOR.
CHICK!

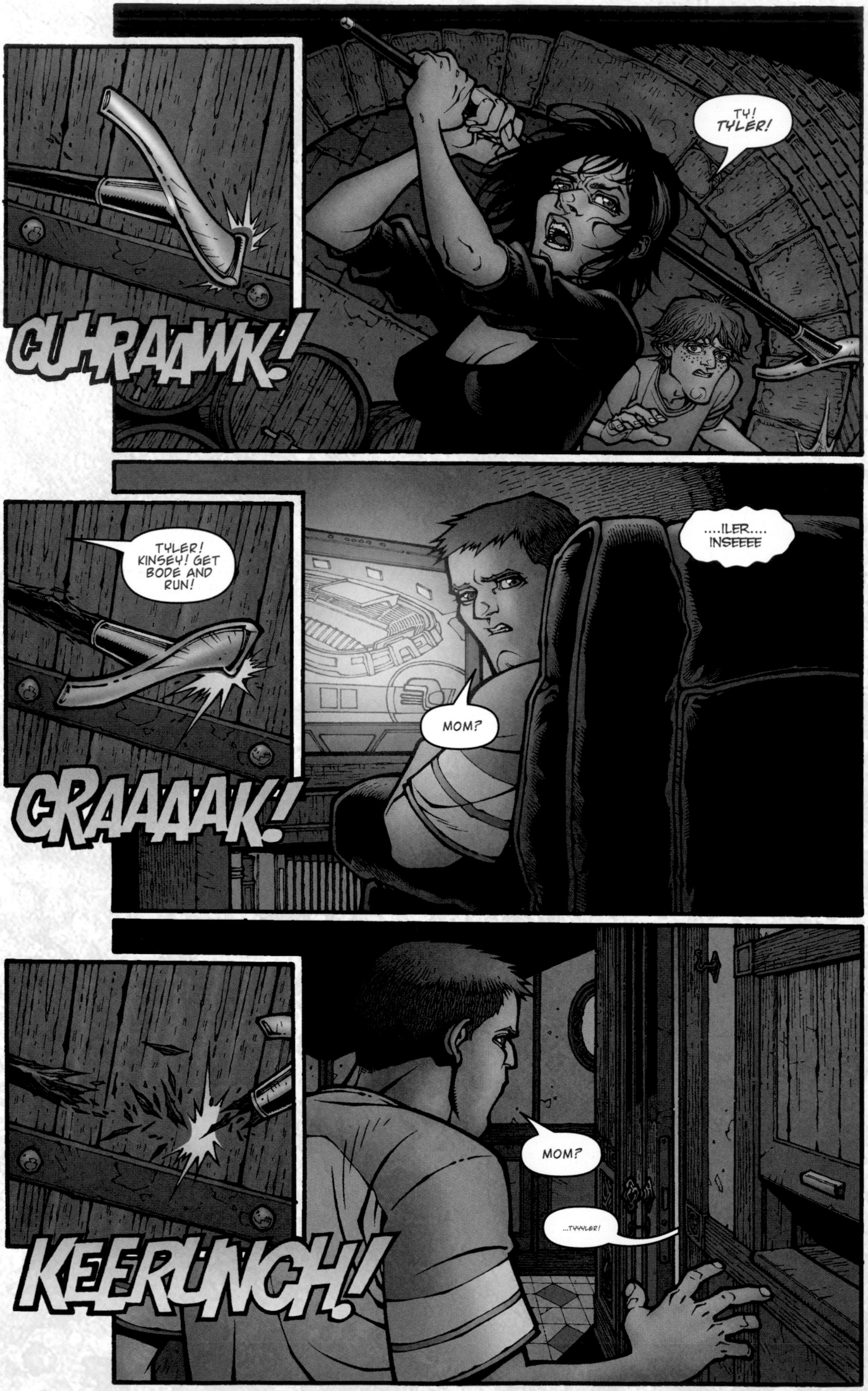
CUHRAAWK!
TY! TYLER!
TYLER! KINSEY! GET BODE AND RUN!
CRAAAAK!
....ILER.... INSEEEE
MOM?
KEERUNCH!
MOM?
...TYYYLER!

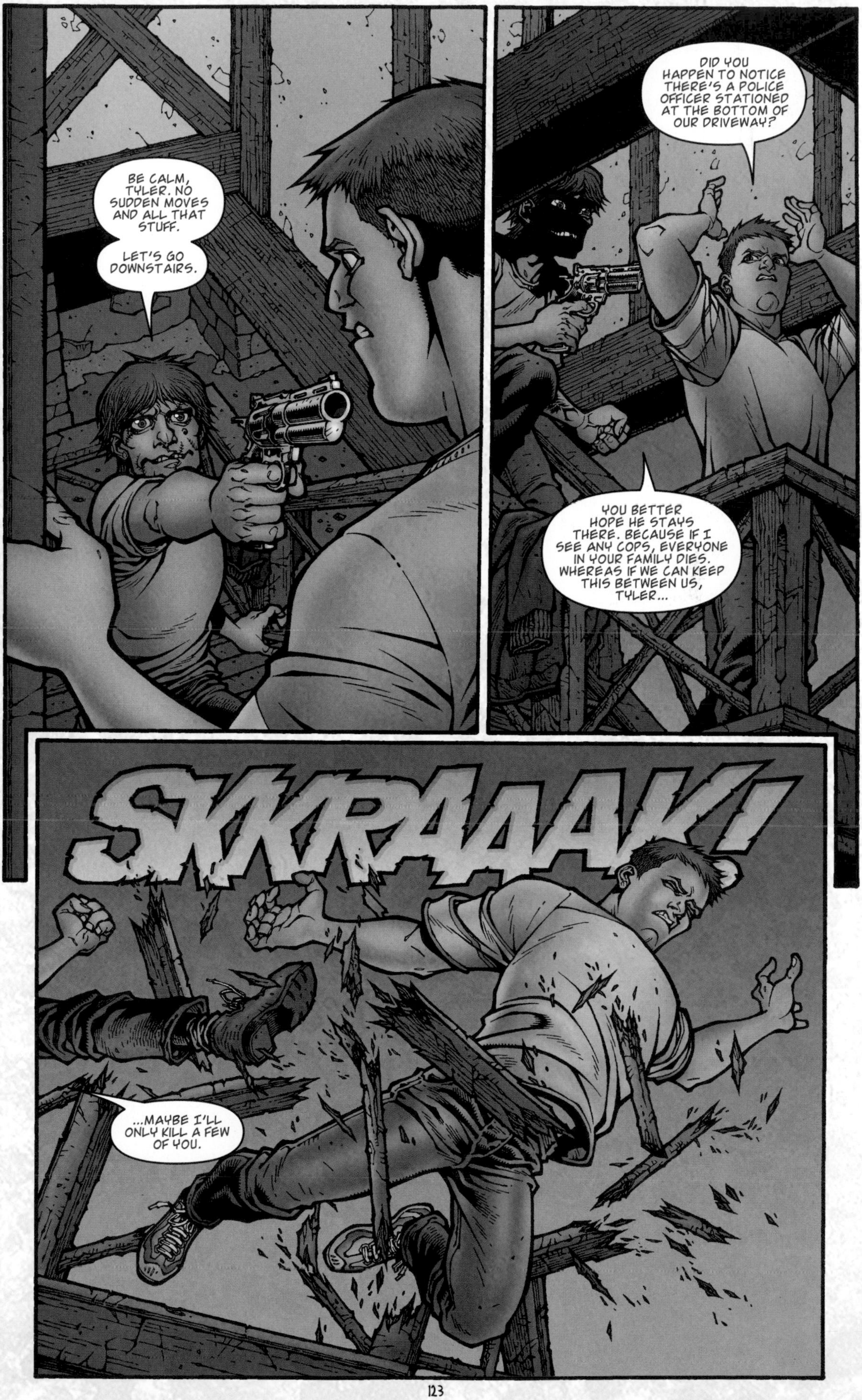
BE CALM, TYLER. NO SUDDEN MOVES AND ALL THAT STUFF.
LET'S GO DOWNSTAIRS.
DID YOU HAPPEN TO NOTICE THERE'S A POLICE OFFICER STATIONED AT THE BOTTOM OF OUR DRIVEWAY?
YOU BETTER HOPE HE STAYS THERE. BECAUSE IF I SEE ANY COPS, EVERYONE IN YOUR FAMILY DIES. WHEREAS IF WE CAN KEEP THIS BETWEEN US, TYLER...
SKKRAAAK!
...MAYBE I'LL ONLY KILL A FEW OF YOU.

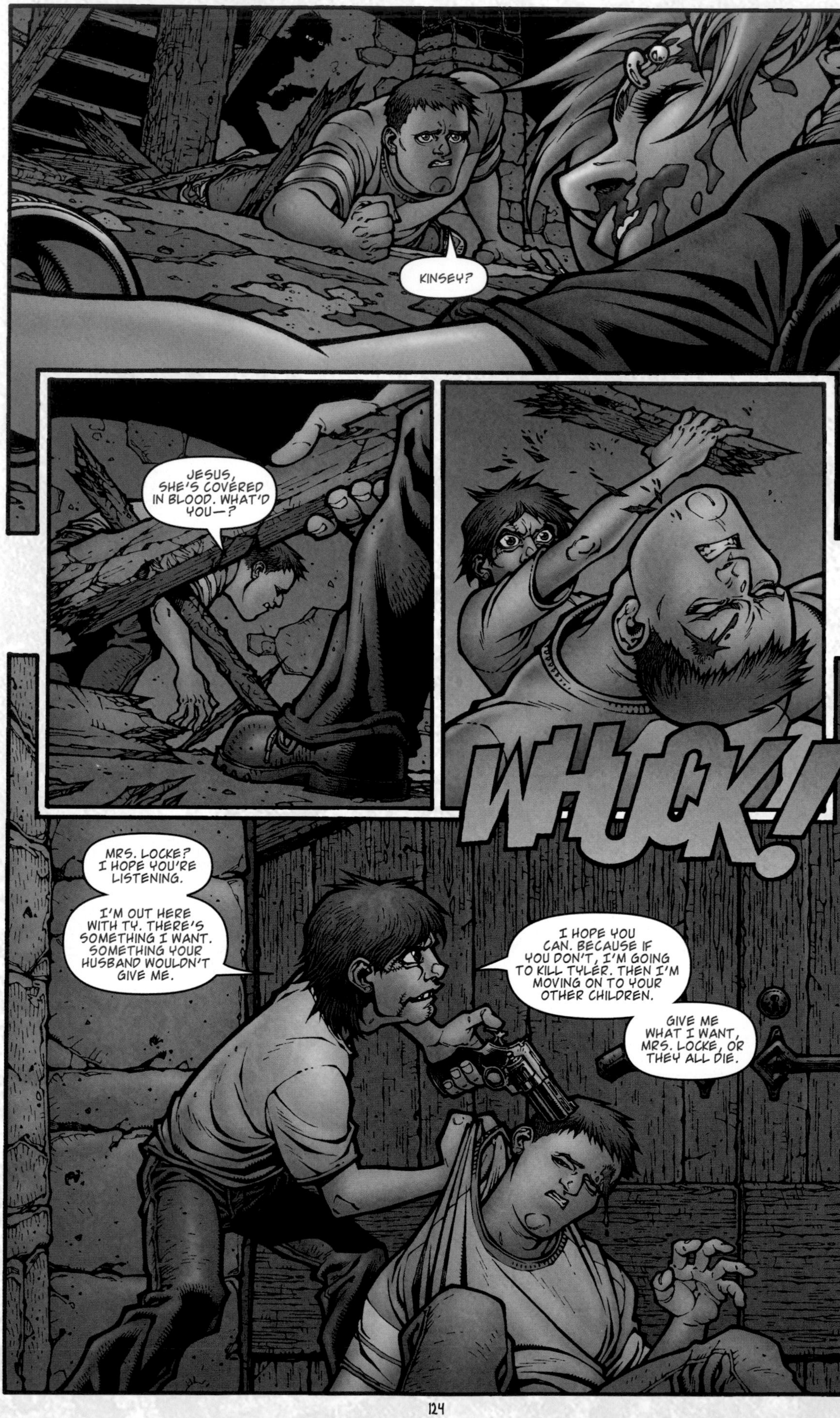
KINSEY?
JESUS, SHE'S COVERED IN BLOOD. WHAT'D YOU—?
WHUCK!
MRS. LOCKE? I HOPE YOU'RE LISTENING.
I'M OUT HERE WITH TY. THERE'S SOMETHING I WANT. SOMETHING YOUR HUSBAND WOULDN'T GIVE ME.
I HOPE YOU CAN. BECAUSE IF YOU DON'T, I'M GOING TO KILL TYLER. THEN I'M MOVING ON TO YOUR OTHER CHILDREN.
GIVE ME WHAT I WANT, MRS. LOCKE, OR THEY ALL DIE.

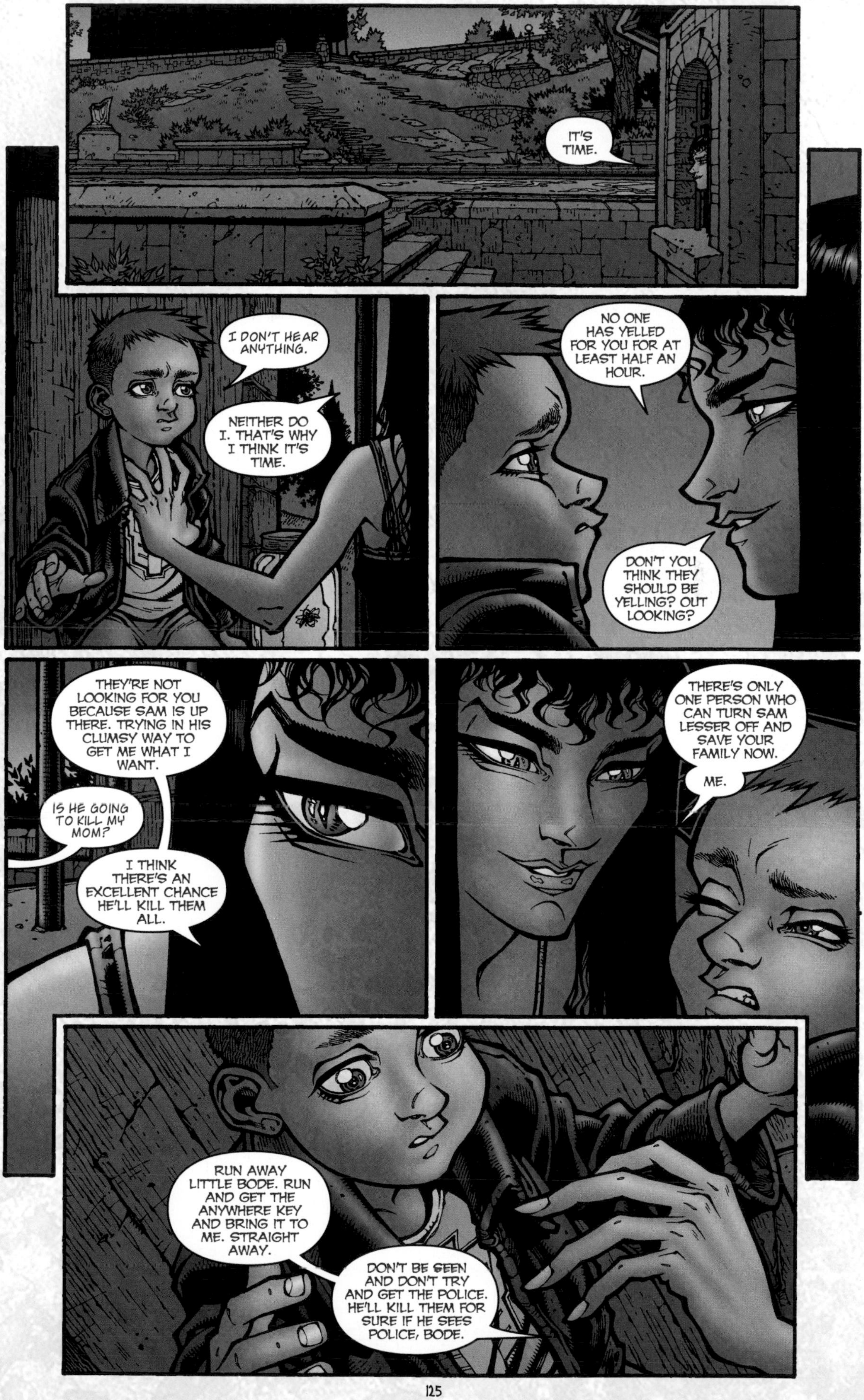
IT'S TIME.
I DON'T HEAR ANYTHING.
NEITHER DO I. THAT'S WHY I THINK IT'S TIME.
NO ONE HAS YELLED FOR YOU FOR AT LEAST HALF AN HOUR.
DON'T YOU THINK THEY SHOULD BE YELLING? OUT LOOKING?
THEY'RE NOT LOOKING FOR YOU BECAUSE SAM IS UP THERE. TRYING IN HIS CLUMSY WAY TO GET ME WHAT I WANT.
IS HE GOING TO KILL MY MOM?
I THINK THERE'S AN EXCELLENT CHANCE HE'LL KILL THEM ALL.
THERE'S ONLY ONE PERSON WHO CAN TURN SAM LESSER OFF AND SAVE YOUR FAMILY NOW.
ME.
RUN AWAY LITTLE BODE. RUN AND GET THE ANYWHERE KEY AND BRING IT TO ME. STRAIGHT AWAY.
DON'T BE SEEN AND DON'T TRY AND GET THE POLICE. HE'LL KILL THEM FOR SURE IF HE SEES POLICE, BODE.

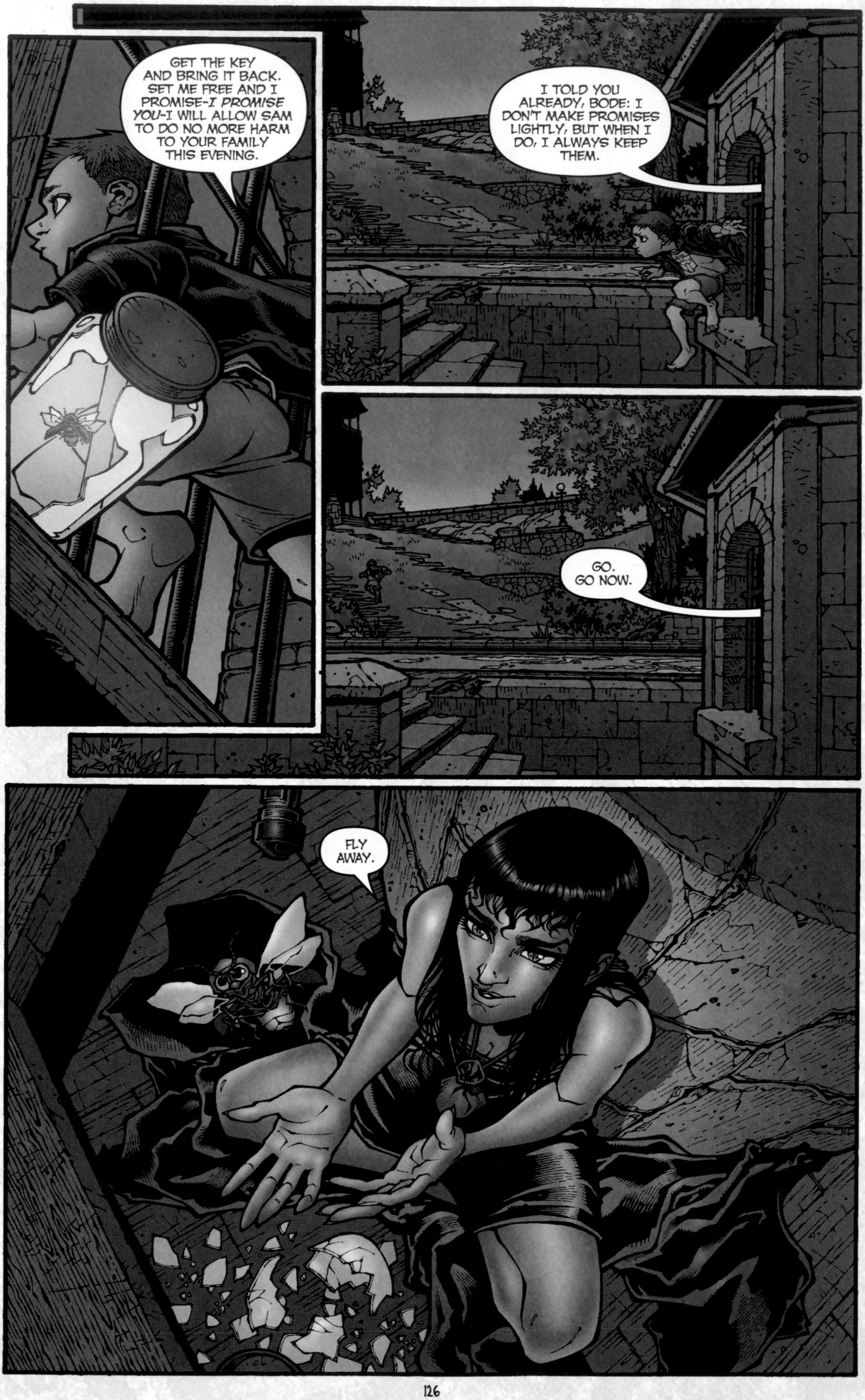
GET THE KEY AND BRING IT BACK. SET ME FREE AND I PROMISE–*I PROMISE YOU*–I WILL ALLOW SAM TO DO NO MORE HARM TO YOUR FAMILY THIS EVENING.
I TOLD YOU ALREADY, BODE: I DON'T MAKE PROMISES LIGHTLY, BUT WHEN I DO, I ALWAYS KEEP THEM.
GO. GO NOW.
FLY AWAY.

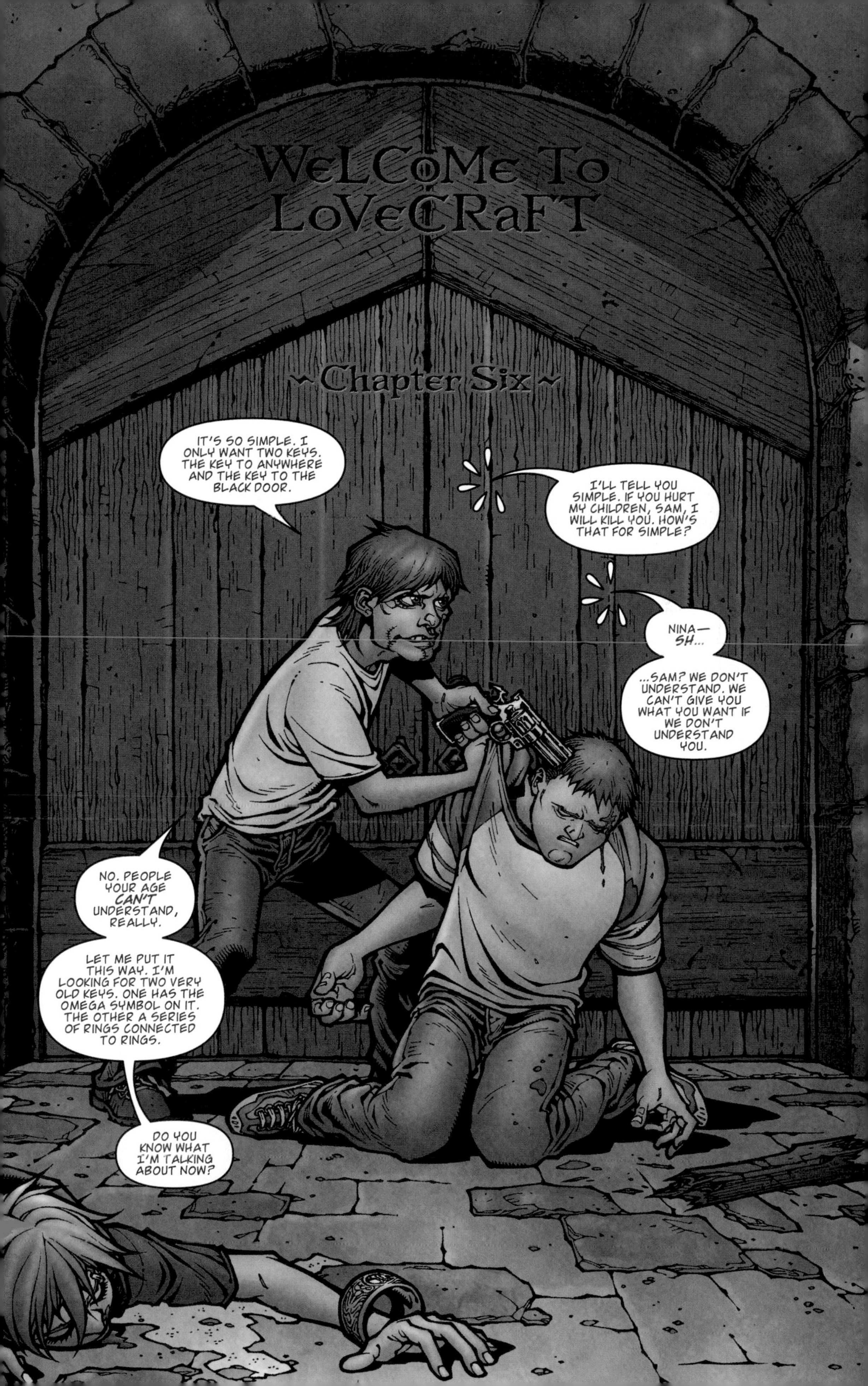
WELCOME TO LOVECRAFT
~Chapter Six~
IT'S SO SIMPLE. I ONLY WANT TWO KEYS. THE KEY TO ANYWHERE AND THE KEY TO THE BLACK DOOR.
I'LL TELL YOU SIMPLE. IF YOU HURT MY CHILDREN, SAM, I WILL KILL YOU. HOW'S THAT FOR SIMPLE?
NINA— SH...
...SAM? WE DON'T UNDERSTAND. WE CAN'T GIVE YOU WHAT YOU WANT IF WE DON'T UNDERSTAND YOU.
NO. PEOPLE YOUR AGE CAN'T UNDERSTAND, REALLY.
LET ME PUT IT THIS WAY. I'M LOOKING FOR TWO VERY OLD KEYS. ONE HAS THE OMEGA SYMBOL ON IT. THE OTHER A SERIES OF RINGS CONNECTED TO RINGS.
DO YOU KNOW WHAT I'M TALKING ABOUT NOW?

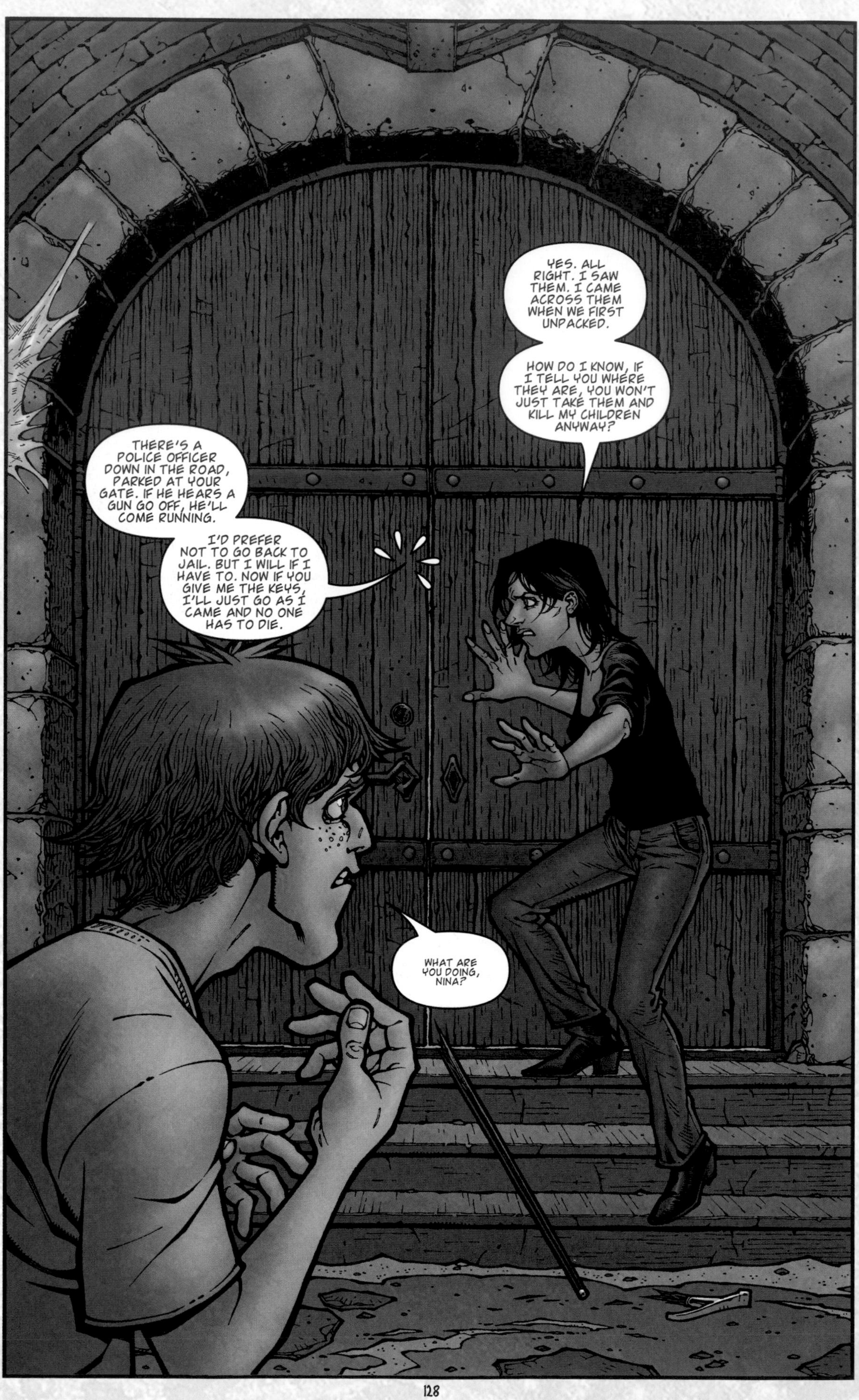
YES. ALL RIGHT. I SAW THEM. I CAME ACROSS THEM WHEN WE FIRST UNPACKED.
HOW DO I KNOW, IF I TELL YOU WHERE THEY ARE, YOU WON'T JUST TAKE THEM AND KILL MY CHILDREN ANYWAY?
THERE'S A POLICE OFFICER DOWN IN THE ROAD, PARKED AT YOUR GATE. IF HE HEARS A GUN GO OFF, HE'LL COME RUNNING.
I'D PREFER NOT TO GO BACK TO JAIL. BUT I WILL IF I HAVE TO. NOW IF YOU GIVE ME THE KEYS, I'LL JUST GO AS I CAME AND NO ONE HAS TO DIE.
WHAT ARE YOU DOING, NINA?

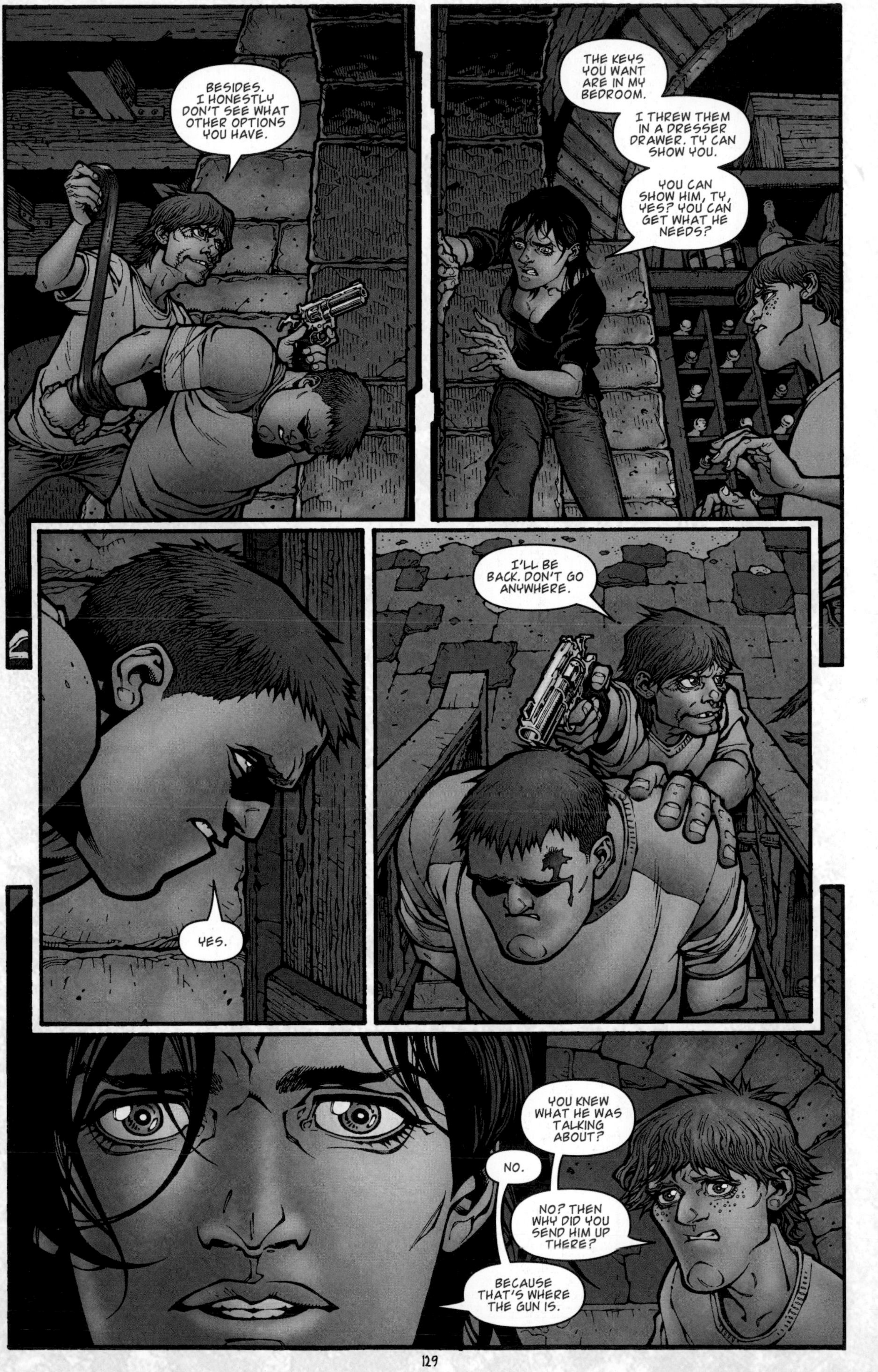
BESIDES. I HONESTLY DON'T SEE WHAT OTHER OPTIONS YOU HAVE.
THE KEYS YOU WANT ARE IN MY BEDROOM.
I THREW THEM IN A DRESSER DRAWER. TY CAN SHOW YOU.
YOU CAN SHOW HIM, TY, YES? YOU CAN GET WHAT HE NEEDS?
YES.
I'LL BE BACK. DON'T GO ANYWHERE.
YOU KNEW WHAT HE WAS TALKING ABOUT?
NO.
NO? THEN WHY DID YOU SEND HIM UP THERE?
BECAUSE THAT'S WHERE THE GUN IS.

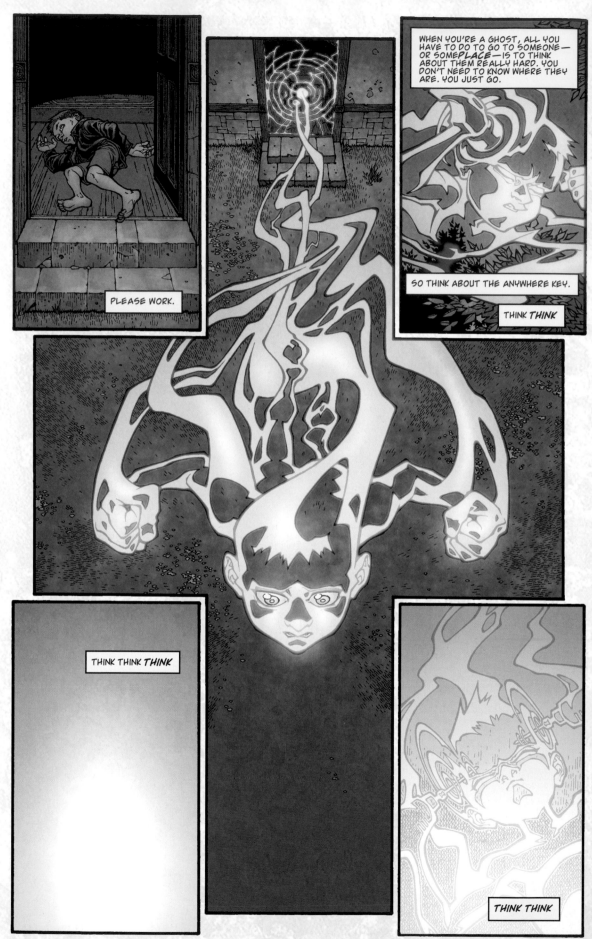

PLEASE WORK.

WHEN YOU'RE A GHOST, ALL YOU HAVE TO DO TO GO TO SOMEONE— OR SOME*PLACE*—IS TO THINK ABOUT THEM REALLY HARD. YOU DON'T NEED TO KNOW WHERE THEY ARE. YOU JUST GO.

SO THINK ABOUT THE ANYWHERE KEY.

THINK *THINK*

THINK THINK *THINK*

THINK THINK

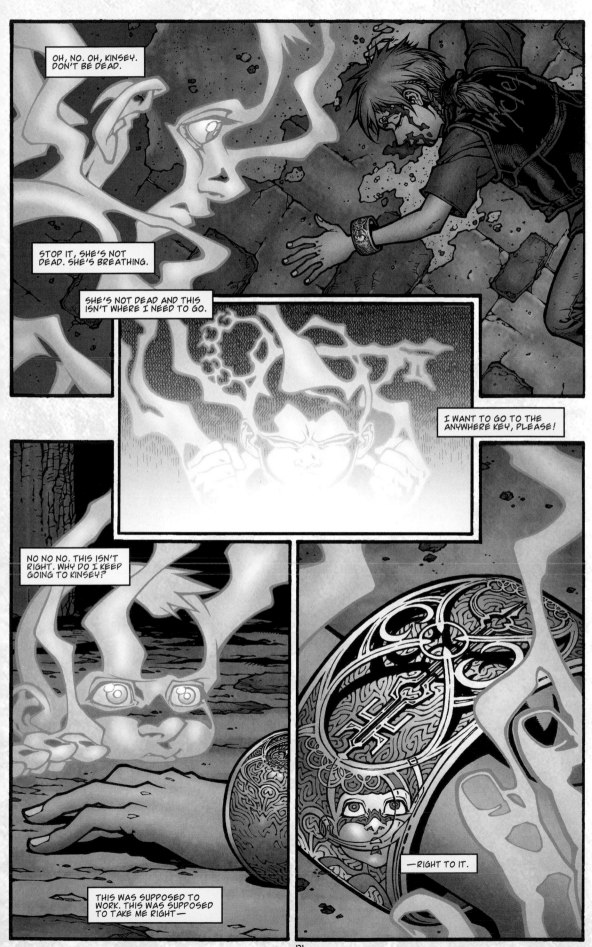

OH, NO. OH, KINSEY. DON'T BE DEAD.

STOP IT, SHE'S NOT DEAD. SHE'S BREATHING.

SHE'S NOT DEAD AND THIS ISN'T WHERE I NEED TO GO.

I WANT TO GO TO THE ANYWHERE KEY, PLEASE!

NO NO NO. THIS ISN'T RIGHT. WHY DO I KEEP GOING TO KINSEY?

THIS WAS SUPPOSED TO WORK. THIS WAS SUPPOSED TO TAKE ME RIGHT—

—RIGHT TO IT.

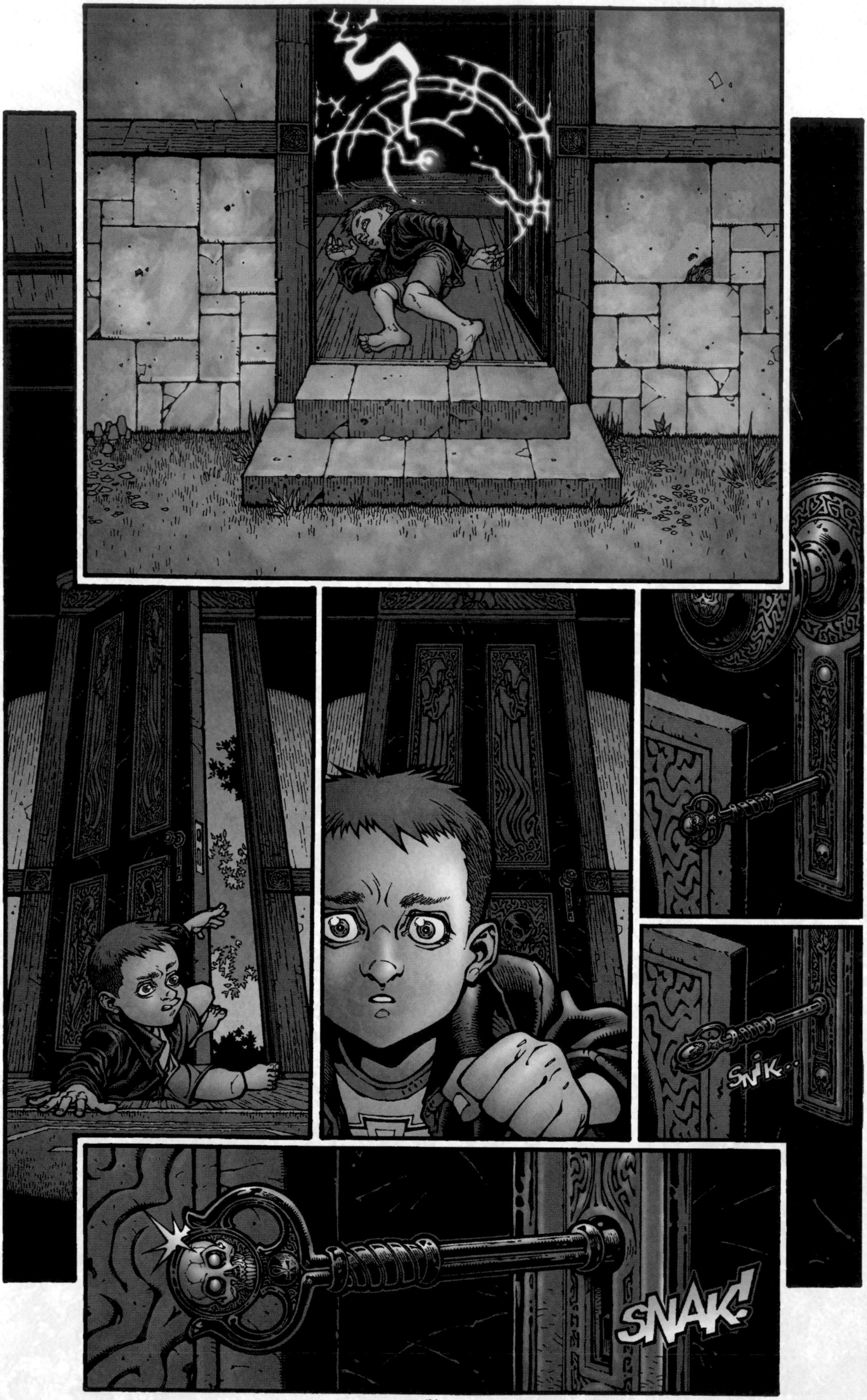
SNIK..
SNAK!

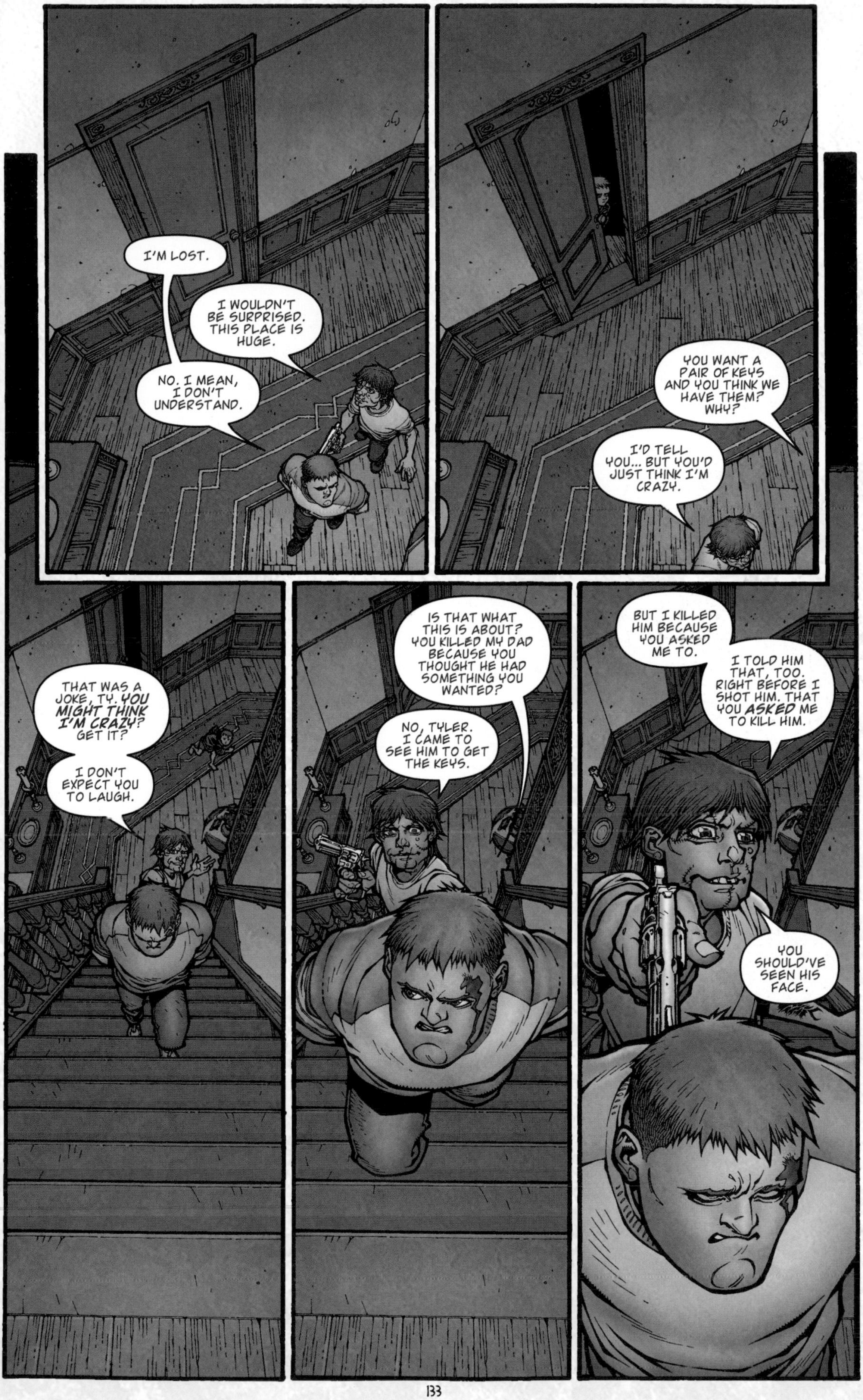
I'M LOST.
I WOULDN'T BE SURPRISED. THIS PLACE IS HUGE.
NO. I MEAN, I DON'T UNDERSTAND.
YOU WANT A PAIR OF KEYS AND YOU THINK WE HAVE THEM? WHY?
I'D TELL YOU... BUT YOU'D JUST THINK I'M CRAZY.
THAT WAS A JOKE, TY. YOU MIGHT THINK I'M CRAZY? GET IT?
I DON'T EXPECT YOU TO LAUGH.
IS THAT WHAT THIS IS ABOUT? YOU KILLED MY DAD BECAUSE YOU THOUGHT HE HAD SOMETHING YOU WANTED?
NO, TYLER. I CAME TO SEE HIM TO GET THE KEYS.
BUT I KILLED HIM BECAUSE YOU ASKED ME TO.
I TOLD HIM THAT, TOO. RIGHT BEFORE I SHOT HIM. THAT YOU ASKED ME TO KILL HIM.
YOU SHOULD'VE SEEN HIS FACE.

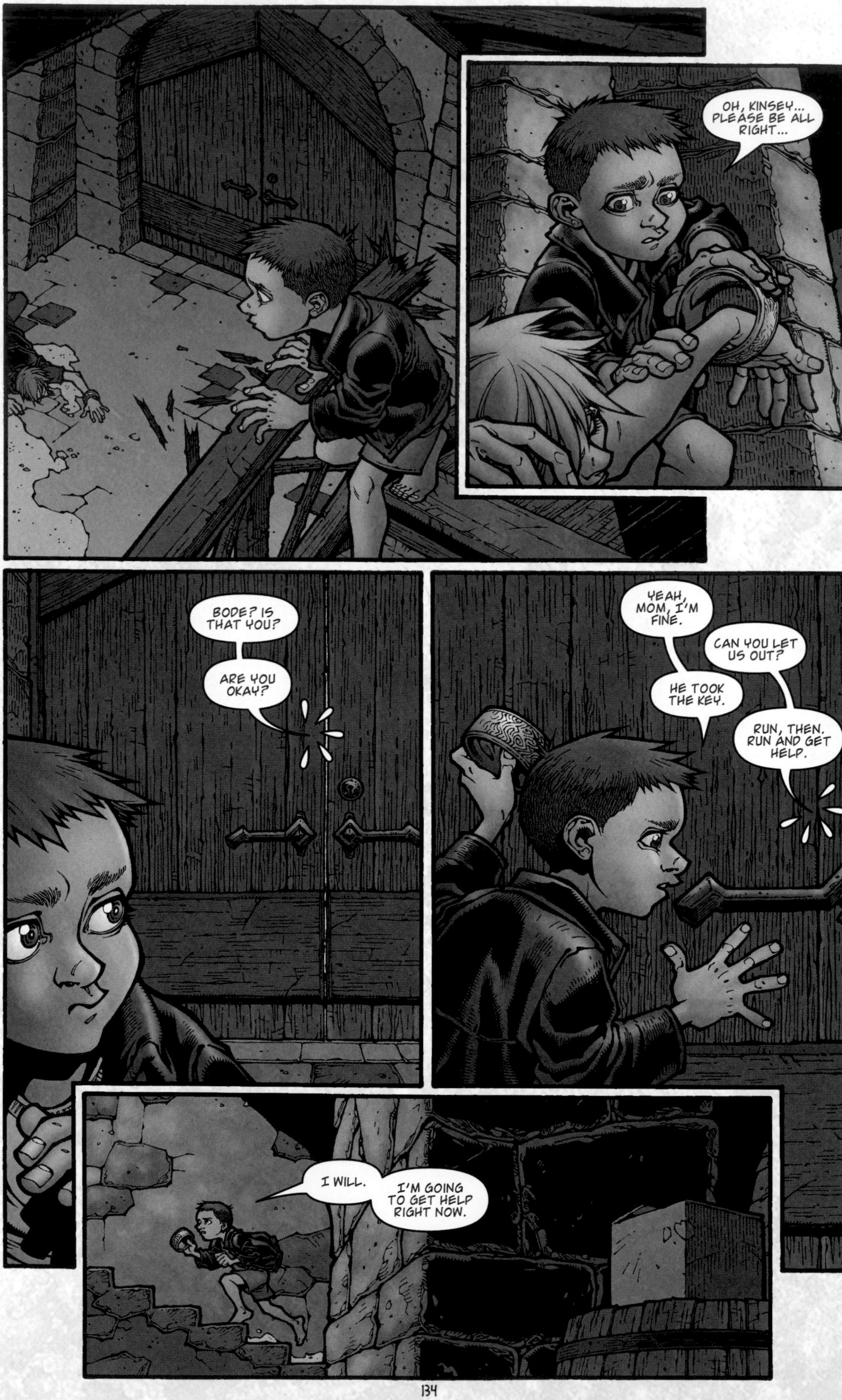
OH, KINSEY... PLEASE BE ALL RIGHT...
BODE? IS THAT YOU?
ARE YOU OKAY?
YEAH, MOM, I'M FINE.
HE TOOK THE KEY.
CAN YOU LET US OUT?
RUN, THEN. RUN AND GET HELP.
I WILL.
I'M GOING TO GET HELP RIGHT NOW.

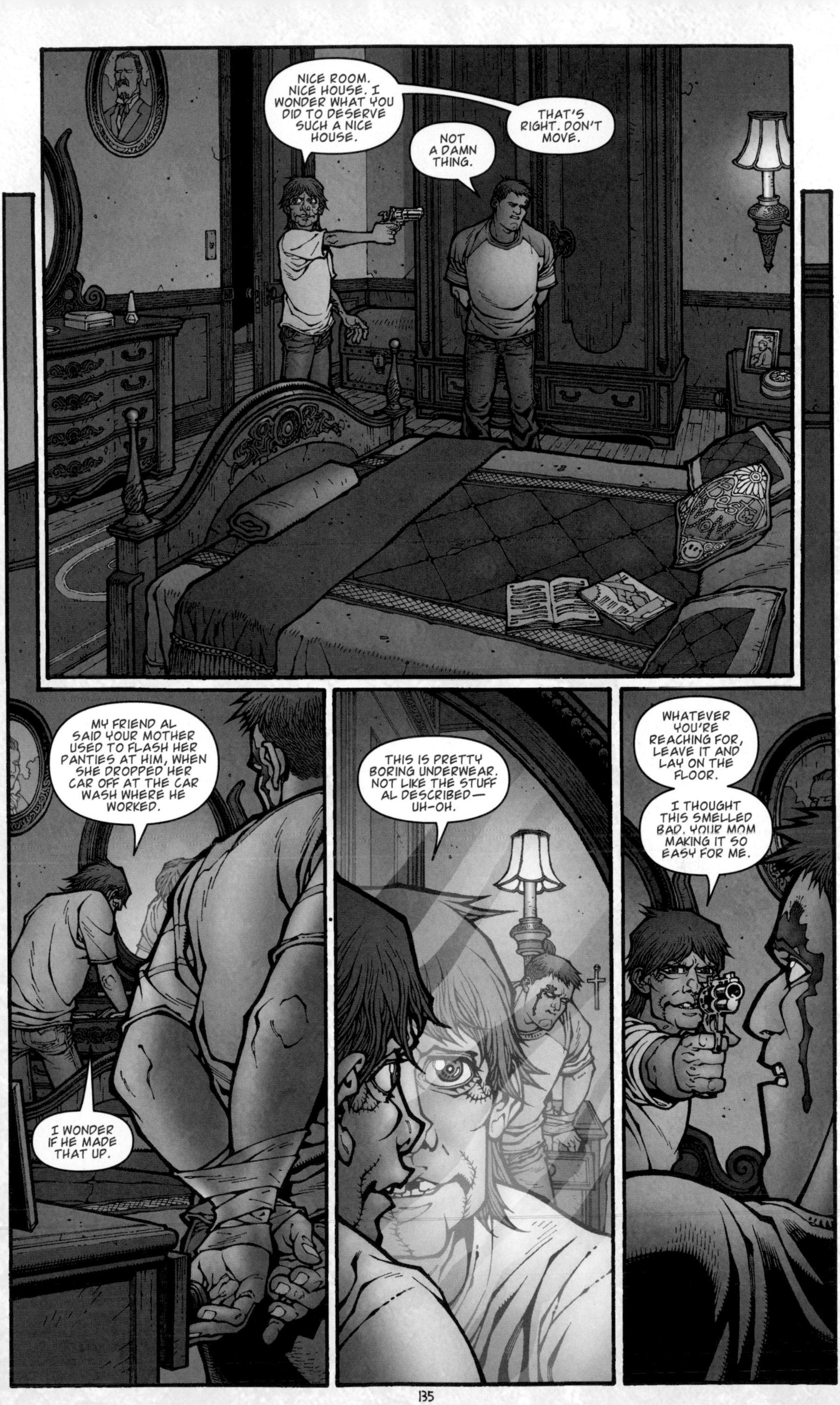
NICE ROOM. NICE HOUSE. I WONDER WHAT YOU DID TO DESERVE SUCH A NICE HOUSE.
NOT A DAMN THING.
THAT'S RIGHT. DON'T MOVE.
MY FRIEND AL SAID YOUR MOTHER USED TO FLASH HER PANTIES AT HIM, WHEN SHE DROPPED HER CAR OFF AT THE CAR WASH WHERE HE WORKED.
I WONDER IF HE MADE THAT UP.
THIS IS PRETTY BORING UNDERWEAR. NOT LIKE THE STUFF AL DESCRIBED— UH-OH.
WHATEVER YOU'RE REACHING FOR, LEAVE IT AND LAY ON THE FLOOR.
I THOUGHT THIS SMELLED BAD. YOUR MOM MAKING IT SO EASY FOR ME.

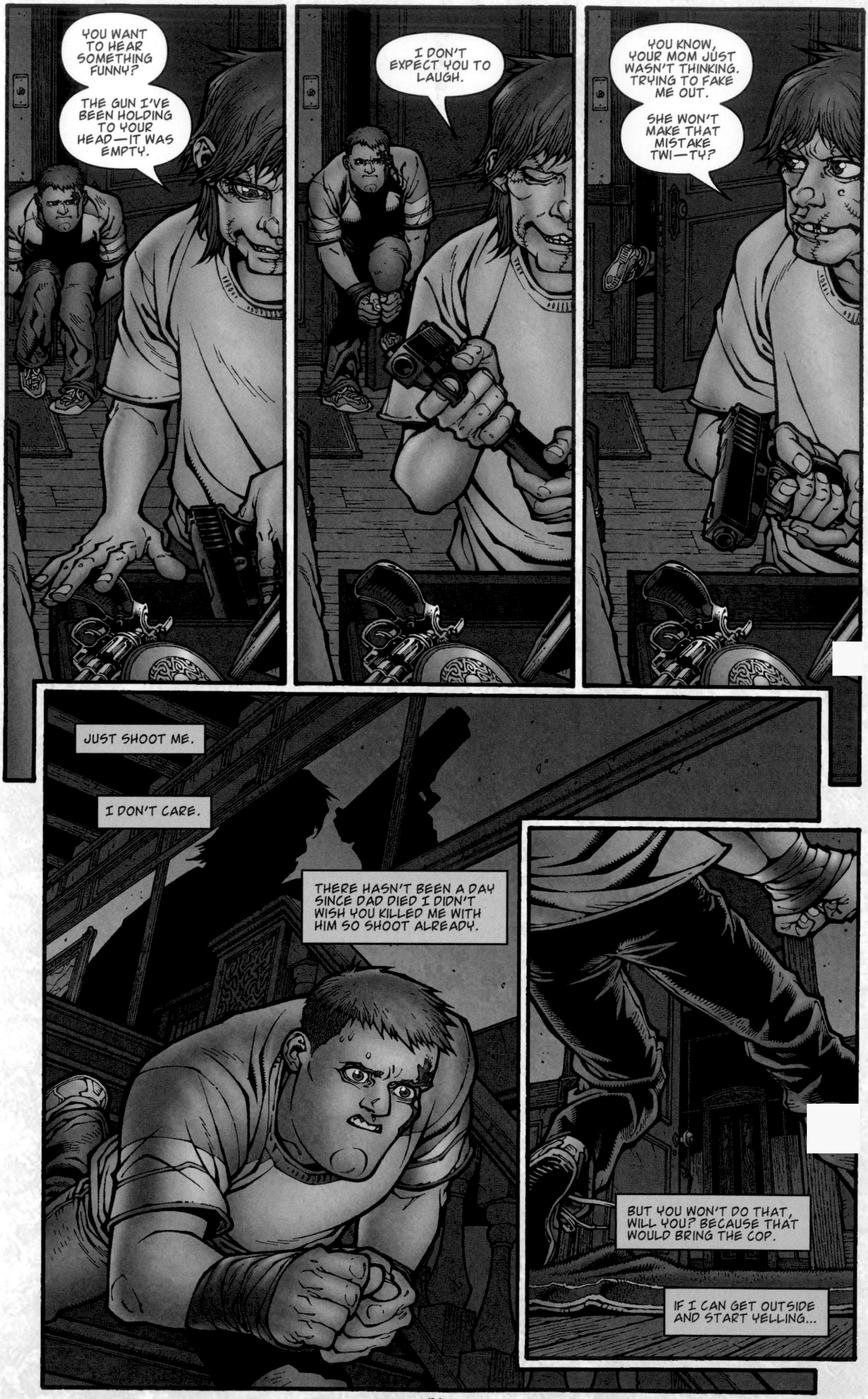
YOU WANT TO HEAR SOMETHING FUNNY?
THE GUN I'VE BEEN HOLDING TO YOUR HEAD—IT WAS EMPTY.
I DON'T EXPECT YOU TO LAUGH.
YOU KNOW, YOUR MOM JUST WASN'T THINKING. TRYING TO FAKE ME OUT.
SHE WON'T MAKE THAT MISTAKE TWI—TY?
JUST SHOOT ME.
I DON'T CARE.
THERE HASN'T BEEN A DAY SINCE DAD DIED I DIDN'T WISH YOU KILLED ME WITH HIM SO SHOOT ALREADY.
BUT YOU WON'T DO THAT, WILL YOU? BECAUSE THAT WOULD BRING THE COP.
IF I CAN GET OUTSIDE AND START YELLING...

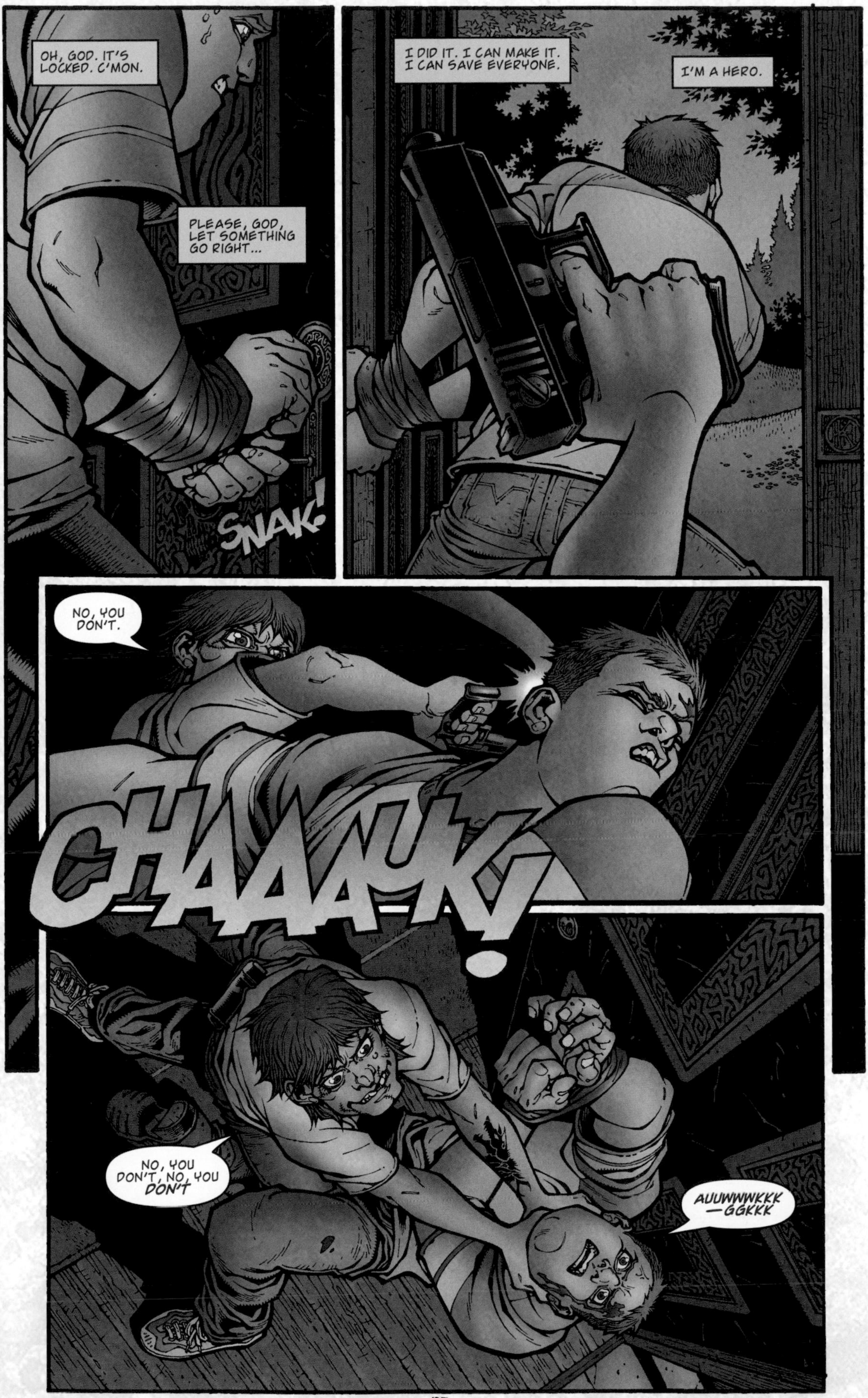
OH, GOD. IT'S LOCKED. C'MON.
PLEASE, GOD, LET SOMETHING GO RIGHT...
SNAK!
I DID IT. I CAN MAKE IT. I CAN SAVE EVERYONE.
I'M A HERO.
NO, YOU DON'T.
CHAAAUK!
NO, YOU DON'T, NO, YOU DON'T
AUUWWWKKK —GGKKK

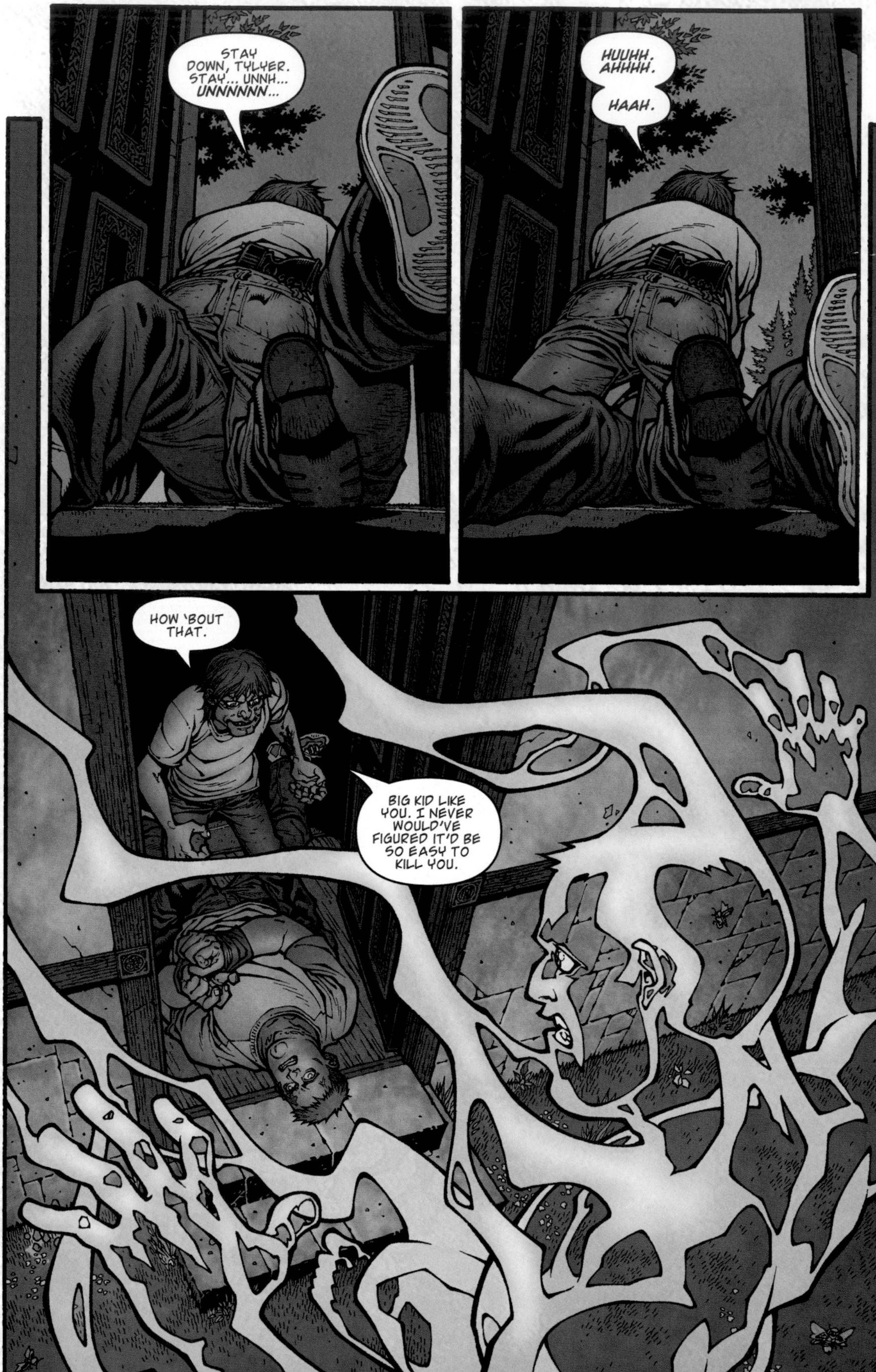
STAY DOWN, TYLYER. STAY... UNNH... UNNNNNN...
HUUHH. AHHHH.
HAAH.
HOW 'BOUT THAT.
BIG KID LIKE YOU. I NEVER WOULD'VE FIGURED IT'D BE SO EASY TO KILL YOU.

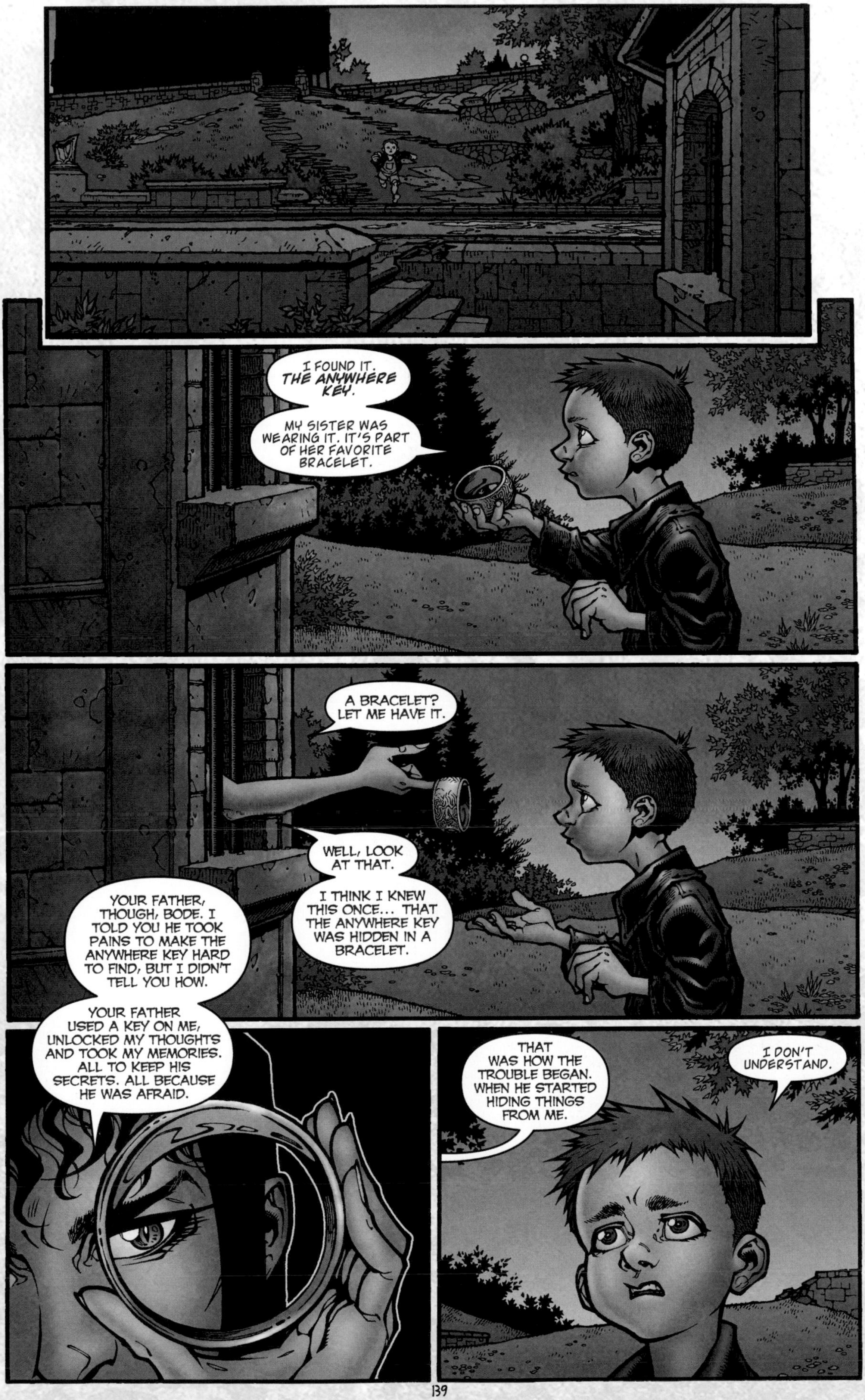
I FOUND IT. *THE ANYWHERE KEY.*
MY SISTER WAS WEARING IT. IT'S PART OF HER FAVORITE BRACELET.
A BRACELET? LET ME HAVE IT.
WELL, LOOK AT THAT.
I THINK I KNEW THIS ONCE... THAT THE ANYWHERE KEY WAS HIDDEN IN A BRACELET.
YOUR FATHER, THOUGH, BODE. I TOLD YOU HE TOOK PAINS TO MAKE THE ANYWHERE KEY HARD TO FIND, BUT I DIDN'T TELL YOU HOW.
YOUR FATHER USED A KEY ON ME, UNLOCKED MY THOUGHTS AND TOOK MY MEMORIES. ALL TO KEEP HIS SECRETS. ALL BECAUSE HE WAS AFRAID.
THAT WAS HOW THE TROUBLE BEGAN. WHEN HE STARTED HIDING THINGS FROM ME.
I DON'T UNDERSTAND.

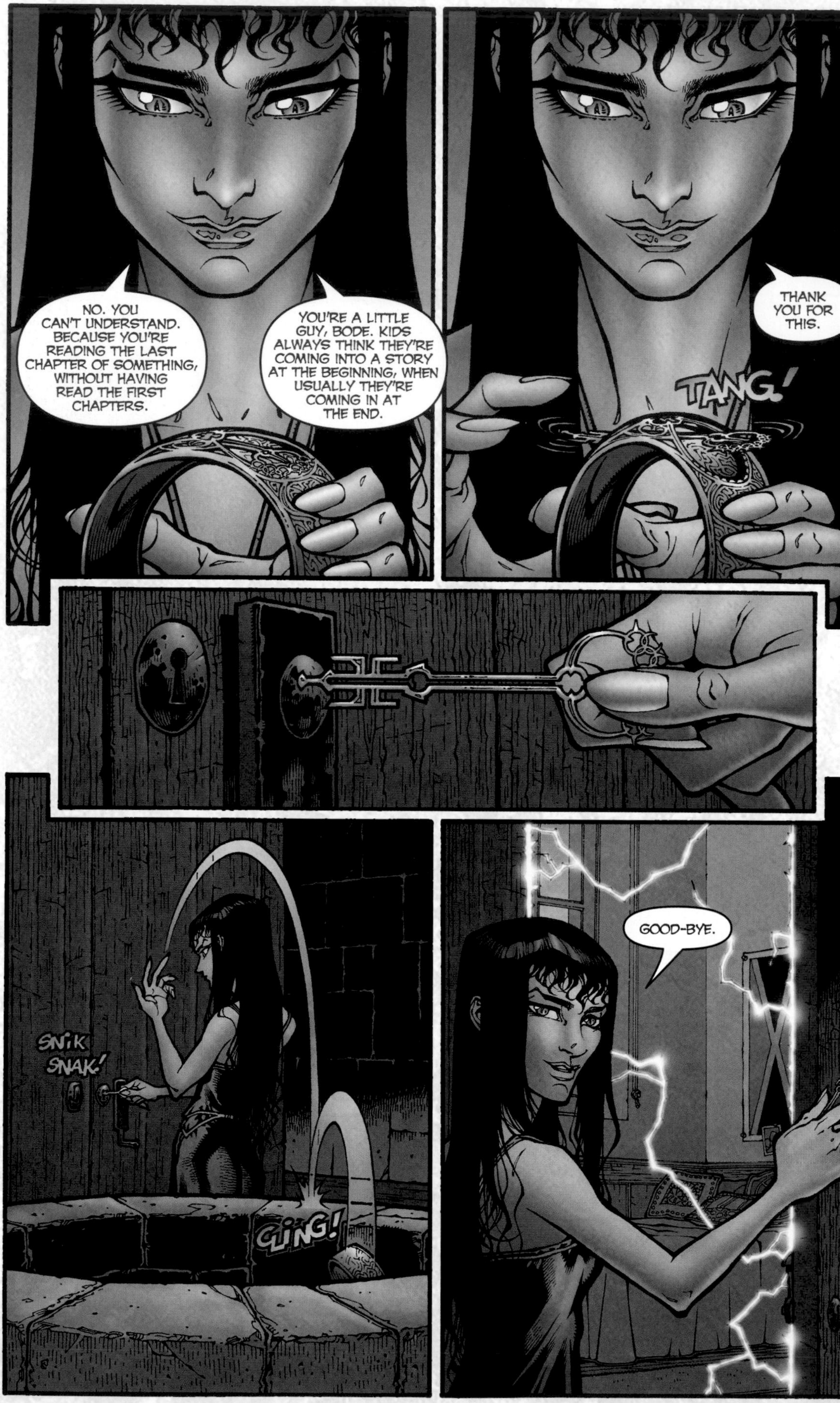

NO. YOU CAN'T UNDERSTAND. BECAUSE YOU'RE READING THE LAST CHAPTER OF SOMETHING, WITHOUT HAVING READ THE FIRST CHAPTERS.
YOU'RE A LITTLE GUY, BODE. KIDS ALWAYS THINK THEY'RE COMING INTO A STORY AT THE BEGINNING, WHEN USUALLY THEY'RE COMING IN AT THE END.
THANK YOU FOR THIS.
TANG!
SNIK SNAK!
CLING!
GOOD-BYE.

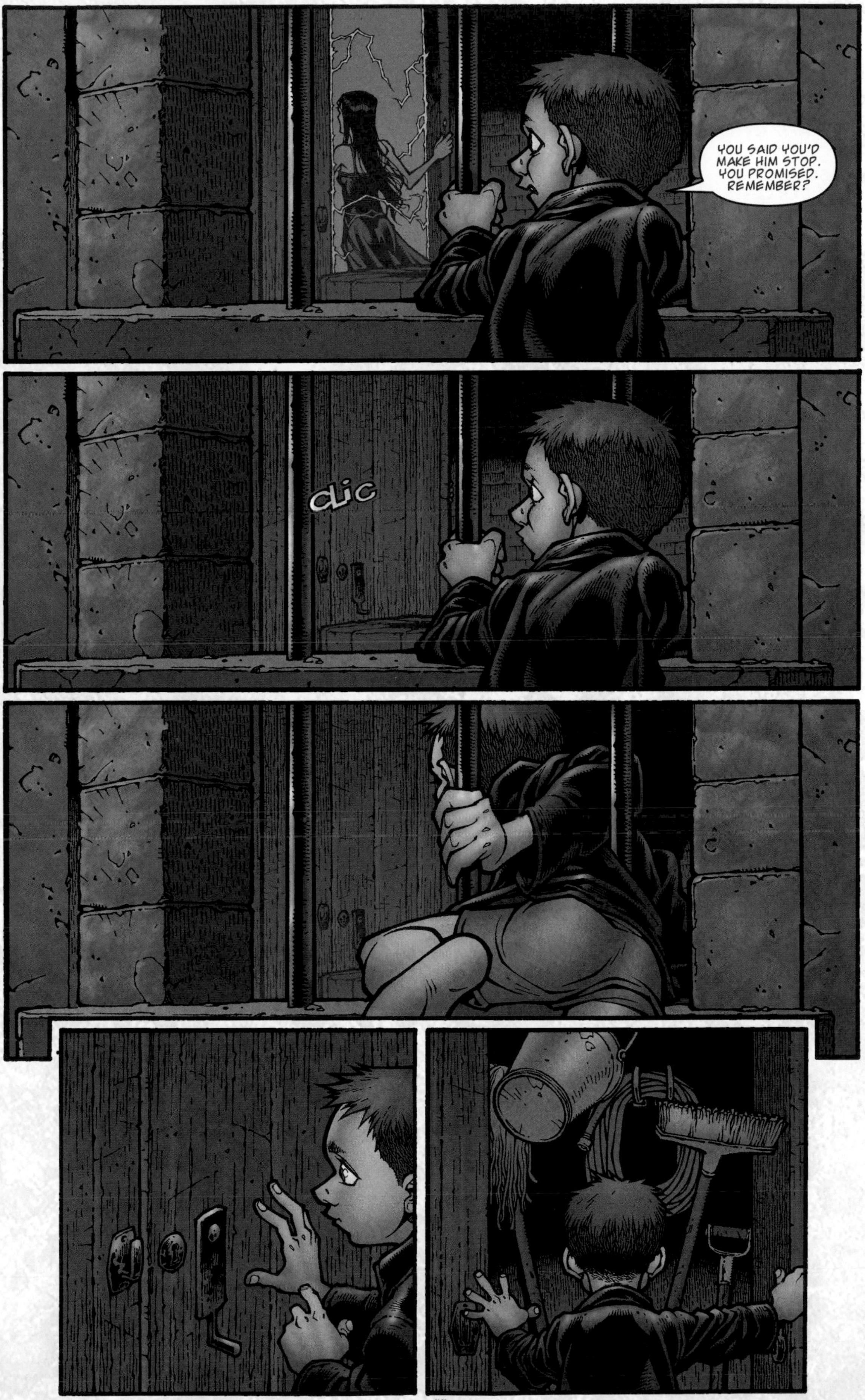

YOU SAID YOU'D MAKE HIM STOP. YOU PROMISED. REMEMBER?
clic

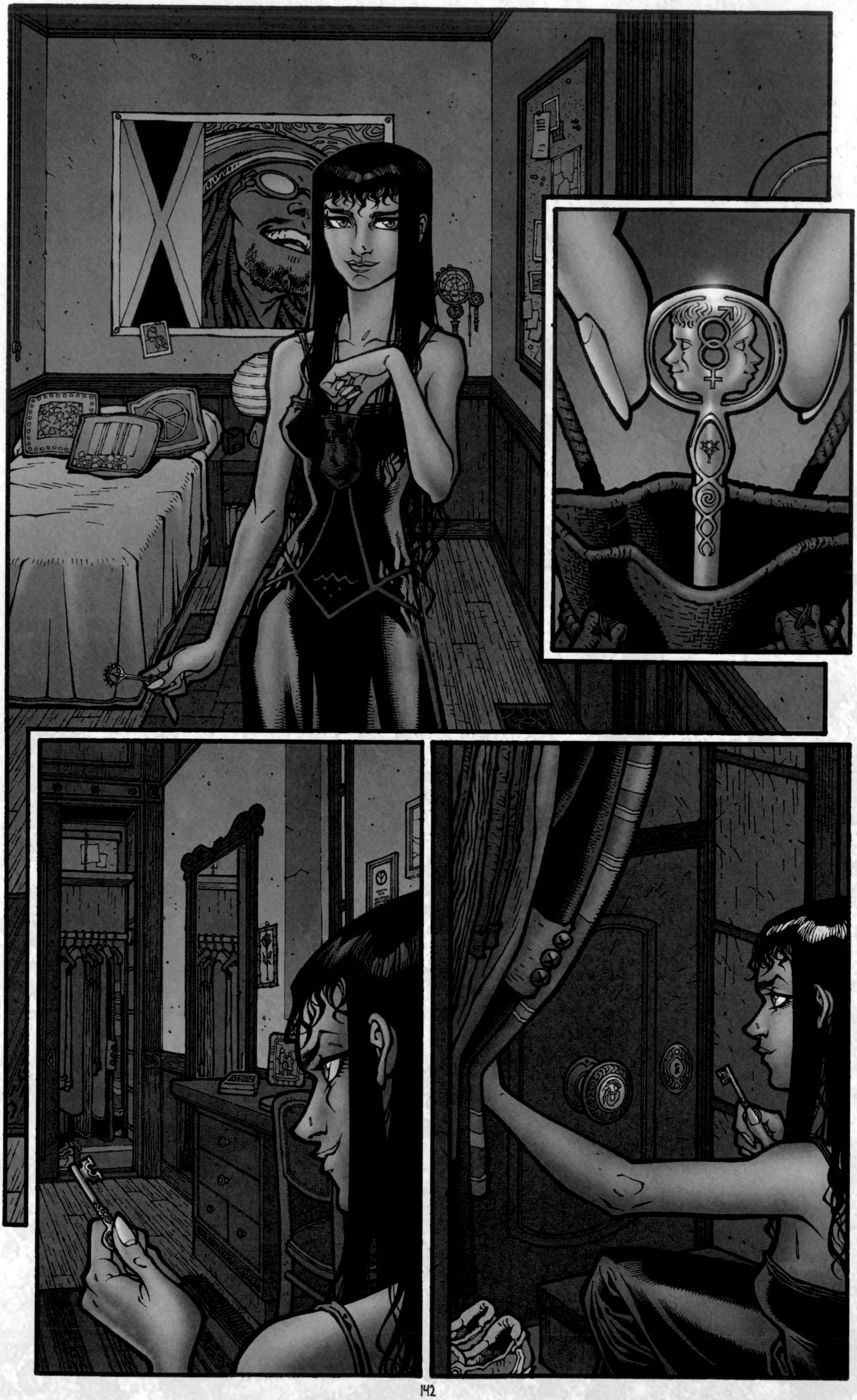

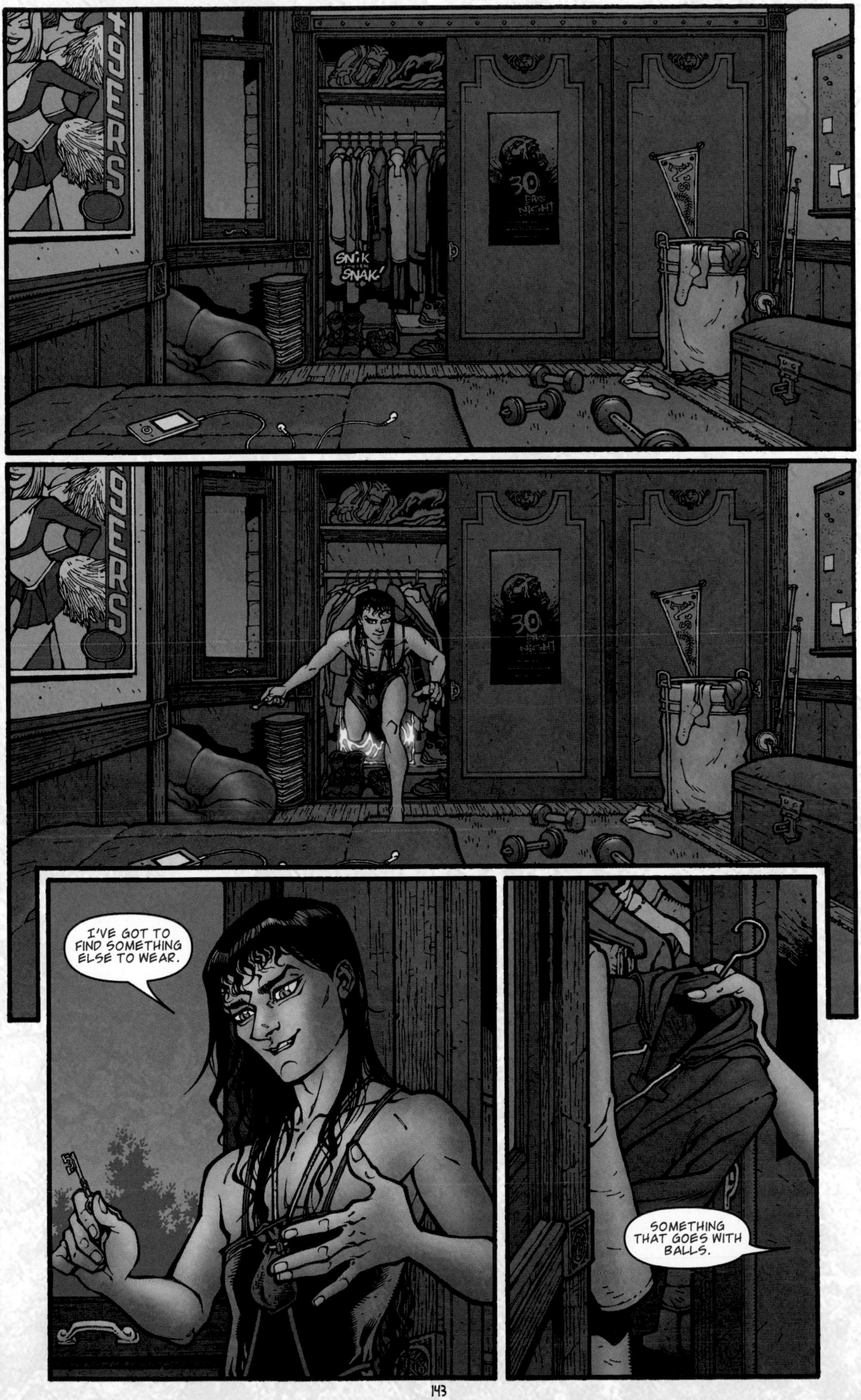
49ERS
30 DAYS NIGHT
SNIK SNAK!
I'VE GOT TO FIND SOMETHING ELSE TO WEAR.
SOMETHING THAT GOES WITH BALLS.

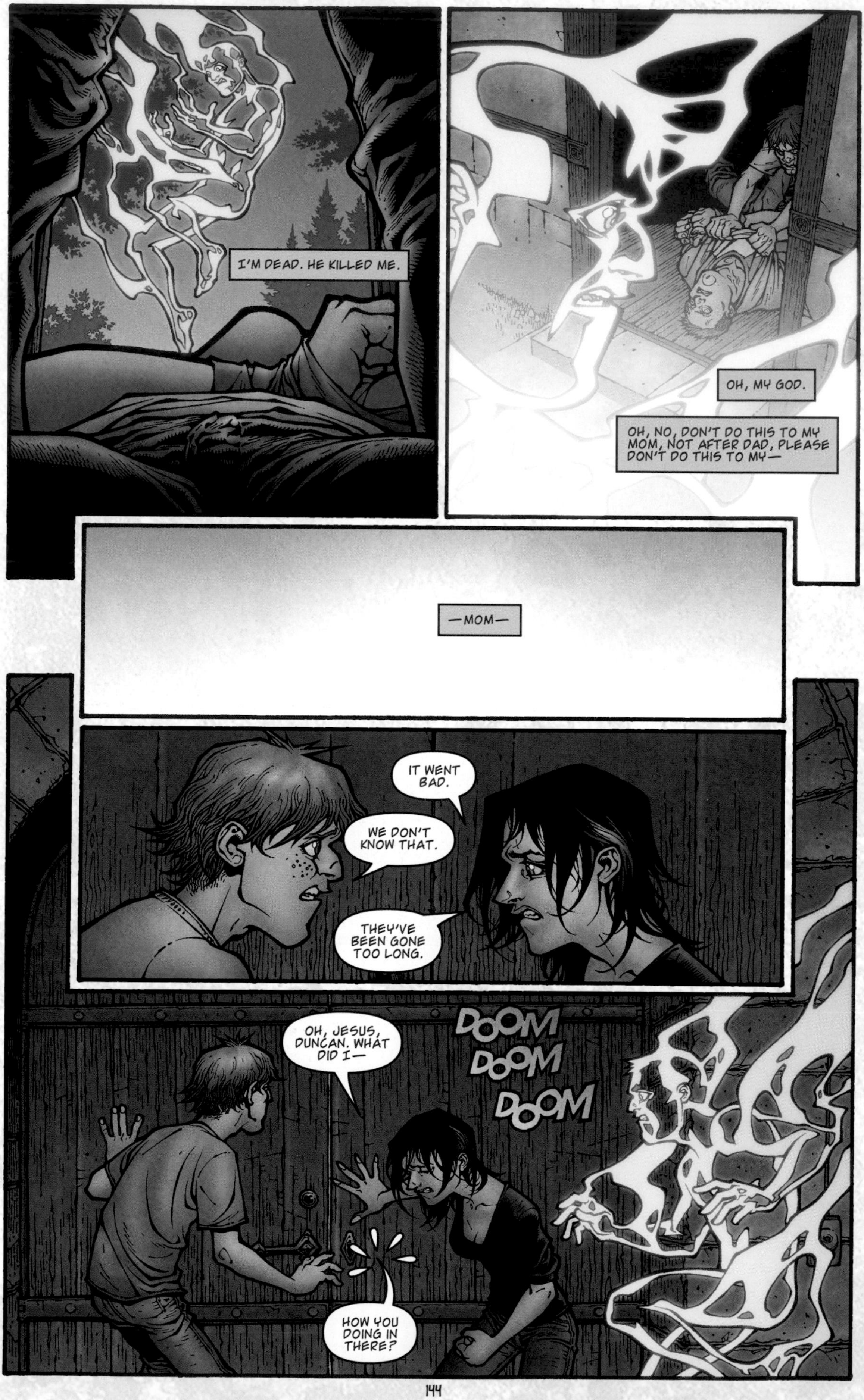
I'M DEAD. HE KILLED ME.
OH, MY GOD.
OH, NO, DON'T DO THIS TO MY MOM, NOT AFTER DAD, PLEASE DON'T DO THIS TO MY—
—MOM—
IT WENT BAD.
WE DON'T KNOW THAT.
THEY'VE BEEN GONE TOO LONG.
OH, JESUS, DUNCAN. WHAT DID I—
DOOM
DOOM
DOOM
HOW YOU DOING IN THERE?

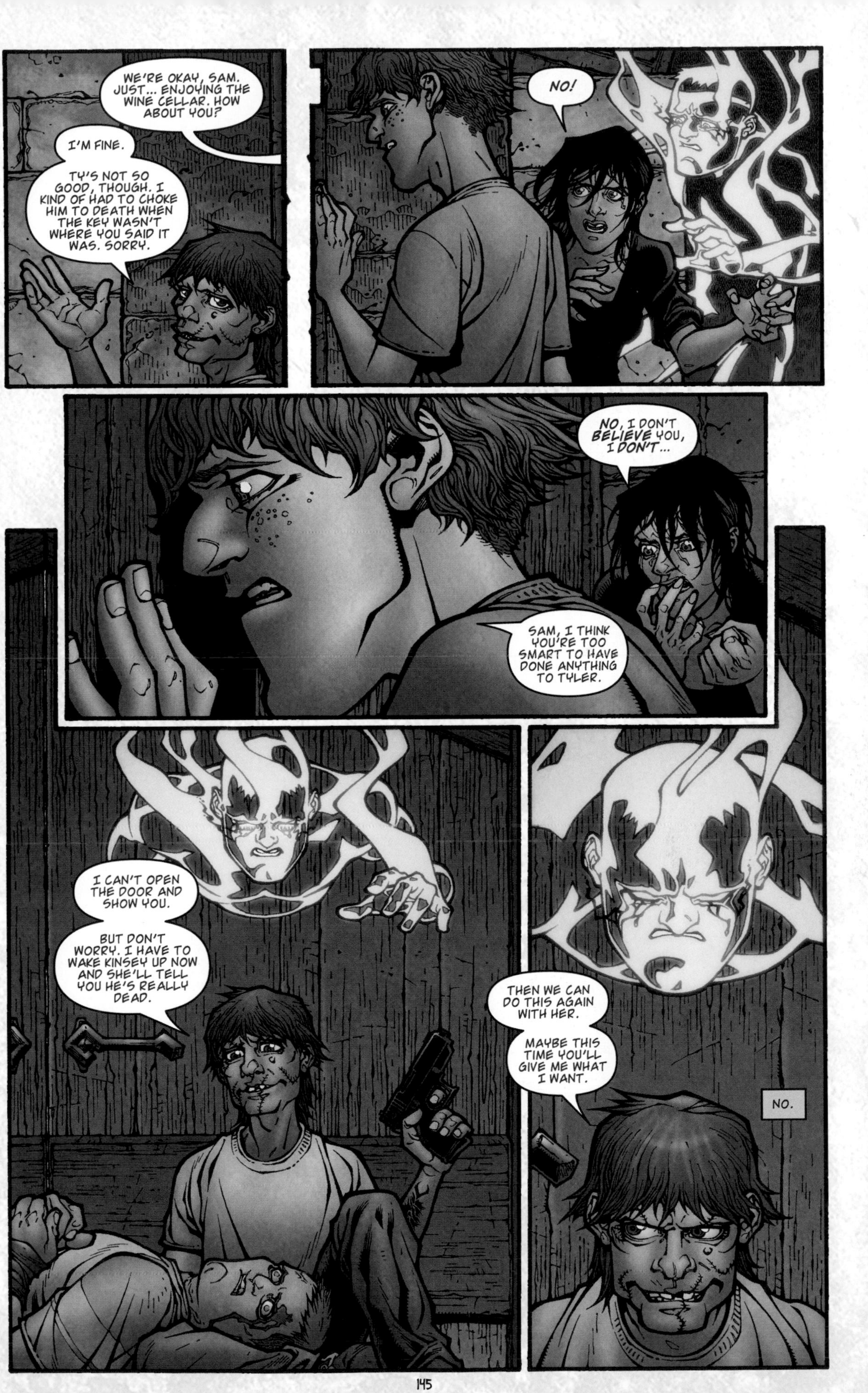
WE'RE OKAY, SAM. JUST... ENJOYING THE WINE CELLAR. HOW ABOUT YOU?
I'M FINE.
TY'S NOT SO GOOD, THOUGH. I KIND OF HAD TO CHOKE HIM TO DEATH WHEN THE KEY WASN'T WHERE YOU SAID IT WAS. SORRY.
NO!
NO, I DON'T BELIEVE YOU, I DON'T...
SAM, I THINK YOU'RE TOO SMART TO HAVE DONE ANYTHING TO TYLER.
I CAN'T OPEN THE DOOR AND SHOW YOU.
BUT DON'T WORRY. I HAVE TO WAKE KINSEY UP NOW AND SHE'LL TELL YOU HE'S REALLY DEAD.
THEN WE CAN DO THIS AGAIN WITH HER.
MAYBE THIS TIME YOU'LL GIVE ME WHAT I WANT.
NO.

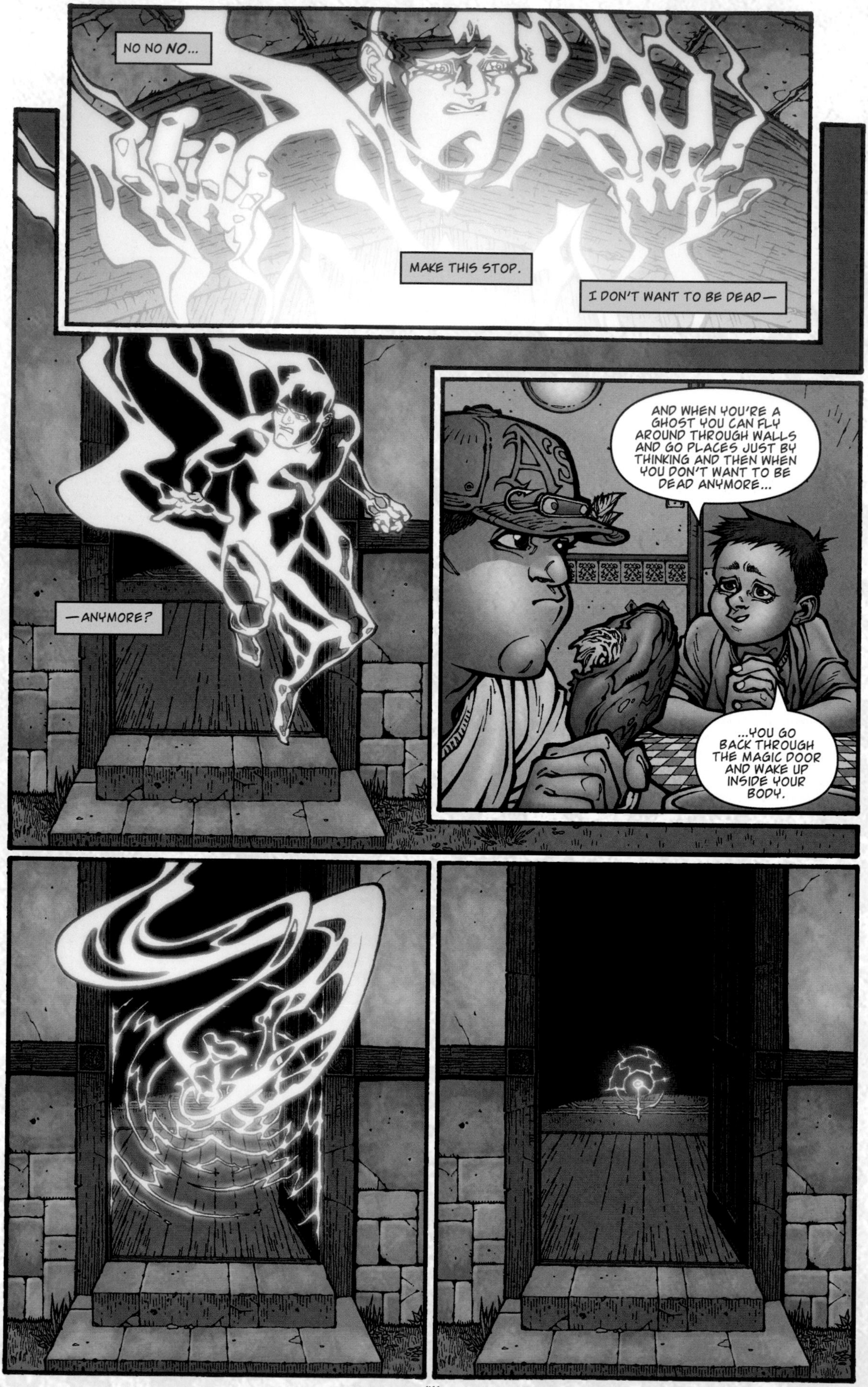

NO NO NO...
MAKE THIS STOP.
I DON'T WANT TO BE DEAD—
—ANYMORE?
AND WHEN YOU'RE A GHOST YOU CAN FLY AROUND THROUGH WALLS AND GO PLACES JUST BY THINKING AND THEN WHEN YOU DON'T WANT TO BE DEAD ANYMORE...
...YOU GO BACK THROUGH THE MAGIC DOOR AND WAKE UP INSIDE YOUR BODY.

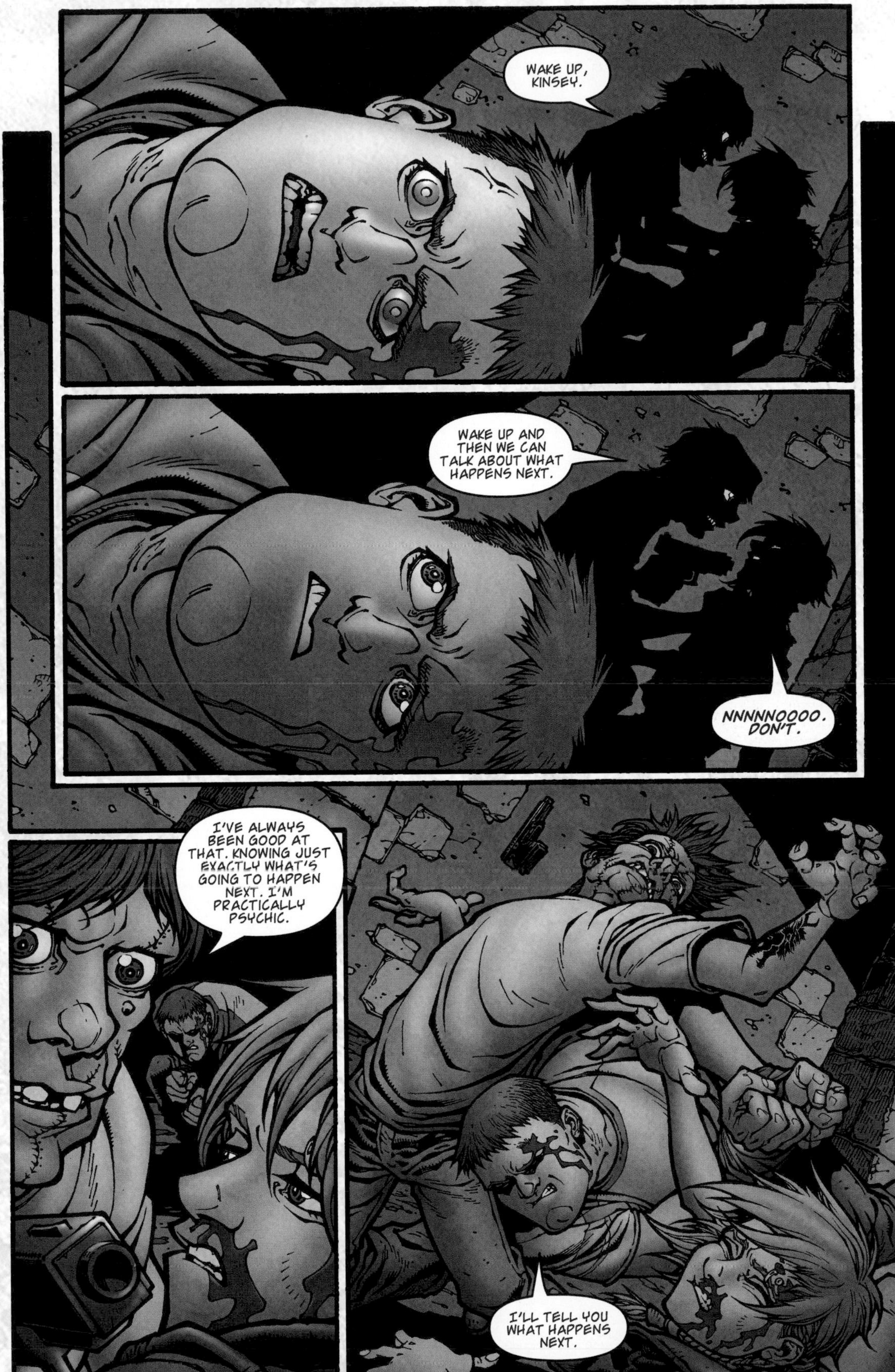
WAKE UP, KINSEY.
WAKE UP AND THEN WE CAN TALK ABOUT WHAT HAPPENS NEXT.
NNNNNOOOO. DON'T.
I'VE ALWAYS BEEN GOOD AT THAT. KNOWING JUST EXACTLY WHAT'S GOING TO HAPPEN NEXT. I'M PRACTICALLY PSYCHIC.
I'LL TELL YOU WHAT HAPPENS NEXT.

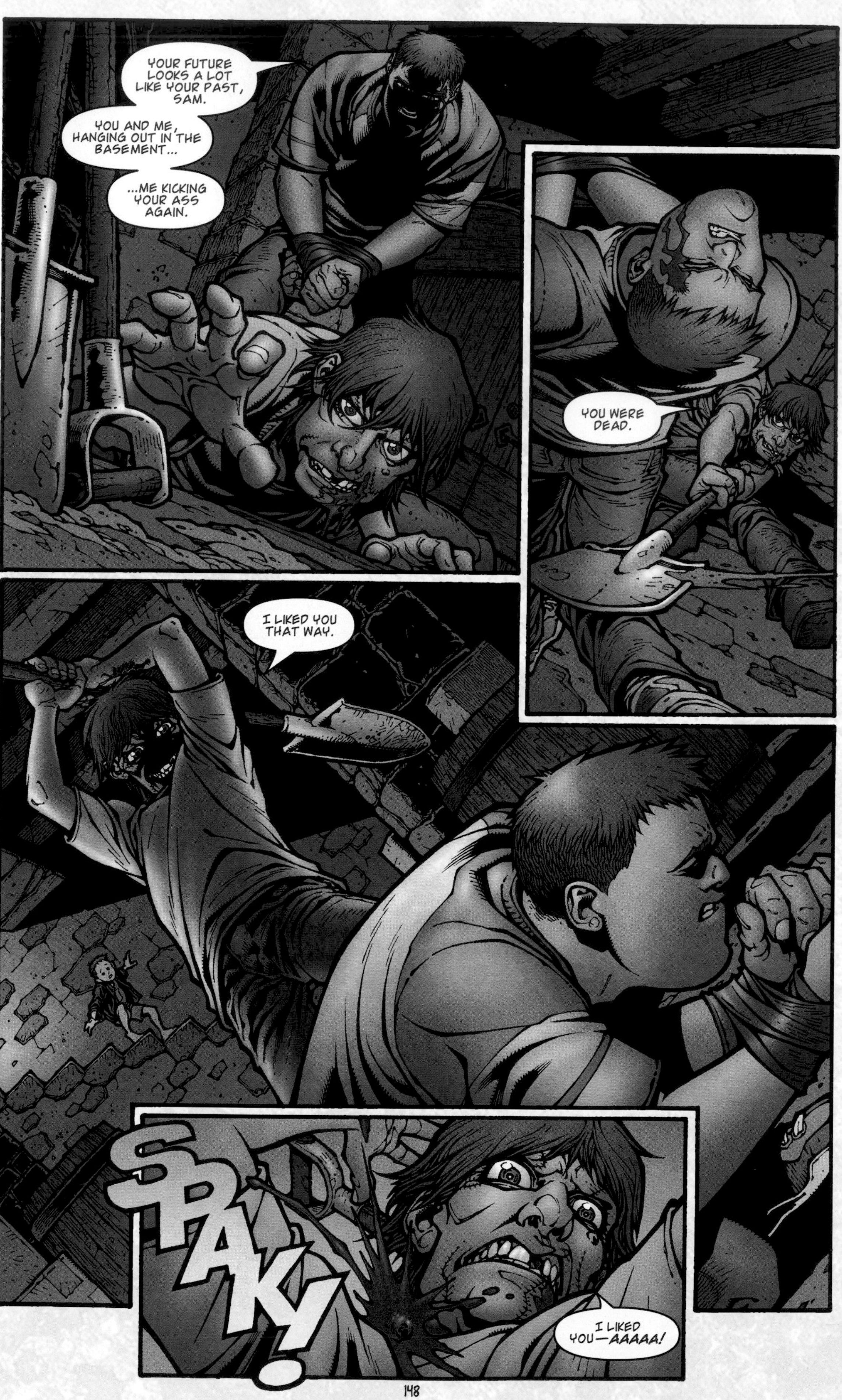
YOUR FUTURE LOOKS A LOT LIKE YOUR PAST, SAM.
YOU AND ME, HANGING OUT IN THE BASEMENT...
...ME KICKING YOUR ASS AGAIN.
YOU WERE DEAD.
I LIKED YOU THAT WAY.
SPAKY!
I LIKED YOU—AAAAA!

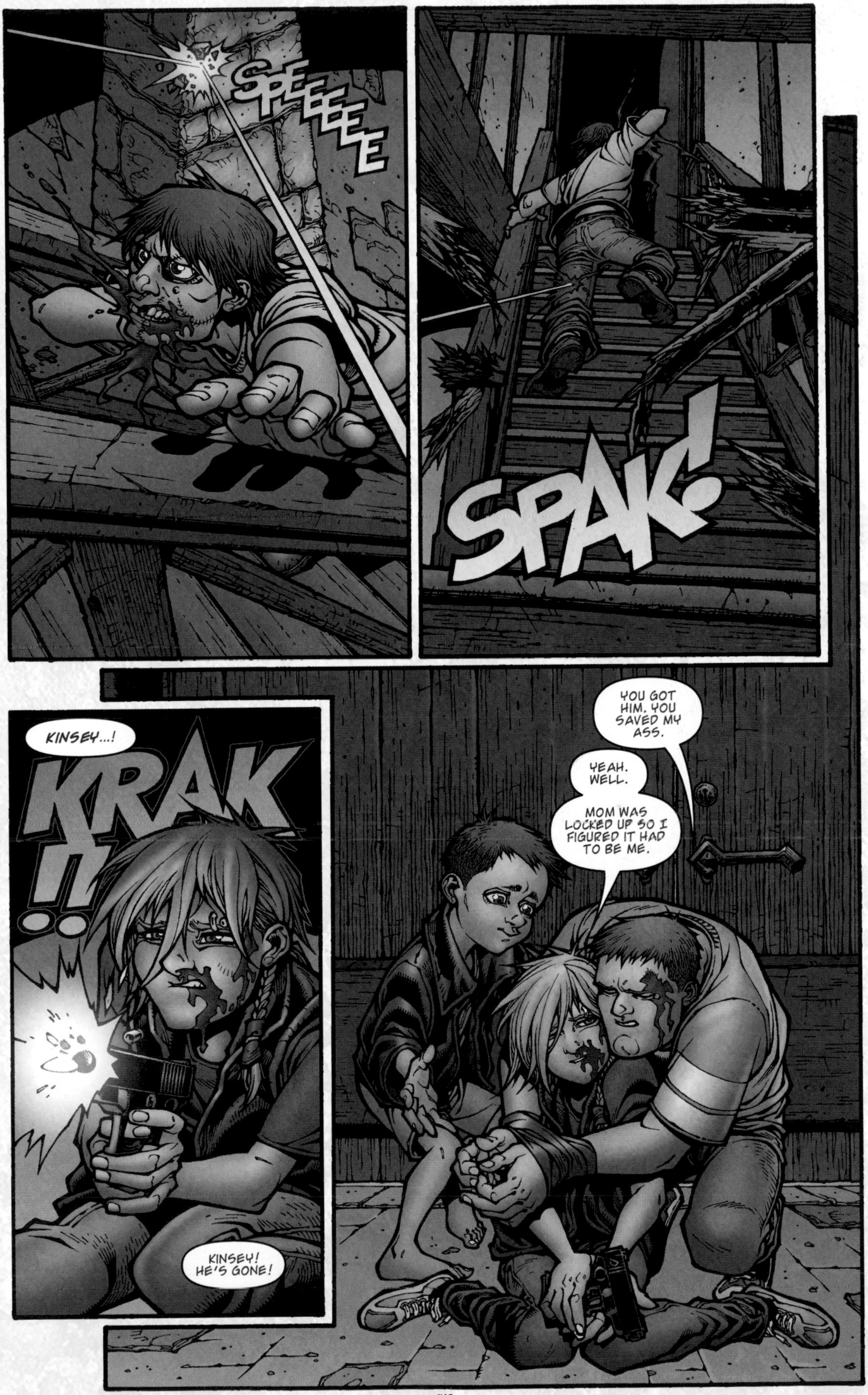
SPEEEEEE
SPAK!
KINSEY...!
KRAKK!!
KINSEY! HE'S GONE!
YOU GOT HIM. YOU SAVED MY ASS.
YEAH. WELL.
MOM WAS LOCKED UP SO I FIGURED IT HAD TO BE ME.

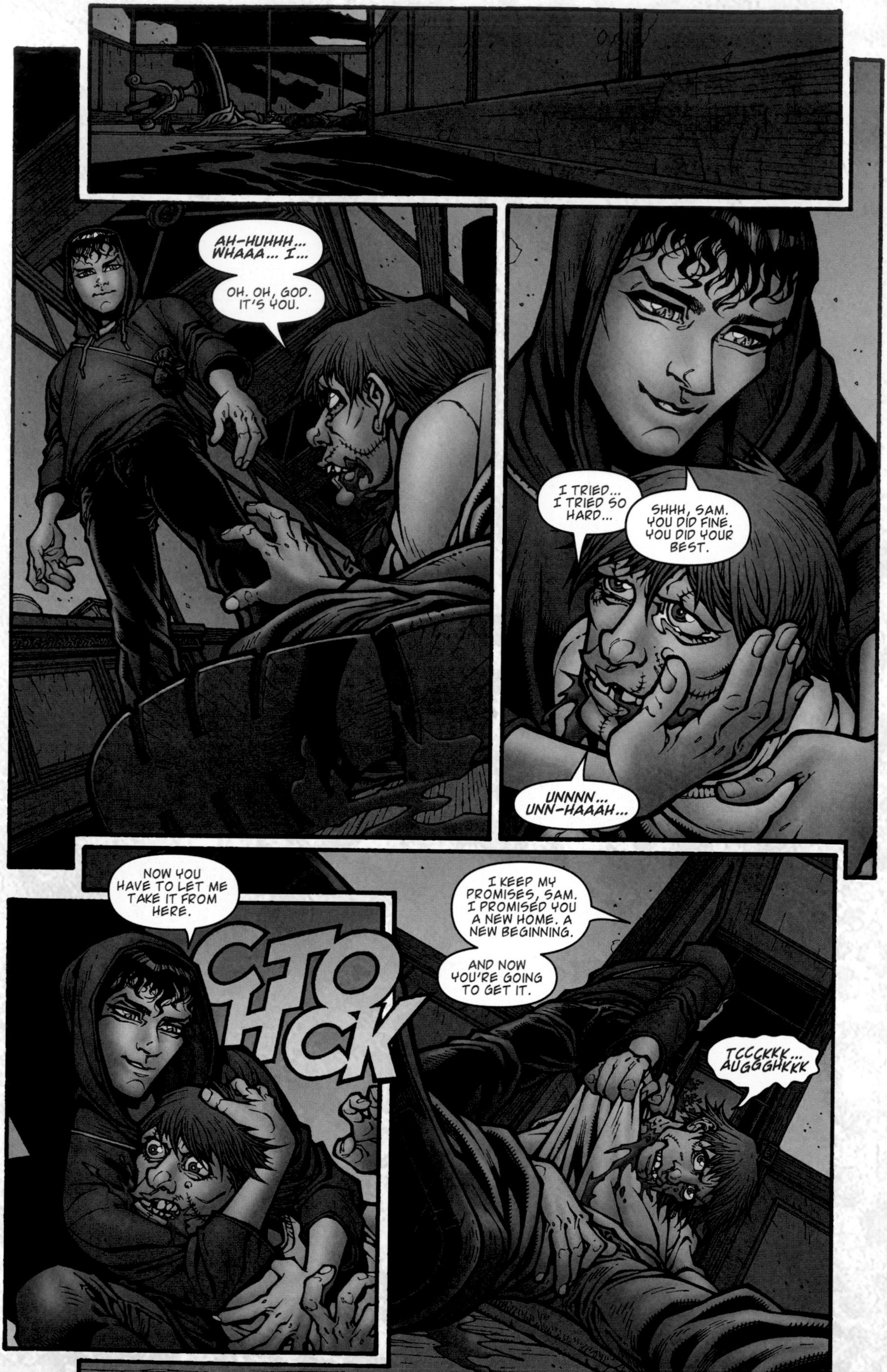
AH-HUHHH... WHAAA... I...
OH. OH, GOD. IT'S YOU.
I TRIED... I TRIED SO HARD...
SHHH, SAM. YOU DID FINE. YOU DID YOUR BEST.
UNNNN... UNN-HAAAH...
NOW YOU HAVE TO LET ME TAKE IT FROM HERE.
CTO HCK
I KEEP MY PROMISES, SAM. I PROMISED YOU A NEW HOME. A NEW BEGINNING.
AND NOW YOU'RE GOING TO GET IT.
TCCCKKK... AUGGGHKKK

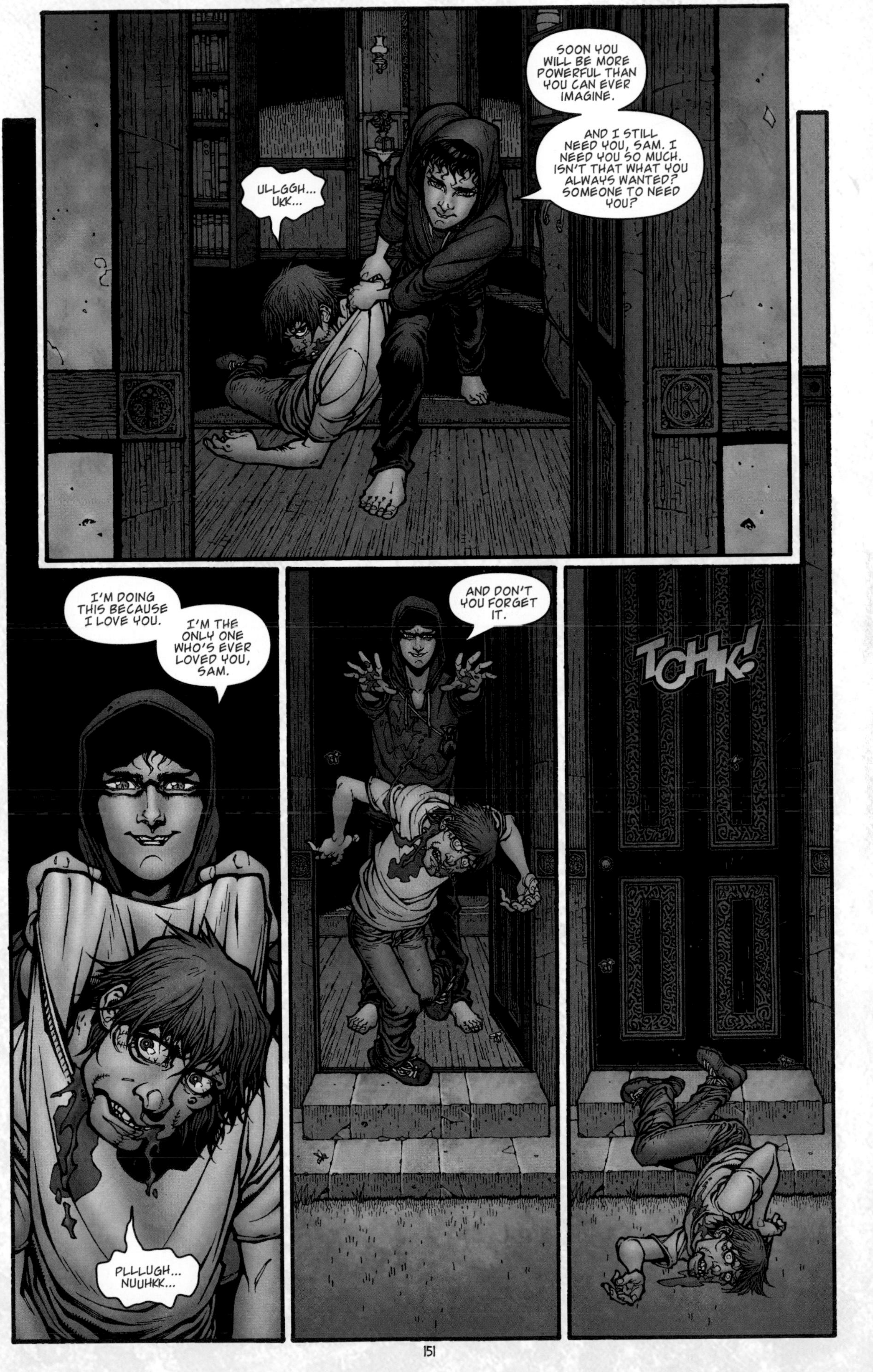

SOON YOU WILL BE MORE POWERFUL THAN YOU CAN EVER IMAGINE.
AND I STILL NEED YOU, SAM. I NEED YOU SO MUCH. ISN'T THAT WHAT YOU ALWAYS WANTED? SOMEONE TO NEED YOU?
ULLGGH... UKK...
I'M DOING THIS BECAUSE I LOVE YOU.
I'M THE ONLY ONE WHO'S EVER LOVED YOU, SAM.
PLLLUGH... NUUHKK...
AND DON'T YOU FORGET IT.
TCHK!

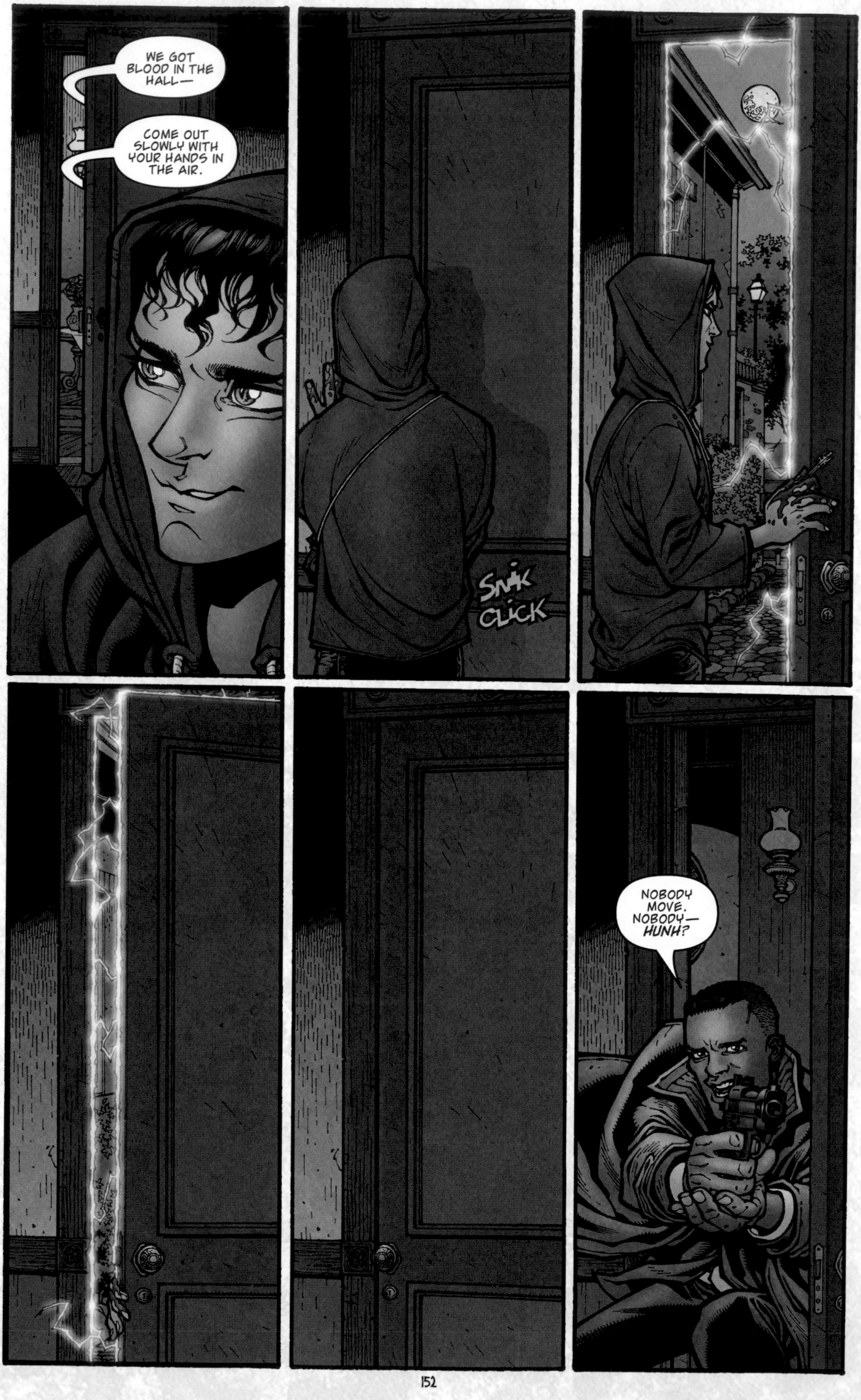
WE GOT BLOOD IN THE HALL—
COME OUT SLOWLY WITH YOUR HANDS IN THE AIR.
SNIK
CLICK
NOBODY MOVE. NOBODY— *HUNH?*

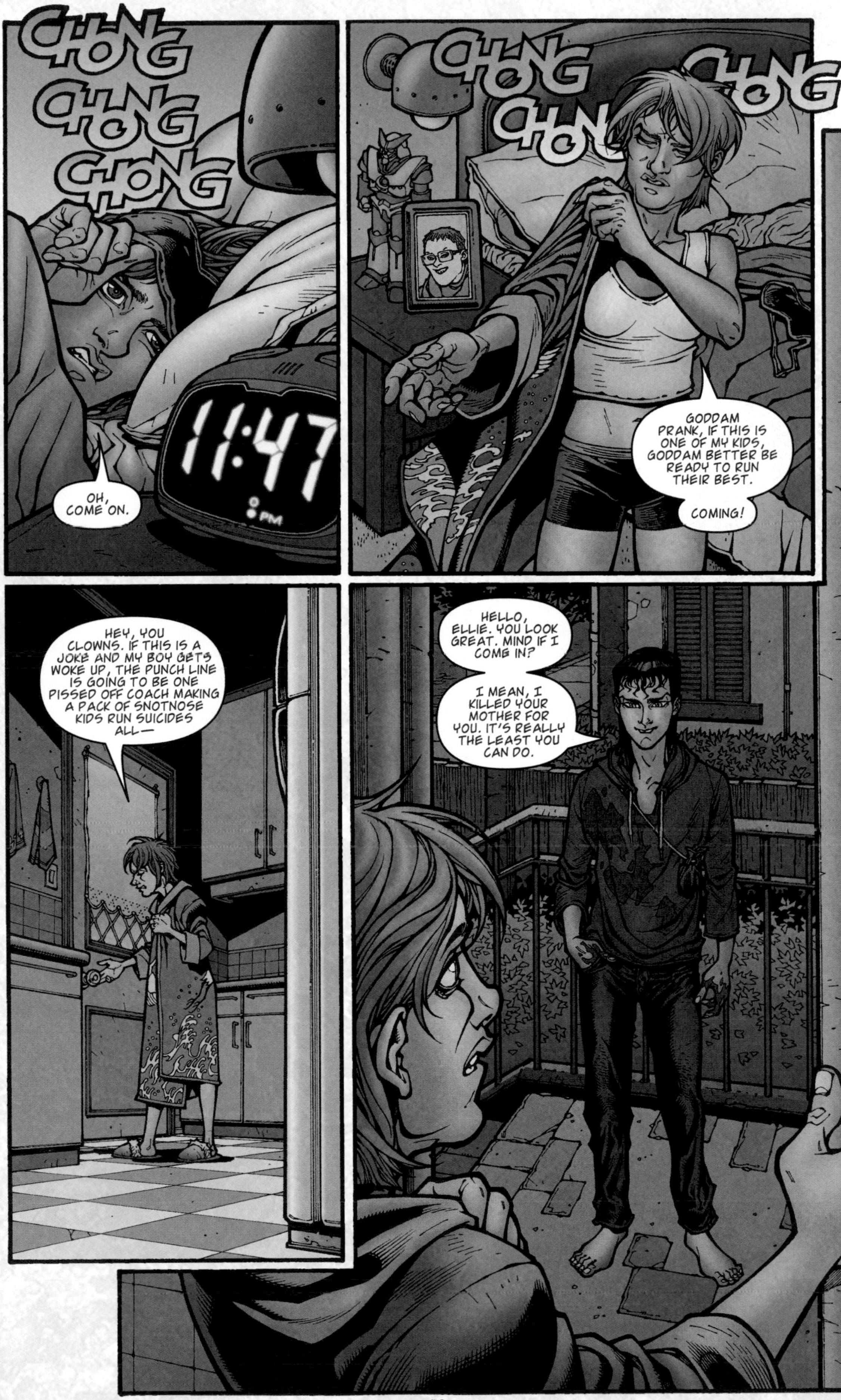
CHONG CHONG CHONG
11:47 PM
OH, COME ON.
CHONG CHONG CHONG
GODDAM PRANK, IF THIS IS ONE OF MY KIDS, GODDAM BETTER BE READY TO RUN THEIR BEST.
COMING!
HEY, YOU CLOWNS. IF THIS IS A JOKE AND MY BOY GETS WOKE UP, THE PUNCH LINE IS GOING TO BE ONE PISSED OFF COACH MAKING A PACK OF SNOTNOSE KIDS RUN SUICIDES ALL—
HELLO, ELLIE. YOU LOOK GREAT. MIND IF I COME IN?
I MEAN, I KILLED YOUR MOTHER FOR YOU. IT'S REALLY THE LEAST YOU CAN DO.

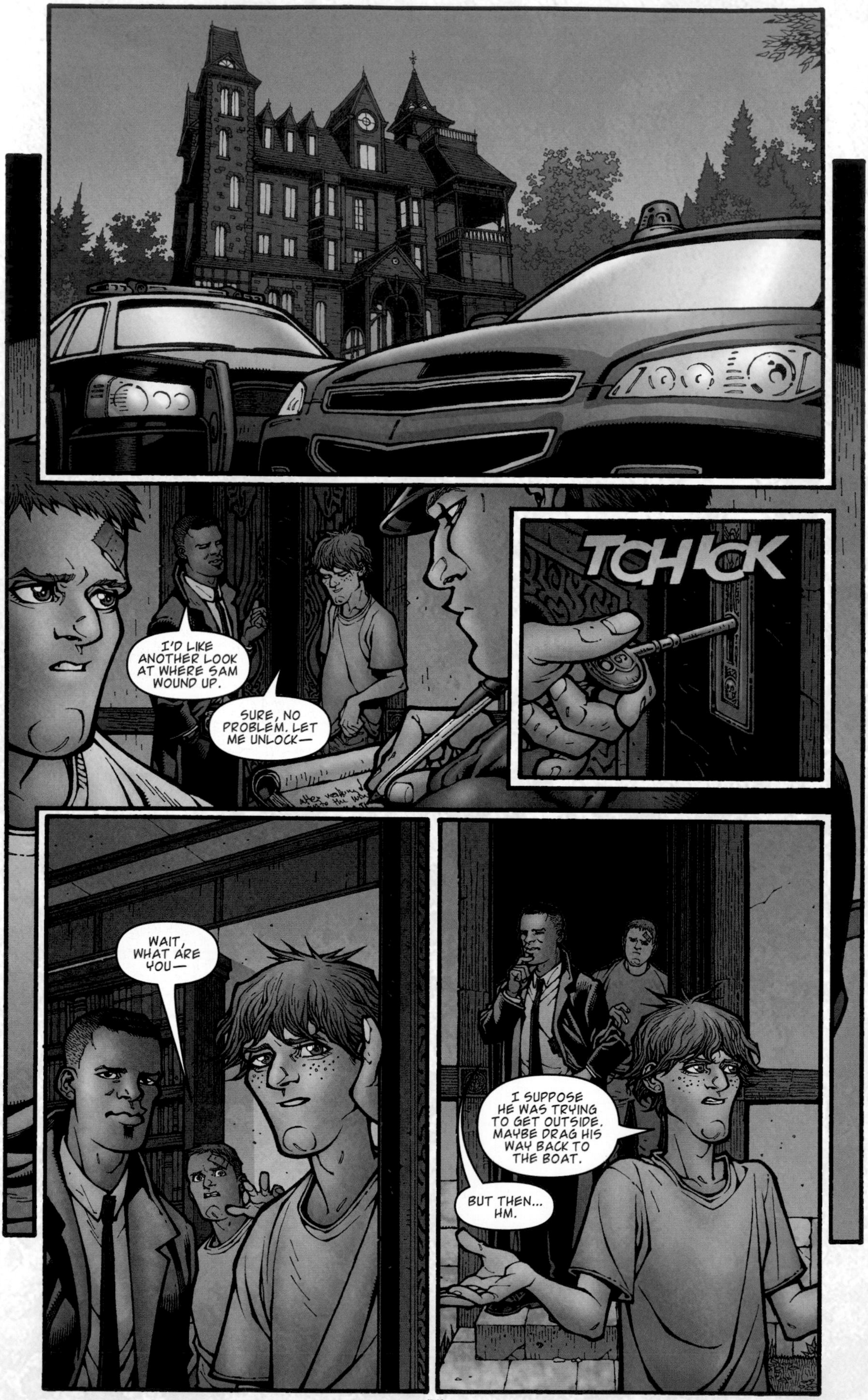
I'D LIKE ANOTHER LOOK AT WHERE SAM WOUND UP.
SURE, NO PROBLEM. LET ME UNLOCK—
TCHICK
WAIT, WHAT ARE YOU—
I SUPPOSE HE WAS TRYING TO GET OUTSIDE. MAYBE DRAG HIS WAY BACK TO THE BOAT.
BUT THEN... HM.

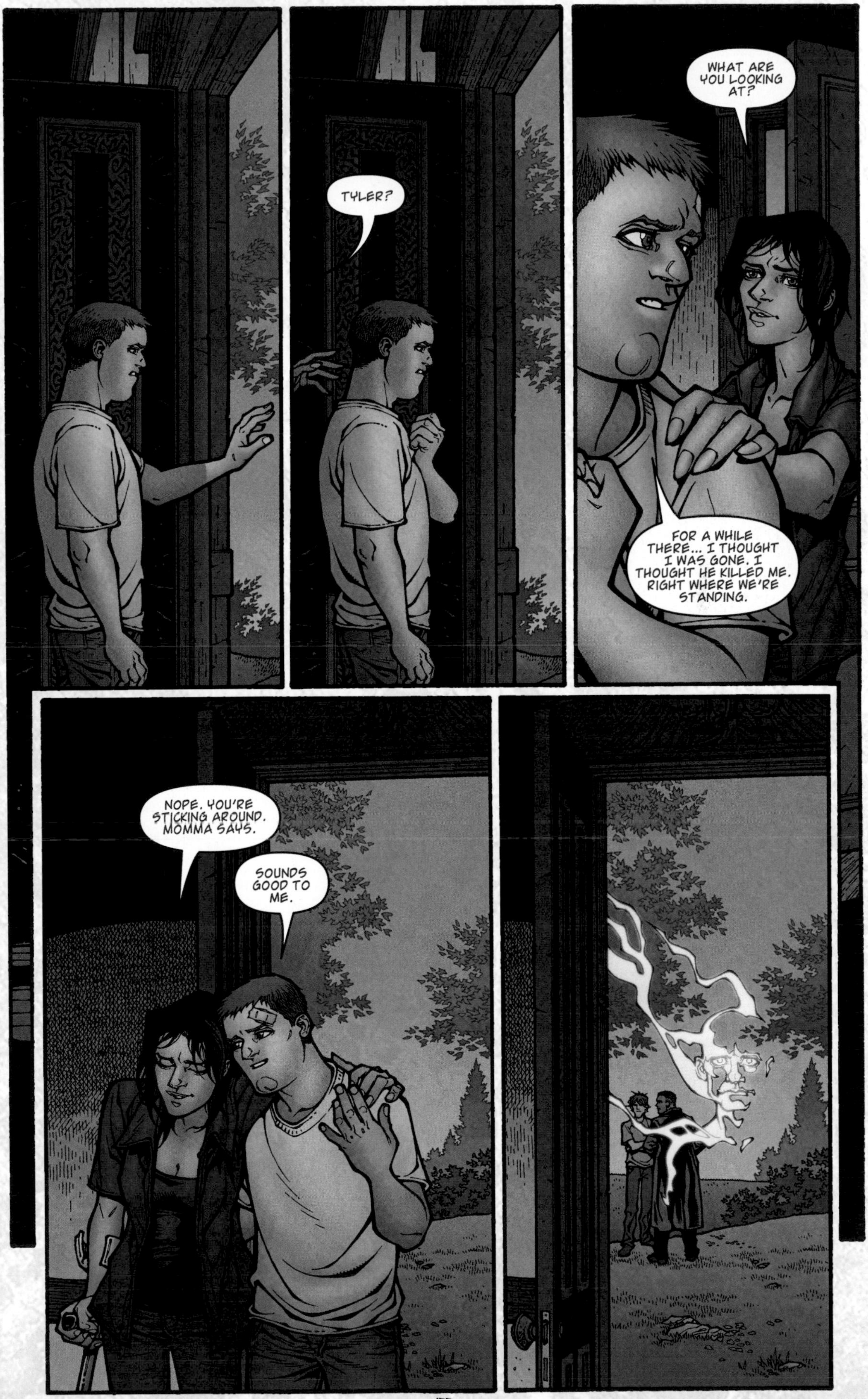
TYLER?
WHAT ARE YOU LOOKING AT?
FOR A WHILE THERE... I THOUGHT I WAS GONE. I THOUGHT HE KILLED ME. RIGHT WHERE WE'RE STANDING.
NOPE. YOU'RE STICKING AROUND. MOMMA SAYS.
SOUNDS GOOD TO ME.

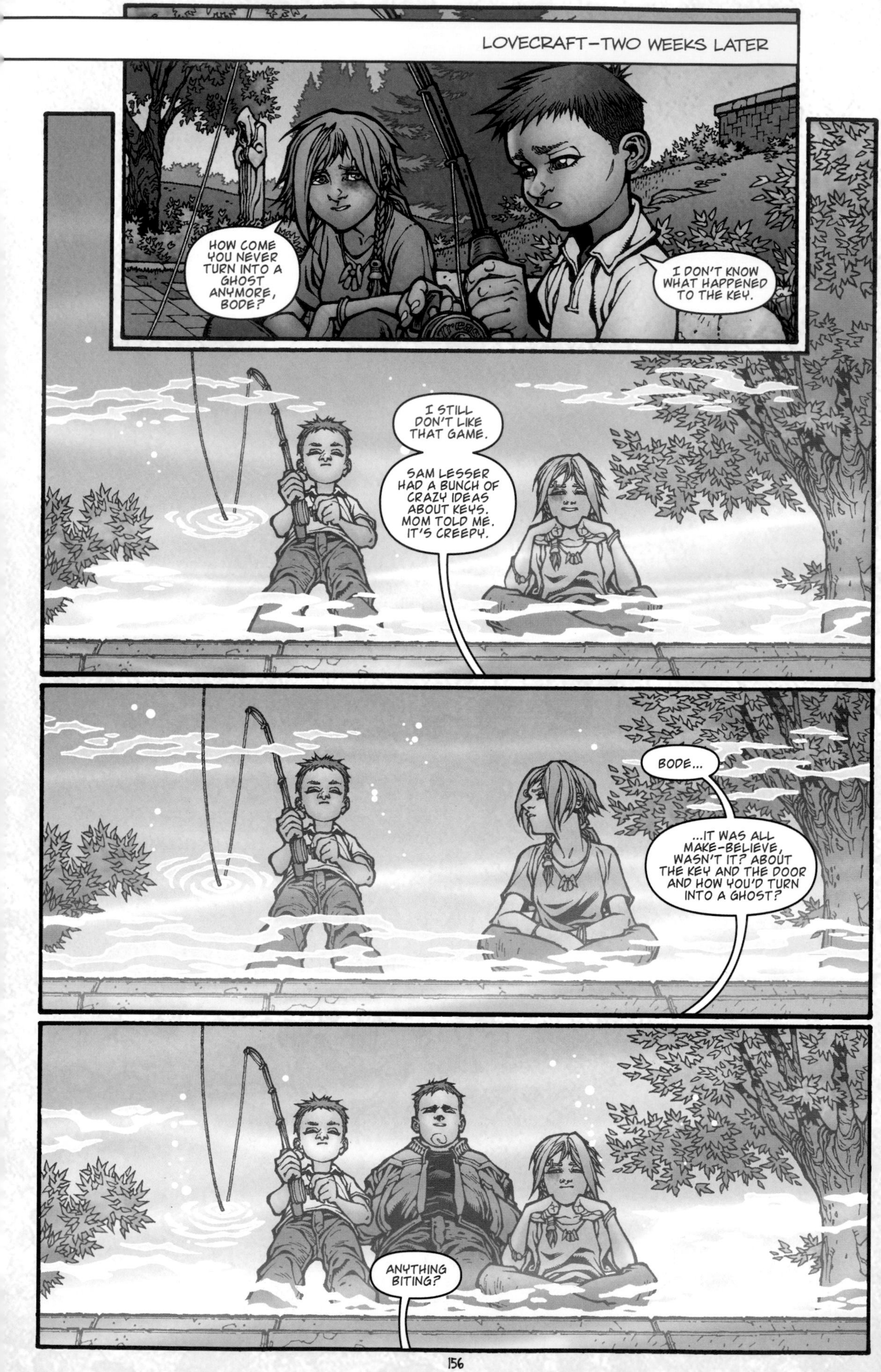

LOVECRAFT—TWO WEEKS LATER
HOW COME YOU NEVER TURN INTO A GHOST ANYMORE, BODE?
I DON'T KNOW WHAT HAPPENED TO THE KEY.
I STILL DON'T LIKE THAT GAME.
SAM LESSER HAD A BUNCH OF CRAZY IDEAS ABOUT KEYS. MOM TOLD ME. IT'S CREEPY.
BODE...
...IT WAS ALL MAKE-BELIEVE, WASN'T IT? ABOUT THE KEY AND THE DOOR AND HOW YOU'D TURN INTO A GHOST?
ANYTHING BITING?

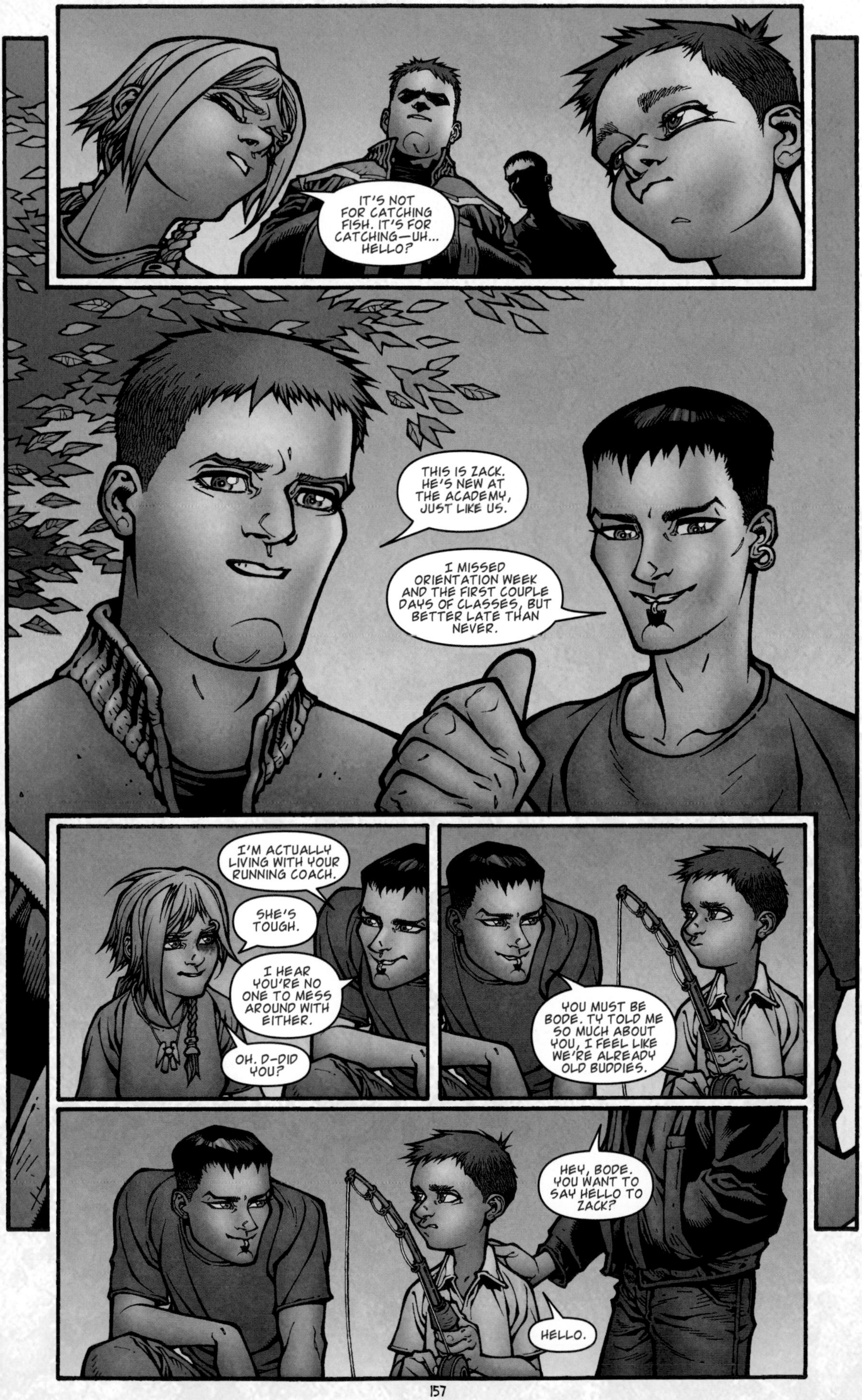
IT'S NOT FOR CATCHING FISH. IT'S FOR CATCHING—UH... HELLO?
THIS IS ZACK. HE'S NEW AT THE ACADEMY, JUST LIKE US.
I MISSED ORIENTATION WEEK AND THE FIRST COUPLE DAYS OF CLASSES, BUT BETTER LATE THAN NEVER.
I'M ACTUALLY LIVING WITH YOUR RUNNING COACH.
SHE'S TOUGH.
I HEAR YOU'RE NO ONE TO MESS AROUND WITH EITHER.
OH. D-DID YOU?
YOU MUST BE BODE. TY TOLD ME SO MUCH ABOUT YOU, I FEEL LIKE WE'RE ALREADY OLD BUDDIES.
HEY, BODE. YOU WANT TO SAY HELLO TO ZACK?
HELLO.

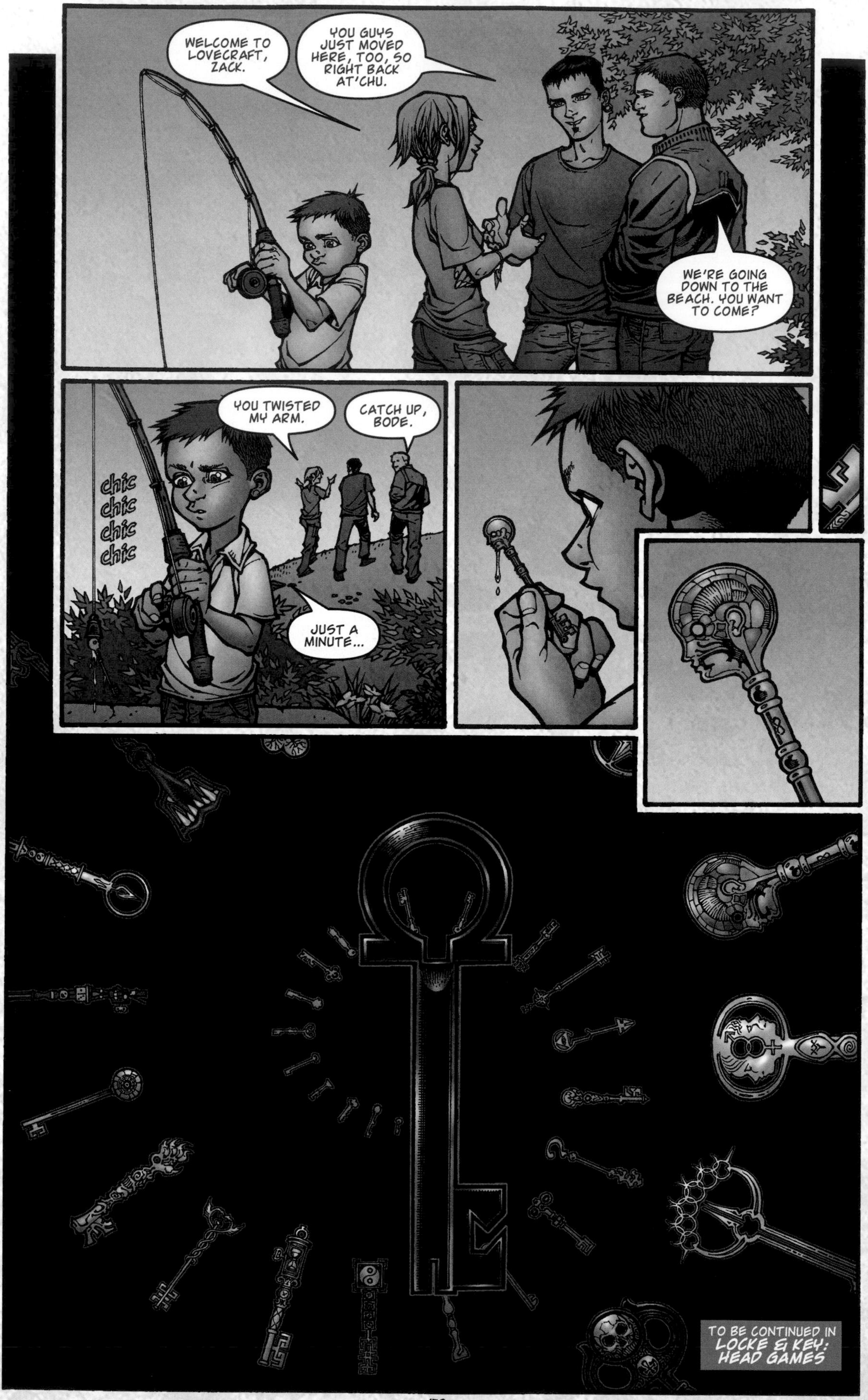
WELCOME TO LOVECRAFT, ZACK.
YOU GUYS JUST MOVED HERE, TOO, SO RIGHT BACK AT'CHU.
WE'RE GOING DOWN TO THE BEACH. YOU WANT TO COME?
YOU TWISTED MY ARM.
CATCH UP, BODE.
chic chic chic chic
JUST A MINUTE...
TO BE CONTINUED IN LOCKE & KEY: HEAD GAMES

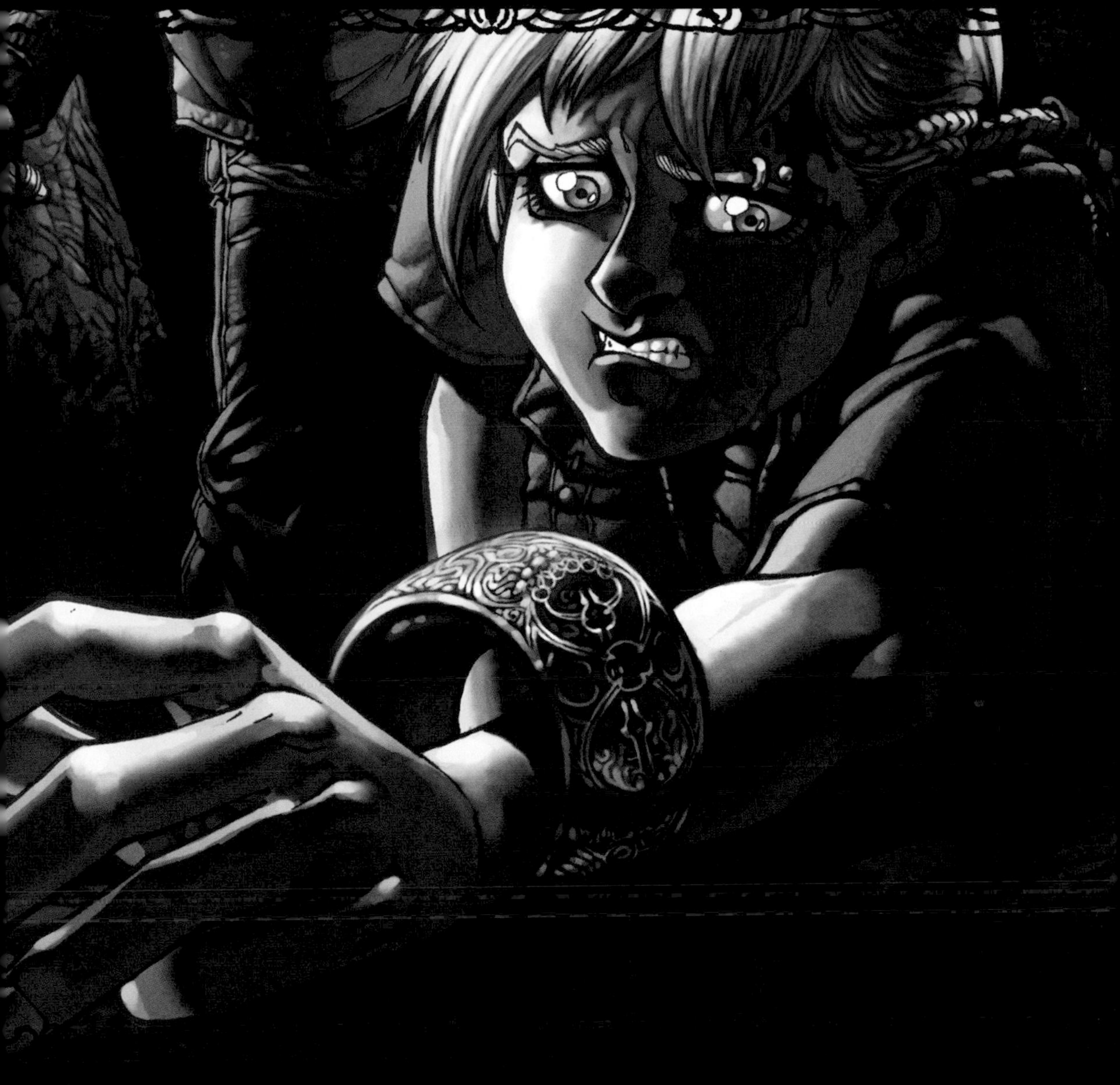

ART GALLERY

BY GABRIEL RODRIGUEZ

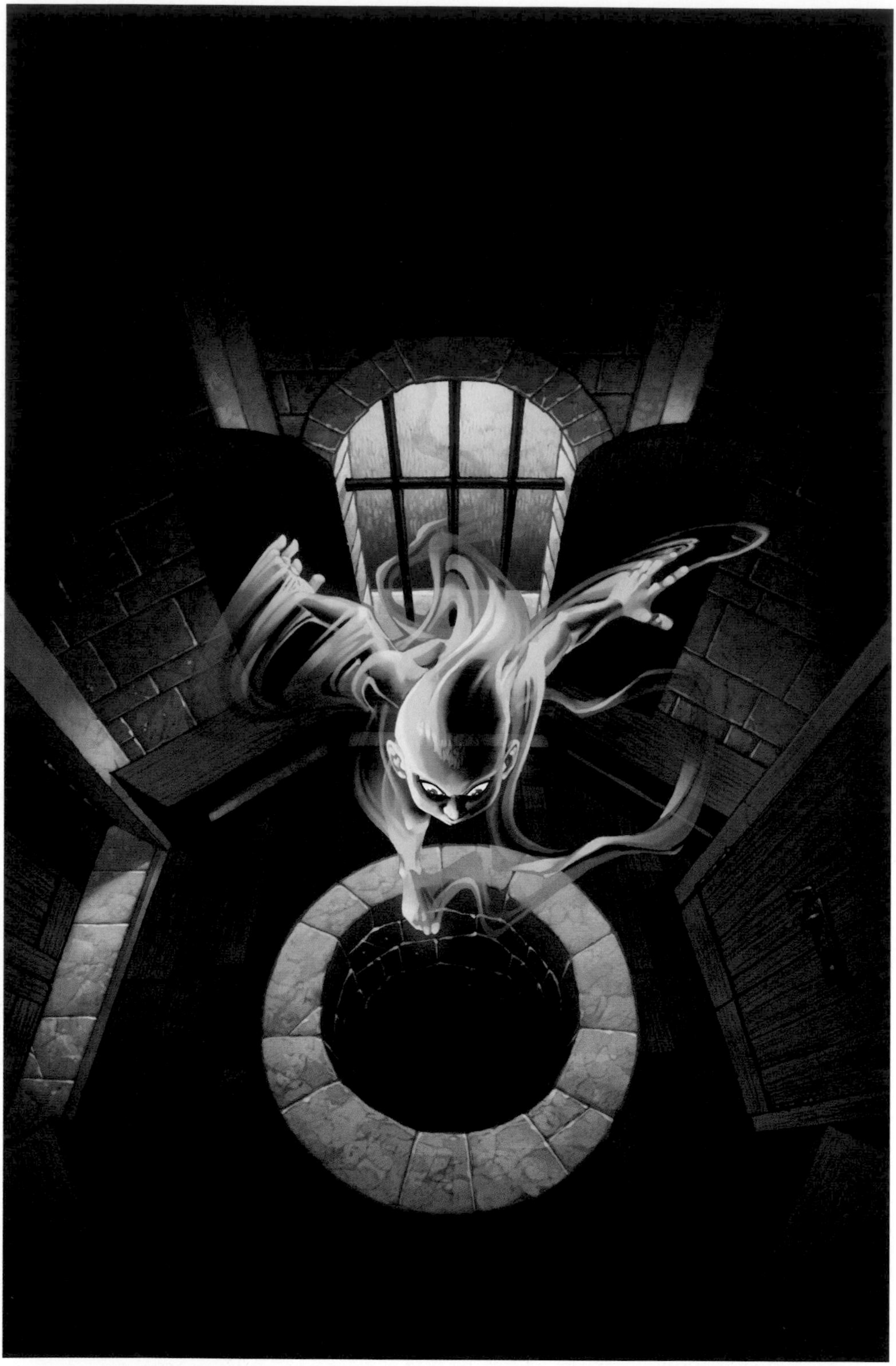

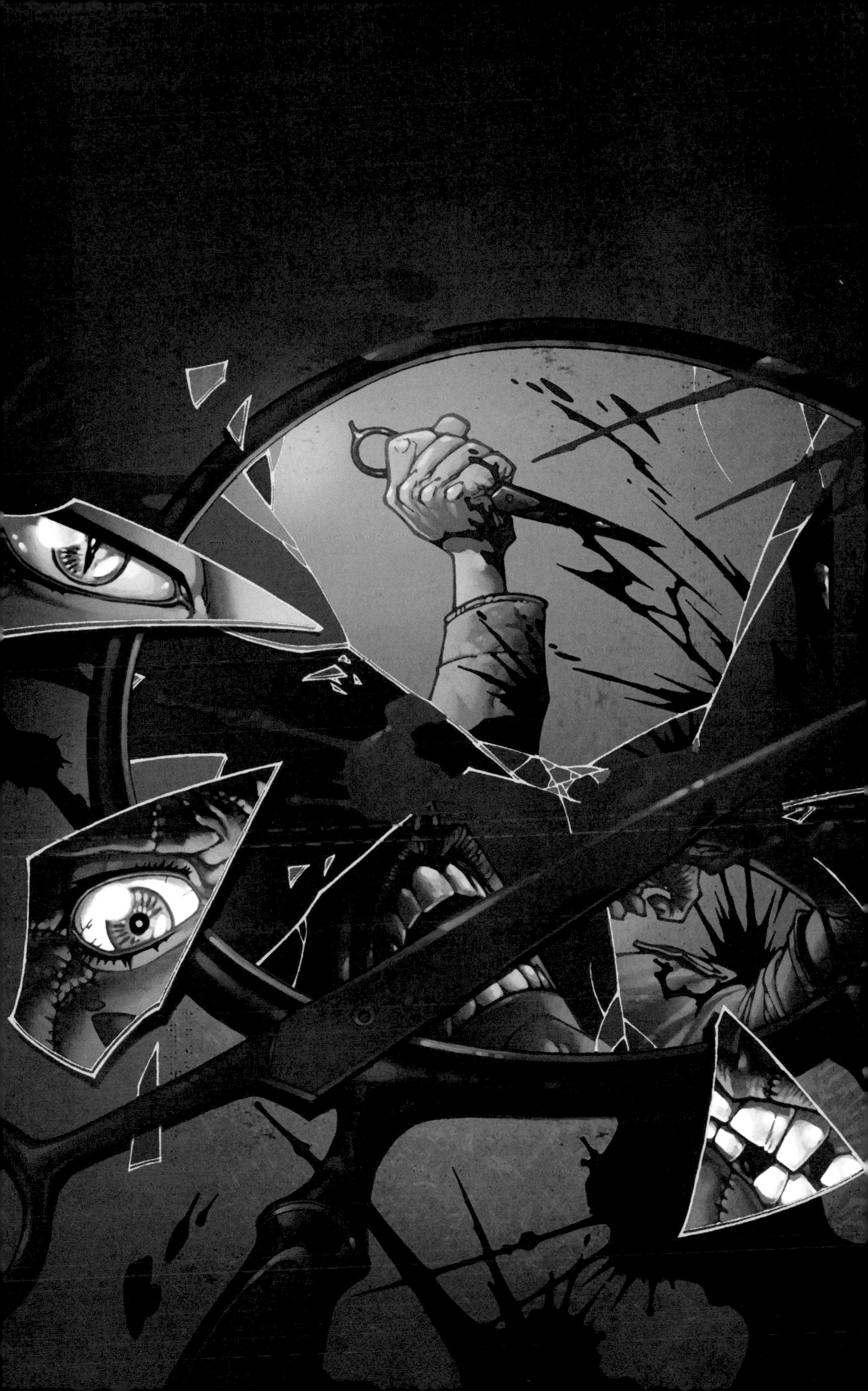

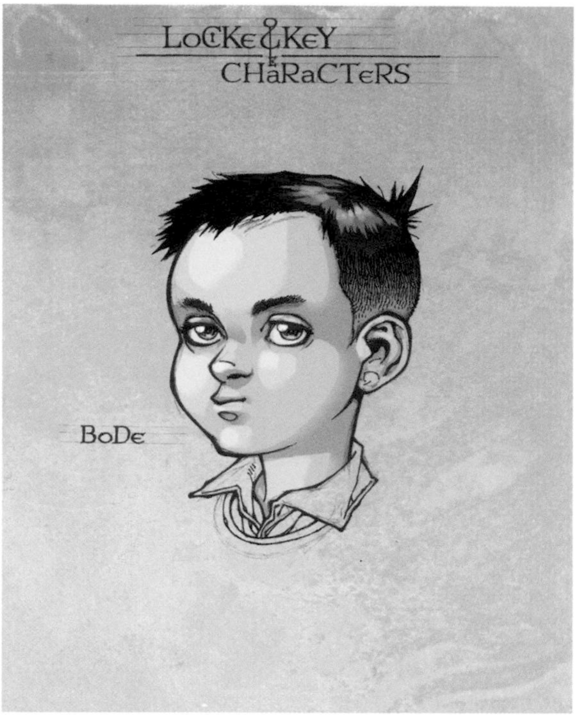
LOCKE & KEY
CHARACTERS
BODE

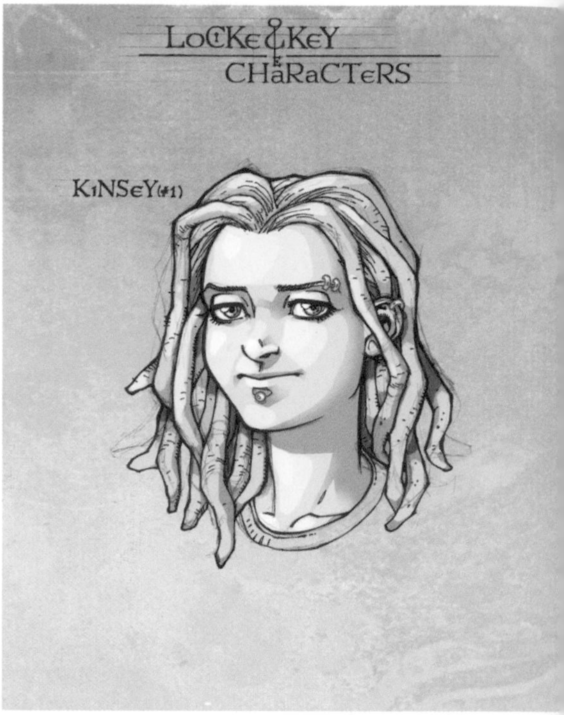
LOCKE & KEY
CHARACTERS
KINSEY (#1)

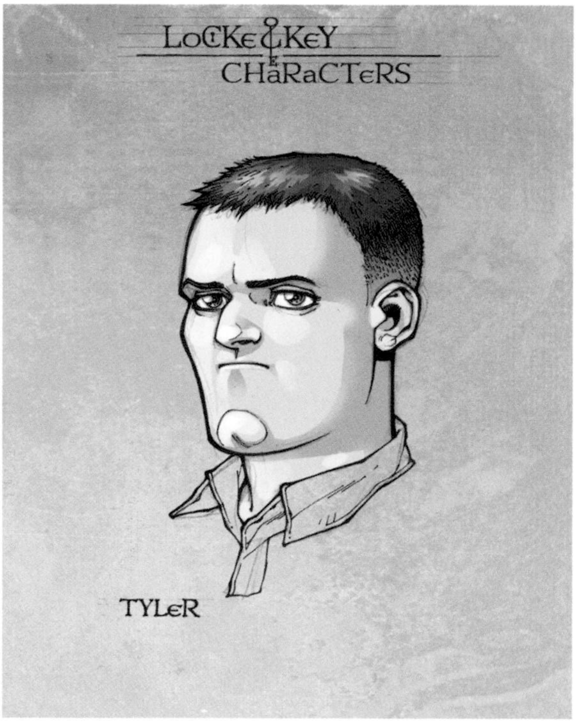
LOCKE & KEY
CHARACTERS
TYLER

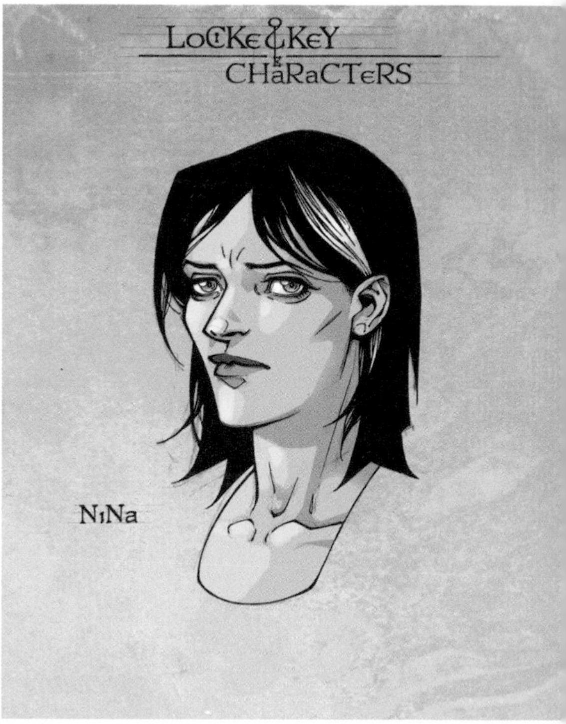
LOCKE & KEY
CHARACTERS
NINA

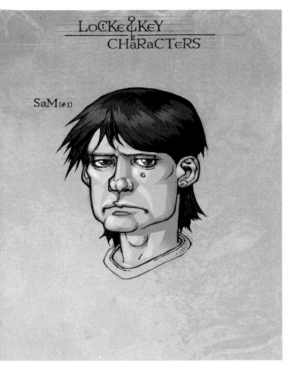

LOCKE & KEY
CHARACTERS

SaM (#1)

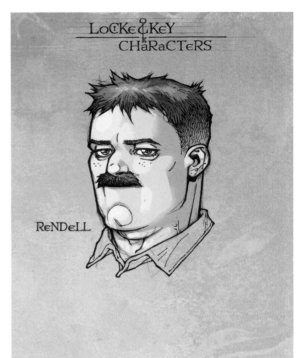

LOCKE & KEY
CHARACTERS

RENDELL

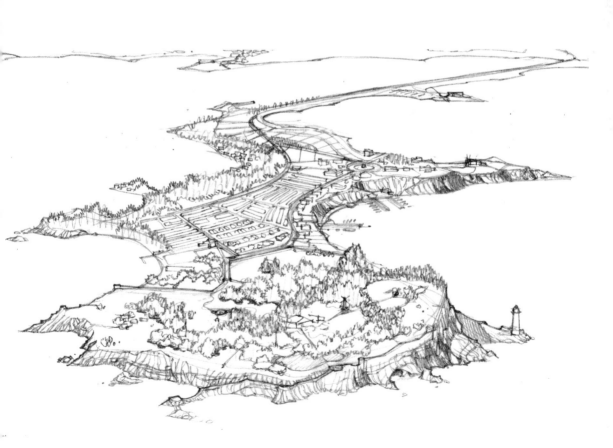

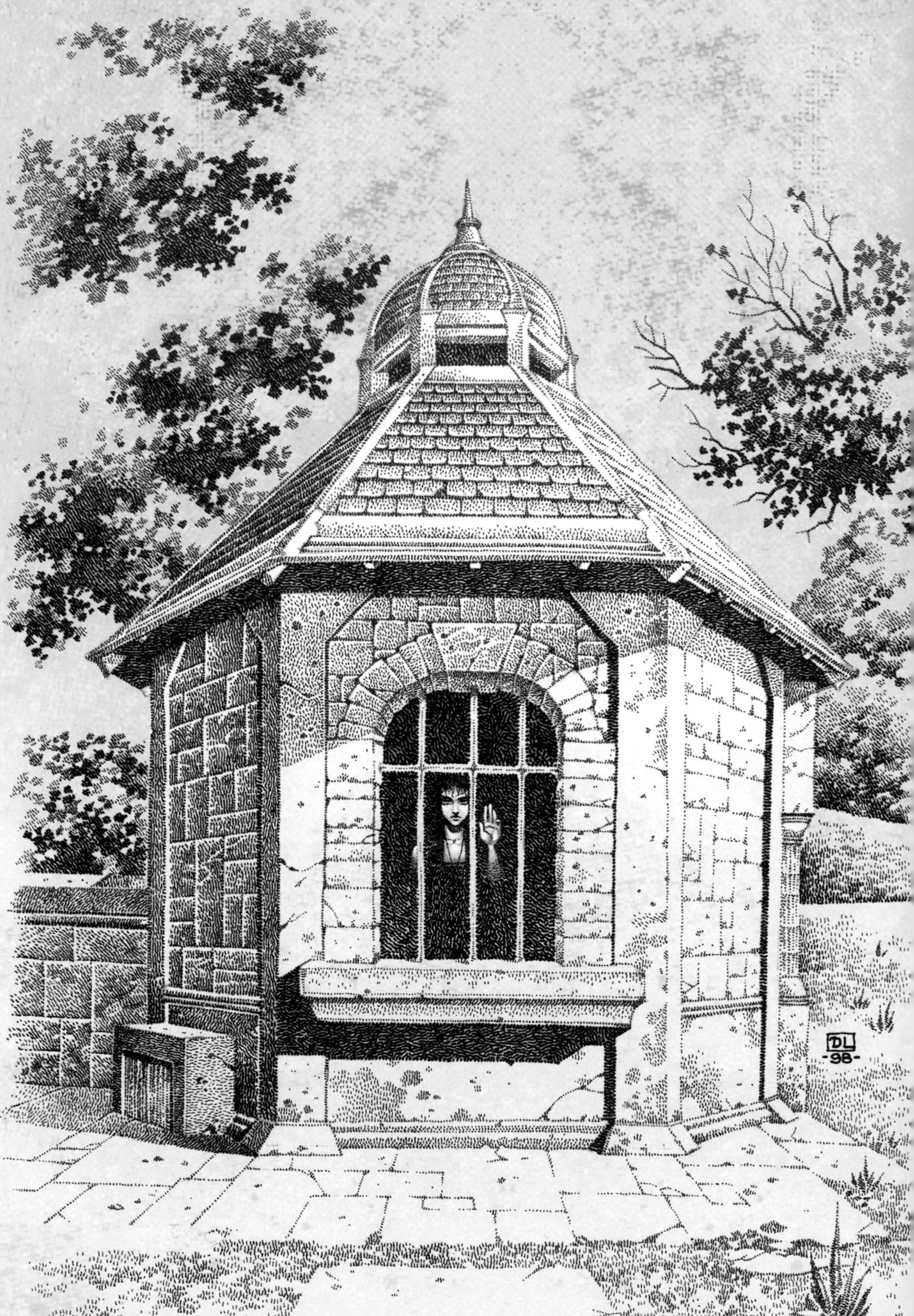
DL
-98-

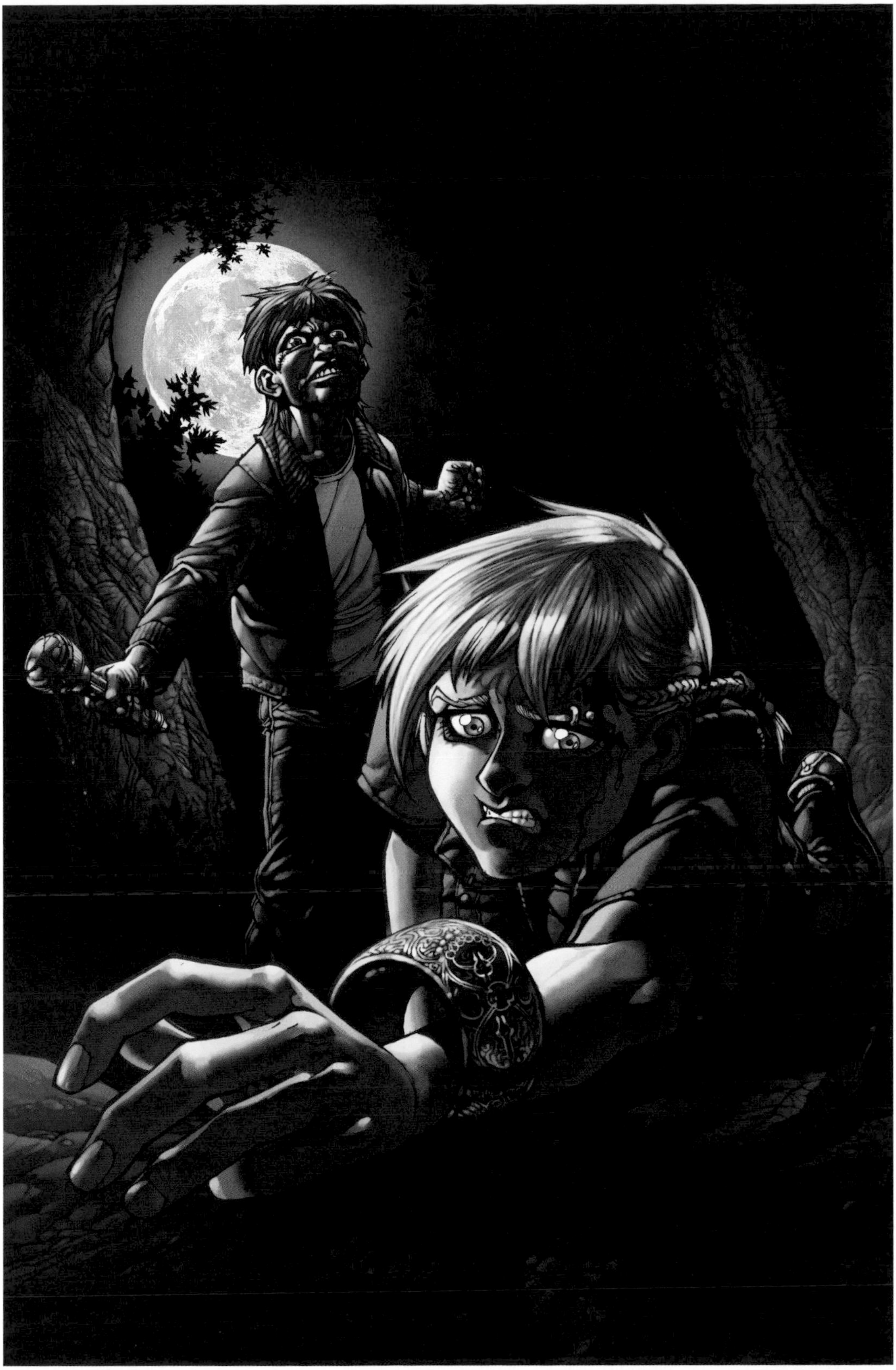

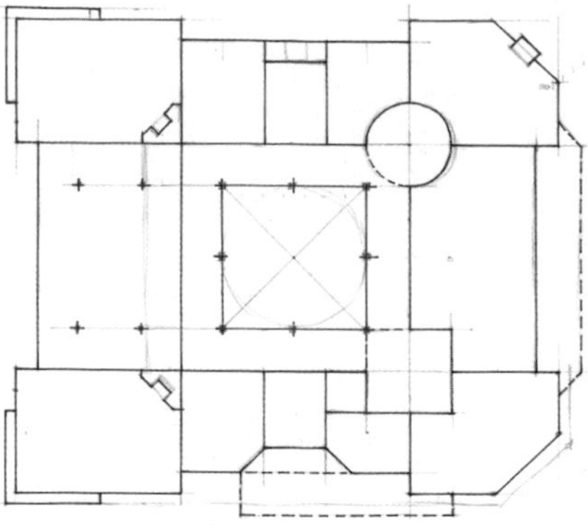

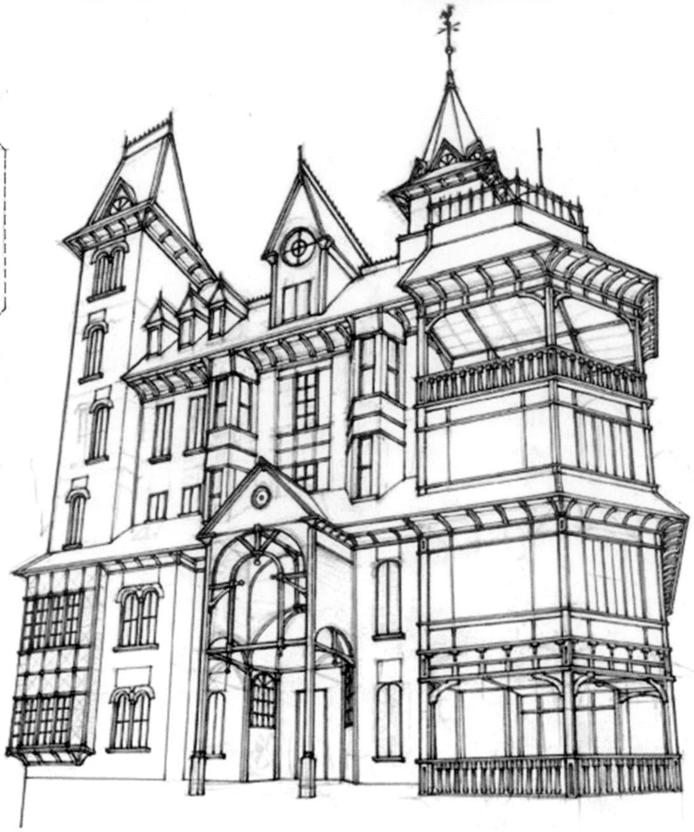

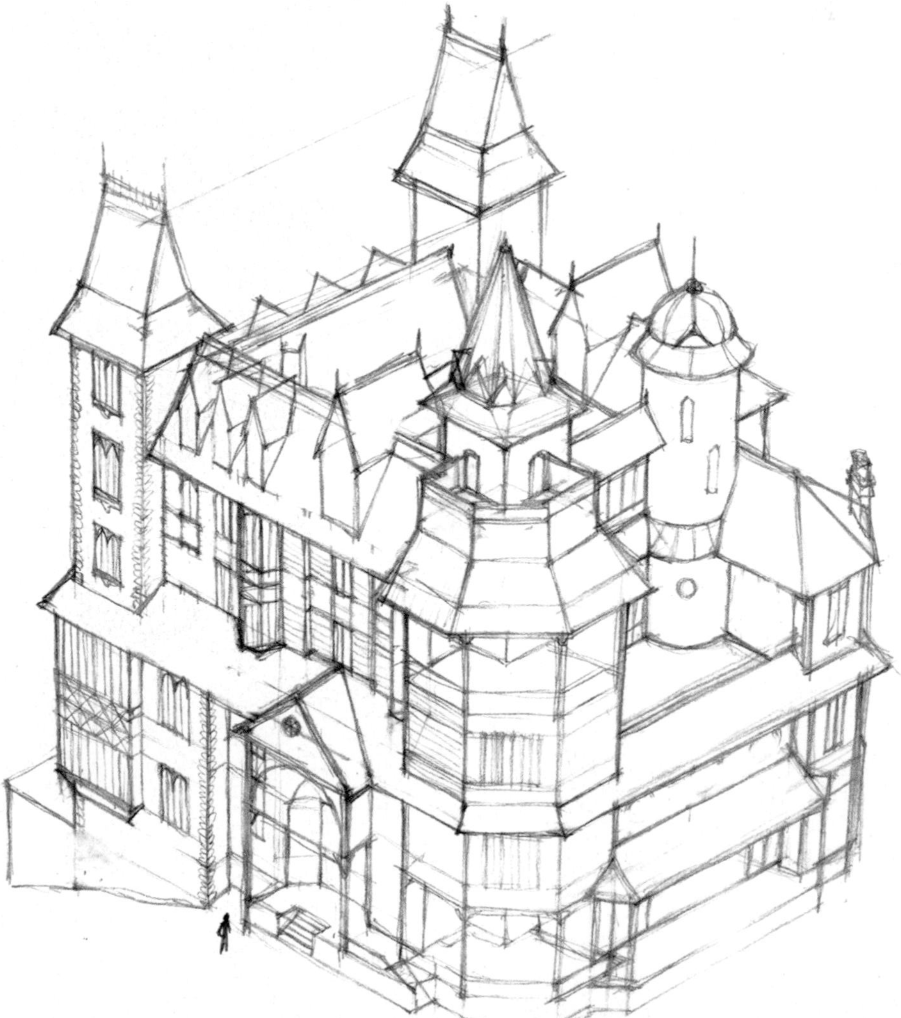

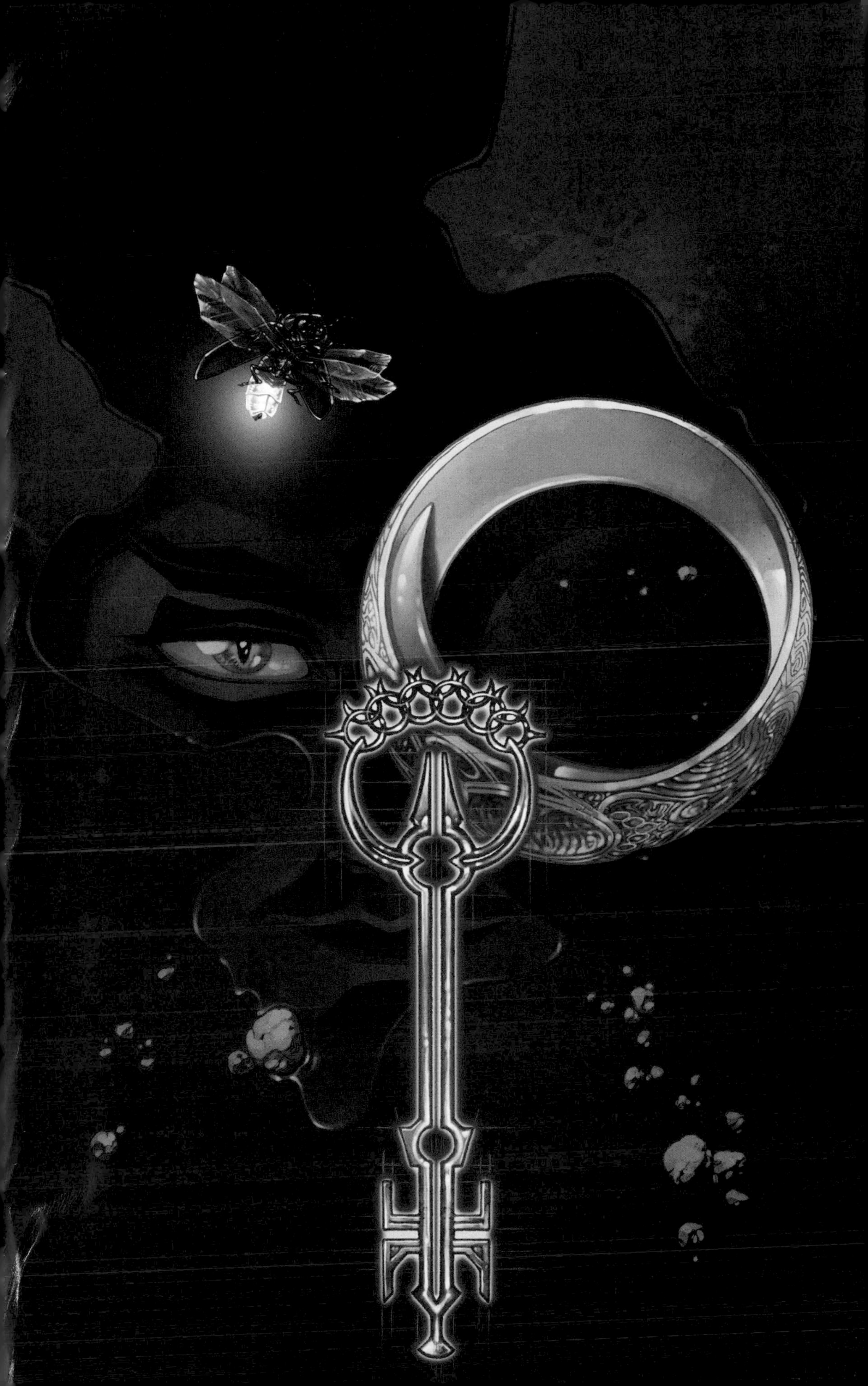

Joe Hill is the author of a novel, *Heart-Shaped Box*, and a collection of stories, *20th Century Ghosts*. He is currently at work on a new novel, *The Surrealist's Glass*. The worst comic book he ever read was still a pretty good time. He has a Web site, joehillfiction.com, where you can find out stuff.

Gabriel Rodriguez is a supremely gifted Chilean artist and co-creator of the twisted but wonderful world of *Locke & Key*. The invitation to participate in the fantastic journey of the surviving members of the Locke family, conceived by Joe Hill, has become a dream project made real for Gabriel. He asks that readers unlock their hearts and minds, and accept an invitation into new realms and tales, thrilling experiences, and secret places that his efforts craft into a vivid universe.

In addition to his current work in *Locke & Key*, Gabriel has collaborated with IDW on *Clive Barker's The Great And Secret Show*, *Beowulf*, and *George A. Romero's Land of the Dead*, as well as several *CSI* comics.

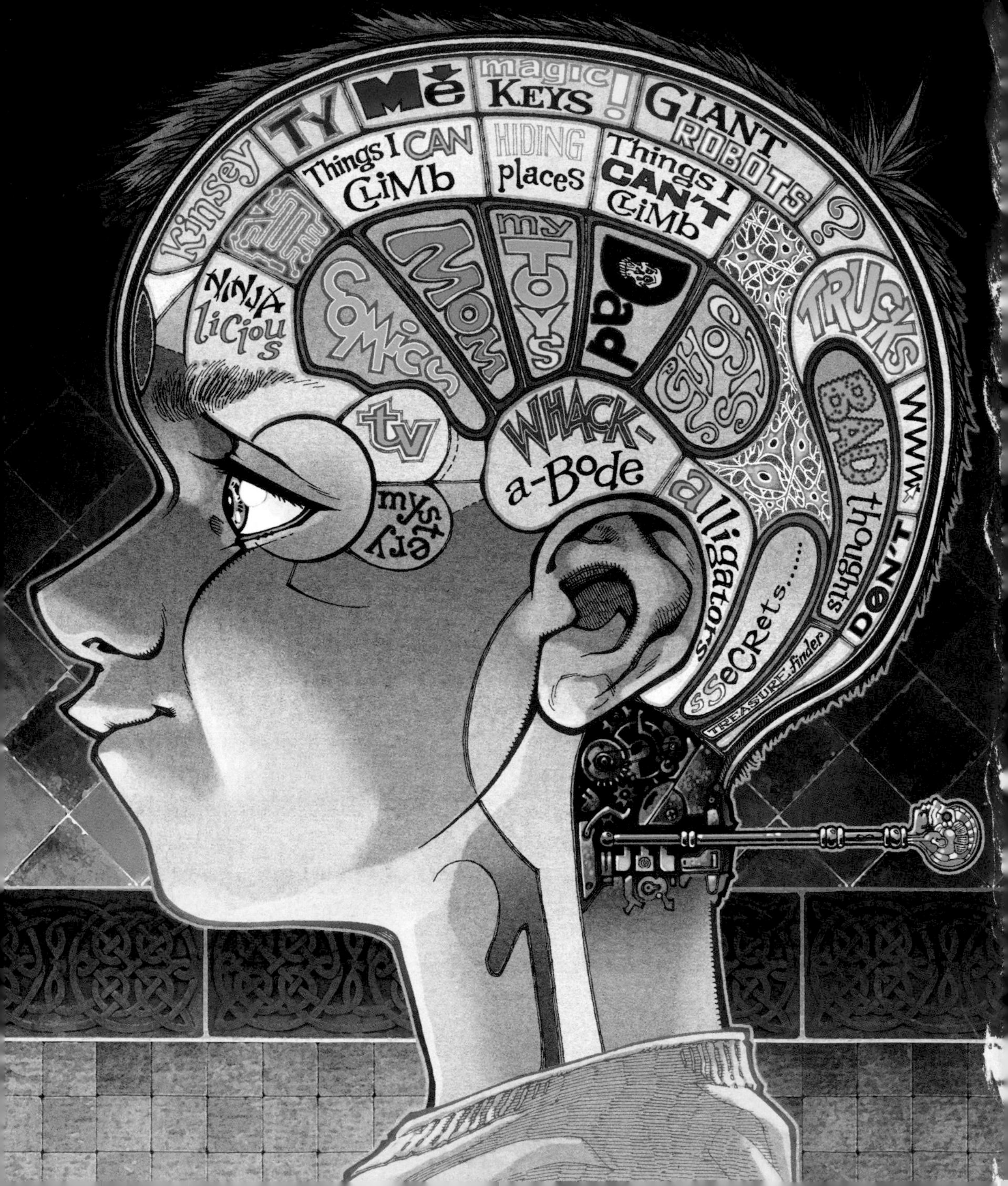
Kinsey
TY
Me
magic
KEYS
!
GIANT
ROBOTS
Things I CAN CLiMb
HIDING
places
Things I CAN'T CLiMb
?
NINJA
licious
COMICS
MOM
my
TOYS
Dad
GHOSTS
TRUCKS
BAD
thoughts
WWW
tv
WHACK-
a-Bode
mystery
alligators
sSeCRets......
TREASURE finder
DON'T